PARTY AUTONOMY IN CONTRACTUAL CHOICE OF LAW IN CHINA

The principle of party autonomy in contractual choice of law is widely recognized in the law of most jurisdictions. It has been more than thirty years since party autonomy was first accepted in Chinese private international law. However, the legal rules provided in legislation and judicial interpretations concerning the application of the party autonomy principle are abstract and open-ended. Without a critical understanding of the party autonomy principle and appropriate interpretations of the relevant legal rules, judges have not exercised their discretionary power appropriately. The party autonomy principle has been applied in a way that undermines its very purpose – that is, to protect the legitimate expectations of the parties and promote the predictability of outcomes in transnational commercial litigation. Jieying Liang addresses the questions of how, when and with what limitations parties' choice of law clauses in an international commercial contract should be enforced by Chinese courts.

JIEYING LIANG is Senior Research Assistant in the Faculty of Law at the University of Hong Kong. She has been engaged in a research project funded by the Research Grants Council in Hong Kong concerning cross-border corporate, financial and securities dealings for several years. The Hague Conference on Private International Law cited Liang in drafting the Hague Principles on Choice of Law in International Contracts. She has received the Fulbright Fellowship and a scholarship from The Hague Academy of International Law.

PARTY AUTONOMY IN CONTRACTUAL CHOICE OF LAW IN CHINA

JIEYING LIANG
The University of Hong Kong

CAMBRIDGE
UNIVERSITY PRESS

CAMBRIDGE
UNIVERSITY PRESS

University Printing House, Cambridge CB2 8BS, United Kingdom

One Liberty Plaza, 20th Floor, New York, NY 10006, USA

477 Williamstown Road, Port Melbourne, VIC 3207, Australia

314–321, 3rd Floor, Plot 3, Splendor Forum, Jasola District Centre, New Delhi – 110025, India

79 Anson Road, #06–04/06, Singapore 079906

Cambridge University Press is part of the University of Cambridge.

It furthers the University's mission by disseminating knowledge in the pursuit of education, learning, and research at the highest international levels of excellence.

www.cambridge.org
Information on this title: www.cambridge.org/9781107169173
DOI: 10.1017/9781316718377

First published 2018

Printed in the United Kingdom by Clays, St Ives plc

A catalogue record for this publication is available from the British Library.

ISBN 978-1-107-16917-3 Hardback

To
Professor Michael Tilbury
My lifelong mentor and friend

CONTENTS

PREFACE

The principle of party autonomy in contractual choice of law gives parties to an international contract the freedom to choose the law to govern their contract. The principle is widely recognized in the law of most jurisdictions. This book is about the application of the party autonomy principle in China. It has been more than thirty years since party autonomy was first accepted in Chinese private international law. The first statute on China's private international law entitled Law on the Application of Laws to Foreign-related Civil Relationships of the People's Republic of China (2010 Conflicts Statute) became effective on 1 April 2011, and the principle is positioned as one of its 'General Provisions'.

Before the 2010 Conflicts Statute, the legal rules provided in legislation and judicial interpretations concerning the application of the party autonomy principle were abstract and open-ended. Several important issues relating to the adjudication of the enforceability of choice of law clauses were ambiguous. The ambiguities were left to be addressed by people's courts in specific cases. But without a critical understanding of the party autonomy principle and appropriate interpretations of the relevant legal rules, judges did not exercise their discretionary power convincingly. As a result, the party autonomy principle was applied in a way that undermined the very purpose underlying the principle, that is, to protect the legitimate expectations of the parties and promote the predictability of outcomes in transnational commercial litigation. The 2010 Conflicts Statute fails to address these ambiguities so that unresolved issues are bound to arise after the Statute became effective.

This book addresses the question of how, when and with what limitations parties' choice of law clauses in an international commercial contract should be enforced by people's courts. It argues that in China, a choice of law clause in contract should only be interfered with or overridden by the *lex fori* when it is necessary to secure a broader public interest, the justification of which should be formed in legislation rather than in administrative rules. In the interests of the predictability and certainty of transnational litigation in China, it is important for the legislature to establish a comprehensive system of legal rules concerning the enforceability of choice of law clauses. It is far more important for the judiciary to interpret and apply those rules in specific cases consistently, respecting the intent of the parties. In doing so, people's courts should consider the theories and principles of private international law, and exercise their discretionary power with caution, demonstrating that they have done so by providing logical and detailed reasoning in their judgments.

ACKNOWLEDGEMENTS

This book is based on my doctoral thesis completed at the Faculty of Law of the University of Hong Kong. The completion of the thesis and this book has been an invaluable experience. I am fortunate to have been helped by so many wonderful people along the way.

I would like to express my deepest gratitude to Professor Michael Tilbury, my respectable supervisor, for his patience, guidance and commitment to teaching and research. I am particularly grateful for the precious time that Professor Tilbury selflessly devoted to reading the earlier drafts of my thesis and this book, and his detailed and insightful comments. His instructive suggestions and questions inspired me to rethink my arguments in fundamental ways. His exemplary scholarship, his heart-warming encouragement, his humility and respect for others have been the greatest source of inspiration for me during these years. Without his unflagging support, I would not have proceeded this far. To me, Professor Tilbury is a lifelong mentor and friend. This book is dedicated to him.

I am indebted to Mr Oliver Jones, my supervisor in the first year of my PhD study, for his thought-provoking suggestions at the very beginning of my research. I wish to express my appreciation to the members of my thesis examination committee, Professor Brian Opeskin, Professor Anselmo Reyes, Professor Zhang Xianchu and Professor Fu Hualing, the chair of the committee, for their profound comments on my thesis, constructive questions and warm encouragement at my oral defence. I am also thankful to Dr Felix Chan W. H. and Dr Maisie Ooi, who offered brilliant suggestions and ideas on my research proposal. I am especially grateful to Maisie, for her unreserved support for my academic endeavours, and her insights on conflict of laws research. I learnt much from discussions with her.

I owe special thanks to Professor Peter Hay at Emory University Law School. During my stay at Emory as a Fulbright Visiting Researcher, I had the opportunity to study conflict of laws under his supervision.

Professor Hay kindly communicated with me his perceptive ideas and analysis concerning the historical background and the most fundamental issues of both American conflicts law and European law. His humour, thoughtful remarks and inspiring words made my stay at Emory a pleasant and rewarding experience.

I extend my thanks to Professor Xingli Liu, Professor Yao Huang and Dr Robert J. Morris. They pointed me to the path of independent academic research. I also wish to acknowledge my gratitude to the University of Hong Kong for offering me the Postgraduate Studentship and the University Postgraduate Fellowship, to the Research Grants Council and the United States Consulate-General in Hong Kong for the Fulbright Fellowship and to The Hague Academy of International Law for granting me a scholarship to take the Summer Courses.

This book has been greatly enriched by the influence of colleagues and friends, who encouraged me and helped make my academic life inspiring and rewarding. I am particularly grateful to Dr Henan Hu, Dr Xiao Pan, Dr Yongxi Chen, Dr Yu Gu, Dr Jingjia Ke, Dr Liang Zhao, Dr Yue Luo, Dr Wenming Xiao, Dr Li Ge, Dr Miaoyan Yang, Dr Huimiao Zhao, Ms Betty Lam, Ms Ivy Chan, Ms Minting Xuan, Ms Runying Liang and Ms Yan Huang.

My sincere thanks go to the editorial team at Cambridge University Press. I would like to thank Mr Joe Ng, Ms Laura Blake and Ms Catherine Rae for their kind help, professional suggestions and enormous patience. I am most appreciative of the comments on the manuscript offered by the anonymous referees.

Above all, I am profoundly indebted to my family. I have been missing my late great-grandmother very much. Her great vision, wisdom and love are always in my heart. I extend my appreciation to my grandmother, for the happiness and unforgettable moments that she brought to me. I owe the utmost gratitude to my dearest parents for their enduring devotion. They put up with all kinds of hardship over the years, and did their best to create a caring and warm environment for me. I am also thankful to my parents-in-law, for their understanding and support for my academic pursuits. Last but not least, I wish to thank my beloved husband and soul mate, Yorkin, for his love and patience, and his trust in me. He is my spiritual companion for life.

I have endeavoured to reflect the law as at 4 November 2017, based on the materials then available to me. All errors or omissions that remain in this book are, of course, entirely my own.

ABBREVIATIONS

1987 Response	Response of the Supreme People's Court to Certain Questions Concerning the Application of the Foreign Economic Contract Law
1988 Opinions	Opinions on Several Issues Concerning the Implementation of the General Principles of Civil Law of the People's Republic of China (Provisional)
1989 Minutes	Minutes of the National Conference on Foreign-, Hong Kong- and Macao-Related Economic Trials in Coastal Areas
1995 Arbitration Notice	Notice on Several Issues Concerning People's Courts' Handling of Foreign-Related and Foreign Arbitration
2004 Guangdong Guiding Opinions	Notice of Issuance of the Guiding Opinions on Several Issues in Foreign-Related Commercial Trials
2004 Responses	Responses to Questions in Foreign-Related Commercial and Maritime Trial (1)
2005 Minutes	Minutes of the Second National Conference on Foreign-Related Commercial and Maritime Trial
2007 Provisions	Provisions on Several Issues Concerning the Application of the Law in Trials of Foreign-Related Civil and Commercial Contract Disputes
2009 Guiding Opinions	Guiding Opinions on Several Issues Concerning the Trial of Civil and Commercial Contract Disputes under Current Circumstances
2010 Conflicts Statute	Law on the Application of Laws to Foreign-Related Civil Relationships of the People's Republic of China
2010 Provisions on FIEs	Provisions of the Supreme People's Court on Several Issues Concerning the Trial of Disputes Involving Foreign-Invested Enterprises (1)
***American President Lines* case**	*American President Lines Ltd.* v. *Feida Appliance Company, Feili Industry Co. Ltd. & Changcheng Industry Company*

Arrangement between the Mainland and Macao on Judicial Assistance	Arrangement for Mutual Entrustment in Civil and Commercial Matters for the Service of Judicial Documents and Investigation and Evidence Obtainment between the Mainland and Macao Special Administrative Region
Brussels Convention	1968 Brussels Convention on Jurisdiction and Enforcement of Judgments in Civil and Commercial Matters
CE	Chief Executive
CEPA	'Mainland and Hong Kong Closer Economic Partnership Arrangement' and 'Mainland and Macao Closer Economic Partnership Arrangement'
Cheshire, North and Fawcett (2008)	Fawcett, J. J. and Carruthers, J. M. (eds), *Cheshire, North and Fawcett: Private International Law* (Oxford: Oxford University Press, 14th edn, 2008)
Circular of the SPC Concerning the Implementation of the CISG	Circular of the Supreme People's Court on Transmitting Certain Issues of the Ministry of Foreign Trade and Economic Cooperation in Connection with the Implementation of United Nations Convention on Contracts for the International Sale of Goods
CISG	The United Nations Convention on Contracts for the International Sale of Goods
Civil Law	The General Principles of Civil Law of the People's Republic of China
CJV	Chinese-foreign cooperative joint venture
COGSA	United States Carriage of Goods by Sea Act 1936
CPG	Central People's Government of the People's Republic of China
DCFR	Draft Common Frame of Reference of the European Community
Dicey and Morris (1987)	Collins, Lawrence (ed), *Dicey and Morris on The Conflict of Laws* (London: Stevens & Sons, 11th edn, 1987)
Dicey, Morris and Collins (2012)	Lord Collins of Mapesbury (ed), *Dicey, Morris and Collins on the Conflict of Laws* (London: Sweet & Maxwell, 15th edn, 2012)
EJV	Chinese-foreign equity joint venture
Evidence Provisions	Some Provisions of the Supreme People's Court on Evidence in Civil Procedure
***Farenco* case**	*Jiangsu Textile Import & Export Group Co. Ltd.* v. *Beijing Farenco Freight Services Co. Ltd. Shanghai Branch & Farenco Freight Services Ltd.*

FIE	Chinese-foreign equity joint venture, Chinese-foreign cooperative joint venture, and wholly foreign-owned enterprise
Fourth Five-Year Reform Outline	Opinion of the Supreme People's Court on Deepening Reform of the People's Courts Comprehensively: Outline of the Fourth Five-Year Reform of the People's Courts (2014–2018)
Hague Rules	International Convention for the Unification of Certain Rules of Law relating to Bills of Lading
Hague-Visby Rules	Protocol to Amend the International Convention for the Unification of Certain Rules of Law Relating to Bills of Lading
Hamburg Rules	United Nations Convention on the Carriage of Goods by Sea
HKCFA	Hong Kong Court of Final Appeal
Hong Kong Basic Law	The Basic Law of the Hong Kong Special Administrative Region of the People's Republic of China
***Hugo Trumpy SpA* Case**	*Trasporti Castelletti Spedizioni Internazionali SpA* v. *Hugo Trumpy SpA*
Interpretation of Contract Law (1)	Interpretation of Supreme People's Court Regarding Law Application Matters of the Contract Law of the People's Republic of China (1)
Interpretation of Contract Law (2)	Interpretation of Supreme People's Court Regarding Law Application Matters of the Contract Law of the People's Republic of China (2)
Interpretation of Security Law	Judicial Interpretation of the Supreme People's Court on Some Issues Regarding the Application of Security law
Interpretation of the 2010 Conflicts Statute (1)	Interpretation of the Supreme People's Court on Certain Issues Concerning the Application of the 'Law on the Application of Laws to Foreign-Related Civil Relations' (1)
Joint Meeting	joint ministerial meeting for the security review of mergers and acquisitions of domestic enterprises by foreign investors
The Kribi	*O.T. Africa Line Ltd.* v. *Hijazy and Others*
Law on the Conclusion of Treaties	Law of the People's Republic of China on the Procedure of Conclusion of Treaties
LegCo	Legislative Council
Macao Basic Law	The Basic Law of the Macao Special Administrative Region of the People's Republic of China

Macao CFA	Court of Final Appeal of Macao Special Administrative Region
Morris (2009)	McClean, David and Beevers, Kisch, *Morris: The Conflict of Laws* (London: Sweet & Maxwell, 7th edn, 2009)
***MSG* case**	*Mainschiffahrts-Genossenschaft e.G. (MSG)* v. *Les Gravières Rhénanes S.a.r.l.*
New York Convention	Convention on the Recognition and Enforcement of Foreign Arbitral Awards
Notice on Private Lending	Notice of the Supreme People's Court on Legally and Properly Hearing Cases on Disputes over Private Lending to Promote Economic Development and Maintain Social Stability
Notice on Security Review	Notice of the General Office of the State Council on the Establishment of the Security Review System for Mergers and Acquisitions of Domestic Enterprises by Foreign Investors
NPC	National People's Congress
NPCSC	Standing Committee of the National People's Congress
Opinions on Case Quality Evaluation Work	Guiding Opinions of the Supreme People's Court on Carrying out the Case Quality Evaluation Work (for Trial Implementation)
PRC	People's Republic of China
Provisions on the Application of Law in Taiwan-Related Cases	Provisions of the Supreme People's Court on the Application of Law in the Trial of Taiwan-Related Civil and Commercial Cases
Provisions on Cross-Straits Judicial Assistance	Provisions of the Supreme People's Courts' Handling of Cases of Mutual Judicial Assistance in Terms of Serving Legal Documents, Investigation and Evidence Collection between Both Sides of the Taiwan Strait
Provisions on Jurisdiction over Foreign-Related Cases	Provisions of the SPC on Certain Issues Concerning Jurisdiction over Foreign-Related Civil and Commercial Cases
Rome Convention	1980 Rome Convention on the Law Applicable to Contractual Obligations
Rome I Regulation	Regulation of the European Parliament and of the Council on the Law Applicable to Contractual Obligations
Rotterdam Rules	Convention of Contracts for the International Carriage of Goods Wholly or Partly by Sea

SAR	Special Administrative Region
***Shantou Hongye* case**	*Bank of China (Hong Kong) Co. Ltd.* v. *Shantou Hongye Co. Ltd. and Shantou Xinye Co. Ltd.*
SPC	Supreme People's Court
The Tilly Russ	*Partenreederei ms. Tilly Russ and Another* v. *Haven & Vervoebedrijf Nova N.V. and Another*
UCC	Uniform Commercial Code
UCP	Uniform Customs and Practice of Documentary Credit
UNIDROIT Principles	UNIDROIT Principles of International Commercial Contracts
URC	Uniform Rules for Collections
WFOE	wholly foreign-owned enterprise

TABLE OF CASES

Australia

Ace Insurance Ltd. *v.* Moose Enterprise Ltd. [2009] NSWSC 724 40, 41–42
Allstate Life Insurance Co. *v.* Australia & New Zealand Banking Group Ltd. [No 6] (1996) 64 FCR 79 212
Oceanic Sun Line Special Shipping Company Inc. *v.* Fay (1988) 165 CLR 197 79, 81

European Court of Justice

Coreck Maritime GmbH *v.* Handelsveem BV and Others, Case C-387/98, [2000] ECR I-9337 75
Mainschiffahrts-Genossenschaft e.G. (MSG) *v.* Les Gravières Rhénanes S.a.r.l., Case C-106/95, [1997] Q.B. 731 65–66, 67, 70, 71, 79
Partenreederei ms. Tilly Russ and Another *v.* Haven & Vervoebedrijf Nova N.V. and Another, Case 71/83, [1984] ECR 2417 70–71, 75
Trasporti Castelletti Spedizioni Internazionali SpA *v.* Hugo Trumpy SpA, Case C-159/97, [1999] ECR I-1636 70–71, 72

Hong Kong SAR

Chen Li Hung and Another *v.* Ting Lei Miao and Others [2000] 1 HKC 461 254
Democratic Republic of the Congo *v.* FG Hemisphere Associates LLC (No. 1) (2011) 14 HKCFAR 95 224
Las Vegas Hilton Corporation *v.* Lo Yuk Leung [1998] HKCU 33 (1997, No. A8739, 19 January 1998) 248–249, 251
Lau Kong Yung *v.* Director of Immigration [1999] 4 HKC 731 225
Ng Ka Ling *v.* Director of Immigration [1999] 1 HKC 291 224
Ng Ka Ling *v.* Director of Immigration (No. 2) [1999] 1 HKC 425 224–225
Vallejos *v.* Commissioner of Registration (2013) 16 HKCFAR 45 224

Mainland China

Supreme People's Court

Higher People's Courts

Intermediate People's Courts and Maritime Courts

Basic-level People's Courts

Permanent Court of International Justice

United Kingdom

United States

TABLE OF STATUTES, JUDICIAL DOCUMENTS AND INTERNATIONAL INSTRUMENTS

1 Statutes and Administrative Rules of the People's Republic of China

2 Judicial Interpretations and Other Documents Issued by the Supreme People's Court of the People's Republic of China

3 International Conventions and EU Legislation

1

The Development of the Party Autonomy Principle in China

The principle of party autonomy in contractual choice of law can be seen as the manifestation in private international law[1] of freedom of contract or of market autonomy.[2] According to this principle, parties to an international contract have the freedom to choose the law to govern their contract.[3] Though this doctrine went through a reaction that reflected an emphasis on state sovereignty during the first half of the twentieth century,[4] it gradually took root both in common law systems and in the rather different soil of civil law countries.[5]

This book is about the application of the party autonomy principle in China.[6] It has been more than thirty years since the principle was first accepted in the Foreign Economic Contract Law in 1985.[7] On 28 October 2010, the Standing Committee of the National People's Congress

[1] Private international law is also commonly referred to as 'conflict of laws'. In this book, the terms 'private international law' and 'conflict of laws' are used interchangeably, meaning the law which deals with cases having a contract with some system of law other than that of the forum.

[2] It is said that, so far as parties are free to enter into whatever contractual bargains they think fit, that freedom is not complete unless they can choose the law by which their agreement will be governed. See Morris (2009) para. 13–003.

[3] Morris (2009) para. 13–003.

[4] In an era when there was 'increased emphasis on the nation state as the sovereign source of legislation', the idea of allowing parties to an international contract a free choice of law was an unwarranted assumption of legislative power by private persons. See Yntema (1952) p. 343.

[5] See Nygh (1999) pp. 13–14; Morris (2009) para. 13–003; Hook (2016) p. 21.

[6] In this book, unless the context otherwise requires, 'China' refers to mainland China, not including the Hong Kong and Macao Special Administrative Regions and the Taiwan District, while 'People's Republic of China' (the PRC) includes the Mainland, Hong Kong, Macao and Taiwan. The interregional conflict of laws issues within the PRC are addressed in Chapter 8.

[7] The history of China's private international law legislation only began with the 1985 Foreign Economic Contract Law (adopted at the 10th meeting of the Standing Committee of the 6th National People's Congress (NPC) on 21 March 1985, effective on 1 July 1985, superseded by the Contract Law on 1 October 1999). Article 5 (1) of this law provided that

(NPCSC) passed a new statute on China's private international law entitled Law on the Application of Laws to Foreign-related Civil Relationships (2010 Conflicts Statute),[8] which became effective on 1 April 2011. The party autonomy principle is positioned in the first chapter as one of the 'General Provisions'.[9]

The practice of adjudicating civil or commercial cases involving more than one jurisdiction in China only began after the state adopted the reform and opening-up policy in 1978, when its door was first opened to the outside world and the state started to place its legal system on a basis appropriate to support its economic development.[10]

This chapter provides a brief overview of the history of China's legislation and judicial practice on the party autonomy principle in contractual choice of law. It examines how the relevant legal rules have evolved and how they have been applied in people's courts in China. The relevant legislation and judicial practice in different periods since 1978 are collated and summarized in a way that illustrates how the party autonomy principle has gradually gained its position in China's private international law of contract and what attitude was held by people's courts in different eras towards its application. This chapter demonstrates that, although the private international law legislation and judicial practice in China has progressed greatly since 1978, most of the legal rules are abstract. They create ambiguities in several respects concerning the practical operation of the party autonomy principle.

A general point should be made at the outset. The sources of Chinese private international law not only include the rules provided in the statutes promulgated by the National People's Congress (NPC) or the NPCSC, the legislature under China's Constitution, but also judicial interpretations issued by the Supreme People's Court (SPC).[11] According

the parties to a foreign-related economic contract may choose the law to resolve their contractual disputes.

8 It was adopted at the 17th meeting of the Standing Committee of the 11th NPC on 28 October 2010 and became effective on 1 April 2011.

9 See Article 3 of the 2010 Conflicts Statute.

10 1978 is seen by Chinese scholars as a turning point in the legal development of China. In the 3rd Plenary Session of the 11th Central Committee of the Communist Party of China, it was declared that a legal system was a necessity for socialist modernization. The importance of law for providing a social order conductive to economic development was repeatedly emphasized by the then Party leaders. For a detailed discussion of the legal experience in post-Mao China, see Chen (2016) pp. 54–75.

11 Unless otherwise indicated, the legal rules discussed in this book are all effective at the time of writing.

to the Constitution and the Law on Legislation,[12] the power of interpreting law is at least formally reserved by the NPCSC. However, the SPC's interpretations are in fact a widespread and important means of legal interpretation. In judicial practice, the SPC plays a very important role in supervising the people's courts in the interpretation and application of statutes when adjudicating cases.[13] The interpretations and other judicial documents issued by the SPC may not have binding force as formal sources of law (because the SPC does not have legislative power according to China's Constitution). They can, however, form the legal basis upon which people's courts decide cases.[14] Moreover, the SPC can

[12] See Article 67(1)(4) of the Constitution (adopted at the 5th Session of the 5th NPC and promulgated for implementation by the Announcement of the NPC on 4 December 1982, amended in accordance with the Amendments to the Constitution of the People's Republic of China adopted respectively at the 1st Session of the 7th NPC on 12 April 1988, the 1st Session of the 8th NPC on 29 March 1993, the 2nd Session of the 9th NPC on 15 March 1999 and the 2nd Session of the 10th NPC on 14 March 2004). It reads: 'The Standing Committee of the National People's Congress exercises the following functions and powers: ... (4) to interpret laws ... ' See also Articles 45 and 50 of the Law on Legislation (adopted by the 3rd Session of the 9th NPC on 15 March 2000, amended at the 3rd Session of the 12th NPC on 15 March 2015). According to Article 61 of the Law on Legislation, in Chinese statutes, an article may consist of paragraphs, subparagraphs and items. When it is necessary to specify a particular provision, the author in this book not only provides the number of the article, but also uses bracketed Arabic numerals to identify the number(s) of the paragraph and even the subparagraph of the identified provision. For example, Article 67(1)(4) of the Constitution means the 4th subparagraph of the 1st paragraph of Article 67 of the law.

[13] See Article 33 of the Organic Law of the People's Courts (adopted by the 2nd Session of the 5th NPC on 1 July 1979, amended for the 1st time at the 2nd Session of the 6th NPC on 2 September 1983, amended for the 2nd time at the 18th Session of the 6th NPC on 2 December 1986 and amended for the 3rd time at the 24th Meeting of the Standing Committee of the 10th NPC on 31 October 2006). It provides: 'The Supreme People's Court gives interpretation on questions concerning specific application of laws and decrees in judicial proceedings.'

[14] The SPC's power to issue binding judicial interpretations is based on one resolution adopted by the NPCSC, the Organic Law of People's Courts and also Provisions of the Supreme People's Court on the Judicial Interpretation Work, which was issued by the SPC itself.

The Resolution of the Standing Committee of the National People's Congress Regarding the Improvement of Interpretation of Law was adopted at the 19th meeting of the Standing Committee of the 5th NPC on 10 June 1981. The 2nd clause of it reads: 'Interpretation of questions involving the specific application of laws and decrees in court trials shall be provided by the Supreme People's Court. Interpretation of questions involving the specific application of laws and decrees in the procuratorial work of the procuratorates shall be provided by the Supreme People's Procuratorate. If the interpretations provided by the Supreme People's Court and the Supreme People's Procuratorate

be regarded as exercising legislative power when it issues interpretations that are wider in scope than the wording of the law.[15] The SPC's judicial interpretations may be issued in various forms and names: provisions, circulars, guiding opinions, replies concerning specific cases, decisions and also conference summaries. Although some of the documents may not be styled as formal 'interpretation', they actually play a similar role.[16] However described, the rules provided in judicial interpretations of the SPC are necessarily involved in the analysis of this book.[17]

A few statutes and judicial documents are significant because they represent milestones in the development of China's general regulative framework on the party autonomy principle. The discussion of the history of the acceptance and operation of the principle in China is accordingly separated into different periods.

are at variance with each other in principle, they shall be submitted to the Standing Committee of the National People's Congress for interpretation or decision.'

Article 33 of the Organic Law of People's Courts confers the powers of making binding interpretations of laws to the SPC.

Moreover, the SPC explicitly provides that it has the power to make judicial interpretations and its judicial interpretations 'shall have full legal force'. See Articles 2 and 5 of Provisions of the Supreme People's Court on the Judicial Interpretation Work (issued on 23 March 2007).

In the Provisions of the Supreme People's Court on Citation of Such Normative Legal Documents as Laws and Regulations in the Judgments (issued on 26 October 2009, effective on 4 November 2009), the SPC also stipulates that judicial interpretations should be cited in civil judgments.

15 For examples and relevant analysis, see the discussion in Section 6.1. See also Finder (1993) pp. 167–169. For a comprehensive analysis of the status and functions of SPC's judicial interpretation in China's legal system and development, see Liu (1997).

16 Before the SPC issued the Provisions on Judicial Interpretation Work in 2007, the judicial documents issued in various forms were all generally regarded to have the same effects as judicial 'interpretations'. See Zhou (1997) p. 17. The different forms and titles of the SPC's judicial documents caused ambiguities as to their effects and functions in judicial practice. See Finder (1993) pp. 164–190. In the 2007 Provisions on Judicial Interpretation Work, the SPC provides for the forms of its judicial interpretations in Article 6: 'Judicial interpretations may be made in four forms, namely, "interpretation", "provision", "reply" and "decision".' Accordingly, other forms of documents issued by the SPC may not bear the effects of 'judicial interpretations' after the Provisions became effective. However, other forms of judicial documents issued by the SPC may in fact also have impact on people's courts' adjudication of cases. See the discussion in the subsequent chapters.

17 For the status of judicial interpretation in China's private international law, see also Huang (1999) p. 165; Tang, Xiao and Huo (2016) section III.2 of chapter 2; Tu (2016) section 2.2 of chapter 2.

1.1 Before the Adoption of the Reform and Opening-Up Policy in 1978

It has been claimed that embryonic conflict of laws legislation was seen in China as early as the Tang Dynasty (618–907).[18] However, for a period of time after 1949, there were barely any choice of law rules governing commercial matters in the country, and no foreign law was applied in the people's courts in China during this period. The principles regulating foreign-related civil or commercial relationships then appeared only in Consular Treaties between China and other countries.[19]

The dominant theory at that time was that judicial sovereignty was absolute and should not yield to any foreign jurisdiction.[20] One possible rationale for this theory was a fear of 'foreign influence'.[21] Such fear came from at least two sources: one was the belief that laws in different countries were mutually exclusive and that no domestic court would directly apply a foreign law;[22] the other was the long-existing bias against

[18] The most acclaimed ancient Chinese choice of law rule is the provision on application of law in the Tang Code (or Yonghui Code). Under the provision, 'a case involving persons who are the subjects of the same foreign sovereignty shall be governed by the law of the said sovereignty, and a case concerning persons who belong to different sovereignties shall apply the code.' This code applied to both civil and criminal cases. See Zhang (2006b) n 1.

[19] The only choice of law rules in China between 1911 and 1979 were perhaps the Act on the Application of Law adopted by the Nationalist government on 5 August 1918 and the application of law provisions scattered in a few Consular Treaties in the 1950s between China and other countries. But in the 1918 Act on the Application of Law, there was nothing about contracts or torts. See Wang (1993) pp. 108–109. There are at least two explanations for the underdevelopment of conflict of laws legislation and literature in China. The first is historical: during more than 2000 years of Chinese history the country was basically a closed and self-sufficient society in which there was little need to engage in 'foreign business transactions'. The second has to do with the philosophy of 'socialist supremacy' that dominated the nation during the period between when the Communist party took power in 1949 and when the country initiated economic reform in 1978. Under this philosophy, state ownership reached almost every corner of the country and no individual or private person was permitted to participate in any business transaction, especially international ones. See Wang (1993) pp. 48–50; Zhang (2006b) pp. 289–290; Tang, Xiao and Huo (2016) section III of chapter 1.

[20] See Zhang (2006b) p. 300. [21] See H. Li (2000) pp. 5–9.

[22] In China, the controlling thought for a long time was that all laws are 'class-based' and could be divided into two primary groups: the laws of the capitalist class and the laws of the proletarian (or socialist) class. There was a well-settled principle that no capitalist class laws or rules should be applied or even recognized in China. Under Chairman Mao's 'class struggle' theory, the law represented and served the will of the dominating class of a given country, and different dominating classes in different countries had different interests that could not be surrendered to each other. For China's legal experience under

Western countries that were perceived to possess a constant desire to move China away from communism.[23] The bias reached its peak in China during the Cultural Revolution (1966–1976), when everything associated with western countries had to be destroyed.[24]

It can be summarized that before and at the very beginning of the adoption of the reform and opening-up policy, there were no private international law rules in China's legislation. When faced with a case involving foreign elements,[25] people's courts would have to seek guidance from the SPC.[26] Sometimes people's courts would also adjudicate civil, commercial or maritime cases with foreign-related elements by applying international customs or practice adopted by a large majority of countries.[27]

1.2 The Partial Acceptance of Party Autonomy before the 1999 Contract Law

Until early 1985, no Chinese conflicts rules governed international contracts in spite of the fact that China's Foreign Trade and Maritime

Mao's leadership, see the discussion in Chen (2016) pp. 47–54. Class struggle ideology, mass campaigns and repressive policies remained features of the nation's political life until the death of Mao Zedong in September 1976. See Chen (2011) p. 41.

23 Traditional China regarded herself as the centre of the world and her civilization and culture as superior to all others. Despite increasing interaction with the West and the reception of Western ideas in the eighteenth and nineteenth centuries, conservative forces against Westernization or modernization were strong. During Mao's era, a very influential ideology prevailed which espoused the idea that the socialism adopted in China and in a few other countries was red (which was good), and that all capitalism was white (which was equivalent to evil). For the legal history of modern China, see Chen (2011) chapter 1.

24 During the Cultural Revolution, virtually all laws and the entire legal system were destroyed. Pronouncements and Party policies replaced law. See the detailed discussions in Tay (1976) pp. 417–423; Chen (2011) pp. 37–41.

25 In the conflict of laws, a 'foreign element' means a contact with some system of law other than that of the forum, that is, the country whose courts are seized of the case. See Morris (2009) para. 1-002; Dicey, Morris and Collins (2012) para. 1-001. In this book, 'foreign-related' cases refer to cases involving contacts with a system of law other than that of mainland China. Even though Hong Kong-, Macao- and Taiwan-related cases are considered to be different from foreign-related cases in Chinese judicial practice, the distinction is not of substantial significance in the discussion of choice of law issues. Therefore, they are also included in 'foreign-related' cases in this book. For the analysis of the distinction, see Sections 8.1.3 and 8.2.

26 See, for example, 'The Reply of the Supreme People's Court Regarding Whether to Protect the Obligation Created in Hong Kong between Xia Qinrui and Wu Zhixiang', in Research Office of the Supreme People's Court (1997) pp. 574–575.

27 See Wan (2002) pp. 45–46.

Arbitration Commissions had been settling disputes arising out of economic relations with foreign countries for almost three decades. However, what conflicts rules were applied by these arbitration commissions are not known: cases were few in number; reasons for awards were normally not given; and proceedings of the commissions were not published.[28] Furthermore, no judgment involving conflicts problems was published by people's courts.[29] The history of Chinese private international law legislation only began with the 1985 Foreign-related Economic Contract Law.

The principle of party autonomy was first accepted in the choice of law rules provided in the Foreign Economic Contract Law. Article 5(1) provided that the parties to a foreign-related economic contract may choose the law to resolve their contractual disputes. Though this was a milestone in China's private international law history, according to Article 2 of that law, the only parties that were entitled to choose the law applicable to their contract were Chinese and foreign enterprises and other economic associations, and foreign individuals.[30] Thus, Chinese individuals were *not* entitled to be a party to foreign-related economic contracts. This was so even though the party autonomy principle was reiterated in Article 145 of the General Principles of the Civil Law (Civil Law).[31] That is to say, party autonomy was *partially* accepted in China during this period.

The rules concerning the party autonomy principle in the previous two statutes were all very abstract. It was generally provided that parties to a foreign-related contract were free to select the applicable law for the settlement of their disputes arising out of the contract, except as otherwise stipulated by law. There were two exceptions to the principle. The first was Article 5(2) of the Foreign Economic Contract Law, which stipulated that Chinese law should apply to contracts that were to be performed within the territory of China, namely contracts for Chinese-foreign equity joint ventures, Chinese-foreign contractual joint ventures and Chinese-foreign cooperative arrangements involving the exploration and development of natural resources.

[28] See Cohen (1984) pp. 298, 312–313. [29] See Chen (1987) p. 462.

[30] Article 2 of the Foreign Economic Contract Law reads: 'The scope of this law includes economic contracts concluded between enterprises or other economic organizations of the People's Republic of China and foreign enterprises and other economic organizations or individuals, but excludes international transport contracts.'

[31] It was adopted on 12 April 1986 at the 4th Session of the 6th NPC, became effective on 1 January 1987, and amended at the 10th Session of the 11th NPCSC on 27 August 2009.

The second was Article 150 of the Civil Law, which provided that if the application of foreign law was against the social public interest of China, it should not be applied by people's courts. Accordingly, it is arguable that the main theme of Article 5 of the Foreign Economic Contract Law was to empower the contractual parties to select the governing law at will as long as the exceptions were not triggered. But neither of the two articles clearly specified what 'the law provides otherwise' meant. In order to clarify that issue and implement the choice of law rules, the SPC issued two judicial documents concerning the determination of applicable law in contractual cases. The relevant rules in legislation and the regulations set out in these judicial documents constituted the whole legal framework under which the principle of party autonomy was applied in this period.

First, the SPC issued its Response to Certain Questions concerning the Application of Foreign Economic Contract Law (1987 Response).[32] This Response contained several rules relating to party autonomy: (1) the time when the parties should make their choice of applicable law; (2) the way in which they should express their choice; (3) the legal rules that can be selected by the parties; (4) the nature of the law chosen by the parties; and (5) the scope of the chosen law.

Second, on 2 April 1988, the SPC issued The Opinions concerning Implementation and Application of the General Principles of the Civil Law of the People's Republic of China (Provisional) (1988 Opinions), which stipulated another restriction on the party autonomy principle, namely, the evasion of law exception. If the parties selected a foreign law with the intent to evade Chinese law that otherwise must be applied, the parties' choice of law would be void.[33]

[32] It was issued on 19 October 1987 by the SPC. Though the Contract Law has been effective since 1 October 1999, it was not until 2000 that the 1987 Response was formally invalidated by the SPC. See 'The Catalogue of the Relevant Judicial Interpretations issued before the End of 1999 which would be Invalidated by the Supreme People's Court (the Third Batch)' (issued by the SPC on 13 July 2000 and effective on 25 July 2000). For the confusion concerning the effect of the 1987 Response after 1 October 1999 and before it was formally invalidated by the SPC, see Lin (2000) pp. 30–31.

[33] Article 194 of the 1988 Opinions reads: 'In case any party has any act of evading the mandatory or prohibitive legal provisions of our country, the foreign law shall not be applied.' Several articles in the 1988 Opinions were invalidated by the SPC on 18 December 2008 because they contradicted the provisions in the Property Law (adopted at the 5th Session of the 10th NPC on 16 March 2007, effective on 1 October 2007). But the articles related to application of laws in foreign-related relations were not invalidated.

In summary, before the enactment of the Contract Law, the rules on the application of the party autonomy principle in China involved the five conditions under which the parties were able to select the applicable law in the 1987 Response, and the three statutory restrictions on the consequences of the parties' choice, which were provided in the Civil Law (the public interest exception), Foreign Economic Contract Law (the contracts where party autonomy was excluded) and 1988 Opinions (the evasion of law exception).

Foreign-related commercial cases were not very complicated during the early period of the adoption of the opening-up policy. People's courts generally tended to confirm the effect of parties' reference to a law in contracts. They did not limit the time within which the parties had to choose the law to govern their contract, nor did they strictly require the law chosen to have any material connection with the contract.[34]

1.3 After the Enactment of Contract Law and before the 2007 Provisions

1.3.1 The Complete Acceptance of Party Autonomy in Chinese Private International Law

Under the Foreign Economic Contract Law, Chinese citizens were not entitled to conclude a contract with foreign legal entities, and thus they did not enjoy the freedom to choose the applicable law. In 1999, the Contract Law was enacted and it superseded the Foreign Economic Contract Law.[35] Article 2 of the Contract Law confirms that Chinese citizens are entitled to become parties to contracts involving foreign elements,[36] and in Article 126, the party autonomy principle is also enshrined in terms similar to Article 5 of the Foreign Economic Contract Law.

The Contract Law is an important milestone in China's private international law legislation, because in combination with Article 145 of the

[34] See, for example, the cases cited in Kong and Hu (2002) pp. 421, 428; Yang (1996) pp. 21–24, 92–95; Institute of Chinese Law of the SPC (1996) pp. 133–138.

[35] See Article 428 of the Contract Law (adopted at the 2nd Session of the 9th NPC on 15 March 1999, effective on 1 October 1999).

[36] Article 2 of the Contract Law confirms that natural persons are also legitimate parties of a contract. It provides: 'For purposes of this Law, a contract is an agreement between natural persons, legal persons or other organizations with equal standing, for the purpose of establishing, altering, or discharging a relationship of civil rights and obligations.'

Civil Law, it meant that the party autonomy principle in contractual choice of law was completely accepted.

Apart from the aforementioned two articles in the Contract Law, there are no other specific rules with respect to party autonomy. Moreover, after the Foreign Economic Contract Law was superseded, the relevant judicial interpretation, the 1987 Response, was later repealed.[37] Therefore, the rules regulating several issues concerning the application of party autonomy were no longer applicable after the enactment of Contract Law. Nevertheless, without further instructions, it was difficult for people's courts to apply the ambiguous articles in the Civil Law and Contract Law. Maybe it was for this reason that the opinions in the 1987 Response remained influential and had a strong effect upon Chinese courts before the issue of the 2007 Provisions.[38]

1.3.2 *Issues Outstanding after the Enactment of Contract Law*

Under the general framework constituted by those rules discussed previously, two important issues remained unsolved.

A Change of the Applicable Law

The first issue was whether the parties may change by a later agreement the applicable law that they had previously chosen, and if so, how the change should be made. Both the Contract Law and the 1987 Response were silent on this issue. There are two important questions. The first concerns the way in which the parties could make a change if they were permitted to do so and how a court could decide that the parties had changed the law they had selected. The second is whether the subsequent change is retroactively effective to the time when the contract was made, because if so, the change may prejudice the formal validity of the contract as well as the interests of third parties.

In practice, the courts, while implicitly accepting parties' ability to change the applicable law, avoided considering the consequences of the alternation of that law by deciding that Chinese law should be applied.

37 See n 32.

38 See Economic Case Trial Division of the SPC (1999) p. 528. This book was written by a group of judges in the Economic Case Trial Division of the SPC and the opinions in the book necessarily reflect the position that the judges took in trials during that period. See also Ding (2004) pp. 306–307.

In *Shengli Shipping Co. (Germany)* v. *Junye International Trade Co. Ltd. (Tianjin)*,[39] the court considered that since both of the parties invoked the Maritime Code[40] and Civil Law of China, it could be concluded that they mutually agreed to choose Chinese law as the governing law of the case. This could be deemed as the parties' agreement and their real intent was thus respected. But in *Shenglun Import and Export Co. Ltd.* v. *Tianjin-Inchon International Passenger & Cargo Co. Ltd. and Tianjin-Inchon International Passenger & Cargo Co. Ltd. (Tianjin)*,[41] where a clause in the bill of lading provided that disputes that may arise concerning the bill should be resolved according to the law of England, the court decided that the law of China was the applicable law because neither of the parties invoked the law of other jurisdictions or submitted relevant evidence of that law to the court during the proceedings. In this case, the parties were assumed to have changed their choice, which seemed against their real intent.

It should be noted that the parties were not required to plead foreign law. That is to say, once they had made a choice as to the applicable law, the people's court should firstly decide on the validity of that choice, and determine the governing law of the contract according to the legal rules in the Civil Law and the Contract Law. The issue of the ascertainment of foreign law would only arise after the court came to the conclusion that a foreign law should apply. In this case, the court obviously neglected that and instead directly held that because the parties had failed to prove the content of foreign law, Chinese law should be applied.[42]

The people's court even accepted the unilateral change of applicable law by one party. In *Xingchen Bank (Hong Kong) Co. Ltd.* v. *Shengwang Clothes-Making Co. Ltd. and Shenzhen Tongyihe Shengwang Clothes Processing Factory*,[43] the plaintiff and the first defendant had selected Hong Kong law to govern their contract (a lease), but neither of the two defendants issued a defence in the proceedings. At trial, the defendants did not appear and the plaintiff argued for the application of Chinese law.

39 30 January 2002, Tianjin Higher People's Court.

40 It was promulgated at the 28th Meeting of the Standing Committee of the 7th NPC on 7 November 1992 and became effective on 1 July 1993.

41 30 July 2002, Tianjin Maritime Court. This case is further discussed in Section 7.1 of Chapter 7.

42 The ascertainment of the foreign law chosen by parties is addressed in Chapter 7.

43 15 September 2006, Yantian District People's Court of Shenzhen. See Deng (2008) pp. 156–160. This case is further discussed in Chapter 4, where the validity of parties' choice of law is addressed.

The court decided that the defendants should be taken as having waived their procedural rights, and since the Mainland had the closest connection with the contract (the place of performance as well as the residence of the defendants were both in mainland China), Chinese law should be applied. Here, the court directly confirmed the effect of the plaintiff's change of the previously chosen law without considering the validity of the choice of law clause in the lease concerned. It seems the only reason that the court did not apply Hong Kong law was the plaintiff's unilateral change of the choice. This decision obviously breached the party autonomy principle.

B Statutory Restrictions on Party Autonomy

The statutory restrictions on party autonomy are provided separately in the Civil Law, the Contract Law and relevant judicial interpretations.

a Mandatory or Prohibitive Rules: Definition and Scope Based on Article 194 of the 1988 Opinions on Civil Law, the conduct of the parties to evade mandatory or prohibitive rules of law would result in the non-application of foreign laws.

The effect of 'mandatory rules' was also articulated in Article 52(1)(5) of the Contract Law: a contract is invalid if it violates the mandatory provision of any law or administrative regulation. Moreover, in Article 4 of Interpretation of the SPC Regarding Law Application Matters of the Contract Law (1) (Interpretation of Contract Law (1)),[44] the SPC pointed out that after the Contract Law became effective, a people's court should only invalidate a contract in accordance with laws adopted by the NPC or its Standing Committee, or administrative regulations adopted by the State Council, and should not invalidate a contract in accordance with any local statutes or administrative rules. However, before the Law on Legislation became effective,[45] there were then no legal rules in China concerning the hierarchy of the binding force of different sources of law. Even after the Law on Legislation became effective, it did not contain any provisions that define 'mandatory or prohibitive rules'. Besides those rules governing the three kinds of contracts identified in Article 126(2) of the Contract Law,[46] it was uncertain what other rules of law bore the nature of being 'mandatory or prohibitive'.

44 It was issued on 19 December 1999 and became effective on 29 December 1999.

45 The Law on Legislation was effective on 1 July 2000.

46 Article 126(2) of the Contract Law reads: 'For the contracts to be fulfilled in the territory of the People's Republic of China on Chinese-foreign equity joint ventures, on Chinese-

b The Boundary of 'Social Public Interest' 'Social public interest' in Article 150 of the Civil Law was another restriction. It was believed that this exception to the party autonomy principle is an expression with Chinese characteristics of the more commonly used term 'public policy reservation' (or *ordre public*) in private international law.[47] In Article 1 (10) of the 1987 Response, the SPC explicitly provided that when the applicable law is a foreign law, the application of which would violate the basic principles of Chinese law and the social public interest, the foreign law should not be applied and the applicable law should then be Chinese law. However, neither of those rules clearly defined the boundary of 'social public interest' or 'basic principles of Chinese law'.

This confusion became manifest in cases involving foreign-related guaranty contracts. In *Starflower Investment Services Co. Ltd.* v. *Hangzhou Jinma Real Estate Co. Ltd. and Hangzhou Weilai Shijie Recreation Co. Ltd.*,[48] the parties chose Hong Kong law as the applicable law in the guarantee. This clause was not enforced because the SPC considered their choice to be an intentional evasion of China's registry rules relating to guarantees on foreign loans, which were seen as mandatory rules by the court. According to Article 4 of the Interpretation of Contract Law (1), a contract can only be deemed invalid on the grounds that it is against the mandatory rules of laws or administrative regulations issued by the State Counsel. However, the registry regulations were only administrative rules issued by the People's Bank of China and thus their binding force was, and is, lower than laws and administrative regulations according to Article 88 of the Law on Legislation. So, the registry regulations cannot be taken as a legal basis for deciding that the parties had the intent to evade law.

In other cases involving foreign-related guaranty contracts, people's courts applied either the evasion of law or the social public interest exception to exclude the foreign law chosen by parties, but their standards were also far from uniform.[49] Thus, the statutory limitations on party autonomy in China were still in a state of confusion.

In summary, the relevant rules in the Civil Law and Contract Law are not clear on several important issues and thus of little practical use.

foreign contractual joint ventures and on Chinese-foreign cooperative arrangements involving the exploration and development of natural resources, the laws of the People's Republic of China shall apply.'

[47] See Liu (2001) pp. 158–165. [48] 21 February 2006, Supreme People's Court.

[49] See the cases cited in Section 5.2.2 of Chapter 5 and the discussions therein.

Moreover, the specific rules concerning the application of party autonomy in the 1987 Response had actually been invalidated in 2000. Those uncertainties needed to be resolved by a framework of comprehensive and clear rules.

1.4 After the 2007 Provisions and before the 2010 Conflicts Statute

In order to address the problems just identified in the application of the party autonomy principle,[50] the SPC issued Provisions on Several Issues Concerning the Application of Law in Trials of Foreign-Related Civil and Commercial Contract Disputes (2007 Provisions),[51] which became effective on 8 August 2008. In two more recent judicial interpretations, the SPC included in each of them an article dealing with the scope and definition of mandatory rules.

1.4.1 The 2007 Provisions

There are several articles in the 2007 Provisions that deal with party autonomy. However, the Provisions simply sum up the previous experience of applying the principle in China's judicial practice.[52] Several issues were still unclear.

A The Parties' Choice Should Be Express

Article 3 of the 2007 Provisions required that the choice of law and the change of this choice should be express. However, it was also provided in Article 4(2) that 'if the parties have not selected the law applicable to their contract dispute but both cite the law of the same country or region and neither has raised an objection to the applicable law, they shall be deemed to have made a selection as to the law applicable to their contract dispute'. The reason for making these two provisions, according to the spokesman of the SPC, was that people's courts have all accepted that the parties' choice of law should be made expressly. However, judicial

[50] See the background to the issuing of the 2007 Provisions in Chen (2008) pp. 259–260.

[51] It was issued on 23 July 2007, became effective on 8 August 2007, and was invalidated by the SPC in 2013. See 'The Catalogue of the Relevant Judicial Interpretations issued between 1 July 1997 and 31 December 2011 That should be Invalidated by the SPC (the Tenth Batch)' (issued by the SPC on 26 February 2013 and effective on 8 April 2013). However, the approaches adopted therein related to party autonomy remain influential in subsequent judicial practice. See the analyses in Chapters 5–7.

[52] See n 50.

practice has always accepted that where the parties have not chosen the applicable law previously, but the plaintiff takes a certain country's law as the legal basis for his pleadings, and the defendant raises no objection and also defends according to the law of that same country, that law would be treated as the law chosen by the parties. Thus, the 2007 Provisions specifically included those two articles.[53]

As just illustrated, the practice of people's courts on this issue is inconsistent and more often than not, they would not distinguish between the parties tacitly choosing a law and the judges inferring the intent of the parties as to the applicable law. The SPC tried to avoid the inconsistencies in Article 4 by clarifying that only when parties 'have *not* selected the applicable law' can the court infer the tacit choice of law from their behaviour. This article might, then, prevent the court from interpreting the parties' failure to invoke a previously chosen law as a change of the applicable law, as was the case in *Shengli Shipping Co. (Germany)* v. *Junye International Trade Co. Ltd. (Tianjin)*.[54]

However, Article 4 contradicted Article 3. To invoke the law of the same origin is obviously different from arriving at an express choice of law agreement, and if the former is allowed, what about other indications of a tacit choice? If a tacit choice of law is permitted, a tacit change of the applicable law should not be excluded, because change is actually a new choice. In fact, Article 4(2) is not necessary. If both of the parties invoke the same law as the governing law of their contract, all the judge has to do is to enquire of both of them and verify whether a new agreement has been concluded.[55]

B Restrictions on Parties' Autonomy

Two articles were relating to restrictions on parties' choice. Article 6 provided that, if the parties select a foreign law with the intent to evade mandatory rules of Chinese law or administrative regulations, their conduct would result in the non-application of foreign laws and the law of China should then be the governing law. Article 7 was about the social public interest.

These provisions, however, are only restatements of the relevant content in the former statutes and judicial interpretations, making no

[53] See the replies to the fourth and fifth questions in n 50. [54] See n 39.

[55] See Guangdong Higher People's Court (2004) p. 13. Article 4(2), combined with Article 9 of the 2007 Provisions, created a further ambiguity concerning the introduction of foreign law into court. See Sections 7.1.2 and 7.3.

attempt to clarify the ambiguities. First, there was no standard to determine which rules have the character of being 'mandatory rules' and thus cannot be evaded by parties by choosing a foreign law. Under Article 126 (2) of the 1999 Contract Law, Chinese law shall apply to three categories of contracts to be performed in China.[56] In Article 8 of the 2007 Provisions, five additional categories of contracts where Chinese law should solely be applied were included.[57] Accordingly, for these eight categories of contracts, the choice of governing law other than Chinese law by the parties would be invalid and unenforceable. Although the legal rules regulating the contracts within those eight categories might be deemed 'mandatory rules', it was still unclear *which* provisions in Chinese legislation are 'mandatory'.

Second, 'social public interest' was not defined in the 2007 Provisions, so it still had an elastic nature and provided people's courts with discretionary power to make decisions on an ad hoc basis, just as it did before.

C The Ascertainment of Foreign Law

Article 9 required that, when parties select a foreign law as the applicable law or change their selection of the law governing their contractual dispute to the law of a foreign country, they shall provide or attest to the relevant provisions of such foreign law, and if the parties fail to ascertain the provisions of the foreign law through suitable means, the people's court may apply the law of China.

Before the 2007 Provisions, the means of ascertaining foreign law were stipulated in the 1988 Opinions where five methods were included and

[56] See n 46.

[57] They are: (1) contracts for the transfer of shares in Chinese-foreign equity joint ventures, Sino-foreign cooperative joint ventures and wholly foreign-owned enterprises; (2) contracts under which foreign natural persons, legal persons or other organizations contract for the operations of Chinese-foreign equity joint ventures or cooperative joint ventures established within the territory of the PRC; (3) contracts for the purchase by foreign natural persons, legal persons or other organizations of equity from shareholders of non-foreign-invested enterprises within the territory of the PRC; (4) contracts for the subscription by foreign natural persons, legal persons or other organizations for capital increases of non-foreign-invested limited liability companies or companies limited by shares within the territory of the PRC and; (5) contracts for the purchase by foreign natural persons, legal persons or other organizations of assets of non-foreign-invested enterprises within the territory of the PRC. This provision is further analysed in Section 6.1.1 of Chapter 6.

both the court and the parties had the responsibility of ascertaining the content of the foreign law chosen by the parties.[58] The 2007 Provisions, however, stipulated that when the parties have selected a foreign law to govern their contract, they bear the burden of proving that law: the parties should provide evidence to the satisfaction of the court, otherwise the court may apply Chinese law instead.

Since the methods to ascertain a foreign law in China are very limited, that article presented a heavy burden on the parties. If they wanted the chosen law to be applied, they would have to follow carefully the instructions on how to prove the content of a foreign law. If they were not able to do that, they would have to rely on Chinese law, with which they may not be familiar or in which they may not have confidence.

Compared with the unsolved issues summarized in the last section, the 2007 Provisions clarified that the parties can change the law they have chosen previously by a later agreement, added the categories of contracts where party autonomy is excluded and only Chinese law should apply, and stipulated the method of ascertaining the content of foreign law chosen by the parties. However, from the analysis in this section, it is clear that the 2007 Provisions could not solve the existing problems and even created new confusion.

1.4.2 *The SPC's Interpretations Relating to Mandatory Rules*

In 2009, the SPC issued Interpretation of Supreme People's Court Regarding Law Application Matters of the Contract Law (2) (Interpretation of Contract Law (2)).[59] According to Article 14, the 'mandatory rules' articulated in Article 52(1)(5) of the Contract Law[60] means mandatory rules 'that affect validity'.

[58] Article 193 of the 1988 Opinions on Civil Law reads: 'The applicable foreign law may be found out through the following ways: (1) provided by the parties; (2) provided by the central organ of the opposite party who has concluded judicial assistant convention; (3) provided by our embassy or consulate in the foreign country; (4) provided by the embassy of the foreign country in China; (5) provided by both Chinese and foreign legal experts. If the applicable foreign law still cannot be determined through the aforementioned methods, the law of the people's republic of China may be applied.' This provision is further discussed in Section 7.1.1.

[59] It was issued by the SPC on 24 April 2009 and became effective on 13 May 2009.

[60] Article 52 of the Contract Law reads: 'A contract is invalid in any of the following circumstances: . . . (5) the contract violates a mandatory provision of any law or administrative regulation.'

Shortly after the issue of this Interpretation, the SPC made another guiding opinion in September 2009, where the definition of 'mandatory rules' is further addressed. In Article 5(15) of Guiding Opinions on Several Issues Concerning the Trial of Civil and Commercial Contract Disputes under Current Circumstances (2009 Guiding Opinions),[61] the SPC requires people's courts to distinguish between mandatory rules 'that affect validity' and mandatory rules 'of an administrative nature' pursuant to Article 14 of the Interpretation of Contract Law (2). The people's court should invalidate those contracts which violate the mandatory rules *that affect validity*, and determine the validity of the contracts which are in violation of the mandatory rules of an administrative nature on a case-by-case analysis.

The distinction provided in the two judicial interpretations looks more like an academic or theoretical construct and are difficult to understand and apply in the context of China's contemporary legal system. They cannot solve the complexities that arise in practice.[62] The scope of 'mandatory rules', one of the important issues mentioned repeatedly in the previous sections, remained uncertain even after the SPC's two interpretations in 2009.

1.5 The 2010 Conflicts Statute

The 2010 Conflicts Statute was passed by the NPCSC after an eight year process of drafting and discussion. Article 1 specifies that the Statute is enacted in order to clarify the application of laws concerning foreign-related civil relationships, reasonably solve foreign-related civil disputes, and protect the legal rights and interests of parties. The party autonomy principle is positioned in Chapter 1 of the Statute, and thus obtained the status of a general principle in China's private international law. Compared with the previous statutes, the application of the party autonomy principle is largely extended in the Statute.

Concerning the party autonomy principle in contract, although the parties are still permitted to choose the applicable law under the Statute, their freedom is restricted or even excluded in two special categories of contracts, namely, consumer contracts and labour contracts. According to Article 42, only the consumer has the right to choose the laws at the

[61] It was issued by the SPC on 7 July 2009.

[62] The relevant provisions in these two interpretations are further analysed in Section 6.2.2.

locality of the provision of goods or services.[63] Pursuant to Article 43, parties are not allowed to select the governing law in labour contracts.[64] Compared with the previous legal rules, the Statute contains special rules in contract to protect the weaker parties in order to safeguard the interests of consumers and labourers.[65]

The enforceability of parties' choice of law clauses is also subject to three provisions. First, the Statute clearly specifies that the mandatory provisions on foreign-related civil relations in the laws of China shall directly apply, and the law chosen by the parties will accordingly not be applied to determine relevant issues.[66] It is noteworthy that this provision has, for the first time, defined the scope of China's mandatory rules in transnational litigation: first, the applicable mandatory rules should be those governing *foreign-related* civil relationships; second, they are provided in *laws*. Accordingly, neither the rules that are only applicable in purely domestic issues, nor those provided in administrative regulations, belong to this category. Compared with Article 52(1)(5) of the Contract Law and the relevant provisions in the SPC's judicial interpretations, the Statute more narrowly defines the mandatory rules that are directly applicable in foreign-related civil litigation. With regard to the party autonomy principle, if parties choose a foreign law to govern an issue within the scope of the mandatory rules as defined in Article 4, their choice will be overridden by those rules. But their chosen law may still be applied to determine other matters.

Moreover, the 'evasion of law' exception, which was stipulated in Article 194 of the 1988 Opinions and Article 6 of the 2007 Provisions,

[63] Article 42 provides: 'The laws at the habitual residence of consumers shall apply to consumer contracts. If a consumer chooses the applicable laws at the locality of the provision of goods or if a business operator does not engage in the relevant business activities at the habitual residence of the consumer, the laws at the locality of the provision of goods or services shall apply.'

[64] Article 43 provides: 'The laws at the working locality of labourers shall apply to labour contracts. If it is difficult to determine the working locality of a labourer, the laws at the main business place of the employer shall apply. The laws at the dispatching place of labour services shall apply to labour dispatch.'

[65] See 'Report on the Main Issues concerning the Draft Law on the Application of Laws to Foreign-Related Civil Relationships of the PRC' (issued on the official website of the NPC on 28 August 2010).

[66] Article 4 provides: 'If a law of the people's republic of China contains mandatory provisions on a foreign-related civil relation, such mandatory provisions should be applied directly.'

is not provided in the Statute.[67] But both the effects of the two provisions and their relationship with Article 4 of the Statute need further investigation.[68]

Second, Article 5 of the Statute also provides for the exception of social public interest: if the application of the selected foreign laws will undermine the social public interest of China, Chinese law shall apply. Article 150 of the Civil Law only articulated that the application of foreign law must not violate the public interest of China, but did not specify which law should be applied after the foreign law concerned is excluded. Article 7 of the 2007 Provisions clarified this issue by providing that Chinese law should be applied instead, and this provision is reiterated in Article 5 of the Statute. However, it is still not clear how to define 'social public interest'.

Third, if parties choose a foreign law, they must 'provide the content' of the laws of that country for the purpose of ascertaining the law. Compared with Article 9 of the 2007 Provisions and Article 193 of the 1988 Opinions, Article 10 of the Statute more specifically provides that people's court also have the responsibility to ascertain the content of foreign law. However, the Statute does not articulate the criteria of assessing the evidence of the foreign law, nor of determining what is to happen if the foreign law is silent on the relevant issues.[69]

Therefore, although China's new Statute on Private International Law makes an improvement on some of the previous legal rules concerning the party autonomy principle in contractual choice of law, it fails to address several obvious existing problems in judicial practice. Moreover, its relationship with the previous rules scattered in different statutes and judicial interpretations is not clear. The efficacy of the new Statute, together with its effects on judicial practice and commercial reality, requires further investigation.

1.6 Overview of the Book

1.6.1 The Structure of the Book

The previous analysis identifies the main problems existing in the relevant rules relating to the application of the party autonomy principle in

[67] However, the evasion of law exception is provided in the SPC's Interpretation of the 2010 Conflicts Statute (1), which, it is submitted, should not be invoked to invalidate parties' choice of foreign law in contract. See Section 5.1.4.

[68] These issues are further addressed in Section 6.2.

[69] These issues are discussed in Chapter 7.

China. It points to the necessity of conducting a comprehensive study of the principle with a focus on people's courts' adjudication of the enforceability of parties' choice of law clauses.

This book addresses the question of how, when and with what limitations, parties' choice of law clauses in an international commercial contract should be enforced by people's courts. It argues that in China, a choice of law clause in contract should only be interfered with or overridden by the *lex fori* when it is necessary to secure a broader public interest, the justification of which should be formed in legislation rather than in administrative rules. In the interests of the predictability and certainty of transnational litigation in China, it is important for the legislature to establish a comprehensive system of legal rules concerning the enforceability of choice of law clauses. It is also important for the judiciary to interpret and apply those rules in specific cases consistently, respecting the intention of the parties. In doing so, people's courts should exercise their discretionary power with caution, demonstrating that they have done so by giving logical and detailed reasoning in their judgments.

Chapter 2 looks at the conceptual debate concerning the party autonomy principle in private international law. It provides the theoretical basis upon which judicial practice in China can be evaluated. The subsequent chapters are then organized in accordance with the issues that arise in the practical operation of the party autonomy principle in China.

Chapters 3 and 4 discuss three main issues preliminary to the application of the principle. Chapter 3 first looks at the question of whether both parties have made a choice of law. Based on the analysis of the difficulties and inconsistence in judicial practice, it takes commercial practice as well as the protection of weaker parties into account in the discussion of how to determine the existence of parties' choice. Second, it deals with the material validity of parties' choice of law and also the governing law of this issue. Chapter 4 then analyses the 'law' that can be chosen by parties and distinguishes between parties' incorporation by reference of foreign law and their choice of the law governing their contract.

Chapters 5 and 6 address the statutory restrictions on party autonomy. By analysing the relevant rules in statutes and judicial interpretations, these chapters discuss in detail the scope of social public interest and the inherent problems and difficulties in the identification of mandatory rules under China's legal system. They demonstrate that only in exceptional cases should social public interest be invoked and that the rules previously taken as being 'mandatory' by people's courts are not mandatory rules in the sense of private international law.

Chapter 7 deals with the ascertainment of the foreign law chosen by parties, which, if not appropriately resolved, can hinder the effective operation of the party autonomy principle. This chapter particularly touches upon three issues: the introduction of foreign law into court, the establishment of the content of the law and the effects of the failure to prove the selected law. It first reveals the uncertainties in the previous rules in the SPC's judicial interpretations, and then examines whether the new rule provided in the 2010 Conflicts Statute can respond to them.

Based on the analyses in the aforementioned chapters, Chapter 8 further considers, from the perspective of people's courts sitting in the Mainland, the impact that the 'One Country, Two Systems' principle may have upon the treatment of the issues addressed in Chapters 5–7. Through the discussion of interregional conflict of laws cases where the social public interest exception has been applied, it analyses the constraints that should be imposed on the application of the exception. Moreover, it discusses the approaches that may be helpful in ascertaining the laws of Hong Kong, Macao and Taiwan.

Chapter 9 summarizes the findings in the previous chapters and touches upon problems more generally relating to the judicial system in China.

1.6.2 Methodology

The book adopts doctrinal, normative and comparative methodologies.

Since the contemporary legal rules concerning party autonomy in China are the starting point of this research, doctrinal (black-letter law) methodology is applied. By looking at the evolving rules under the legal system of China, the author intends to find out the relevant legal framework within which the party autonomy principle is being applied in people's courts for the determination of the law governing international contracts. This is the basis for further analysis of whether the relevant rules are applied appropriately.

The doctrinal research is followed by case study to further illustrate the actual implementation of the rules in people's court. Both Chapter 1 and other studies have shown that a significant gap exists between the written law and law in practice in China, particularly during its market transition.[70] Therefore, case analyses are carried out to gain a thorough understanding of the judicial practice and empirically verify the contentious issues.

[70] For other studies on the implementation and the role of laws in the economic development in China, see Chen (1996) pp. 7–9; Peerenboom (2002) pp. 192–199; Chen (2016) chapter 21.

Although adjudicated cases are not binding on people's courts in China, they reflect the development of legislation. Given that Chinese private international law rules are usually ambiguous and open-ended, adjudicated cases, particularly the judgments made by the SPC, serve as a reference, and assist people's courts in applying the relevant rules to identify the governing law.[71] Moreover, cases can illustrate the difficulty and inconsistency in the interpretation and application of the rules regarding party autonomy in people's courts.

The case studies in this book refer to a wide array of available materials in the area and are based on both primary and secondary sources. The primary sources contain the adjudicated cases reported in the official publications issued by the SPC and lower people's courts and on the websites of *China Foreign-related Commercial and Maritime Trial*,[72] and of people's courts. The secondary sources target books, journal articles and conference papers by both academics and practitioners which comment on the topic.

Based on the black-letter law research and case studies, a general picture is obtained and controversial issues surrounding legislation and judicial practice on the party autonomy principle are exposed. The book then considers how the contemporary situation can be improved. In law, the term 'normative' is used to describe the way something ought to be done according to a value position.[73] Normative research aims at improvement, which means that it includes evaluation of the present state of things and also of the direction of future development.[74] In the analysis of the party autonomy principle in China, the book situates the normative evaluation between two important values in private international law: the predictability and certainty of law as required by commercial transactions and the protection of public interest as is necessary in the transformational era of China's move towards market economy.

Some comparative study is also conducted. As far as international conflicts problems are concerned, comparative law is important, if only because the rules that 'conflict' are those of different legal systems. Since

[71] See Kong and Hu (2002) p. 415.

[72] See the website of China Foreign-Related Commercial and Maritime Trial: www.ccmt.org.cn/.

[73] Normative research may also be referred to as 'reform-oriented research', which intensively evaluates the adequacy of existing rules and recommends changes to any rules found wanting. See Pendleton (2007) p. 159.

[74] It has been argued that the normative analysis approach should be given a proper position in the Chinese juristic research. See Xie (2009).

party autonomy did gradually gain acceptance in private international law with the development of transnational commercial activities, an international and comparative perspective is necessary for an in-depth study of this principle.[75] The comparative study of this book mainly touches upon two systems of rules: one is international instruments such as the 1980 Rome Convention as well as the Rome I Regulation, the Brussels Regime and other instruments on international trade; the other is the common law system, including the traditional private international law rules in the United Kingdom, and also the conflict of laws rules in the United States, due to their vital roles as the model of shaping and developing a harmonious system of private international rules in contract,[76] and in the transformation and evolution of the conflict of laws approaches respectively.[77]

Historically, the continental doctrine of party autonomy only permitted parties to subject their contract to a system of law with which it was internally connected, while the English doctrine allowed parties' choice of any legal system that seemed convenient for business purposes and reasonable.[78] However, the difference between the two doctrines is actually not great. It is practically negligible if the conception of internal connection is not too rigidly framed.[79] After the adoption of the Rome Convention and subsequently the Rome I Regulation within the European Union (EU), the rules concerning the party autonomy principle in contractual choice of law have been unified among the member states, and the difference thus becomes unimportant.[80] In this regard, even though some scholars may insist on viewing the legal system of mainland

[75] For a discussion of the importance of comparative approach to the conflict of laws problems, see Juenger (1999).

[76] Briggs pointed out that the practice of the European Union does offer a valuable and alternative insight into common contemporary problems in international commercial litigation. See Briggs (2008) para. 1.11.

[77] For a detailed discussion of the choice of law revolution in America, see Symeonides (2006a).

[78] See Wolff (1950) pp. 417–420. [79] See Wolff (1950) p. 420.

[80] On 24 June 2016, the people of the United Kingdom (UK) voted by a narrow majority (51.9 per cent to 48.1 per cent) to leave the EU. The decision to leave is likely to have a significant impact on the UK's civil justice system and, in particular, on the rules of private international law. Considerable uncertainty does exist concerning the future development of the rules. For a discussion of the legal baseline of applicable private international law rules under international, EU and national law following the withdrawal, see Dickinson (2016). However, the UK's decision to leave the EU would not undermine the importance of the practice of EU in international commercial litigation. See n 76.

China as one deriving from the civil law tradition,[81] that would not substantially affect how the party autonomy principle is viewed and applied in China. The book focuses on the certainty of the relevant legal rules and the consistency of their application in judicial practice. The comparative study of the EU regime and the common law approach is therefore helpful.

[81] In fact, the external influences that have contributed to shaping the contemporary legal system in mainland China include Soviet law, civil law and common law. See Chen (2000) pp. 55–74.

2

The Background to the Development of Party Autonomy

This chapter looks at the main lines of conceptual debate concerning the party autonomy principle and considers how the development of the principle in China is related to the international debate.

2.1 The Historical Development of the Party Autonomy Principle

The principle of party autonomy is 'almost as ancient as conflicts law itself'.[1] It seems that party autonomy was recognized, albeit indirectly, by what may be regarded as the earliest known conflicts rule. An edict promulgated in Hellenistic Egypt from 120 to 118 BC provided that contracts written in the Egyptian language were subject to the jurisdiction of Egyptian courts, which applied Egyptian law, whereas contracts written in Greek were subject to the jurisdiction of Greek courts, which applied Greek law. In specifying language as the pertinent connecting factor for jurisdictional purposes, it implicitly recognized the principle of party autonomy: by choosing the language, the parties could directly choose the forum and indirectly, the applicable law.[2]

In the Middle Ages the French commentator Dumoulin resurrected party autonomy, which has since been an important concept in continental conflicts doctrine and practice.[3] But Dumoulin did not understand the parties' intention as an independent connecting factor. His main concern appeared to have been with the marriage contract, and the implied intention of the parties was taken as a device which would point to the place of performance rather than of contracting.[4] In the seventeenth century, the writings of Huber also contained the idea of resorting

[1] Symeonides, Perdue and von Mehren (2003) p. 338.
[2] See Juenger (1993) pp. 7–8; Juenger (1983) p. 137.
[3] See Juenger (1993) pp. 16–17; Lipstein (1972) p. 119.
[4] See Nygh (1999) pp. 4–5; Lando (1976) para. 10.

to the intention of the parties. But like Dumoulin, he gave the example of a marriage contract and made an acknowledgement that the place of contracting may not always be relevant. As with Dumoulin, the presumed intention of parties appeared to be a device, much as it was later used in English law, to justify a 'proper law' approach.[5]

Early in the nineteenth century the Danish writer Ørsted referred to the intention of the parties as the basis of the rules which he established and so did most continental and American scholars.[6] The emphasis on the parties as private legislators in their contractual relationships was introduced in the nineteenth century, when the conception of contract changed. Whereas originally it was seen as an obligation imposed on the parties by the general law arising out of their transaction, it came to be seen as an obligation created by the parties themselves.[7] In relation to choice of law, the approach that was later followed was more directly concerned with what rules the parties intended to impose upon their relationship.

It was the Italian jurist Mancini, who, in 1874, founded the theory of party autonomy as we know it today, by submitting the question of choice of law to the provision and express choice of the parties. He rejected territoriality on which previous conflict of laws theories had been largely based, and argued that nationality should be the primary connecting factor in private international law. Mancini's nationality theory was one of the sources from which the party autonomy principle and choice of law was developed. The importance of the national school of law for the law of obligations and, in particular, for the problem of defining the scope within which the contracting parties have the possibility of freely choosing the applicable law, lay in the distinction it made

5 Thus Huber was cited in *Robinson* v. *Bland* (1760) 2 Burr. 1077, one of the first English cases where the question of the application of foreign law was raised and where Lord Mansfield is reported to have said (at [1078]): 'The parties had a view to the laws of England. The law of the place can never be the rule, where the transaction is entered into with an express view to the law of another country, as the rule by which it is to be governed ... ' No conflict of laws was found to arise between English and French law in any event. But Lord Mansfield, citing Huber, explored the position which might have arisen if there had been, although it is unlikely that the parties had any view. The intention of the parties was thus once again taken as an implied fictional intention. Westlake pointed out that the line of English decisions which this remark initiated was in reality based on the objective test of the most real connection. See Nygh (1999) pp. 5–6; Lando (1976) paras. 11, 27; Westlake (1925) p. 304.

6 See the writings cited in Lando (1976) nn 77 and 78.

7 See Atiyah (1979) pp. 141, 420.

between 'necessary' and 'voluntary' private law.[8] In cases where the regulation of parties' affairs was left to them, as in the determination of the terms and conditions of a contract, they should be free to determine for themselves which law should apply. Territoriality only remained relevant as such by way of *ordre public*.[9]

Indeed, in the latter part of the nineteenth century, the place of contracting lost its paramount significance for reasons of economics and commercial convenience.[10] Reliance on the intention of the parties then became the governing principle. Party autonomy was also supported by the laissez-faire philosophy of the nineteenth century.[11] In accordance with that philosophy, the intention of the parties played a great part in the English law of contracts.[12] 'Autonomy' was then taken as a principle of self-ordering that gave parties the freedom to regulate their own affairs, and focus shifted to the intention of individuals as a source of obligation or legal effect, whether in the law of obligations, property or probate. The development of the party autonomy rule was a clear manifestation of the liberal values that gained acceptance in those days.[13]

However, during the first half of the twentieth century, an era when there was 'increased emphasis on the national state as the sovereign source of legislation', a reaction set in and the idea of allowing parties to an international contract a free choice of law was seen as an unwarranted assumption of legislative power by private persons.[14]

The rise of the classical liberal interpretation of party autonomy started with the famous decision of the Privy Council in *Vita Food Products Inc.* v. *Unus Shipping Co. Ltd.*, where Lord Wright asserted the freedom of the parties to choose the applicable law in the broadest

[8] See Kalenský (1971) pp. 88–89.

[9] See Nygh (1999) p. 8. According to Mancini's disciplines, the distinction between optional and mandatory rules could not be eliminated by a mere manifestation of the will of the parties. Therefore, party autonomy is limited by the mandatory rules of the forum. See Chapters 5 and 6.

[10] For the declining importance of the *locus contractus*, see Lando (1976) para. 13.

[11] See Lando (1976) para. 30. [12] See Graveson (1974b) p. 406.

[13] See Hook (2016) p. 21.

[14] See Yntema (1952) p. 343. The doctrine of autonomy was besieged in the interbellum and post-Second World War periods in the twentieth century. Critics complained that it was logically impossible to elevate the will of the parties above the law, as there was no law outside legal systems that could give effect to it. See Nygh (1999) pp. 8–10; Lando (1976) paras. 27–60. The source of party autonomy is further discussed in Section 2.3.

terms.[15] Since then, the principle of party autonomy has gradually been accepted in different jurisdictions and international instruments as the primary rule in contractual choice of law.[16]

2.2 The Justifications of Party Autonomy

Parties' freedom to choose the law applicable to their international commercial contract is generally supported by two main considerations: the need of the parties for freedom and the need for certainty and predictability in cross-border transactions.[17]

Freedom of contract is considered to be an essential part of the market economy.[18] The party autonomy principle in contractual choice of law can be seen as the conflict of laws aspect of freedom of contract.[19] In fact, the development of the general principles of English contract law was closely associated with liberal views of political freedom and the free market economy.[20] As the previous section indicates, in the history of private international law, there was also a parallel movement concerning the autonomy of parties. The earlier writings on this subject were not concerned with the subjective intention of parties, but rather with the results which flowed from what they had done or what they proposed to do. The later approach in conflict of laws was more directly concerned with what rules the parties intended to impose upon their relationship.

Parties' freedom is magnified in the context of international commercial contracts. Normally a plaintiff has several fora available and can choose a more favourable forum.[21] Concerning the law governing their contract, parties have creditable motives, which justify their choice:[22]

[15] [1939] A.C. 277 (P.C.), 290. Lord Wright said: 'Where the English rule that intention is the test applies, and where there is an express statement by the parties of their intention to select the law of the contract, it is difficult to see what qualifications are possible, provided the intention expressed is bona fide and legal, and provided there is no reason for avoiding the choice on the ground of public policy.' See also Lando (1976) para. 32.

[16] See Nygh (1999) pp. 10–13.

[17] See Lando (1976) paras. 61–62; Nygh (1999) pp. 2–3; Takeshita (2015) pp. 198–199.

[18] For a more detailed discussion of freedom of contract, see Atiyah (1979); Nygh (1999) pp. 7–8.

[19] Takeshita (2015) p. 199.

[20] For an extensive description of the process, see Atiyah (1979).

[21] Nygh (1999) p. 2.

[22] Lando (1976) para. 62.

> They may want to use a certain formula which is internationally known. They may want to submit the contract to the law of the country that dominates the market. They may want to select a 'neutral' law in which each of them has more confidence than in that of the domicile of the other party. A certain legal system may be well developed and well suited to the contract in question. The parties may wish to refer to a law which they have used in earlier transactions with each other. The contract may have a close relationship to some other contract which is governed by a certain law.

Second, the choice of law clause ensures certainty and predictability in cross-border commercial transactions. Where several fora are available and several laws potentially applicable, the parties should be able to avoid such uncertainties through a choice of law clause.[23] As the party autonomy principle has developed, there is almost unanimous agreement between the laws of different jurisdictions that the choice of law clause should be respected in principle. This uniformity ensures that parties' choice of law will relieve the parties of their uncertainty as to the law governing their contract.[24]

2.3 The Source of Parties' Autonomy

Critics of party autonomy once complained that it was logically impossible to elevate the will of the parties above the law, as there was no law outside legal systems that could give effect to it.[25] This criticism is concerned with the question of the source of parties' autonomy: what gives the parties permission to make a choice of law at all? This section discusses the issue.

2.3.1 The Law of the Forum Provides the Entry Point

Proponents of party autonomy reasoned that the parties' choice did not place them within a lawless vacuum because it operated as a connecting factor given effect to by the forum. As Ehrenzweig said:[26]

> Party autonomy is, of course, not an independent source of conflicts rules, but is effective only in so far as it is recognized by such a rule.

[23] See Nygh (1999) pp. 2–3, 34; Takeshita (2015) p. 198. [24] See Lando (1976) para. 61.
[25] See n 14. [26] Ehrenzweig (1972) p. 44.

It is now a general consensus that the law of the forum must provide the entry point for the operation of party autonomy.[27] Vischer said:[28]

> The forum state, which ultimately controls the choice of law, has to determine the conditions, the limits and the scope of the parties' autonomy in international contracts.

In spite of the general acceptance of the party autonomy principle, divergence still exists concerning the circumstances in which the choice of the parties may be ignored.[29] The difficulty with applying the national law approach may be that, the fate of parties' choice of law may not be ultimately determined until the plaintiff files suit and a forum is seized with jurisdiction.[30] This is nothing new in private international law. As Nygh pointed out, 'it shows that autonomy in a pragmatic sense ultimately rests with the parties, to be exercised jointly if they agree on an exclusive forum, and severally, if they do not'.[31]

The concept underlying the national law approach is the conventional idea of the territorial sovereignty of the nation state and its ability to command its courts. On that basis, the rules of the forum which specify when its courts are competent and what choice of law rules they shall apply are part of its own territorial law.[32] As a result, private international law, contrary to its name, is characterized as part of *national* law, rather than *international* law.[33]

27 See Lando (1976) para. 63; Kahn-Freund (1980) p. 197; North (1993) pp. 184–187; Nygh (1999) p. 32.

28 Vischer (1992) p. 139. Therefore the parties are highly unlikely to promise one another in the nature of providing a warranty that the chosen law would apply to *all* issues falling within the choice of law clause. See Yeo (2010) pp. 196–197. The nature of parties' choice of law is further discussed in Section 2.4.

29 Yeo (2010) p. 197 pointed out that the effect and scope of a choice of law clause varies from jurisdiction to jurisdiction. The variations may occur in respect of whether it can apply to non-contractual obligations; whether it will be given effect to and with what limitations; and what overriding laws may be applied. Briggs (2008) paras. 2.11–2.12 also argued that the recognition of parties' consent in private international law was driven by the development of the rule of consent in the substantive rules of commercial law, and therefore the extent to which a court will honour the parties' choice of the law governing their contract will be affected by how much the consent of the parties is honoured in the commercial litigation and by the judges within a country. The statutory restrictions on party autonomy are discussed in Chapters 5 and 6.

30 See Nygh (1999) p. 34.

31 Nygh (1999) p. 34.

32 Nygh (1999) p. 35; Cheshire, North and Fawcett (2008) p. 3.

33 As Mills pointed out: 'A sharp distinction is usually drawn between public international law, concerned with the rights and obligations of states with respect to other states and individuals, and private international law, concerned with issues of jurisdiction,

This characterization reflects the influence of the positivist theory of sovereignty on the subject.[34] It indicates that any freedom the parties may possess is one granted by the sovereign. This 'received wisdom' is increasingly subject to criticism by scholars from an international perspective,[35] and is further discussed in the next section.

2.3.2 International Law as a Source and the Idea of 'Individual Sovereignty'

The source of party autonomy is also viewed from a perspective beyond national law. Parties' autonomy is considered to arise from some form of international consensus. Lowenfeld has written: 'It is fair to say . . . that party autonomy – both for choice of law and for choice of forum, including an arbitral forum – is now part of an international customary law of dispute settlement.'[36]

Some degree of judicial and doctrinal support for such an international view could be found earlier in the twentieth century in some countries,[37] and later in the Preamble to the Resolutions adopted by the Institute of International Law at Basel in 1991 entitled 'The Autonomy of the Parties in International Contracts Between Private Persons or Entities'.[38] Professor Jayme, the Rapporteur of the Report accompanying the Resolutions, subsequently explained that the foundation of autonomy lies in the principle of the liberty of the individual which is a human right. According to that view, the freedom to choose the applicable law is not

applicable law and the recognition and enforcement of foreign judgments in international private law disputes before national courts. Private international law is viewed as national law, which is and ought to be focused on resolving individual private disputes based on domestic conceptions of justice or fairness . . . Thus, public and private international law are viewed as distinct disciplines, as two separate intellectual streams running in parallel.' Mills (2009) pp. 1–2.

34 The positivist territorial theory of sovereignty and its influence upon the status of the party autonomy principle in private international law are critically analysed in Section 2.3.2.

35 Nygh (1999) p. 35 doubted 'whether this received wisdom is a realistic view of today's world'. See further, Section 2.3.2.

36 Lowenfeld (1996) pp. 208–209.

37 See Nygh (1999) pp. 35–36.

38 It declared, *inter alia*: 'Considering that the autonomy of the parties is one of the fundamental principles of private international law; recognizing that the autonomy of the parties has also been enshrined as a freedom of the individual in several conventions and various United Nations resolutions . . . ' This document is available at: http://www.idi-iil.org/app/uploads/2017/06/1991_bal_02_en.pdf.

merely a connecting factor; it is the parties who insert their agreement into the legal system they have freely chosen.[39]

The acceptance of party autonomy in private international law is further perceived as reflecting the recognition of the 'sovereignty' of individuals in international law.[40] Mills argued that the principle gives individuals the power to determine the substantive law which applies to them, and thus to 'self-determine' an aspect of their own regulation, recognizing that not only states but also individuals possess a form of 'sovereignty'.[41]

Mills' argument is made from an 'international systemic perspective' on private international law. On that basis, he challenged the conventional distinction between public and private international law[42] by exploring the ways in which norms of public international law shape and are given effect to through private international law. After a detailed analysis of the history of private international law theories, Mills concluded that the idea of private international law as purely a part of national law may be understood as a product of two late nineteenth century phenomena: on the one hand, it is a product of the fact of increased diversity in national legal systems; on the other hand, it is a product of the positivist theoretical emphasis on sovereignty.[43]

39 See Jayme (1995) pp. 147–148, cited at Nygh (1999) p. 36. See also Takeshita (2015) p. 199.

40 This is taken as an 'essential explanation' for the principle. See Mills (2009) pp. 291–292, 308.

41 See Mills (2009) pp. 305–306.

42 See n 33.

43 See the discussion in Mills (2009) chapter 2. The application of scientific methods to the study of social science is referred to as positivism. See Kelly (1992) p. 331 for the origins of the term. Positivism is more a methodology than a theory. When it is applied to law, it prescribes the study of laws as if they were natural phenomena, to be observed and evaluated, detached from preconceived ideas and dogma. See Mills (2009) pp. 37–38; Neff (2006) p. 38; Kelly (1992) pp. 223 ff. According to positivist ideas, theorizing should be based on the observation of behavior from which rules are developed through inductive reasoning. A positivist approach to international law means the study of the behaviour or practice of states, and the derivation of rules from that practice. The conclusions that the positivist theorists derived from their account of international law therefore came from their observation of the behaviour among states. Although these conclusions constituted what is known as the 'positivist theory of international law', they are only the result of applying a positivist methodology to studying the behaviour of states in the eighteenth and nineteenth centuries (Mills (2009) pp. 38, 40). The application of this methodology to international law in the present day may not lead to such an emphasis on state sovereignty, because the way in which states behave has changed. See Mills (2009) chapter 3; Henkin (1979). For a more detailed discussion of the development of the positivist theory of international law and its impact on the subject, see Mills (2009) section 2.3; Hu (2015)

The 'international systemic' approach looks at the consistency of private international law as a whole rather than at any national policies or objectives.[44] It views private international law as an international system and focuses on the functioning of this system in an international context.[45] Mills argued:[46]

> From this perspective, the problem of private international law is the problem of the appropriate allocation of regulatory authority: which state should hear a dispute, whose law should be applied, and whether a foreign judgment should be enforced locally ... The distribution of regulatory authority is itself a matter of justice – perhaps 'meta-justice' – operating within the framework of justice pluralism. The answer to a problem of private international law involves the determination of which idea of justice (which state law) would be most just to apply. Private international law, properly understood, is about determining the most 'just' distribution of regulation authority.

The fact that individuals are able to choose the jurisdiction or applicable law governing their dispute, Mills analysed, does not deny that private international law rules serve the function of ordering regulatory authority. It merely demonstrates that private international law recognizes, as does contemporary public international law, the polycentric existence of a range of contesting 'authorities' in international law.[47]

The idea of private international law as part of the structural ordering of the international system indicates that the regulatory authority of each

section 5.1; Hu (2016) pp. 77–78. For the critiques on positivism in international law, see Mills (2009) sections 3.2–3.4.

44 Mills (2009) p. 17. 45 Mills (2009) pp. 12, 16.

46 Mills (2009) p. 18. 'Meta-justice' is suggested by Mills as an allusion to 'meta-ethics', the concern of 'value pluralism' in philosophy. Concerning the idea of justice, Mills considered that since the rules of private law of each state contain and embody a different determination about what the 'just' outcome of a dispute would be, the usual meaning of 'justice' cannot provide a justification for choice of law rules because the problem for choice of law is determining which state's law should be applied, that is, which idea of 'justice' should be applied. Under the conception of 'justice pluralism', Mills presumed that 'the variety of legal cultures represent significant and distinct sets of norms which should be independently valued'. In this regard, the justification for the application of foreign law in private international law is 'a question of context – of determining the appropriate circumstances for the application of local or foreign standards of justice, the appropriate "connections" between the dispute and the forum or legal system.' Therefore, a central problem in choice of law is 'the determination of what standards could be applied to identify when the application of foreign law is "just"'. See Mills (2009) pp. 5–6.

47 For the idea of contesting authorities in international law, see Mills (2009) chapter 3.

state is not only limited by the horizontal recognition of the authority of other states, but also influenced by the development of public international law related to private rights of individuals.[48]

The concept of 'individual sovereignty'[49] or identity is increasingly recognized as part of international law.[50] The most obvious examples are the very extensive agreement that individuals possess a range of rights under international law,[51] the emergence of international minimum standards of due process and procedural fairness,[52] and the specific individual rights and freedoms defined by international economic law.[53] The recognition of these ideas in private international law theory is reflected in the use of residence and domicile as connecting factors in choice of law rules, which involve a subjective component.[54] The popularity of tests based on these factors challenges the traditional international law attitude to jurisdiction as an issue purely of state territorial or personal power,[55] partially devolves the power of determining identity from the state to the individual, and thus enhances the ability of the individual to 'self-determine' the law applicable to them.[56]

The deference to party autonomy in private international law was once described as reflecting 'the sovereign will of the parties'.[57] If the notion of 'individual sovereignty' is acknowledged, Mills reasoned, then 'the widespread recognition of party autonomy is clearly compatible with an argument that the foundations of private international law lie in broader international norms'.[58]

48 For the ways in which private international law rules reflect and give effect to international private rights, see Mills (2009) section 5.4.

49 The idea of individual sovereignty has a long history. It can be seen, for example, in the widespread recognition of human rights norms, which constitutes a limitation on state sovereignty, in their recognition of a superior 'sovereignty of the individual'. Lauterpacht (1950) p. 70 argued that 'International law, which has excelled in punctilious insistence on the respect owed by one sovereignty State to another, henceforth acknowledges the sovereignty of man.' See also the references in Mills (2009) p. 84, n 45.

50 See Mills (2009) p. 233.

51 See the discussion in Mills (2009) section 3.3.1 and pp. 266–267.

52 See the discussion in Mills (2009) pp. 267–268.

53 See Mills (2009) section 5.5.

54 See McClean (1996) pp. 36ff; Mills (2009) section 5.5.3.

55 See the discussion in Mills (2009) section 5.5.4.

56 Mills (2009) p. 257.

57 See the dissenting opinion by Judge De Bustamante in the *Serbian and Brazilian Loans* cases, (1929) PCIJ Serious A, Nos. 20–21, Judgment No. 14, p. 53.

58 Mills (2009) pp. 291–292. The idea of 'individual sovereignty' is further discussed in the next section.

2.3.3 *Implications of the International Approach*

The source of parties' autonomy is an issue on which wide agreement in judicial practice contrasts with contrariety in theoretical debate. The fundamental divergence between the national and international approaches lies in their different understanding of whether the principle of state sovereignty is the exclusive basis of private international law, and the status of individuals in private international law rules.

The idea of 'individual sovereignty' makes a contrast with the positivist approach to public international law, which, in Mills' criticism, 'cannot be accepted as providing a successful descriptive or normative framework for the contemporary international legal system'. In his view, the positivist conception of international law as purely the product of relations between *a priori* state sovereigns 'is unable to account for the widespread recognition of fundamental individual rights'.[59]

The weakness of the positivist approach mainly lies in its reliance on the concept of sovereignty.[60] With the process of globalization, regional economic and political integration, the rise of non-state actors and the flourishing of the notion of human rights, the concept of sovereignty in international positivism is increasingly subject to criticism regarding its incompatibility with the development of a legally regulated international community.[61]

[59] Mills (2009) p. 87.

[60] Positivist international theory entails a core commitment to certain essential ideas. States are viewed as the key actors in the formation of international law and are independent, free and equal. The positivist idea of state sovereignty implies that states possess some unrestricted freedoms as an *a priori* consequence of their statehood. This freedom is said to exist 'prior' to law. Thus, positivists (and their descendants, 'realist' international relations scholars) argue that international law can only exist where it is an expression of state sovereign will. Indeed, the origin and limitations of such a conception of sovereignty can be explained as an overstretch of the analogy between the individual and the state. Brand (2002) pp. 280–285; Brand (2006) pp. 38–39. Mills (2009) p. 67 argued that the idea of *a priori* or 'absolute' sovereignty is a myth which has never been meaningful outside the pages of the theorist. Radon (2004) pp. 195–196 argued that sovereignty 'has always been a term in search of a definition' which has 'become so powerful and so emotive as a political slogan that it has been rendered meaningless in the international law discourse'. Henkin (1995) p. 43 objected to 'the "shibboleth" of sovereignty'. Sadat (2005) p. 335 pointed out that 'the notion of absolute sovereignty is a fallacy'.

[61] See the brief survey of the scholarly arguments on the decline of sovereignty in Rudolph (2005) pp. 1–2. For the incompatibility of the concept of sovereignty with the development of the international community, see Kalmo and Skinner (2010).

When viewed from the perspective of resolving specific cross-border disputes, the function of private international law may be seen as the application of the conflicts rules of the forum to ultimately determine the rights and obligations of parties. But if the subject is examined against the background of the regulation of international commercial transactions, then its function is not confined to a particular jurisdiction – it is actually concerned with the relationships among states in the regulation of the conduct of private parties. As Brand has argued, when we discuss jurisdiction, applicable law or recognition of judgments, 'we are dealing with the way in which different sets of internal legal rules, developed by different sovereign entities, should be applied to private party relationships in a judicial context'.[62]

In this regard, the focus of the national approach on sovereign states as the sole basis of private international law would be an obvious ignorance of its function in international ordering. This justifies the reassessment of the concept of sovereignty.

Contrary to the reliance of the positivist theory of sovereignty on the authority of nation state, the human being is the essential element in the original conception of sovereignty. Indeed, the historical characteristic of sovereignty used to be based on the individual.[63] After a historical[64] and conceptual analysis of sovereignty in international law, Hu summarized that sovereignty, from historical theories to debates in contemporary international law, is a conception related to 'the different priority in the relationships of human with the God, the ruler or the State'. However, 'on the road to modernity, we have seen the gradual disappearance of the humans, swallowed by the leviathan, in the theory of sovereignty'.[65] Therefore, the concept of sovereignty in international legal positivism, as Mills argued, may be 'a mockery, not a fulfilment, of the deepest aspirations of humanity'.[66]

Although the positivist theoretical approach has its weakness, it would be too much to claim that the concept of sovereignty is itself meaningless, because the term 'sovereignty' still 'retains a symbolic significance, representative of international law's respect for the diverse values of national

62 Brand (2006) p. 39.

63 See Brand (2002) pp. 280–285; Brand (2006) pp. 38–39; Hu (2015) section 4.3.

64 Laski (1921) p. 314 said: 'Nothing is today more greatly needed than clarity upon ancient notions. Sovereignty, liberty, authority, personality – these are the words of which we want alike the history and the definition; or rather, we want the history because its substance is in fact the definition.'

65 Hu (2015) p. 167.

66 Mills (2009) p. 88.

communities'.[67] When speaking of the function of private international law in the 'allocation of regulatory authority', Mills did not ignore the authority of states. Under his conceptual framework, 'to define the appropriate boundaries of party autonomy would be to strike a balance between individual freedom and the respect for state "regulatory authority"', that is, a balance 'between the vertical and horizontal dimensions' of private international law.[68]

Mills' argument that individuals possess a form of 'sovereignty' reveals both the interaction between public and private international law, and the historical characteristic of the conception of sovereignty.[69] However, further elaboration is needed as to how the recognition of parties' private rights has affected the acceptance and operation of the party autonomy principle in different fields of private international law, and, concerning choice of law, how parties' 'individual sovereignty' could reconcile with the fact that the forum state, through legislation or judge-made law, has set down the choice of law rules to be applied, which may permit party autonomy in some areas but not others.[70]

As will be seen in the subsequent chapters of this book, the characteristics of the legal and judicial systems of the forum and the public policies prevailing in that jurisdiction still substantively determines the extent to which parties are free to choose the law applicable to their contract. Diversity still exists in the practical application of the party autonomy principle. Therefore, more extensive attention is needed as to how the recognition of the 'authority' of individuals in international law influences the approaches that different jurisdictions adopt towards the specific issues in the practical application of the party autonomy principle.[71]

More importantly, although human rights and parties' freedom to choose the law applicable to their international contract have both been recognized in international instruments, it is not clear to what extent different jurisdictions accepted the party autonomy principle on the basis that they consider themselves to be bound by an 'international customary

[67] Mills (2009) p. 88.

[68] Mills (2009) pp. 294–295. 'Regulatory authority' means the application of a legal order to an event or set of facts. See *ibid.* p. 4.

[69] See Hu (2015) section 4.3 for the historical and conceptual analysis of sovereignty.

[70] See the critical review of Mills' book in Knight (2010) p. 351.

[71] Mills also considered that 'the international law rules on statehood are thus deferential to domestic political and legal institutions', and that this idea 'may be better expressed and developed as a recognition of a general principle of "subsidiarity" as part of international law'. See Mills (2009) sections 3.5.3 and 4.6.4.

law' to this effect.[72] That is to say, while the international approach provides important perspective for the examination of the source of parties' autonomy, it cannot be taken as an incontrovertible response to the issue.

2.3.4 *Summary*

The earlier analyses demonstrate that, on the one hand, the international approach does not totally ignore the authority of states; on the other hand, the national law approach cannot precisely describe the source of parties' autonomy without taking into account the status of individuals and the protection of their rights in international law. In the discussion of the source of parties' autonomy, the significance of the international approach is twofold.

First, it indicates that, the almost universal acceptance of the party autonomy principle in contractual choice of law should be viewed not only as a response to the needs of international commercial transactions,[73] but also as a reflection of the trend in international law of recognizing and protecting individual rights. In this regard, the examination of the operation of party autonomy in a particular jurisdiction should not be confined to the context and policies of that jurisdiction, but should be conducted with the awareness that the party autonomy principle connects the current discussions in private international law to the wider debate on the relationship between the 'sovereignty' or authority of states and that of individuals in international law.[74]

[72] While Nygh considered that party autonomy represents a rule of 'international customary law', he also admitted that 'there is as yet an insufficient consensus to establish an international rule or *lex mercatoria* to give authority to the parties to choose the applicable law directly'. Nygh (1999) pp. 44–45. Mills (2009) p. 293 also admitted that whether there is an international norm requiring adherence to party autonomy in national law remains a controversial issue.

[73] The intention of the parties obtained its importance when the place of contracting lost its paramount significance in the nineteenth century both in large parts of the European continent and in England. This was partly due to a change in the habits and the techniques of international trade. See Lando (1976) para. 13.

[74] For a detailed analysis of the way in which the party autonomy principle provides support for the fiction of an autonomous private transnational legal order, and how the principle connects the current tribulations of private international law to the wider debate on the future of law beyond the state, see Muir Watt (2015). For a critical approach to private international law in the context of global governance, see Muir Watt and Fernández Arroyo (2014).

Second, the international approach serves as a critical reminder that the justification and proper explanation of private international law should not be blind to the reality that it 'stems from the law of nations',[75] and that its rules continue to reflect and replicate the ideas underlying international ordering.[76] In the words of Graveson, private international law is 'both within and outside the individual legal system'. Although it is formally national law, 'sociologically, economically and in terms of international relations, private international law is the common language of private international legal association'.[77]

Based on the discussions in this section, while the formal source of parties' freedom to choose the law governing their contract is the relevant choice of law rules of the forum, the development of the party autonomy principle can only be appropriately comprehended in the broader context of the integration of different jurisdictions in a common legal order serving the needs of international commerce.[78]

2.4 The Nature of Parties' Choice of Law

A choice of law clause is itself an agreement that is usually contained in the contract that the clause purports to submit to the chosen law.[79] It has been variously considered to be a 'factual' agreement,[80] a bargain,[81] a 'declaratory' act,[82] creating a 'promissory obligation'[83] and a 'contract'.[84] Despite the differences in terminology, the conflicts rules of most countries or international instruments generally share the basic requirement that parties should validly *agree* upon a choice of law and that the necessary *consensus ad idem* should be present.[85] Before a court decides that the party autonomy principle should be applied to determine the governing law of a contract,

[75] Jennings (1957) p. 173. Story (1834) para. 9 considered that the jurisprudence 'arising from the conflict of the laws of different nations, in their actual application to modern commerce in intercourse, is a most interesting and important branch of public law'. Lowenfeld (1996) pp. 2–3 agreed with Story's conception of conflict of laws as part of the law of nations, and argued that the term 'private international law' is misunderstood by those who regard it as sharply distinct from public law or public international law.

[76] For a detailed description of the origins of private international law, see Mills (2009) section 2.2.

[77] Graveson (1974a) p. 198. [78] See Yntema (1952) p. 358.

[79] Hay, Borchers and Symeonides (2010) p. 1129. [80] Anton (1967) p. 189.

[81] *Akai Pty Ltd.* v. *People's Insurance Co. Ltd.* [1999] I.L.Pr. 24, [57] (Thomas J.).

[82] *Ace Insurance Ltd.* v. *Moose Enterprise Ltd.* [2009] NSWSC 724, [47] (Brereton J.).

[83] Briggs (2008) para. 11.43. [84] Hook (2016) pp. 33–43.

[85] See Lando (1976) para. 81; Hook (2016) pp. 21–22.

it must first verify whether a choice of law agreement exists, and whether the consent of one of the parties is vitiated by a defect. The existence and validity of a choice of law agreement are therefore important issues preliminary to the application of the party autonomy principle.[86]

Concerning the nature of parties' choice of law agreement, two scholars have attempted to approach the issue in a more 'contractualized' context.[87]

2.4.1 *Choice of Law Agreement as a 'Promise'*

Briggs argued that 'an agreement on choice of law is a promise by which contracting parties undertake reciprocal obligations'.[88] Where the court hearing a dispute applies the law chosen by the parties, no problem arises. The difficulty may come 'when the court seized with jurisdiction does not apply, or does not simply apply, the selected law'.[89] When such a circumstance occurs, the promissory obligation may be shown to have been broken, with the further consequential question of whether the party who brought proceedings before the court in question can be said to have breached the agreement on choice of law.[90] Briggs further discussed the possibility of enforcing the adherence to a governing law clause by an action for breach of contract.[91]

It has been judicially doubted that a choice of law clause is promissory, creating a contractual obligation. It has been held that such terms are usually declaratory of the intent of the parties for choice of law purposes but not about covenants or promises that a particular legal system will apply, and it would require very clear language for the court to infer promissory content in a choice of law clause.[92]

86 See Lando (1976) paras. 81–85; Hay, Borchers and Symeonides (2010) §18.8. The existence and validity of a choice of law agreement is further discussed in Chapters 3 and 4.

87 In the case of Briggs, 'the question is how far the conflict of laws has become contractualized, or been rendered liable to being restated in contractual terms'. Briggs (2008) para. 1.10. Hook analysed the party autonomy rule within a contractual framework and argued that a choice of law agreement is best described as a contract. See Hook (2016) pp. 12, 23. Their arguments are further discussed in the subsequent sections.

88 Briggs (2008) para. 1.19. He considered that 'after all, there is no reason in principle why such a promise could not be made'.

89 Briggs (2008) para. 11.45. 90 See Briggs (2008) paras. 11.09, 11.32 and 11.45.

91 See Briggs (2008) para. 11.45 *et seq.*

92 *Ace Insurance Ltd.* v. *Moose Enterprise Pty. Ltd.* [2009] NSWSC 724 [47], [51] and [53]. Brereton J.'s starting point was clear ([47]): 'No doubt a contractual obligation could be

There may be a number of reasons why the law selected by the parties is not applied by a court.[93] For the reasons arising from the statutory limitations of the conflict of laws of the forum, it seems not appropriate to blame the party who brought proceedings before the court in question for breaching the choice of law agreement.[94] It may only be plausible in principle to see such clauses as creating an enforceable obligation when it is accompanied by an agreement to the exclusive jurisdiction of a given court.[95] Moreover, it would be more uncertain as to whether one party can be required to indemnify the other for non-compliance with a governing law clause.[96]

The methodology advocated by Briggs is sound in that it involves the simple proposition of contract law that 'it is good for parties to make contracts, good for parties to perform contracts, and good for courts to enforce contracts'.[97] Nevertheless, it remains to be seen whether Briggs' approach to the choice of law agreement will be supported in judicial practice,[98] and whether, in other jurisdictions, parties' consent and agreement could play a role in the development of private international

framed which unambiguously contained a promise to do nothing that might result in some other system of law becoming applicable.' Nevertheless, his honour concluded that this was not ordinarily the effect of a choice of law clause, and not the result in this case.

93 See Briggs (2008) para. 11.45.

94 In *Ace Insurance Ltd.* v. *Moose Enterprise Pty. Ltd.* [2009] NSWSC 724 [52], Brereton J. also held that parties' entitlement to select the governing law is not absolute; a court hearing the case may not give effect to the express choice, and may apply its own mandatory rules. Yeo (2010) p. 197 argued: 'Because the effect and scope of application of a choice of law clause varies from jurisdiction to jurisdiction (and the contracting parties presumably know this), it will generally be difficult to ascertain what, if anything, the parties have promised each other in respect of the application of the chosen law to their disputes.' The statutory restrictions on party autonomy are addressed in Chapters 5 and 6.

95 This may presumably constitute an agreement that the conflicts rules of the forum shall apply, including those giving effect to any choice of law clause. But if such a clause is tied to a non-exclusive jurisdiction agreement, or contains no jurisdiction agreement at all, this suggests that the parties are content that the effect of the clause is subject to the conflicts rules of any court seized of proceedings. See Fentiman (2015) paras 3.15–3.16.

96 See Briggs (2008) paras. 5.51–5.52; Fentiman (2015) para. 3.17.

97 Briggs (2008) para. 1.01. Brereton J. also affirmed the soundness of such a methodology. See the quotation in n 92.

98 As Yeo (2010)p. 200 has pointed out, what the parties have promised one another in respect of a choice of law clause is a question of construction of their contract, and difficulties will arise in determining the terms of any promise. Briggs also admitted that common law authority is almost non-existent concerning the matter and therefore he had to approach it as one of principle. See Briggs (2008), paras. 11.03, 11.46, 11.47 and 11.49.

law rules similar to the one that Briggs considered them to have played in the common law principles of private international law.[99]

2.4.2 *Choice of Law Agreement as a 'Contract'*

Hook analysed the party autonomy rule within a contractual framework that fuses principles of choice of law and contract. She argued that a choice of law agreement is a legally binding agreement; and, although it does not feature some of the usual hallmarks of a contract, it is best described as a contract.[100] However, her reasoning does not sufficiently explain the reasons for such a categorization.

First, as Hook mentions, in most legal systems, the choice of law agreement does not have obviously contractual characteristics because it does not create, modify or extinguish rights or obligations.[101] She also considers that contrary to Briggs' argument, choice of law agreements are 'inherently non-promissory', and that 'it is the court that has to give effect to it'.[102] But if a choice of law agreement creates neither *in personam* rights and obligations, nor promissory obligation, then it seems difficult to categorize it as a 'contract' simply because 'contracts are known in all legal systems', and such a categorization would 'have the advantage of a certain form of universality'.[103]

Second, Hook argues that 'a mutual intention to be bound is at the heart of both the law of contract and the party autonomy rule', and thus 'it is the law of contract that must provide many of the principles and rules that determine the scope, existence and validity of choice of law agreements'. She maintains that since 'there is no separate regime of rules that deals only with legally binding agreements that are not contracts', 'choice of law agreements are best treated as contracts'.[104]

It is true that the law of contract provides the principles and rules for the determination of the existence of parties' mutual intention or agreement on choice of law, and also the substantive effect of their agreement.[105] However, 'contract' has its particular meaning in

[99] See Briggs (2008) chapter 2. Briggs argued that (para. 2.10) 'a significant part of the common law conflict of laws can and should be explained in terms of the consent or agreement of the parties' and that (para. 2.01) the roles of consent and agreement are 'central' and 'fundamental'.

[100] See Hook (2016) pp. 12, 23. [101] Hook (2016) p. 42. [102] Hook (2016) p. 32.

[103] Hook (2016) p. 42. [104] See Hook (2016) p. 42.

[105] For the existence of a choice of law agreement and its substantive validity, see Chapters 3 and 4.

law.[106] That parties' choice of law agreement bears certain characteristics of a contract does not mean that it can be categorized as a contract. In fact, what Hook has argued is *not* that the nature of a choice of law agreement satisfies all the elements involved in the definition of 'contract' in law – she only considers that the meaning of contract *may* be understood as a 'fluid concept', and choice of law agreements are at least 'like' contracts.[107] Without convincing analysis to justify the labelling of a choice of law agreement as a 'contract' in law, it seems that such a 'contractual framework' is not substantially different from the previous discussion of the party autonomy principle in conflict of laws.[108]

Third, Hook considers that 'the sole function of the choice of law contract is to opt out of the applicable objective choice of law rule and select the law governing the underlying relationship'.[109] Therefore, the evaluation of the scope of party autonomy depends on the determination of 'whether the objective choice of law rule is mandatory in nature'.[110] In this way, Hook adopts, in the conflict of laws, the distinction between default and mandatory rules in substantive law. Although the existence of such a distinction has been described as 'doubtful' on the basis that all choice of law rules are mandatory in the sense that 'parties cannot replace them by a rule of their own making',[111] Hook argues that 'there is no need for such a formalistic interpretation of mandatory rules'.

[106] As Hook (2016) p. 33 points out, in both civil and common law jurisdictions, the conventional understanding of contract is founded on obligation: a contract creates rights and duties between the parties. Here the term 'right' is to be understood in its narrow sense, meaning 'an interest recognized and protected by a rule of rights . . . respect for which is a duty, and the disregard of which is a wrong'. See Salmond (1907) p. 182. Justinian considered an obligation to be a 'legal bond, with which we are bound by a necessity of performing some act according to the laws of our State'. See Moyle (1913) Book III, Title XIII. In his *Commentaries on the Laws of England*, Blackstone (1768, Chapter XXX, Part IX) wrote: 'A contract, which usually conveys an interest merely in action, is thus defined: "an agreement, upon sufficient consideration, to do or not to do a particular thing."'

[107] See Hook (2016) pp. 42–43.

[108] Hook (2016) pp. 9–10 argues: 'a fundamental manifestation of this problem [that the contractualization of choice of law has been unduly divorced from the principles and the law of the contract] is the failure, in legal scholarship and practice, to engage with the contractual nature of the parties' agreement on choice of law. This is particularly true of common law jurisdictions. . . [D]iscussion of the choice of law agreement is typically framed by a narrow focus on its scope and effect as a connecting factor.' However, as the analysis in Chapter 3 reveals, the existence and validity of parties' agreement on choice of law have been the subject of discussion in a number of scholarly writings and court decisions.

[109] Hook (2016) p. 13. [110] Hook (2016) p. 46. [111] See Boer (1996) pp. 348–349.

She reasons that 'in exercising their freedom to choose the applicable law, the parties necessarily set aside the objective choice of law rule'.[112] In her view, 'it is immaterial that they rely on the party autonomy rule to do so and that this rule is not a 'rule of their making': 'If the objective choice of law rule is *ius cogens*, the parties do not have the freedom to set it aside.'[113]

It is submitted that this analysis is not convincing. Choice of law rules are mandatory in the sense that they determine which law should be applied in cross-border disputes. Even in the common law approach where the application of foreign law is dependent upon the consent of at least one of the parties to the litigation,[114] it is still the choice of law rules of the forum that primarily determine whether a foreign law should be introduced into court at all.[115] Concerning the relationship between the party autonomy rule and other objective choice of law rules, it is not the parties' choice of law agreement that 'sets aside' the objective rules, but simply that when there is an effective choice of law agreement, the party autonomy rule becomes applicable and therefore the other objective rules do not apply. Since the formal source of parties' power to choose the applicable law is the forum's choice of law rules,[116] the party autonomy rule is also mandatory in the sense that once an effective choice of law agreement is made, the selected law should be determined to be applicable within the scope prescribed by the choice of law rules of the forum.[117] Contrary to Hook's analysis, if party autonomy is prohibited in a particular area or limited to a certain extent, that is because the forum's choice of law rules stipulate to that effect, but *not* because 'the objective choice of law rule is *ius cogens* '.[118]

2.4.3 Summary

Both Briggs and Hook consider that the choice of law agreement can be viewed independently of the substantive dispute between the

[112] Hook (2016) p. 47. [113] See Hook (2016) p. 47. [114] Briggs (2008) para. 2.22.

[115] See Fentiman (1998) pp. 66–67. See further, Section 7.4 of Chapter 7.

[116] See Lando (1977) para. 63; Nygh (1999) p. 32; Section 2.3. Hook also agreed that parties are free to choose the law applicable to their relationship because it is the choice of law rule of the forum that prescribes that effect be given to the choice. See Hook (2016) pp. 21, 46.

[117] But how the selected foreign law is introduced into court and how it can be proved to the satisfaction of the court are separate issues and should be determined by the rules of the forum in relation to the ascertainment of foreign law. See Chapter 7.

[118] See Hook (2016) p. 47. The statutory restrictions on party autonomy are discussed in Chapters 5 and 6.

parties.[119] Their views concerning the nature of parties' choice of law do not currently represent the law, especially in contract, where choice of law clauses are traditionally considered as simply a part of the contract between the parties. As the discussions in Chapters 3 and 4 reveal, this is true of judicial practice in China. However, the approaches adopted by Briggs and Hook have the potential to explain many of the difficulties to which party autonomy gives rise in the conflict of laws. Indeed, they provide important theoretical perspectives on the party autonomy principle.

The framework established by Hook is particularly important in her analyses of how the existence and validity of parties' choice of law agreement should be placed on a more principled footing, taking the basic principles of contract law into account.[120]

The innovative approach adopted by Briggs is relevant to the topic of this book in that, by distinguishing between choice of law by parties and choice of law by courts, Briggs provides a new perspective for the explanation and analysis of two key issues in the operation of party autonomy: the function and application of mandatory rules,[121] and the influence of the rules on pleading and proof of foreign law on the ultimate fate of parties' choice of law.[122] These issues are discussed in subsequent chapters.

This book focuses on the application of the party autonomy principle in China. For its purpose, parties' choice of law clause is understood as an agreement, which is part of the mechanism set up by the parties for the resolution of disputes.[123]

2.5 The Relevance of International Debate to the Development of Party Autonomy in China

2.5.1 The Evolution of Freedom of Contract in China

Chapter 1 demonstrates that, the acceptance and development of party autonomy in China's private international law is in line with the evolution of the conception of freedom of contract, which clearly reflects

[119] See Briggs (2008) part VIII of chapter 3; Hook (2016) chapter 4.

[120] See Hook (2016) chapters 4–6. See further, Chapter 3 on the existence and validity of parties' choice of law agreement.

[121] See Briggs (2008) paras. 10.03–10.04.

[122] See Briggs (2008) section IV of chapter 2.

[123] See Briggs (2008) paras. 1.07, 10.40; Hook (2016) p. 42, n 127. The existence and validity of choice of law agreements are discussed in Chapter 3.

China's politico-economic and ideological transformation towards a market-oriented economy.

The anti-foreign sentiments that dominated China from the 1950s to 1970s became untenable after the reform and opening-up policy was adopted. With the development of external economic cooperation and trade, increasing numbers of disputes involving foreign factors arose, and were brought to Chinese courts. The 1985 Foreign Economic Contract Law, where parties' autonomy to choose the law governing a contract was first accepted, was actually promulgated against this background. The purpose of introducing a special choice of law rule for foreign economic contracts was to reduce the anxiety of foreign investors and facilitate direct foreign inward investment in China.[124] The autonomy of parties permitted under this Law was considered to be more in line with Western capitalist practice than with socialism. The Law is therefore considered to have initially started a sort of a 'plural' approach in the drafting of legislation in China to drawing experience from foreign and international sources.[125] The significant influence of foreign and international jurisprudence was more obvious in the drafting of the 1999 Contract Law, which commenced after progress in reforming China's politico-economic system had been made.[126]

Under the Contract Law, a contract is defined as an agreement between citizens, legal persons, and other organizations of equal status. This finally extends freedom of contract to individuals. The development from the Foreign Economic Contract Law to the Contract Law illustrated the process of China's transformation from a planned to a market economy, which itself redefines the role of the State in economic management and activities.[127] Permitting the parties to choose the law governing their foreign-related contract can also be seen as the reflection

[124] See Armfelt (1987) p. 151; Xu (1989) p. 648.

[125] See the discussions in Potter (2000) pp. 190–196.

[126] Concerning the nature of the politico-economic system in China, Chen (2016) p. 116 stated: 'Economic development and opening up to foreign investment have challenged another important and central tenet of socialism, namely the insistence on public ownership and its priority protection by law. In fact, the most substantial revisions since 1988, though only made incrementally, have been those defining the nature of the politico-economic system in China. These changes clearly reflect the gradual transformation of the Chinese politico-economic system, a process short of full privatisation but nevertheless allowing the gradual introduction of "capitalist" practices in economic spheres. Here significant changes have occurred in relation to the description of socialism and to equal protection of public and private property.'

[127] See the detailed discussions in Chen (1995) chapters 2 and 5.

of freedom of contract in China's private international law.[128] Indeed, the drafting of the 2010 Conflicts Statute has also been strongly influenced and much inspired by modern foreign legislation and international instruments, and thus incorporates many of the most advanced developments in the field.[129]

2.5.2 The Nature of Private International Law: A Chinese Perspective

There was once a concern in China that the application of foreign law in people's courts would mean the surrender of sovereignty to a foreign country.[130] The past decades have witnessed a substantial change in China's attitude towards the application of foreign law: the country has moved from sovereignty-sensitive exclusion of foreign law to reform-served openness regarding the application of foreign law.[131]

The nature of private international law is explored by Chinese scholars through the examination of the evolutionary process of the subject. An international perspective is adopted by many private international law scholars.[132] In their views, private international law in the twenty-first century is a blend of national and international law: while its current sources are primarily and formally domestic legislation and case law, the discipline is moving towards the realm of international law.[133]

In judicial practice, while the trial of foreign-related commercial and maritime cases is considered to be closely related to the protection of the sovereignty of China and the advancement of the long-term interests of the country,[134] the Supreme People's Court (SPC) has also emphasized the importance of adopting an international perspective in the adjudication of foreign-related cases. The SPC urged people's courts to equally

128 Tang, Xiao and Huo (2016) para. 8.05.

129 According to the report from the NPCSC concerning the drafting of the 2010 Conflicts Statute and the main issues therein, the most advanced developments in private international law have been absorbed into the Statute, and the conflicts codification of other countries, conventions of the Hague Conference on Private International Law and some regulations of the European Union have been consulted. See 'Report on the Main Issues concerning the Draft Law on the Application of Laws to Foreign-relatd Civil Relationships of the PRC' (issued on the official website of the NPC on 28 August 2010).

130 See the discussion in Section 1.1.

131 See Zhang (2006b) p. 304; Liu (2001) pp. 37–40; Huang (1999) pp. 161–169.

132 See Zhang (2006b) pp. 304–308.

133 Shen (2006) p. 674.

134 See Shen (2015) p. 17.

protect the legitimate interests of both Chinese and foreign parties, and create a more competitive investment environment.[135]

Subsequent chapters of this book will further analyse the operation of the party autonomy principle in China. They critically examine whether, and to what extent, the resolution of issues related to the principle in judicial practice reflects international development in the field, and is responsive to the needs of international commerce.

[135] See Opinions of the Supreme People's Court on Comprehensively Carrying Forward the Strategy of Producing Fine Works on the Trial of Foreign-Related Commercial and Maritime Cases to Provide Effective Judicial Safeguard for Establishing an Open Economic System and Building up a Maritime Power (issued by the SPC on 14 July 2015).

3

The Existence and Validity of Parties' Choice of Law

Article 3 of the Law on the Application of Laws to Foreign-related Civil Relationships (2010 Conflicts Statute) provides: 'Parties may, in accordance with laws, expressly choose the law that is to govern their foreign-related civil relationship.'[1] Some Chinese scholars consider this to be a 'declaratory provision', which, on the one hand, indicates the legislative purpose of the Statute, and on the other hand, provides the two general conditions on the exercise of party autonomy.[2] The first is that parties should make their choice expressly, whether in written or oral form. The second is that parties should make their choice in accordance with statutory provisions.[3] With regard to contractual choice of law, Article 41 of the 2010 Conflicts Statute stipulates: 'Parties may choose by agreement the law applicable to their contract. In the absence of a choice by parties, the contract shall be governed by the law of the place of habitual residence of the party whose performance of obligations best reflects the characteristics of the contract or other laws that have the closest connection with the contract.' Accordingly, in determining the governing law of a contract, a court should begin with the examination of whether the parties have made an effective choice of law. Three main issues are involved: (1) whether the parties have made a choice; (2) whether the parties' choice of law is vitiated; and (3) whether the 'law' referred to by the parties in contract can be applied as the governing law to solve their dispute.

Chapters 3 and 4 address the issues preliminary to the application of the party autonomy principle. Chapter 3 first looks at the question of

[1] The Statute was adopted at the 17th meeting of the Standing Committee of the 11th NPC on 28 October 2010 and became effective on 1 April 2011.

[2] See Huang and Jiang (2011) p. 13. But Huang argued that since there are specific provisions concerning the party autonomy principle in succeeding chapters of the statute, Article 3 is unnecessary. See Huang (2011) p. 12.

[3] See Huang and Jiang (2011) pp. 13–14. The statutory restrictions on party autonomy are discussed in Chapters 5 and 6.

whether both parties have agreed on an express choice of law clause. This can normally be treated as an autonomous issue of fact. In China, most of the disputes on this issue have arisen in cases concerning bills of lading.[4] Since bills of lading are drafted by a carrier in advance, a dispute may arise as to whether the counterparty (a shipper or holder of the bill) has also agreed to the choice of law clause, or the clause only represents the unilateral intention of the carrier. People's courts have adopted inconsistent approaches to the determination of this issue. Difficulties may also arise where a third party is involved or where a choice of law clause is incorporated from another document. Moreover, in the situations where an economically weaker party is involved, it is necessary to treat parties' consent on the choice of law clause as a legal issue as well to ensure that the weaker party is notified of the clause as required by law and that the choice is not procured by duress or fraud. Chapter 3 then discusses the material validity of parties' choice of law. In judicial practice, people's courts have vitiated parties' choice of law on the basis of one of the parties' failure to appear in court, or the typographical error in a choice of law clause. The inappropriateness of their approaches is to be demonstrated and the law governing the validity of parties' choice is analysed. Chapter 4 discusses the 'law' that can be chosen by parties. It makes the distinction between parties' incorporation by reference of national laws or international instruments in contract and their choice of a legal system as the governing law, and further touches upon the outstanding problems in Chinese judicial practice.

3.1 Identification of the Existence of Parties' Consent on Choice of Law

3.1.1 Inconsistent Approaches in Determining Parties' Consent in Bills of Lading

In determining whether the party autonomy principle is applicable, a court should begin with a preliminary factual inquiry to identify the apparent existence of mutual consent on choice of law. The questions to be asked are: whether, as a question of fact, a nomination of applicable

[4] In judicial practice, most of the disputed issues concerning parties' intention on choice of law arose in bills of lading. Therefore, the discussion in Chapter 3 mainly focuses on cases involving bills of lading. However, the analysis is also relevant to other categories of contracts. See Section 3.1.4.

law was made and it is reasonable in the circumstances to assume that the other side accepted it.[5] In Chinese judicial practice, disputes in this field mostly arise in cases involving bills of lading.

Normally, a bill of lading is issued by a carrier upon the request of a shipper. A carrier or its agent signs a bill of lading acknowledging that goods have been shipped on board a specific vessel that is bound for a particular destination and stating the terms on which the goods are to be carried.[6] A bill of lading is thus considered to be evidence of the contract of carriage of goods by sea between the shipper and carrier.[7] However, since the clauses on the back of a bill are not the result of a negotiation between a shipper and a carrier, people's courts have adopted different assumptions in determining whether a choice of law clause therein represents the mutual consent of the original parties to a bill of lading. This is illustrated in *Jiangsu Textile Import & Export Group Co. Ltd.* v. *Beijing Farenco Freight Services Co. Ltd. Shanghai Branch & Farenco Freight Services Ltd.* (the *Farenco* case).[8]

In 2002, Jiangsu Textile Import & Export Group Co. Ltd. (Jiangsu Co. Ltd.) acknowledged with the carrier, Farenco Freight Services Ltd. (Farenco Ltd.) shipment on board textiles for carriage to and delivery at Laredo (Texas, the United States of America) for payment. Farenco Ltd. issued bills of lading which specified Jiangsu Co. Ltd. as shipper and RAFAEL MORALES as consignee. Jiangsu Co. Ltd. did not receive the payment for the goods from the consignee, and still possessed the original bills of lading. But it later found that the cargoes were released at the destination harbour and sued the two defendants for the payment in Shanghai Maritime Court.

Clause 33 of the bills of lading provided: 'No matter the Carriage includes Carriage to, from or through a port in the United States of America, the Carrier's responsibility under this Bill of Lading shall be subject to the United States Carriage of Goods by Sea Act 1936

[5] See Nygh (1999) p. 93. [6] Schoenbaum (2004) p. 546.

[7] Article 71 of China's Maritime Code (adopted at the 28th Meeting of the Standing Committee of the 7th NPC on 7 November 1992, effective on 1 July 1993) provides: 'A bill of lading is a document which serves as an evidence of the contract of carriage of goods by sea and the taking over or loading of the goods by the carrier, and based on which the carrier undertakes to deliver the goods against surrendering the same. A provision in the document stating that the goods are to be delivered to the order of a named person, or to order, or to bearer, constitutes such an undertaking.'

[8] 20 May 2004, Shanghai Maritime Court; 11 November 2004, Shanghai Higher People's Court.

(COGSA).' Clause 36 provided: 'The carriage of goods by sea contract, as is evidenced by this bill of lading, should be construed in accordance with Hong Kong law.'

In the first trial, Farenco Ltd. argued for the application of US law. Jiangsu Co. Ltd. disagreed and argued that Clause 33 did not represent its intention as it did not agree to the clause. The Shanghai Maritime Court found first, that the 1936 US COGSA did not contain provisions concerning the release of cargoes without the production of original bills of lading; second, Farenco Ltd. could not prove either that Jiangsu Co. Ltd. had agreed to use the bills of lading in question, or that the relevant choice of law clauses represented the real intention of the parties.[9] Therefore, the court rejected the argument of Farenco Ltd. and applied the closest connection principle to determine that the applicable law was the law of China. Based on China's Maritime Code, judgment was entered for the plaintiff.

Farenco Ltd. insisted that the application of Chinese law was wrong and appealed to Shanghai Higher People's Court. Farenco Ltd. argued that: first, whether the COGSA was applicable should not be determined on the basis of whether there were relevant provisions regulating the disputed issue of the case; second, the SPC had once applied the COGSA for the adjudication of a similar case;[10] third, since there was no evidence that Jiangsu Co Ltd. had been obliged to use the bills of lading by Farenco Ltd., the court should affirm that both parties had agreed to use the bills and thus the choice of law clauses should be deemed to be the agreement of the parties; and fourth, even if the closest connection principle should be applied, the law most closely related to the case was US law rather than Chinese law.

Shanghai Higher People's Court affirmed the facts as identified in the first trial. It decided that according to Article 269 of China's Maritime Code, parties were free to choose the applicable law of their contract.

[9] As is analysed in Chapter 4, the reference to a specific act of the United States of America in Clause 33 should not be taken as a choice of the law governing the bill of lading: it only incorporates the provisions of the act into the bill. The court's finding on this point is therefore not right. But the focus of Section 3.1 is on the ascertainment of parties' apparent consent on a clause in contract which refers to a set of rules that may be applied to solve the disputes between parties. For the 'law' that can be chosen by parties as the governing law of a contract, see Chapter 4, where this case is further analysed.

[10] Here, Farenco Ltd. was actually referring to *American President Lines Ltd.* v. *Feida Appliance Company, Feili Industry Co Ltd. & Changcheng Industry Company* (25 June 2002 Supreme People's Court), where the SPC applied the 1936 US COGSA and 1916 Shipping Act. However, the SPC's application of law in this case is problematic. See, Section 4.3.1 of Chapter 4 and Section 6.2.2 of Chapter 6.

The party autonomy principle should be applied to a bill of lading as it served as evidence of the contract for carriage of goods by sea. Although the choice of law clauses were printed on the back of the bills of lading and were drafted by the carrier in advance, they were issued at the request of the shipper. Therefore, both parties had voluntarily agreed to use the bills of lading. As Jiangsu Co. Ltd. could not prove that there was any difference between the terms and conditions in the bills of lading and those in the contract for carriage of goods by sea which was made previously, the former should be seen as the result of the mutual agreement of the parties, and the choice of law clauses therein should be held effective.[11]

3.1.2 Burden of Proof in a Bill of Lading Taken as a Contract

In the aforementioned case, the parties were only in disagreement about whether the shipper Jiangsu Co. Ltd. should be bound by the choice of law clause on the back of the bills of lading, which was drafted by the carrier Farenco Ltd. in advance. Except for the original copy of the bill of lading concerned,[12] neither of the parties produced additional evidence to support their respective arguments, and the two courts based their decisions on different assumptions. One question was not clearly addressed by either of the courts: which party should bear the burden of proving that both of them had agreed to the choice of law clause.

The Civil Procedure Law provides that people's courts should take the facts as the basis and the laws as the criterion in trying civil cases, and parties should be responsible for providing evidence for their respective allegations.[13] Article 2(2) of Some Provisions of the Supreme People's Court on Evidence in Civil Procedure (Evidence Provisions)[14] specifies

[11] However, the court did not apply Hong Kong law or US law, as referred to in Clauses 33 and 36. It considered that the relevant rules on carrier's responsibility provided in China's Maritime Code were mandatory and should be applied directly in this case. For further discussion of this issue, see Section 6.2.2 of Chapter 6.

[12] Farenco Ltd. submitted the original bill of lading that it issued to the court.

[13] See Articles 7 and 64 of the Law (adopted at the 4th Session of the 7th NPC on 9 April 1991; amended for the first time at the 30th Meeting of the Standing Committee of the 10th NPC on 28 October 2007; amended for the second time at the 28th Meeting of the Standing Committee of the 11th NPC on 31 August 2012; amended for the third time at the 28th Meeting of the Standing Committee of the 12th NPC on 27 June 2017).

[14] It was issued by the SPC on 21 December 2001, became effective on 1 April 2002 and was revised on 16 December 2008. Article 2(2) of it is the same as Article 90(2) of Interpretation of the Supreme People's Court on the Application of Civil Procedure Law (issued by the SPC on 30 January 2015, effective on 4 February 2015).

that where any party cannot produce evidence or the evidence produced cannot support the facts on which the allegations are based, a court may make a decision unfavourable to the party that bears the burden of proof on the relevant issues.

Concerning contractual disputes, Article 5(1) of the Evidence Provisions provides that the party that claims the establishment of a contractual relationship and the effectiveness of the contract shall be responsible for producing evidence to prove that the contract has been concluded and that it has taken effect; the party that claims that the contract has been altered, dissolved, terminated or cancelled shall be responsible for producing evidence to prove the facts causing the change of the contractual relationship. If a choice of law clause in a bill of lading is taken as an agreement or part of an agreement between the parties and a dispute arises as to whether the clause is accepted by both parties, the burden of proof should then be determined according to this provision.

Based on Articles 2(2) and 5(1) of the Evidence Provisions, the carrier Farenco Ltd. in the case just mentioned should have completed its burden of proving that the shipper had accepted the terms on the bill of lading by submitting the original bill to the court. The shipper Jiangsu Co. Ltd. bore the burden of proving that it did not accept the choice of law clause on the bill. As it did not attempt to do so, the Shanghai Higher People's Court was right in treating the bill of lading as a contract between the parties.

The first trial decision by the Shanghai Maritime Court actually represented another approach: to treat a bill of lading as a standard contract and impose on the carrier the burden of proving that the terms on it have been accepted by the shipper. The inconsistency in judicial practice exists because of the nature of a bill of lading: first, it is a standard contract drafted by a carrier in advance; second, a shipper normally does not sign it upon acceptance; third, it can be negotiated to other parties. That explains why most of the disputes on contractual choice of law clauses in China concern bills of lading.

3.1.3 *Special Issues in a Bill of Lading Taken as a Standard Contract*

Reflecting the UNIDROIT Principles of International Commercial Contracts (UNIDROIT Principles),[15] Article 39(2) of the Contract

[15] The first edition of the UNIDROIT Principles was published by the International Institute for the Unification of Private Law in 1994. The Contract Law reflects Article

Law[16] provides that 'standard terms' are contract provisions which are prepared in advance for general and repeated use by one party, and which are not negotiated with the other party in concluding the contract. The critical legal characteristic of a standard contract is that it is 'prepared-in-advance' by one party.[17] Since standard terms are normally not the product of negotiations of the parties, a contract that contains all standard terms is often concluded on a 'take-it-or-leave-it' basis. To protect the equal legal status of contractual parties and fairness,[18] there are some rules in the Contract Law governing the use of standard terms.

Article 39(1) of the Contract Law stipulates that where standard terms are adopted when entering a contract, the party who supplies the standard terms shall define the rights and obligations between the parties according to the principle of fairness, shall make the other party aware of the exclusion or limitation of the supplying party's liabilities in a reasonable way and shall explain these terms in response to the other party's request. Furthermore, Article 40 specifies several situations in which standard terms are invalid.[19]

Since a bill of lading is usually prepared by a carrier in advance, it is a typical type of standard contract.[20] The question that often arises is: was a nomination of applicable law made and is it reasonable in the circumstances to assume that the other side accepted it? The object of this inquiry is to ensure that a choice of law clause is not inserted into a contract by one of the parties primarily for his own advantage or inserted without the actual knowledge of the other party. The issue becomes critical in a bill of lading, where one of the parties may not have sufficient bargaining concerning the choice of law clause before it accepts the bill.

2.19 (2) of this edition. The latest edition of the Principles was published in 2016. The analysis in Section 3.1.4 refers to the latest edition.

16 It was adopted by the 2nd Session of the 9th NPC on 15 March 1999 and became effective on 1 October 1999.

17 See Zhang (2006a) p. 138; Wang (2003) pp. 157–158.

18 Article 3 of the Contract Law provides: 'The parties to the contract have equal legal status, and neither party may impose its will on the other.' Article 5 stipulates: 'The parties shall observe the principle of fairness in defining each other's rights and obligations.'

19 Article 40 provides: 'Standard clauses shall become invalid if they fall under any of the circumstances set forth in Articles 52 and 53 of this Law or if the party that provides the standard clauses exempts itself from the liability, imposes heavier liability on the other party or precludes the other party from its main rights.' Article 52 stipulates the circumstances under which a contract becomes invalid. Article 53 lists the situations where a clause on liability exemption becomes invalid.

20 See Tetley (2001) p. 366. Tetley noted that bills of lading are sometimes, misleadingly, regarded as contracts of adhesion. Cf the cases cited in nn 69 and 70.

The Shanghai Maritime Court has in some cases refused to recognize that a shipper had consented to a choice of law clause in a bill of lading.

In *Nanjing Jindao Clothing Co. Ltd.* v. *The Ultimate Freight Management Corporation*,[21] the plaintiff and shipper, Nanjing Jindao Clothing Co. Ltd. (Jindao Co. Ltd.), claimed that the defendant and carrier, the Ultimate Freight Management Corporation (Ultimate Corporation), had released the goods to the consignee without the presentation of the original bill of lading.

In the first trial, the defendant argued that the law of the US should be applied since there was a clause on the back of the bill of lading referring to the US COGSA. The Shanghai Maritime Court held that on the one hand, the evidence put before it could not prove that both parties had negotiated on the choice of law issue; on the other hand, the plaintiff Jindao Co. Ltd. had never expressed its consent to that clause. Therefore, the court decided that the plaintiff was not bound by the clause referring to the COGSA. The Shanghai Maritime Court then determined that the governing law was Chinese law according to the closest connection principle, and decided for the defendant. The plaintiff appealed to the Shanghai Higher People's Court. The appellate court did not touch upon the effect of the choice of law clause,[22] but confirmed that the court of first trial was right in applying Chinese law as the governing law.

In *Hangzhou Shengke Electrics Co. Ltd.* v. *Westconsolidators Inc. and Shenzhen Hualian International Transportation Agency Co. Ltd.*,[23] the plaintiff and shipper, Hangzhou Shengke Electrics Co. Ltd. (Shengke), sued the carrier Westconsolidators Inc. for releasing the cargoes without presentation of the original bill of lading. Clause 20 of the bill provided that any litigation conducted against the non-vessel-operating carrier should be governed by the law of the state of the carrier's principal place of business. The defendant argued that since its principal place of business was in the United States, American law should be applied. The Shanghai Maritime Court held that Westconsolidators Inc. did not

[21] 9 April 2010, Shanghai Higher People's Court. The Ultimate Corporation was permitted to be engaged in non-vessel-operating services in the United States, but was not qualified to do that in mainland China. The goods were shipped from Shanghai to Los Angeles. So this case was foreign-related.

[22] That may be because neither of the parties disagreed with the determination in the governing law in the first trial.

[23] 20 April 2010, Shanghai Maritime Court. Westconsolidators Inc. was registered in the United States and the goods were shipped from Shanghai to Los Angeles. This case was foreign-related.

produce evidence to prove that the plaintiff and it had any express agreement on the governing law. Therefore, the applicable law was determined based on the closest connection principle.

In *Jiangsu Hongye Co. Ltd.* v. *CTS International Logistics Co. Ltd.*,[24] there was also a clause in the bill of lading referring to the US COGSA. The Shanghai Maritime Court held that the clause was a standard clause drafted in advance by the defendant carrier; and that, when a consigned bill of lading contained a clause referring to the COGSA, that clause would have substantial effect on the rights of a shipper. Since the defendant did not print the clause on the front of the bill, nor did it sufficiently remind the plaintiff of the clause, the court decided that the plaintiff's action of accepting the bill of lading should not be taken as indicative of its acceptance of that clause. The court then applied Chinese law according to the closest connection principle.

In all the aforementioned cases, there was no dispute between the parties on the fact that the shippers had accepted the bills of lading issued by the carriers. The only issue in each case concerning the effect of the choice of law clauses was whether the shipper's acceptance of the bill of lading without objection meant that it also agreed to the choice of law clause on the back of it. The Shanghai Maritime Court seemed to assume that besides providing the original bill of lading identifying the shipper, the carrier should bear the additional burden of proving that the shipper had actually consented to the choice of law clause.

3.1.4 Trade Usage and the Formation of Contract

The notion underlying the special rules on standard contracts is to guarantee that the party who is in a take-it-or-leave-it position will not be bound by the terms that he or she is not aware of. These rules are set out particularly for the protection of weaker parties such as consumers.[25] However, as between a carrier and a shipper, both of whom are usually professionals in international business transactions, the consideration should be different.[26] Bills of lading are a creation of mercantile custom

[24] 29 March 2011, Shanghai Maritime Court. The Shanghai Maritime Court held that since the cargo was shipped from Shanghai to Savannah, Atlanta, and released outside the territory of China, this was a foreign-related case.

[25] Zhang (2006a) pp. 139–140; Wang (2003) p. 161.

[26] One Chinese scholar suggests that Article 39 of the Contract Law should distinguish between commercial contracts and consumer contracts, and should restrict the scope of the article to consumer contracts. See Su (2004) p. 191.

dating back at least to medieval times, and they came into general use in the sixteenth century.[27] A bill is signed by the carrier and typically contains the names of the shipper and consignee, a description of the goods, including shipping marks used for identification purposes, stipulations for payment of freight, and details of conditions of carriage.[28] Given the long history of the use of bills of lading and its typical clauses, people engaged in international trade should be aware that there are many clauses on the back of a bill of lading. Therefore, when a dispute arises as to whether the shipper should be bound by the choice of law clause on a bill of lading, the key question to be asked is: *can a trade usage mean that the shipper is bound by that clause even when it did not know or was not aware of the clause?* It is submitted that, as between professional parties, people's courts should determine the existence of practice between parties or a trade usage by looking at such elements as the nature of the trade or industry in which parties are involved, their respective experience in the trade, the previous dealings between them, the accessibility of the clauses concerned and other facts relevant to their transaction.

A Trade Usage in China's Contract Law

China's Contract Law accepts 'trade usage' as determinative of the form that an acceptance should take and of the time when an acceptance becomes effective.[29] Article 22 provides that an acceptance shall be made in the form of a notice unless, in light of trade usages or as indicated by the offer, the offeree may indicate the assent by performing an act. Article 26(1) further confirms that if an acceptance needs no notice, it becomes effective when an act of acceptance is performed in light of trade usages.[30] Concerning the determination of 'trade usages', Article 7 of Interpretation of the Supreme People's Court Regarding Law Application

[27] For the history of bills of lading, see Bennett (1914).

[28] See Schoenbaum (2004) pp. 546–547.

[29] Trade usage is also mentioned in the clauses concerning the supplement of the content of a contract (Articles 60 and 61), the duties of notification, assistance and confidentiality after the termination of a contract (Article 92), the interpretation of contract terms (Article 125) and parties' obligations under sales contracts (Article 136), passenger transportation contracts (Article 293) and contracts of deposit (Article 368).

[30] Article 26(1) reads: 'The acceptance becomes effective when the acceptance notice reaches the offeror. If an acceptance needs no notice, it becomes effective when an act of acceptance is performed in light of trade usages or as indicated by the offer.'

Matters of the Contract Law of the PRC (2) (Interpretation of Contract Law (2))[31] provides:

> The people's court may determine any of the following circumstances as the 'trade usages' mentioned in the Contract Law provided such circumstances do not violate the mandatory provisions of laws and administrative regulations:
>
> (1) Practice which is generally adopted in the place where the trading is conducted or by a certain field or industry, and which is known or ought to have been known by the other party to the trading at the time of the conclusion of contract;
> (2) Customary practice that is frequently adopted by both parties.
>
> With respect to trade usages, the party that puts forward the claim shall bear the burden of proof.

Article 7(1)(1) concerns the two requirements for the establishment of a regional or industrial usage: first, it should be generally adopted in the trading place or by a certain field or industry; second, it is known or ought to have been known by the other party at the time of the conclusion of contract. As to the first requirement, the practice can be adopted either nationally or in a specific district (for example, in the northeastern district or the Pearl River Delta district of China). Whether a practice is 'generally' adopted is determined according to the trading history, scope of the trade, opinions of the industrial associations and so on.[32] The second requirement concerns the knowledge of the practice on the part of the other party. It does *not* require that *both* parties know or ought to have known the practice, but that the party invoking the practice should assure that the other party knows or ought to have known it. Accordingly, knowledge of a practice may be either actual or presumed. Article 7 (1)(2) recognizes the previous customary practice between the parties. That is to say, concerning a shipper's consent to the choice of law clause in a bill of lading, a carrier may argue that as a general trade usage or as a customary practice between it and the shipper, the shipper's action of accepting the bill without objection should be taken as the shipper having agreed to the choice of law clause contained in the bill.

While trade usage has been accepted as an important element concerning the formation of an agreement in several international instruments, its role in the ascertainment of parties' intention on choice of law

[31] It was issued by the SPC on 24 April 2009 and became effective on 13 May 2009.
[32] See Feng (2010) p. 49.

has not received much attention in academic research,[33] and it is still not clear how a court should embark upon the investigation of this issue in China, particularly how to determine whether a practice 'ought to have been known' by the other party in international trade. Some Chinese judges and scholars consider that the requirement concerning the other party's knowledge aims at protecting the parties who do not know about a certain practice or who do not have sufficient experience in a certain field or industry. Therefore, they argue that the party who does not know about a general usage or who is a newcomer to a market or trade should not be bound by the usage.[34] As is analysed shortly, this understanding is too restrictive especially in international commercial transactions. The analysis in the following parts first looks at the relevant provisions in the United Nations Convention on Contracts for the International Sale of Goods (CISG),[35] the UNIDROIT Principles and the Draft Common Frame of Reference of the European Community (DCFR).[36] Second, the Brussels regime, where specific rules on trade usage and the formation of a dispute resolution agreement are provided, is discussed. Third, the author elaborates on the elements referred to in cases and looks at other possible criteria.

B Trade Usage and the Formation of Contract in International Instruments

Trade usage is accepted as an important element in the formation of international contracts in the CISG, the UNIDROIT Principles and the DCFR. Article 18(3) of the CISG, Article 2.1.6(3) of the UNIDROIT Principles and Article II.- 4:205(3) of the DCFR all stipulate that as a result of practices which the parties have established between themselves or of usage, the offeree may indicate assent by performing an act, and the contract is concluded upon performance of that act. Concerning

[33] Although two Chinese scholars have been aware of this issue in their writings, they have not provided detailed analysis as to how this issue should be resolved by looking at the relevant facts in a specific case. See Qin (2010) pp. 235–237; Liu (2008) pp. 82–87, 167–173.

[34] See Feng (2010) p. 50; Shen and Xi (2009) p. 68.

[35] It was prepared by the United Nations Commission on International Trade Law (UNCITRAL) and adopted by a diplomatic conference on 11 April 1980.

[36] See Von Bar and Clive (2010). One purpose of the DCFR is to serve as a draft for drawing up a 'political' Common Frame of Reference (CFR) which was first called for by the European Commission's Action Plan on A More Coherent European Contract Law of February 2003. For other purpose of the DCFR and the background of this project, see Von Bar and Clive (2010) Introduction.

practices and usage between parties, Article 9(1) of the CISG, Article 1.9 of the UNIDROIT Principles, and Article II - 1:104(1) of the DCFR provide that they refer to any usage to which parties have agreed and practices which they have established between themselves. As to an international trade usage, both the CISG and UNIDROIT Principles require that it should be a usage in international trade that is widely known and regularly observed by parties in the particular trade concerned. The DCFR looks at whether a general usage would be considered generally applicable by persons in the same situation as the parties. Article 9(2) of the CISG further provides that a usage is one that parties to a contract knew or ought to have known, while Article 1.9(2) of the UNIDROIT Principles and Article II.-1:104(2) of the DCFR do not require any knowledge of the usage on the part of parties, but only exclude a usage in circumstances where the application of it would be unreasonable.[37]

a A Particular Trade or Industry Since this requirement does not concern a universal trade usage, it must be met for the particular trade concerned. This is to secure the application of specific rules developed in actual practice. Therefore, distinctions regarding industry, party and place are necessary. The transaction concerned should also have a sufficient relation to the usage's sphere of observance (whether place or industry).[38]

A particular trade sector is that part of a business that is characteristic for its commercial activities and makes up most of its transactions. Typical trade sectors in international commerce include oil trade, the export or import business, the commodities trade and the retail sector.[39]

b General Adoption or Regular Observance Worldwide observance of the usage is not required, but the trade usage must be observed by the majority of those involved in the particular industry and there must be no considerable group unaware of such usage.[40] The group of persons establishing the usage have to be businessmen, merchants, traders, or more specifically, those engaged in a particular international trade.

[37] See also the analysis in Bederman (2010) pp. 129–131.

[38] See Schwenzer (2010) p. 190.

[39] See Working Group for the Preparation of Principles for International Commercial Contracts, *Summary Records of the Meeting Held in Miami from 6 to 10 January 1992* (P.C. – Misc. 18) p. 89; Vogenauer and Kleinheisterkamp (2009) p. 197.

[40] See Schwenzer (2010) pp. 190–191.

The observance must be widespread and regular amongst the kind of parties that operate in the very trade sector to which the parties to a given transaction belong.[41]

c Knowledge or Imputed Knowledge of the Parties Although Article 7(1)(1) of the Interpretation of Contract Law (2) acknowledges that the other parties' knowledge on trade practice can be imputed, some Chinese scholars and judges argue that the party who does not actually know a practice should not be bound by it.[42] This interpretation is unconvincing. It is clear from the Chinese provision and the international instruments that a party to a contract may be bound by a trade usage of which he or she is not in fact aware, as long as the usage satisfies the previously mentioned requirements.[43] Implied knowledge may arise from a party's residence in an area where the usage is observed. A party's regular activity in the relevant usage's sphere of observance may also be sufficient.[44] A local or national usage which operates at the place of business of one of the parties but not at that of the other party can only bind the latter if this would be reasonable. A party who comes into a market of the other party will often be bound by the local usages. Commercial acceptance by regular observance by business people is *prima facie* evidence that the usage is reasonable.[45]

C Trade Usage in the Formation of a Dispute Resolution Agreement: The Brussels Regime

a General Provision Established commercial usage was also accepted for the determination of parties' consensus on a dispute resolution clause by the 1978 and 1989 Amendments to Article 17 of the 1968 Brussels Convention on Jurisdiction and Enforcement of Judgments in Civil and Commercial Matters (Brussels Convention).[46] The purpose of the

[41] Vogenauer and Kleinheisterkamp (2009) pp. 194, 197.

[42] See Feng (2010) p. 50; Shen and Xi (2009) p. 68.

[43] See Schmitthoff (1987) p. 17. Lando also pointed out that to provide otherwise would hamper world trade. See Working Group for the Preparation of Principles for International Commercial Contracts, *Summary Records of the Meeting Held in Miami from 6 to 10 January 1992* (P.C. – Misc. 18), pp. 83, 85.

[44] See Schwenzer (2010) p. 191. [45] See Von Bar and Clive (2010) p. 140.

[46] See Article 11 of the 'Council Convention on the Accession of the Kingdom of Denmark, Ireland and the United Kingdom of Great Britain and Northern Ireland to the Convention on Jurisdiction and the Enforcement of Judgments in Civil and Commercial Matters and to the Protocol on its Interpretation by the Court of Justice' (signed on 9 October 1978, 78/884/EEC) and Article 7 of the 'Convention on the Accession of the Kingdom of

1978 Amendment was to take account of the specific practices and requirements of international trade.[47] Article 17 provided:

> If the parties, one or more of whom is domiciled in a Contracting State, have agreed that a court or the courts of a Contracting State are to have jurisdiction to settle any disputes which have arisen or which may arise in connection with a particular legal relationship, that court or those courts shall have exclusive jurisdiction. Such an agreement conferring jurisdiction shall be either:
>
> (a) in writing or evidenced in writing, or
> (b) in a form which accords with practices which the parties have established between themselves, or
> (c) in international trade or commerce, in a form which accords with a usage of which the parties are or ought to have been aware and which in such trade or commerce is widely known to, and regularly observed by, parties to contracts of the type involved in the particular trade or commerce concerned.
>
> Where such an agreement is concluded by parties, none of whom is domiciled in a Contracting State, the courts of other Contracting States shall have no jurisdiction over their disputes unless the court or courts chosen have declined jurisdiction.

Spain and the Portuguese Republic to the Convention on Jurisdiction and the Enforcement of Judgments in Civil and Commercial Matters and to the Protocol on its Interpretation by the Court of Justice with the adjustments made to them by the Convention on the accession of the Kingdom of Denmark, of Ireland and of the United Kingdom of Great Britain and Northern Ireland and the adjustments made to them by the Convention on the Accession of the Hellenic Republic' (signed on 26 May 1989, 89/535/EEC).

The Brussels Convention was superseded by the 'Council Regulation (EC) No 44/2001 of 22 December 2000 on Jurisdiction and the Recognition and Enforcement of Judgments in Civil and Commercial Matters' (Brussels I Regulation) as of March 2002. The Brussels I Regulation has also been replaced by the 'Regulation (EU) No 1215/2012 of the European Parliament and of the Council of 12 December 2012 on Jurisdiction and the Recognition and Enforcement of Judgments in Civil and Commercial Matters (Recast)' (Brussels I Regulation Recast). The Brussels I Regulation Recast entered into force in January 2013, but only applies from 10 January 2015 to legal proceedings instituted (and to judgments rendered) on or after that date. The requirements concerning the establishment of trade practice under the Brussels I Regulation Recast and the Brussels I Regulation are the same as those of Article 17(1) of the Brussels Convention. See Article 25(1)(c) of the Brussels I Regulation Recast and Article 23(1)(c) of the Brussels I Regulation. The analysis in this section mainly refers to the jurisprudence on Article 17(1)(c) of the Brussels Convention.

[47] See *Mainschiffahrts-Genossenschaft e.G. (MSG)* v. *Les Gravières Rhénanes S.a.r.l.*, Case C-106/95, [1997] Q.B. 731, 754. Schmitthoff considered that compared with the CISG, the Brussels Convention went further in that it admitted a derogation by the parties of the forum normally provided by the Convention, even if such derogation was done in a form which accorded with the practices of the trade in which the parties were engaged. See Schmitthoff (1987) p. 13.

b Criteria Set out by the European Court of Justice In *Mainschiffahrts-Genossenschaft e.G. (MSG)* v. *Les Gravières Rhénanes S.a.r.l.* (the *MSG* case),[48] the Court of Justice of the European Communities set out the principles governing the determination of the existence of a commercial practice under Article 17(1)(c) of the Brussels Convention.

The plaintiff, MSG, was domiciled in Germany. It chartered an inland-waterway vessel to the defendant, a French company, by an oral agreement. The agreement contained no jurisdiction clause. Subsequently, however, MSG sent a letter of confirmation which stated that the place of performance of the contract was Würzburg and that the courts of Würzburg would have exclusive jurisdiction over any dispute relating to the contract. The invoices it sent, and which were paid by the defendant, contained a similar statement. After damage to the vessel was allegedly caused by the defendant, the plaintiff brought an action for damages in Würzburg against the defendant. One of the main issues in the *MSG* case was whether the defendant's paying the invoices and not raising any objections to the choice of court statement could constitute agreement to the clause if such behaviour corresponded to a practice which prevailed in the area of international trade or commerce in which the parties operated, and if they knew of it or ought to have known of it.

The Court held that the national court must decide the following issues: first, whether a given contract concerned international trade or commerce; second, whether a relevant practice existed in the particular area of international trade or commerce in which the parties operated; and, third, whether the parties were or ought to have been aware of it.[49] Although these issues were ultimately for the national court to decide, the Court of Justice set out the relevant criteria.[50] A contract concluded in an area of commercial activity between two companies established in different contracting states may be regarded as concerning international trade or commerce. It then said that the existence of a practice must be determined on the basis of the particular area in which the parties are carrying on their activities. A practice may be regarded as existing, in particular, where businessmen in that area generally and regularly behave

[48] Case C-106/95, [1997] Q.B. 731. [49] [1997] Q.B. 731, 755.

[50] Article 1 of the 'Protocol on the Interpretation by the Court of Justice of the Convention of 27 September 1968 on Jurisdiction and the Enforcement of Judgments in Civil and Commercial Matters' (the Brussels Convention Protocol) conferred jurisdiction to the Court of Justice of the European Communities to give rulings on the interpretation of the Convention and the Protocol annexed to that Convention.

in a certain way when concluding contracts of a certain type.[51] Finally, the actual or presumed knowledge of such a practice on the part of the parties may be regarded as established where: (1) they have previously entered into commercial relations with each other or with other parties in the same area of business; or (2) in that area of business, a particular course of conduct is sufficiently well known because it is generally and regularly followed when a particular type of contract is concluded, with the result that it may be regarded as being a consolidated practice.[52]

c Criteria Applied in a Specific Case The principles set out in the *MSG* case were applied in *O.T. Africa Line Ltd.* v. *Hijazy and Others* (*The Kribi*).[53] *The Kribi* arose out of a carriage of goods by sea, which resulted in claims for short delivery against the shipowner. Two parallel cases were brought before the Commercial Court, each involving the same shipowner and some of the same defendants. The shipowner argued in each case that the short delivery was engineered by the Liberian first and second defendants – who were shippers in one of the cases and consignees in the other. The other defendants were the Belgian receivers of one of the shipments and their insurers. The defendants commenced proceedings in Antwerp. The shipowner then brought proceedings in the Commercial Court seeking a declaration of non-liability, substantive relief and anti-suit injunctions to restrain the Belgian proceedings.

In *The Kribi*, a jurisdiction and choice of law clause was contained in the bill of lading concerned, which provided:

> Clause 25 Any claim or dispute whatsoever arising in connection with the carriage under this Bill of Lading shall exclusively be governed by English law and determined by the High Court in London.

One question for the court to decide was, as between the original parties (the shipowners and the Liberian defendants), whether Clause 25 of the bill fulfilled the requirements of Article 17(1)(c) of the Brussels Convention.

Aikens J. held that this form of bill of lading, including Clause 25, is one that would normally be encountered in a modern day international liner service. Similar forms (including English jurisdiction clauses) are used by six other international shipowners or carriers, including carriers on a liner basis to West Africa. It was not challenged that the English jurisdiction clauses were regularly observed and that parties to bills of

[51] [1997] Q.B. 731, 755. [52] [1997] Q.B. 731, 755–756. [53] [2001] 1 Lloyd's Rep. 76.

lading containing English jurisdiction clauses regularly complied with them if disputes arose and thus commenced proceedings in England. There was also the unchallenged evidence that the first two defendants regularly engaged in the West Africa liner trade and had been parties to contracts of carriage evidenced by bills of lading on the same form containing the English jurisdiction clause. Clause 25 was therefore held to be a jurisdiction clause in a form which accorded with a usage of which the shipowners and the Liberian defendants were, or ought to be, aware. Moreover, Clause 25 was a jurisdiction clause that was in a form that was widely known to and regularly observed by parties to bill of lading contracts of carriage in the international liner services, including liner services between Europe and West Africa. Based on the decision of the European Court of Justice in the *MSG* case, Aikens J. decided the court was entitled to presume that there was agreement to the jurisdiction clause as between the Liberian defendants and the shipowners.[54]

As can be seen from the *MSG* case and *The Kribi*, the two courts identified the elements to be taken into account for the establishment of a trade practice: the branch of trade or commerce in which the parties to the contract are operating,[55] a party's experience in commerce,[56] the previous dealings between parties[57] and patterns of bills of lading used in a certain branch of trade.[58] The next section elaborates on these elements and looks at other possible criteria which people's courts in China may take into account.

D Elements to Be Considered in the Determination of the Existence of Trade Usage

a The Branch of Trade Where Parties Are Involved: Taking International Carriage of Goods by Sea as an Example Bills of lading have been used in international commerce since the sixteenth century, and the practice in this field also led to the development of the law merchant.[59] By the end of the nineteenth century divergences in the regulation of the carriers' liability under contracts of affreightment evidenced by bills of lading had attracted attention and had caused concern. The most

[54] [2001] 1 Lloyd's Rep. 76, 90. Aikens J. also confirmed (at pp. 90 – 91) that the lawful holders of the bills of lading and the insurers in this case were also bound by Clause 25 because they succeeded the rights and obligations of the shippers. This issue is further discussed in Section 3.1.5.

[55] [1997] Q.B. 731, 755; [2001] 1 Lloyd's Rep. 76, 90.

[56] [2001] 1 Lloyd's Rep. 76, 90.

[57] [2001] 1 Lloyd's Rep. 76, 89.

[58] [2001] 1 Lloyd's Rep. 76, 90.

[59] See Bennett (1914) chapter 1.

spectacular conflict in that regard involved the question of the validity of 'negligence' clauses, namely clauses designed to exonerate the carrier from liability for his or his servants' negligence in connection with damage to cargoes.[60]

Large scale international trade needs a certain measure of security and predictability with regard to the enforcement of obligations. The contract for the carriage of goods by sea under bills of lading was one of the first areas of commercial law to attract attention for possible unification of law. Unification of law in that area was highly necessary because of the great importance of maritime transportation for the economy of different countries.[61] The international conventions concerning the unification of laws in this area include four important documents: the Hague Rules,[62] the Hague-Visby Rules,[63] the Hamburg Rules[64] and most recently, the Rotterdam Rules.[65]

Many countries have included in their Hague Rules statutes a provision which requires the parties to bills of lading governed by the statute to include therein an express statement that the bill of lading is to have effect subject to the provisions of the Hague Rules enacted by that statute.[66]

Given the influence of the international conventions,[67] business people in this field should be aware of these mechanisms, and if one is concerned about the relevant clauses in a bill of lading, he or she should look into

[60] Knauth (1953) p. 116. [61] See Yiannopoulos (1962) chapter 2.

[62] International Convention for the Unification of Certain Rules of Law Relating to Bills of Lading (Brussels, 25 August 1924).

[63] Protocol to Amend the International Convention for the Unification of Certain Rules of Law Relating to Bills of Lading (Brussels, 23 February 1968).

[64] United Nations Convention on the Carriage of Goods by Sea (Hamburg, 31 March 1978).

[65] United Nations Convention on Contracts for the International Carriage of Goods Wholly or Partly by Sea (adopted by the United Nations General Assembly on 11 December 2008). The Convention extends and modernizes the existing international rules relating to contract of maritime carriage of goods. The aim is that the Convention will replace the Hague Rules, the Hague-Visby Rules and the Hamburg Rules and that it will achieve uniformity of law in the field of maritime carriage. The Convention will come into force one year after ratification by the 20th United Nations member state.

[66] For example, Section 13 of the United States 1936 COGSA requires that an outbound bill of lading contain a 'clause paramount', reciting that the bill is to be governed by the provisions of the Act. This was an addition by Congress to the Rules. No provision is to be found for enforcing this requirement. For the effect of a carrier's omission of this clause in an outbound bill of lading and the policy underlying that provision, see Gilmore and Black (1975) pp. 185–186. In 2006, the 1936 US COGSA was re-codified as a historical and statutory note to 46 U.S.C. §30701. It previously was codified at 46 U.S.C.A. §§1300–1315.

[67] As to the measure of the success of the Hague Rules, see Yiannopoulos (1962) chapter 6.

the clauses in the bill carefully.[68] When determining the existence of trade practice in international carriage of goods by sea, people's courts should be aware of the widespread unification of laws in this area.

b A Party's Experience in Commerce Although bills of lading have often been treated as contracts of adhesion that are construed against the drafter,[69] when no ambiguities exist in the bill, the non-drafting but sophisticated party will still be held to be bound by the clauses in the bill, absent evidence that it was prevented from negotiating the provisions.[70]

It is critically important to distinguish between two issues here: the difficulty in the interpretation of a contract because its terms are unclear or ambiguous, and whether a party has agreed to a clause of a contract drafted in advance by the other party. The principle that ambiguities should be resolved against the drafter of a contract only applies to the first issue.[71] As to the second issue, the non-drafting party should be bound by the clauses in a standard contract especially when it is a large, sophisticated corporation with experience in international business transactions if it cannot provide evidence to prove that it was in fact unaware of the terms.

Guangzhou Maritime Court adopted this approach in *Shenzhen Yihe Import & Export Co. Ltd.* v. *MSC Mediterranean Shipping Company SA, Go-Trans (Hong Kong) Co. Ltd. and Go-Trans Express Co. Ltd.*[72] The 'Application of Laws' clause on the back of the bill of lading concerned referred to the COGSA. The plaintiff shipper said that the

68 The patterns of bills of lading and their availability are discussed later. See Part d.

69 See, for example, *Navieros Oceanikos, S.A.* v. *S.T. Mobil Trader* 554 F.2d 43, 48 (2nd Cir. 1977); *Associated Metals & Minerals Corp.* v. *M/V Vishva Shobha* 530 F.2d 714, 718 (6th Cir. 1976) (resolving ambiguity in the bill of lading 'against the party ... which prepared the instrument').

70 Courts do not hesitate to rule in favour of carriers in this situation. See, for example, *Gamma-10 Plastics, Inc.* v. *American President Lines, Ltd.* 32 F.3d 1244, 1253 (8th Cir. 1994) (noting that '[a]lthough a bill of lading is a contract of adhesion, the language in APL's bills is clear and we can only interpret it to mean what it says'); *Mori Seiki USA, Inc.* v. *M.V. Alligator Triumph* 990 F.2d 444, 448 (9th Cir. 1993) (holding that although a bill of lading is a contract of adhesion and ambiguities must be construed against the carrier, no such ambiguity existed in the bill of lading in question).

71 Article 41 of China's Contract Law provides: 'If a dispute arises over the understanding of a standard clause, the clause shall be interpreted in accordance with its common understanding. If a standard clause has more than one interpretation, the clause shall be interpreted in a manner unfavourable to the party providing the clause. If a standard clause is inconsistent with the non-standard clause, the non-standard clause prevails.'

72 25 December 2003, Guangzhou Maritime Court.

carriers did not provide to it the terms on the reverse of the bill in the negotiation, that the terms were printed in very small characters and thus hard to recognize, and that the clause was incorporated into the bill unilaterally by the carriers. It therefore argued that it should not be bound by the clause. The court pointed out that it is a practice in international trade and the maritime industry that there are clauses on the front and back of a bill of lading. Although the characters were small, it was not impossible to identify them. As a professional company in international trade, the plaintiff shipper should have been aware of the practice and the existence of clauses on the back of the bill even though the carriers did not provide those clauses in their negotiation. The plaintiff should have asked the carriers about the clauses if it wanted to know the terms. More importantly, there was no evidence showing that the plaintiff had expressed its disagreement to the clauses on the back of the bill when it accepted the bill. Based on these facts, the court held that the plaintiff should be taken as having impliedly agreed to the choice of law clause.

c The Previous Dealings between Parties The actual or presumed awareness of a usage on the part of the parties to a contract can be made out by showing either that the parties previously had commercial or trade relations between themselves or with other parties operating in the sector in question.[73]

The previous dealings between the parties concerned are generally decisive when the same or similar forms of bills of lading have been used between them. In these circumstances, it would be very difficult for the non-drafting party to prove that it was not aware of the clause concerned.

In *Partenreederei ms. Tilly Russ and Another* v. *Haven & Vervoebedrijf Nova N.V. and Another* (*The Tilly Russ*), the European Court of Justice was asked to decide firstly whether the jurisdiction clause contained in the bills of lading satisfied the conditions laid down in Article 17 of the Brussels Convention as regards the relationship between the shipper and the carrier.[74] The Court held that in order to satisfy the original version

[73] See the *MSG* case [1997] Q.B. 731,748–749; *Trasporti Castelletti Spedizioni Internazionali SpA* v. *Hugo Trumpy SpA* (the *Hugo Trumpy SpA* Case), Case C-159/97, [1999] ECR I-1636, para. 43.

[74] Case 71/83, [1984] ECR 2417. The second question before the Court was the effect of the jurisdiction clause as between the carrier and the third-party holder. See the discussion in Section 3.1.5.

of Article 17,[75] it was not sufficient for the jurisdiction clause merely to be printed on the back of the bill of lading. It was necessary for the shipper to have expressed his consent in writing to the clause, whether on the bill of lading or in a separate document. If, however, the jurisdiction clause in the bill of lading was the formal manifestation of a prior oral agreement, Article 17 would be satisfied where the bill of lading was signed by the carrier alone. If neither of the aforementioned requirements were satisfied, then the jurisdiction clause would only be valid 'provided that the bill of lading comes within the framework of a continuing business relationship between the shipper and the carrier, in so far as it is thereby established that that relationship is governed as a whole by general conditions containing the jurisdiction clause drawn up by the author of the written confirmation, in this case the carrier . . . and provided that the bills of lading are all issued on pre-printed forms systematically containing such a jurisdiction clause'.[76]

The continuing business relationship between parties is not only helpful in determining the customary practice frequently adopted by them, as is provided for by Article 7(1)(2) of the Interpretation of Contract Law (2) in China, but also indicative of parties' knowledge of that practice.

d General and Regular Observance in a Particular Trade and the Assessment of Parties' Knowledge of the Usage Parties' actual or presumed knowledge of a usage can also be proved by showing that in a trade sector, a particular course of conduct is sufficiently well known because it is generally and regularly followed when a particular type of contract is concluded, so that it may be regarded as being an established usage.[77] Therefore, the more well known a particular market or trade

[75] It should be noted that at issue was the interpretation of Article 17 in the original 1968 Brussels Convention, and not as it was amended by the 1978 Convention of Accession by Denmark, Ireland and the United Kingdom. In its original form, Article 17 required that the agreement as to jurisdiction should be 'in writing or by an oral agreement evidenced in writing', requirements which had been strictly interpreted by the European Court, whose decisions led to the more generous terminology of the amended Article 17. See North (1985) pp. 177–178.

[76] [1984] ECR 2417, para. 18. North (1985) p. 178 considered that this rather more liberal requirement marked a step away from earlier national court decisions, which had held that jurisdiction clauses in bills of lading did not satisfy Article 17, and was more in line with the broader approach of the amended Article 17.

[77] See the *MSG* case [1997] Q.B. 731, 748–749; the *Hugo Trumpy SpA* Case [1999] ECR I-1636, para. 43.

sector is, the harder it will be to claim ignorance of its practices.[78] Moreover, a course of conduct satisfying the conditions indicative of a usage does not cease to be a usage because it is challenged before the courts, whatever the extent of the challenges, provided that it still continues to be generally and regularly followed in the trade with which the type of contract in question is concerned.[79]

In *The Kribi*, Aikens J. looked at the forms of bills of lading in a modern day international liner service, and held that a similar form of bill containing Clause 25 would normally be encountered.[80] Accordingly, if a choice of law clause in a bill of lading is one that would usually be encountered, such as one referring to the Hague Rules or the relevant statutes in the contracting states, it would be easy to establish that it has become part of a trade practice.

The publicity of bills of lading can make it easier to prove parties' awareness and is also an important element for determining whether the non-drafting party is aware of the clauses in the bill. Nowadays, corporations involved in international carriage of goods by sea usually make their bills of lading accessible on websites. Moreover, publications on bills of lading also contain different patterns of bills for the readers' reference.[81] When a bill of lading is easily accessed on the Internet or is widely used in international commerce, it would be contrary to ordinary commercial practice and common expectation if a shipper claims that it is not aware of a choice of law clause contained in it. This approach has been adopted by people's courts.

In *Fujian Provincial Arts & Crafts Xiamen Import and Export Corp.* v. *Greating Marine Ltd. and Xiamen Yuli Container Services Ltd.* (Yuli Ltd.),[82] there was a choice of law clause referring to Hong Kong law on the back of the bills of lading concerned. As to the effect of this clause, the Xiamen Maritime Court held that since the carrier Yuli Ltd. was a non-vessel carrier registered in the Communications Department of the State Council, and the bill of lading it used in this case was the same as the one

78 Newton (2002) p. 259.
79 The *Hugo Trumpy SpA* Case [1999] ECR I-1636, para. 29.
80 [2001] 1 Lloyd's Rep. 76, 90.
81 See, for example, Gaskell, Asariotis and Baatz (2000); Wilson (2010).
82 20 December 2004, Xiamen Maritime Court; 20 March 2005, Fujian Higher People's Court. In this case, the defendants released the cargoes at the port of destination to the consignee of the bills of lading without the production of original bills, and the plaintiff sued them for the loss of payment for goods. Both courts, based on Hong Kong law, determined that the carrier's releasing cargoes to the consignee was not in breach of his obligations, and made decisions for the defendants.

it had registered for record,[83] this clause could be applied to determine the governing law of this case. This holding was confirmed by Fujian Higher People's Court.

In *Kogee International Group and Kogee Co. Ltd.* v. *DSL Star Express Inc., Maersk Logistics (China) Co. Ltd., Panama Greencompass Marine SA, Copenhagen A. P. Moller-Maersk and CMA CGM SA*,[84] the 'Applicable Law and Jurisdiction' clauses in all the bills of lading concerned referred to the COGSA and English law. The standard bills of lading in this case had also been registered for record in the Communications Department, and the shipper Kogee International Group did not express any disagreement with the terms in the bills when accepting them. The Guangzhou Maritime Court therefore confirmed that the choice of law clauses in the bills were effective.

In the *Farenco* case,[85] the standard bill of lading of the carrier had in fact been registered in the Communications Department of the State Council and could be easily accessed by the public on the website. Given that, the shipper would have to provide very strong evidence if it wanted to prove that it did not have the opportunity of discovering the clauses in the bills of lading for itself. The appellate decision in this case would have been much more convincing had the Shanghai Higher People's Court taken this important fact into account.

E Summary

The analysis in Section 3.1.4 focuses on contracts between commercial parties in international transactions. Although it begins with the situations involving a bill of lading, the discussion is also relevant to other commercial contracts. Commercial practice should be taken into consideration in determining whether the apparent consent of the non-drafting party on a clause in a standard contract can be proved. The consideration behind this is that the existence of trade usages is so common that a duty lies on the other party to inquire in each case whether or not, and what kind of, practices are employed.[86] The elements identified earlier can be

[83] This is required by the Regulation of the PRC on International Maritime Transportation (issued by the State Council on 11 December 2001, effective on 1 January 2002; revised for the first time on 18 July 2013, revised for the second time on 6 February 2016).

[84] 18 December 2007, Guangzhou Maritime Court.

[85] See n 8 and the discussion of this case in Sections 3.1.1 and 3.1.2.

[86] See Prausnitz (1937) pp. 79–80.

applied cumulatively for the determination of the existence of commercial practice and parties' knowledge of it.

First, the general applicability of a practice indicates the inference which may properly be drawn regarding the parties' knowledge of its existence: the more generally applicable and well established a practice is, the stronger is the inference that a party knew or had reason to know of it.[87] The practice must, if not actually known, be so general and notorious that a person of ordinary prudence in the exercise of reasonable care would be aware of it.[88]

Second, a party's engagement in a particular business or trade may also make it reasonable to presume that he or she is informed of the general practice of the trade.[89] 'Where both parties to a transaction are engaged in the same occupation, or belong to the same group of persons, the usages of that occupation or group are operative, unless one of the parties knows or has reason to know that the other party has an inconsistent intention.'[90] Moreover, a party is always held to conduct generally observed by members of his or her chosen trade because the other party is justified in so assuming unless he or she indicates otherwise.[91]

Third, practices in a trade, however, are not automatically binding on persons *not* in that trade or business.[92] A trader cannot normally be expected to be aware of particular trade usages that are limited to a

[87] *Pacific Grape Products Co.* v. *C.I.R.* 219 F.2d 862, 866 – 867 (9th Cir. 1955) (the more general and notorious a usage is, the more clearly will either party to a contract be justified in assuming the other is contracting with reference to the usage).

[88] See *Federal Reserve Bank of Richmond* v. *Malloy* 264 U.S. 160, 169–171 (US Supreme Court, 1924); *Eames* v. *H. B. Claflin Co.* 239 F. 631, 634–635 (C.C.A. 2nd Cir. 1917); *Mullins Lumber Co.* v. *Williamson & Brown Land & Lumber Co.* 246 F. 232, 235 (C.C.A. 4th Cir. 1917); *Continental Coal Co.* v. *Birdsall* 108 F. 882, 884–885 (C.C.A. 4th Cir. 1901).

[89] See *Elijah Goodenow* v. *John E. Tyler* 7 Mass. 36, 46–47 (1810); *US Naval Institute* v. *Charter Communications, Inc.* 687 F. Supp. 115 (S.D. N.Y. 1988), judgment reversed, 875 F.2d 1044 (2nd Cir. 1989) (publisher was held to have knowledge of trade usage with respect to the meaning of the term 'publication date' as used in contract licensing paperback edition of a particular book, where it had engaged in the business of publishing for nearly a century and had previously contracted for paperback licenses).

[90] *Joseph N. Ermolieff* v. *R.K.O. Radio Pictures, Inc.* 19 Cal. 2d 543, 550–551(1942).

[91] *Nanakuli Paving and Rock Co.* v. *Shell Oil Co., Inc.* 664 F.2d 772, 32 U.C.C. Rep. Serv. 1025 (9th Cir. 1981).

[92] *US Shipping Board Emergency Fleet Corp.* v. *Levensaler* 290 F. 297, 325–328 (App. D.C. 1923), affirmed, 1 F.2d 1021 (App. D.C. 1924).

geographical area that is foreign to it.[93] Therefore, proof of actual knowledge on the part of a person *outside* the trade or business is necessary.[94]

3.1.5 *Contracts Where a Third Party Is Involved or Another Document Is Incorporated*

When a third party is involved or a choice of law clause is incorporated from another contract, a question that arises is whether a choice of law originally made between two parties can bind a third party in a dispute with one of the original parties.

In *The Tilly Russ*,[95] the purchaser acquired from the shipper a bill of lading which contained a jurisdiction agreement. Could the jurisdiction agreement be enforced against the purchaser although the purchaser, as a third party, had made no separate contract with the carrier? The Court's approach was essentially that in so far as a jurisdiction clause in a bill of lading was valid under Article 17 of the Brussels Convention as between the original parties, and that in so far as a third party, under the applicable law, had succeeded to the shipper's rights and obligations by acquiring the bill of lading, it would be 'alien' to the purposes of Article 17 not to enforce the clause. The Court held that in agreeing to transfer the bill the shipper could confer no more rights than it had, and the third party therefore took the rights subject to the obligations including the jurisdiction clause.[96] Briggs considered this approach to be 'sensible', and further explained that if a transferee does succeed to the rights and obligations of a transferor, it would be a manifestation of bad faith for him to claim to have succeeded to the substantive rights and liabilities, but not to have ratified the jurisdictional framework.[97] This approach must surely depend upon the terms of the jurisdiction clause. If the clause excluded claims by the third party presumably it would not be enforced against the third party.[98] Article 78(1) of China's Maritime Code stipulates that the relationship between the carrier and the

[93] See Vogenauer and Kleinheisterkamp (2009) p. 197.

[94] *Frigaliment Importing Co.* v. *B.N.S. International Sales Corp.* 190 F. Supp. 116, 119–120 (S.D. N.Y. 1960); *US Shipping Board Emergency Fleet Corp.* v. *Levensaler* 290 F. 297, 301–303 (App. D.C. 1923), affirmed, 1 F.2d 1021 (App. D.C. 1924).

[95] Case 71/83, [1984] ECR 2417.

[96] [1984] ECR 2417, paras. 24–25. This approach was also applied in *The Kribi* [2001] 1 Lloyd's Rep. 76 and *Coreck Maritime GmbH* v. *Handelsveem BV and Others*, Case C-387/98, [2000] ECR I-9337.

[97] See Briggs (2012) pp. 379–380.

[98] See Cox, Merrett and Smith (2006) para. 5.71.

consignee or the holder of the bill of lading with respect to their rights and obligations shall be defined by the clauses of the bill of lading. Therefore, if the consent of both the carrier and shipper to a choice of law clause in a bill exists, then a subsequent holder of the bill would normally be bound by the clause provided that the circumstances or the clause do not indicate otherwise.

When a dispute resolution clause is incorporated from a charterparty into a bill of lading, a court should also consider whether the parties have clearly expressed their intent. In *Siboti K/S* v. *BP France S.A.*,[99] the principal issue was the effect of the incorporation of a jurisdiction clause. Gross J. pointed out that Article 17 of the Brussels Convention recognized the validity of incorporation by reference, provided that the body of terms to be incorporated was clearly identified and that it was available to the contracting party at the time of entry into the contract. For the purposes of Article 17, jurisdiction clauses were regarded as ancillary to the substantive provisions of the contract. In many cases, Gross J. recalled, general words of incorporation would only suffice to incorporate terms germane to the subject matter of the contract but not terms ancillary thereto. The reason is that in the absence of specific language, a court would not be able to conclude that the parties have demonstrated clearly and precisely the existence of a consensus to incorporate clauses which are ancillary to the subject matter of their contract. Moreover, Gross J. held that a court must in each case construe the language of the contract against the commercial background and inquire whether a consensus on the subject matter of the jurisdiction clause had been clearly and precisely demonstrated.[100]

This approach is adopted by people's courts. In *Shenzhen Cereals Group Co. Ltd.* v. *Future E.N.E*,[101] the defendant Future E.N.E. (Future Company) was the owner of the vessel 'Alpha Future' and the carrier under the relevant bill of lading. The plaintiff, Shenzhen Cereals Group Co. Ltd. (Cereals Group), was the holder of the bill. Future Company concluded a time charter of 'Alpha Future' to Bunge S.A., and Bunge S.A. then sub-chartered the vessel to Noble Grain Pte. Ltd. (Noble Grain). In 2004, tons of beans were shipped on board Alpha Future and a 1994 version of a Congen bill of lading was issued on behalf of the shipowner, the Future Company. The bill specified that the shipper was Noble Grain,

[99] [2003] EWHC 1278 (Comm); [2003] 2 Lloyd's Rep. 364.

[100] See [2003] EWHC 1278 (Comm); [2003] 2 Lloyd's Rep. 364, 372–374.

[101] 20 November 2004, Qingdao Maritime Court.

consignee to order, the noticer was the plaintiff, Cereals Group, and the goods were shipped from Santos (Brazil) to Qingdao (China). The bill was later negotiated to the plaintiff. At the destination port, Qingdao, the plaintiff found the beans were mouldy and thus sued the defendant carrier for damages in the Qingdao Maritime Court in China.

Clause 1 on the back of the bill of lading provided: 'The terms and conditions, liberties and exceptions of the Charter Party, dated as overleaf, including the Law and Arbitration Clause, are herewith incorporated.' Clause 17 of the Charter Party said: 'Any dispute arising out of this Charter Party shall be referred to Arbitration in London.' Based on this arbitration clause, the defendant raised an objection to the jurisdiction of the Qingdao Maritime Court and argued that the dispute should be solved through arbitration.

One of the issues before the court was whether, pursuant to Clause 1, the arbitration clause in the Charter Party could be incorporated into the bill. The court held that when an arbitration clause in another contract was incorporated into the bill of lading, the validity of the clause of incorporation (Clause 1) was a question of law and should be determined by its governing law. After the plaintiff had filed an action to this court, the issue of whether an arbitration agreement existed between both parties was not only related to the examination of the agreement, but also to the rights of suit of the parties and to the jurisdiction of the court. Therefore, that was a question concerning litigation procedure and the forum law should be applied. The Qingdao Maritime Court then applied Article 95 of China's Maritime Code and decided that the clauses in the time charter of this case could not be incorporated into a bill of lading[102] and thus there was no arbitration agreement between the parties in the case. The defendant's objection was not supported.

As to the effect of a clause incorporating the terms of a charterparty into a bill of lading, the Supreme People's Court (SPC) has stated that an arbitration clause, jurisdiction clause or choice of law clause in a charterparty can only be incorporated into a bill of lading provided that the incorporation clause in the bill *expressly and specifically* stipulates to that

[102] Article 95 of the Maritime Code provides: 'Where the holder of the bill of lading is not the charterer in the case of a bill of lading issued under a voyage charter, the rights and obligations of the carrier and the holder of the bill of lading shall be governed by the clauses of the bill of lading. However, if the clauses of the voyage charterparty are incorporated into the bill of lading, the relevant clauses of the voyage charterparty shall apply.' The court accordingly considered that only a voyage charter can be incorporated into a bill of lading.

effect; otherwise, the dispute resolution clauses in a charterparty cannot bind a holder of the bill who is not the charterer.[103]

Although the circumstances in which charterparty provisions are incorporated into a bill are considered to be 'special and possibly unique',[104] the aforementioned approach may even be applied to other situations where another contract is incorporated if the parties intend that the subject matter of the two contracts shall be the same. This was the case in *AIG Europe (UK) Ltd. and Others* v. *The Ethniki*, where the court held that in a reinsurance contract, what may be called the scope of the insurance was identical with that in the underlying policy.[105] This was a good and sufficient reason for asking the same question as in a bill of lading: did the parties to the contract in which the general words of incorporation appear intend that their contract should include the particular term from the other contract referred to?[106]

As can be seen from the analysis, a court should determine the effect of a choice of law clause in a contract on a third party by looking at whether the clause represents the consent of the original parties and whether the third party succeeds to the rights and obligations from one of the original parties. When a choice of law clause is incorporated from another contract between two other parties or between one of the parties in the dispute and a third party (such as a bill of lading, building contract and reinsurance and insurance contract), a court should carefully construe the incorporation clause against the commercial background and examine whether the parties have precisely identified the clause to be incorporated and clearly expressed their intent.[107]

[103] See Responses to Questions in Foreign-related Commercial and Maritime Trial (1) (issued by the Fourth Division of Civil Case Trial of the SPC in 2004).

[104] *AIG Europe (UK) Ltd. and Others* v. *The Ethniki* [2000] 2 All ER 566, 575 (C.A.).

[105] [2000] 2 All ER 566, 575.

[106] [2000] 2 All ER 566, 575–576. This approach was adopted in *AIG Europe S.A.* v. *QBE International Insurance Ltd.* [2001] 2 Lloyd's Rep. 268, 273 ('In many cases the answer will be that in the absence of specific language the court will not be able to infer with confidence that the parties did intend to incorporate any terms other than those which are germane to their own contract . . . ').

[107] See also *Habas Sinai ve Tibbi Gazlar Isthisal Endustri AS* v. *Sometal SAL* [2010] EWHC 29 (Comm); [2010] 1 Lloyd's Rep. 661. For a further discussion of incorporating a charterparty's applicable law clause into a bill of lading and a recent decision from the High Court of Singapore on this issue, see Zhao and Chan (2012). For other practical problems concerning the construction of a linking clause, see Fentiman (2015) paras. 5.119–5.127.

3.1.6 *Standard Contracts Involving Weaker Parties*

The earlier discussion focuses on contracts between commercial parties. In contracts where weaker parties are involved, the considerations should be different. It is obvious that a choice procured by duress and fraud would not be regarded as effective. What is more open to question is the effect of the use of superior bargaining power.[108] In the *MSG* case, the European Court of Justice pointed out that the aim of Article 17 of the Brussels Convention was to ensure that there was real consent on the part of the persons concerned. The underlying purpose was to protect the weaker party to the contract by avoiding jurisdiction clauses, incorporated into a contract by one party, going unnoticed.[109] In *Oceanic Sun Line Special Shipping Company Inc.* v. *Fay*, one of the disputed issues was whether the passenger, Fay, should be bound by the exclusive jurisdiction clause which was inserted into the cruise ticket by the carrier after Fay had paid for the fare. The High Court of Australia held that a mere statement in the carrier's brochure that the carrier contracted on its conditions of carriage was not enough to make those conditions, including the jurisdiction clause, terms of a contract subsequently made with a passenger.[110]

Modern law is sensitive to the need to protect the economically weaker party, most notably the consumer, the employee and the insured.[111] As to choice of law clauses, special rules should also be applied to ascertain the weaker party's consent. In the 2010 Conflicts Statute, the party autonomy principle is restricted or even excluded in two contexts, namely consumer contracts and labour contracts.[112] However, the scope of protection provided in the Statute is vague, and it is not clear what kind of relationship is covered by the provisions therein. Their scope is to be determined by people's courts on a case-by-case basis.[113] Moreover, no particular conflicts rule is provided concerning insurance contracts in the Statute.[114] Consequently, there are some categories of contracts where a weaker party is involved and where the party autonomy principle may be

108 Nygh (1999) p. 69. 109 [1997] Q.B. 731, 754–755.
110 (1988) 165 CLR 197, 228–230. 111 Nygh (1999) p. 69.
112 See Articles 42 and 43 of the 2010 Conflicts Statute.
113 For the restrictions on party autonomy in consumer contracts and labour contracts in the 2010 Conflicts Statute and the inherent uncertainties, see Liang (2012) pp. 98, 100–103.
114 Some Chinese scholars have suggested that a particular conflicts rule should be provided concerning international insurance contracts for the purpose of protecting the interests of the insured. See Qu and Zhang (2006) p. 40.

regarded applicable by a court. When there is a choice of law clause in these contracts, it is still necessary to apply the particular rules in the Contract Law to determine whether the weaker party has consented to the clause.

Article 39(1) of the Contract Law and Article 6(1) of the Interpretation of Contract Law (2) both provide that when entering a contract, the party who supplies the standard terms shall make the other party aware of the clauses concerning the exclusion or limitation of the supplying party's liabilities in a reasonable way. Five factors are relevant: (a) the appearance of the notice document – it should be legible enough to attract the other party's attention; (b) the method of giving the notice; (c) degree of explicitness of the language used; (d) time to give the notice – the notice must be given before the contract is concluded or in the process of concluding the contract; and (e) degree of the awareness of the other party – the notice must make the other party fully aware.[115] According to the two provisions, the supplying party is *not* required to notify the other party of all the standard clauses,[116] and thus it is not clear whether a choice of law clause is required to be notified to the other party. The Insurance Law of China[117] provides a better rule in this respect. Article 17(1) of the law stipulates that where an insurance contract is entered into using the standard clauses of the insurer, the insurer shall provide an insurance policy with the standard clauses attached and explain the contents of the contract to the insurance applicant. The Insurance Law does not restrict the scope of standard clauses of which the supplying party is required to notify the other party. Since the governing law of a contract determines the rights and obligations of the parties, people's courts should also carefully look at the aforementioned elements to decide whether a choice of law clause can be taken to have been assented to by the weaker party.

Section 3.1 identifies the elements that people's courts need to take into account when ascertaining the existence of parties' consent to a choice of law clause. For contracts between professional merchants, a court should look at the trade usages and commercial practice to ascertain parties' intention on choice of law. Under the circumstances where a

[115] See Wang (2002) pp. 394–395. [116] See Feng (2010) p. 42; Shen and Xi (2009) p. 63.
[117] It was adopted at the 14th Meeting of the Standing Committee of the 8th NPC on 30 June 1995, amended for the first time on 28 October 2002, revised on 28 February 2009, amended for the second time on 31 August 2014 and amended for the third time on 24 April 2015.

third or a weaker party is involved, or where a choice of law clause is incorporated from another document, people's courts should be more careful in the assessment of the non-drafting party's consent.

3.2 Determination of the Validity of Parties' Choice of Law

The analysis in Section 3.1 is based on Chinese law as the law of the forum. Following the remarks that Brennan J. made in *Oceanic Sun Line Special Shipping Company Inc.* v. *Fay*, if the choice of law rule of the forum allows parties to agree on the applicable law, then until they agree, there is no choice. Therefore, the existence of any agreement as to choice of law (or jurisdiction, as it was in this case) is a preliminary issue which cannot be determined by assuming that the parties have agreed on such a choice.[118] It is hard to see how a court can solve the issue, before it has identified the *lex causae*, by reference to anything other than its own conception of what amounts to an agreement.[119] The issue of whether there has been a consensus between the parties as regards a choice of law, no matter the consensus exists as a matter of fact or as a matter of contract construction, is thus determined by the forum law.[120]

As to the validity of a choice of law clause, three issues need to be distinguished.[121] The first is whether parties are permitted to choose the law governing their contract. This is related to the permissibility of party autonomy in contractual choice of law and also the scope of party autonomy, namely whether there are any statutory restrictions on their choice. This issue is subject to the private international law of the forum.[122] The second is parties' consent to a choice of law, which is, as analysed in Section 3.1, determined by the forum law. The third issue concerns the material validity of the choice, that is, whether there is

[118] (1988) 165 CLR 197, 225. See also *Mackender and Others* v. *Feldia A. G. and Others* [1967] 2 Q.B. 590, 602–603 (per Diplock L. J.); Libling (1979) p. 170.

[119] See Briggs (2008) para. 10.29.

[120] See Nygh (1999) pp. 87–90, 92–93; Dicey and Morris (1987), Vol. 2, pp. 1176–1178 (this was the position in English law prior to the incorporation of the Rome Convention in England; see also *Compagnie Tunisienne de Navigation SA* v. *Compagine d'Armement Maritime SA* [1971] AC 572, 603); Briggs (1989) pp. 219–220.

[121] In Chinese literature on private international law, the meaning of 'validity of a choice of law clause' is usually ambiguous as it encompasses two of, or all the three issues to be mentioned shortly. See, for example, J. Xu (2010) pp. 76–83.

[122] The issue is addressed in Chapters 5 and 6.

duress, fraud, misrepresentation or any other situations that would make a choice of law clause void. This section discusses the third issue.

3.2.1 *Criteria Adopted by People's Courts*

The issue has arisen in cases where one of the parties unilaterally chooses or changes the governing law, and where the choice of law clause is ambiguous.

A A Party's Unilateral Change or Choice of the Governing Law

In *DBS Bank (Hong Kong) Ltd.* v. *Shengwang Clothes-Making Co. Ltd. and Shenzhen Tongyihe Shengwang Clothes Processing Factory*,[123] the plaintiff and the first defendant had selected Hong Kong law to govern their lease, but neither of the two defendants issued a defence in the proceedings. At trial, the defendants did not appear and the plaintiff argued for the application of Chinese law. The court decided that the defendants' failure to appear in court should be taken as having waived their procedural rights, and since the Mainland had the closest connection with the contract, Chinese law should be applied. The court directly confirmed the effect of the plaintiff's change of the previously chosen law without considering the validity of the choice of law clause in the lease concerned. It seems the only reason that the court did not apply Hong Kong law, which was mutually selected by the parties, was the plaintiff's unilateral change of the choice.

In *Industrial and Commercial Bank of China (Shenzhen Branch)* v. *Karsing (Holding) Ltd., Karsing Investment Co. Ltd. and Guangzhou Dongyi Real Estate Co. Ltd.*,[124] the plaintiff and Karsing Investment Co. Ltd. selected the law of Macao to govern the Agreement on Quota for Opening a Letter of Credit between them. Karsing Investment Co. Ltd. did not appear at trial, and the plaintiff said that it waived the selection of Macao law and pleaded Chinese law. Guangdong Higher People's Court held that the failure of the second defendant to appear in court proceedings indicated that it had waived the right to choose the governing law. Since the Agreement was signed in China and notarized by the Shenzhen Notary Public Office, and that the plaintiff was a Chinese legal person,

[123] 15 September 2006, Yantian District People's Court of Shenzhen.
[124] 26 March 2002, Guangdong Higher People's Court.

the plaintiff's selection of Chinese law should be approved according to the principle of closest connection.

The approach in the previous two cases was also adopted by other people's courts in confirming a plaintiff's unilateral choice of law in court proceedings.[125] In these cases, the courts either accepted the plaintiffs' unilateral change of the law previously selected by both parties, or confirmed that the law chosen by the plaintiff before the court should be applied, even though the defendant did not appear in court to express the intention on the change or choice of the governing law.

This approach is against the principle of due process. Article 144 of the Civil Procedure Law only stipulates that when the defendant refuses to appear before court upon being summoned and without justified reasons or leaves the courtroom during the court session without the approval of the court, a default judgment may be made by the court. Article 3(6) of Minutes of the National Conference on Foreign-, Hong Kong- and Macao-Related Economic Trials in Coastal Areas (1989 Minutes) issued by the SPC also contains a similar provision that the defendant's failure to appear in court only indicates that he or she gives up the right to defend.[126] Accordingly, a defendant's failure to appear in court should not affect the validity of parties' previous choice of law in contract as far as the choice represents both parties' intention at the time of the conclusion of the contract. Nor should the failure be taken as an 'implied' consent to the plaintiff's choice of law in court proceedings.

In *Kreditanstalt für Wiederaufbau* v. *Abu Dhabi Container Lines P.J.S.C.*,[127] the loan contract between the parties referred to English law. The defendant did not appear in court and the plaintiff pleaded Chinese law in the proceedings. The Shanghai Maritime Court held that the parties' choice of law in the contract was effective according to the Civil Law and Contract Law and represented the mutual consent of them.

[125] In *Standard Chartered China (Beijing Branch)* v. *Tian Qixin* (19 August 2011, The Second Intermediate People's Court of Beijing), the defendant did not appear in court. The court held that 'since the plaintiff chooses Chinese law, Chinese law should be applied according to the party autonomy principle'. In *Kwak Yong Pil* v. *KMC Co. Ltd.* (23 November 2005, Shanghai Maritime Court), the court held that the defendant's failure to appear in court indicated that it had waived the right to choose the applicable law; since the plaintiff selected Chinese law, that law should be applied.

[126] It was issued by the SPC on 12 June 1989. Although this document is labeled as conference minutes, it represents the opinions of Chinese judges on the issues mentioned therein.

[127] 21 June 2002, Shanghai Maritime Court.

Although the plaintiff wanted to change the selected law before the court, the court noted that the defendant could not express its intention on the change and its silence should not be taken as an acceptance of the change. Therefore, the court held that English law should be applied to the loan contract.[128] This is the appropriate approach that should be adopted.

B Typographical Errors in a Choice of Law Clause

In *Shanghai Dongshen Import & Export Corporation* v. *The Shanghai Branch of the Jiangsu Unite Transport Co. and Oceanic Bridge International Inc.*,[129] the carrier Oceanic Bridge International Inc. (Oceanic Bridge) was a corporation registered in the United States. On the bills of lading it issued, there was a clause that provided: 'The Contract evidenced by or contained in Bill of Lading shall be governed by the law of the United States of Anerica . . . ' The defendant Oceanic Bridge did not appear before the court, and the defendant Shanghai Branch of the Jiangsu Unite Transport Co. argued that the word 'Anerica' actually meant 'America' and thus American law should be applied, as was stipulated in the bills. The Shanghai Maritime Court held that since that clause was a standard clause pre-printed in the bills issued by Oceanic Bridge, it should clarify whether the word 'Anerica' was in fact a typographical error. Since Oceanic Bridge did not appear in the proceedings, this question could not be determined. The court considered that a choice of law clause in a contract would ultimately determine parties' rights and responsibilities and therefore, Oceanic Bridge should be prudent and careful when drafting this clause so as not to make it ambiguous. Moreover, the court said that the error in the bills would lead to the holder's misunderstanding on that clause. Since it was unclear which law the choice of law clause referred to, and that Oceanic Bridge did not appear to explain this, the court held that the choice of law clause on the bills of lading was not effective and that the parties did not arrive at an agreement on the governing law. The court then applied the closest connection principle and determined that Chinese law was applicable.

[128] However, English law was not applied in the end because the parties did not provide the evidence on English law. The court thus applied Chinese law to resolve the dispute over the loan contract. The ascertainment of the foreign law chosen by parties is discussed in Chapter 7.

[129] 24 October 2005, Shanghai Maritime Court.

In this case, the parties had no dispute over their consent to the choice of law clause. According to Article 125 of the Contract Law, the court should interpret the meaning of the clause on the basis of the words and sentences used in the bill, related clauses of the bill, aim of the bill, trade practices and the principle of good faith. Even though the court considered the clause to be a standard one, it should interpret the clause in accordance with its common understanding.[130]

C Summary

As can be seen from the analysis, people's courts have adopted inappropriate criteria in determining the validity of parties' choice of law. Their decisions look more like punitive sanctions on a party's failure to appear in court or its carelessness in drafting the choice of law clause. It seems that these decisions did not really focus on the analysis of the material validity of parties' choice of law, but were made for the purposes of ignoring the selected foreign law and of applying Chinese law. People's courts should look at the elements mentioned in Section 3.1 to determine the existence of parties' consent to a choice of law clause. If further disputes arise as to whether the clause is vitiated, they should be determined by the law governing the material validity of the clause.

3.2.2 *The Law Governing the Material Validity of Parties' Choice*

Article 3(2)(2) of the 1989 Minutes provides that the voidness of a foreign-, Macao- or Hong Kong-related contract should not render void a dispute resolution clause therein, no matter whether it is an arbitration, a jurisdiction or a choice of law clause, and that these clauses should be applied to resolve the disputes that arise after a court has held the contract void. Article 57 of the Contract Law also confirms that if a contract is null and void, rescinded or terminated, the validity of the dispute settlement clause independently existing in the contract shall not

[130] Article 41 of the Contract Law provides: 'If a dispute arises over the understanding of a standard clause, the clause shall be interpreted in accordance with its common understanding. If a standard clause has more than one interpretation, the clause shall be interpreted in a manner unfavourable to the party providing the clause. If a standard clause is inconsistent with the non-standard clause, the non-standard clause shall be adopted.'

be affected.[131] Both provisions clarify that the validity of a choice of law clause is separated from that of the contract of which it forms a part, but they do not specify what should be the law governing the validity of a choice of law clause itself. Moreover, it is not clear whether the law governing a choice of law clause should be different from the one governing the contract of which the clause forms a part. There is no particular rule in Chinese law covering this issue.

As to the validity of an arbitration clause, Article 18 of the 2010 Conflicts Statute provides that the parties concerned may agree upon the law applicable to an arbitration agreement.[132] The notion underlying this provision is that since parties are allowed to choose the law to govern their contract, they should also be permitted to do so for an arbitration clause, which is also an agreement between them.[133] However, based on the principle of severability, the SPC stipulates that the law chosen by parties for a contract is *not* applicable to the validity of an arbitration clause associated with that contract. If the parties want to have the same law apply to the arbitration clause, they should *specifically stipulate to that effect.*[134]

Article 18 indicates that parties can also choose a law applicable to the validity of their dispute resolution agreement, but the approach provided by the SPC should *not* be adopted for choice of law clauses. On the one hand, a choice of law clause is substantially different from an arbitration clause in that the former does not involve the competence problem and therefore, a court does not need to consider its jurisdiction over a dispute. On the other hand, even for an arbitration agreement or clause, it is recognized that parties in commercial practice *seldom* choose a law particularly applicable to it.[135] Therefore, it is highly impractical, if not

[131] Here, the independence is described to mean three things: (a) when the contract is avoided, the dispute settlement clause remains effective; (b) if the contract is rescinded, the rescission does not apply to the dispute settlement clause; and (c) in case the contract is terminated, the effectiveness of the dispute settlement clause stays unchanged. See Zhang (2006a) p. 129; cf Tang (2012b) p. 461. Tang pointed out that Chinese legislation does not explicitly accept the doctrine of severability for a jurisdiction clause.

[132] This provision has its origin in Point 58 of Minutes of the Second National Conference on Foreign-related Commercial and Maritime Trial (2005 Minutes, issued by the SPC on 26 December 2005). However, it is not clear which issues relevant to an arbitration clause are governed by the law chosen by parties. See Wan (2011a) p. 143.

[133] See Wan (2011a) p. 138.

[134] See Wan (2011a) p. 139; see also Point 58 of the 2005 Minutes.

[135] Wan (2011a) p. 139.

impossible, for parties to make another particular agreement as to the law governing their choice of law clause, which already stipulates the governing law of their contract.

Under the Regulation (EC) No 593/2008 of the European Parliament and of the Council of 17 June 2008 on the Law Applicable to Contractual Obligations (Rome I Regulation), the material validity of a contract, or any term of it, including a choice of law clause, depends on the law that would govern the contract if it were valid.[136] Where parties have made an apparent agreement on the applicable law, the material validity of the choice of law clause is governed by the alleged chosen law.[137]

The 2010 Conflicts Statute of China does not contain a specific rule on this issue. Compared with the previous rules on party autonomy in contractual choice of law, Article 41 of the Statute provides that parties can choose the law applicable to their 'contract', rather than 'the settlement of contractual disputes'.[138] According to Point 46 of the 2005 Minutes and Article 2 of the Provisions on Several Issues Concerning the Application of the Law in Trials of Foreign-related Civil and Commercial Contract Disputes (2007 Provisions),[139] the term 'contractual disputes' in the previous rules includes disputes over whether a contract has been concluded, the date of its conclusion, the validity, performance, amendment, interpretation, suspension, rescission, transfer and termination of a contract as well as liability for breach of contract. One Chinese scholar considers that disputes over the material validity of a jurisdiction clause are also included.[140] Since a more general term 'contract' is used in the 2010 Conflicts Statute, and on the basis of the previous rules, the validity of a contract term is governed by the chosen law, the scope of

[136] See Articles 3(5) and 10(1) of the Rome I Regulation; see also the comments on Article 8 (1) of the Convention on the Law Applicable to Contractual Obligations (Rome Convention) in *The Giuliano-Lagarde Report* (Official Journal C 282, 31/10/1980). Article 8 (1) of the Rome Convention is the same as Article 10(1) of the Rome I Regulation.

[137] See Calliess (2011) p. 211.

[138] See Article 5 of the Foreign-related Economic Contract Law, Article 145 of the Civil Law, Article 126 of the Contract Law and the relevant discussions in Sections 1.2 and 1.3 of Chapter 1. All of these provisions stipulate that parties can choose the law applicable to 'the settlement of contractual disputes'.

[139] It was issued by the SPC on 23 July 2007 and became effective on 8 August 2007. Although the SPC has invalidated this judicial interpretation and consequently it became void as of 8 April 2013, Article 2 in fact did not contradict the 2010 Conflicts Statute. As can be seen in Point 46 of the 2005 Minutes, Article 2 represented the understanding of 'contractual disputes' by Chinese judges.

[140] See X. Liu (2011) p. 105.

the law selected by parties should extend to the material validity of a choice of law clause itself.[141]

This chapter demonstrates that the ascertainment of parties' consent on choice of law should begin with a preliminary factual inquiry to identify the apparent existence of mutual consent on the governing law, taking into account trade usage in international commercial transactions and the specific circumstances of a case. If further disputes arise concerning the validity of a choice of law clause, that is, whether both parties have given effective consent in law, the putative applicable law should be applied.

[141] Hook (2016) p. 78 also argues that the choice of law clause and the putative chosen law are intrinsically linked and there is nothing wrong, in principle, with reliance on the putative chosen law to determine the validity of parties' choice of law. Cf Briggs (2008) para. 3.05 and n 9 considers that the choice of law clause is 'the only provision of the contract which is not tested for its validity by reference to the law which governs the contract', because application of the *lex contractus* would 'allow the principle of renvoi into choice of law for contracts'.

4

The 'Law' That Can Be Chosen by Parties

According to Articles 3 and 41 of the Law on the Application of Laws to Foreign-related Civil Relationships (2010 Conflicts Statute),[1] parties are free to choose the 'law' applicable to their contract. The use of the term 'law' is in line with all the statutory rules concerning party autonomy before the Statute: all the previous rules adopted the term 'law', rather than 'rule of law'.[2] This is considered by some Chinese scholars as indicating that parties are only permitted to choose national laws to govern their contract.[3] Article 1 of the Provisions on Several Issues Concerning the Application of the Law in Trials of Foreign-related Civil and Commercial Contract Disputes (2007 Provisions)[4] stipulated that the law applicable to foreign-related civil and commercial contracts referred to the substantive law of the relevant country or region, exclusive of the conflict of laws and procedural law. Although the subject of this provision was to exclude *renvoi* in contractual cases, it is taken to have affirmed that parties are not allowed to choose supranational rules to govern their contract.[5]

The meaning of 'law' is not specified in the 2010 Conflicts Statute. As to the exclusion of *renvoi*, a more simplified rule is included, which supersedes Article 1 of the 2007 Provisions. Article 9 of the Statute states that the foreign laws applicable to foreign-related civil relations shall not include the conflict of laws rules of foreign countries. While parties'

1 It was adopted at the 17th meeting of the Standing Committee of the 11th NPC on 28 October 2010 and became effective on 1 April 2011.

2 See Article 5 of the Foreign-Related Economic Contract Law, Article 145 of the General Principles of Civil Law, Article 269 of the Maritime Code, Article 188 of the Civil Aviation Law, Article 126 of the Contract Law and the relevant discussions in Sections 1.2 and 1.3 of Chapter 1.

3 See Xiao and Long (2009) p. 196.

4 It was issued by the SPC on 23 July 2007, became effective on 8 August 2007 and invalidated by the SPC on 8 April 2013.

5 See Xiao and Long (2009) pp. 196–197.

choice of supranational rules is not expressly prohibited in the Statute, it is not completely clear whether parties are permitted to choose international treaties, practice or instruments as the 'governing law' of their contract. In judicial practice, people's courts have adopted inconsistent approaches to determining the effect of parties' reference in contract to these supranational rules. This chapter first looks at the previous provisions concerning party autonomy and analyses whether the 'law' that could be chosen by parties encompassed sources other than national laws. It then further examines the meaning of 'law' in the 2010 Conflicts Statute. Second, it analyses the status and application of international treaties and practice in China. Third, it discusses the effect of parties' reference to supranational rules and the *lex mercatoria* in contract, and the possibility of parties' choosing them as the governing law.

4.1 The Meaning of 'Law' in the 2010 Conflicts Statute

4.1.1 The 'Law' That Can Be Chosen by Parties in the Previous Rules

Article 145 of the Civil Law and Article 126(1) of the Contract Law both provide that parties to a foreign-related contract may choose the *law* applicable to the settlement of contractual disputes, unless stipulated otherwise by law; if the parties to a foreign-related contract fail to make such a choice, the *law of the state* that has closest connection with the contract shall apply (emphasis added). The different wording under party autonomy and the closest connection principle seem to imply that the scope of the 'law' that can be selected by parties as governing law may be broader than that of the law referred to through the closest connection principle: the latter can only be a state law.[6] Point 39 of the Responses to Questions in Foreign-related Commercial and Maritime Trial (1) (2004 Responses)[7] stipulates that the governing law chosen by parties includes international treaty, international practice, foreign law or the law of the relevant district. Even before the 2004 Responses, this approach had been adopted by people's courts in judicial practice.

In *Shanghai Lansheng Co. Ltd.* v. *Citibank N.A. and OCBC Bank Shanghai Branch*,[8] Shanghai Lansheng Co. Ltd. (Lansheng) was the

6 See Tang (2012a) p. 606.
7 It was issued by the Fourth Division of Civil Case Trial of the SPC in 2004.
8 25 April 2000, Shanghai Second Intermediate People's Court; 2 August 2001, Shanghai Higher People's Court.

principal who entrusted the handling of a collection of payment for goods to the OCBC Bank Shanghai Branch (OCBC Bank). The OCBC Bank instructed Citibank N.A. (Citibank) to do the collection in the United States. Based on the instructions from Lansheng, the OCBC Bank made the Collection Instruction and sent it to Citibank. The Instruction stipulated: 'Where applicable subject to the Uniform Rules for Collections (ICC Publication No. 322)'. Without the authorisation from the OCBC Bank or Lansheng, Citibank dealt with the bill of exchange payable at a future date as one payable at sight, and failed to send without delay the advice of payment to the OCBC Bank. Lansheng lost the goods and also the payment for them. It therefore sued the two banks for its loss.

In the first trial, both Lansheng and the OCBC Bank agreed that the Uniform Rules for Collections (URC), as referred to in the Collection Instruction, should be applied as the governing law. Citibank objected, arguing that according to the Instruction, URC should only be applied 'where applicable', that according to Article 99 of the 1995 Negotiable Instruments Law,[9] the Uniform Commercial Code (UCC) of the United States should be the governing law of this case, and since the provisions on fault in the UCC were different from those in the URC, UCC should be applied.

The Shanghai Second Intermediate People's Court ruled that based on Article 145 of the Civil Law, parties were free to choose the law applicable to their dispute. Since both Lansheng and the OCBC Bank agreed that the URC should be applied, and that Citibank neither expressed its objection to the reference to the URC in the Collection Instruction when it received it, nor refused to do the collection, the URC should be applied to solve the dispute. The court accordingly made a judgment that Citibank should compensate for Lansheng's loss. Citibank then appealed to the Shanghai Higher People's Court. One of its arguments was that the URC only represented international practice and could not be taken as a governing law; it was not applicable because according to Article 150 of the Civil Law, the application of international practice was different from

[9] It provided: 'For acts of endorsement, acceptance, payment and guaranty for negotiable instruments, the law of the place of the act shall apply.' The Negotiable Instruments Law was adopted at the 13th Meeting of the Standing Committee of the 8th NPC on 10 May 1995, and amended at the 11th Meeting of the Standing Committee of the 10th NPC on 28 August 2004. Article 99 of the 1995 Negotiable Instrument Law was the same as Article 98 in its 2004 version.

that of the governing law.[10] The law governing the case should be determined by Article 99 of the Negotiable Instruments Law but not Article 145 of the Civil Law.

Concerning the governing law in this case, the Shanghai Higher People's Court decided as follows. First, the disputed issue in this case was whether the two banks were in breach of the Collection Instruction from Lansheng. Therefore, the issue should be characterized as one concerning the agreement between the parties, but not the parties' acts in relation to negotiable instruments. The applicable law should be determined by the choice of law rules on obligations, that is, Article 145 of the Civil Law. Second, Article 150 did not deny that international practice could be the governing law. On the contrary, this provision demonstrated that international practice could become an applicable law under Chinese law. The court held that a governing law could be a domestic law, a foreign law and also an international treaty or practice. It therefore decided that the UCR should be applied and dismissed the appeal.

While the Shanghai Second Intermediate People's Court did not clarify the nature of the UCR in the first instance, the Shanghai Higher People's Court particularly ruled that the UCR, as international practice, could be applied as the governing law. In other more recent cases, the Uniform Customs and Practice of Documentary Credit (UCP) have also been applied by people's courts as the governing law.[11]

This interpretation of the scope of 'law' that could be chosen by parties has not been adopted in other judicial sources. Article 2(2) of the Response of the Supreme People's Court to Certain Questions Concerning the Application of the Foreign Economic Contract Law (1987 Response)[12] specified that the law selected by the parties to a contract

[10] Article 150 of the Civil Law provides: 'The application of foreign laws or international practice in accordance with the provisions of this chapter shall not violate the public interest of the People's Republic of China.' The Civil Law was adopted at the 4th Session of the 6th NPC on 12 April 1986, became effective on 1 January 1987 and was amended at the 10th Meeting of the Standing Committee of the 11th NPC on 27 August 2009.

[11] See, for example, *Zhoushan Shichuang Seafood Co. Ltd.* v. *Kyungnam Bank* (2009, Zhoushan Intermediate People's Court; 17 June 2010, Zhejiang Higher People's Court) and *Lianyungang Koufu Food Co. Ltd.* v. *Industrial Bank of Korea Seoul (Head Office Seoul) and Bank of China (Lianyungang Nuclear Power Station Branch)* (30 December 2002, Nanjing Intermediate People's Court; 23 December 2003, Jiangsu Higher People's Court). Both the Zhejiang Higher People's Court and Jiangsu Higher People's Court in these two cases ruled that UCP 500 should be applied as the governing law to determine the rights and obligations of the parties. The latter case is further discussed in Section 4.3.3.

[12] It was issued on 19 October 1987 and invalidated on 25 July 2000 by the SPC.

may be the law of China, the law of the District of Hong Kong or Macao or the law of a foreign country. Article 1 of the 2007 Provisions in fact followed the approach adopted in the 1987 Response.[13] Moreover, Point 48 of the 2005 Minutes particularly provided that the governing laws selected by parties only included the substantive laws of the relevant countries or regions, excluding conflicts or procedural rules.

The scope of 'law' that could be chosen by parties as the law governing their contract was not, therefore, settled before the 2010 Conflicts Statute. People's courts tended to adopt a flexible interpretation of the term 'law' under the party autonomy principle.

4.1.2 The Meaning of 'Law' in the 2010 Conflicts Statute

Article 41 of the 2010 Conflicts Statute provides:

> Parties may choose by agreement the law applicable to their contract. In the absence of a choice by parties, the contract shall be governed by the law of the habitual residence of the party whose performance of obligations best reflects the characteristics of the contract or other laws that have the closest connection with the contract.

Compared with Article 145 of the Civil Law and Article 126(1) of the Contract Law, Article 41 does not specify that under the closest connection principle, the applicable law should be the law of a state. Does it mean that in the Statute, the meaning and scope of 'law' that can be selected as the governing law of a contract encompasses international treaties and other supranational rules? It is submitted that, although non-state norms are not expressly excluded from the scope of 'law' in Article 41 of the 2010 Conflicts Statute, they should not be taken as encompassed in the term 'law' either.[14]

First, a literal interpretation of the term 'law' indicates that non-state norms are not included in it. In Chinese domestic statutes, the term 'law' or its plural form 'laws' is both a generic word, which means all the norms laid down by the State,[15] and a specific term with particular

[13] See Chen (2008) p. 261.

[14] The analysis in this section focuses on the interpretation of the 2010 Conflicts Statute. For further discussions concerning the effect of parties' reference to non-state norms in theory and practice, see Sections 4.2 and 4.3.

[15] Under this meaning, 'law' includes the Constitution, laws enacted by the NPC or NPCSC, regulations issued by the State Council or its commissions and ministries, and local regulations issued by the local people's congresses and so on. See Von Senger (2000)

reference to enactments by the National People's Congress (NPC) or its Standing Committee (NPCSC), that is, one of the categories of legislative documents under the former meaning.[16] In the 2010 Conflicts Statute, only the term 'law' (*falü*) is used and no reference is made to other sources. Concerning the purpose of the Statute,[17] the term 'law' therein refers to two different categories of rules depending on the subject and content of the provision in which the term exists. On the one hand, when 'law' is used to stipulate the statutory restrictions on party autonomy and the application of mandatory rules, it should be interpreted as meaning the Chinese domestic statutes enacted by the NPC or NPCSC.[18] On the other hand, in other provisions concerning the determination of the legal rules governing a foreign-related relationship, the term encompasses more rules than those applicable in purely domestic cases. Based on Articles 9 and 10,[19] the term 'law' in the latter capacity undoubtedly includes foreign law. The problem remains whether it also encompasses international treaties, practice and other non-state norms.

Although Article 41 of the 2010 Conflicts Statute does not specify that the law with which a contract has its closest connection should be the law *of a state*, in the search for the governing law according to the characteristic performance doctrine, it is impossible for a court to take into

p. 41. The Law on Legislation (adopted at the 3rd Session of the 9th NPC on 15 March 2000, and amended at the 3rd Session of the 12th NPC 15 March 2015) classifies legislative documents into law, administrative regulations, local regulations, autonomous regulations, departmental rules and local governmental rules, and provides further rules concerning the effects and procedures of making those documents.

16 Article 7 of the Law on Legislation provides: 'The National People's Congress enacts and amends basic laws governing criminal offences, civil affairs, the State organs and other matters. The Standing Committee of the National People's Congress enacts and amends laws other than the ones to be enacted by the National People's Congress, and when the National People's Congress is not in session, partially supplements and amends laws enacted by the National People's Congress, but not in contradiction to the basic principles of such laws.'

17 Article 1 of the 2010 Conflicts Statute provides: 'This Law is formulated to specify the application of laws to foreign-related civil relations, resolve foreign-related civil disputes in a reasonable manner, and safeguard the legitimate rights and interests of the parties concerned.'

18 See Liang (2012) pp. 104–106. The statutory restrictions on party autonomy are further discussed in Chapters 5 and 6.

19 Article 9 concerns the exclusion of *renvoi* and Article 10 deals with the ascertainment of foreign law.

account non-state norms.[20] The law selected on this basis is therefore the law of a state, no matter whether the Statute stipulates so or not. In this regard, the term 'law' in the second sentence of Article 41 only encompasses state laws, not including non-state norms. The same interpretation should also be adopted concerning the determination of governing laws in other categories of relationships because the laws to which the objective connecting factors refer cannot generally be non-state norms. If a uniform and consistent approach of interpretation is to be adopted concerning the meaning and scope of 'law' in all the choice of law provisions in the 2010 Conflicts Statute (except the first term 'law' in Article 3 and the term 'laws' in Article 4),[21] the 'law' that can be selected by parties should only encompass state law.

Second, this interpretation does not exclude the possibility that parties may refer to non-state norms in their contracts. Briggs has mentioned that the menu of laws which may be expressly chosen may be longer than that from which the most closely connected law may be identified. From this perspective, if the parties express a choice, their choice should be given effect, subject to proof of content of the law chosen.[22] Moreover, the weight to be attached to the literal interpretation of the term 'law' in Chinese statutes is considered to be 'indecisive' because the use of the terms 'law', 'law of a state' and 'rule of law' is inconsistent in Chinese statutes and these terms are misleading in the proper construction of legislation.[23] This argument is unconvincing. It should be noted that the issue being discussed here is *not* whether parties are allowed to invoke non-state norms in their contract – as is discussed shortly, normally their incorporation of these rules should be respected. The issue at stake is: whether parties are allowed to select non-state norms *as the governing law* of their contract.[24] In fact, the so-called 'inconsistent language used in legislation' only existed in the draft of the 2010 Conflicts Statute.[25] Article 2 of the draft stated that 'applicable law' referred to the substantive law of a relevant country, while Article 50(1) provided that parties to a foreign-related contract may choose the law, international treaty or practice that is applicable to their

[20] According to Articles 3 and 41 of the Statute, a court should determine the law of *the place* that has the closest connection with the contract on the basis of the quality and quantity of the connecting factors. See Wan (2011a) pp. 23–27, 299–301.

[21] The first term 'law' in Article 3 and the term 'laws' in Article 4 refer to the former category of rules, that is, Chinese domestic statutes enacted by the NPC or NPCSC.

[22] See Briggs (2008) para. 10.10.

[23] See Tang (2012a) p. 608.

[24] See Sections 4.2 and 4.3.

[25] See the analysis in Tang (2012a) p. 608.

contract.[26] This contradiction does not exist in the 2010 Conflicts Statute as Article 41 does not refer to sources other than 'law'.

The previous analysis demonstrates that even though non-state norms are not expressly excluded from the scope of 'law' that can be chosen by parties to govern a contract, they are not included in it either. The next two sections further address the existing problems in judicial practice concerning the status and effect of non-state norms referred to in foreign-related contracts.

4.2 The Application of International Treaties and Practice in Foreign-Related Commercial Litigation

Articles 4 and 5 of the Interpretation of the Supreme People's Court on Certain Issues Concerning the Application of the 'Law on the Application of Laws to Foreign-related Civil Relations' (1) (Interpretation of the 2010 Conflicts Statute (1)) provide that Article 142(2) and (3) of the Civil Law are still binding concerning the application of international treaties and international practice.[27] Accordingly, even after the 2010 Conflicts Statute, the most important provision concerning the status of international treaties and practice in Chinese private international law is Article 142 of the Civil Law.[28] It is the first provision in

[26] See Articles 2 and 50 of part 9 of the 'Draft of the Civil Law of the People's Republic of China' concerning the Application of Laws in Foreign-Related Civil Relations, reproduced in Wang (2007) appendix.

[27] The Interpretation of the 2010 Conflicts Statute (1) was issued by the SPC on 28 December 2012 and became effective on 7 January 2013. The 2010 Conflicts Statute does not touch upon the application of treaties because this issue was considered to be too complicated, and one on which many different opinions were presented. See 'Report on the Main Issues concerning the Draft of Law on the Application of Laws to Foreign-related Civil Relations' (issued on the official website of the NPC on 28 August 2010).

[28] It should be noted that, the General Principles of Civil Law (adopted at the 4th Session of the 6th NPC on 12 April 1986, effective on 1 January 1987, amended at the 10th Meeting of the Standing Committee of the 11th NPC on 27 August 2009, referred to as 'Civil Law' in this book) continues to be effective even after the General Provisions of Civil Law (adopted at the 5th Session of the 12th NPC on 15 March 2017, effective on 1 October 2017) entered into force. In the event of a discrepancy between these two statutes, the rules in the General Provisions of Civil Law shall apply. However, the General Provisions of Civil Law does not contain rules stipulating the status and application of international treaties or practice in China. Therefore, Article 142 of the Civil Law remains binding. See Committee of Civil and Commercial Matters under the Society of Chinese Trial Theories (2017) pp. 3–4; Li (2017) p. 10.

Chapter 8 of the Civil Law entitled 'Application of Law to Foreign-related Civil Relations'. The article reads:

> The law to be applied in foreign-related civil relations shall be determined in accordance with the provisions of this Chapter.
>
> Where an international treaty that the People's Republic of China has concluded or acceded to contains provisions different from those in the civil laws of the People's Republic of China, the provisions in the international treaty shall apply, except for the provisions to which the People's Republic of China has made a reservation.
>
> Where the laws of the People's Republic of China or international treaties which the People's Republic of China has concluded or acceded to do not contain a relevant provision, international practice may be applied.

4.2.1 The Application of International Treaties Concluded or Acceded to by China

The wording of Article 142(2) is ambiguous and several points should be made before further analysis.

First, according to Articles 67(1)(14), 81 and 89 (1)(9) of the Constitution and Article 3 of the Law on the Procedure of Conclusion of Treaties (Law on the Conclusion of Treaties),[29] the State Council has the power to conclude treaties and agreements with foreign states, the NPCSC decides on the ratification of treaties concluded by the State Council and the President ratifies treaties according to the decision of the NPCSC. Therefore, even though the word 'concluded' (*dijie*) is used in Article 142(2) of the Civil Law, only those treaties that China has ratified or acceded to upon the decision of the NPCSC can have the effect described in Article 142.[30]

Second, as Article 2[31] and the title of Chapter 8 of the Civil Law indicate, Article 142(2) applies to international treaties dealing with

[29] The Constitution was adopted by the 5th Session of the 4th NPC on 4 December 1982, amended for the first time at the 1st Session of the 7th NPC on 12 April 1988, amended for the second time at the 1st Session of the 8th NPC on 29 March 1993, amended for the third time at the 2nd Session of the 9th NPC on 15 March 1999 and amended for the fourth time at the 2nd Session of the 10th NPC on 14 March 2004. The Law on the Conclusion of Treaties was adopted at the 17th Meeting of the Standing Committee of the 7th NPC on 28 December 1990 and became effective on 28 December 1990.

[30] See Tang (2012a) p. 609, n 52.

[31] Article 2 of the Civil Law reads: 'The Civil Law of the People's Republic of China shall adjust property relationships and personal relationships between civil subjects with equal

foreign-related civil relations between individual parties.[32] It therefore does not govern the status of the treaties which focus on the duty and obligations between state sovereignties.[33]

Third, within the scope of treaties covered by Article 142(2), there are three categories: substantive law treaties, private international law treaties and also mixed treaties which provide substantive as well as conflict of laws rules. Article 142(2) applies to all the three types of treaties.[34]

Fourth, based on the wording of Article 142(2), it is not clear whether treaties acquire prevailing force over domestic law *only when* the relevant provisions in treaties are *different* from those in the civil laws of China. The word 'different' has been subject to two different interpretations in judicial practice and has therefore created uncertainty.[35] It is submitted that the difference between domestic civil laws and international treaty provisions should *not* be taken as a prerequisite concerning the prevailing force of international treaties under Article 142.

On the one hand, the basis of Article 142(2) is that as a party to the 1969 Vienna Convention on the Law of Treaties, China should comply with its treaty obligations in good faith and should not use its internal law as a justification for evading its international obligations, as provided in Article 27 of the Convention.[36] On the other hand, Article 142(2) only stipulates that the provisions in international treaties prevail whenever the relevant domestic rules conflict with them: it does *not* require that only treaties containing different provisions can have prevailing binding force.[37] In the Notice concerning Several Issues in the Adjudication and Enforcement of Foreign-related Civil and Commercial Cases, the SPC

status, that is, between citizens, between legal persons and between citizens and legal persons.'

32 That is, treaties falling within the scope of civil and commercial laws involving foreign-related civil relations and disputes. See Xue and Jin (2009) p. 305.

33 See Tang (2012a) p. 622. There is no provision in the Constitution of China concerning the status of international treaties in Chinese legal system and their implementation. For the status of international treaties in China, see generally Xue and Jin (2009).

34 See Tang (2012a) pp. 622–623; for the status of treaties containing conflicts rules, see also Chen (2013) pp. 181–183.

35 See the cases cited in Huang (2008) pp. 109–116.

36 See Xue and Jin (2009) p. 305; Tang (2012a) p. 623. The Vienna Convention on the Law of Treaties was concluded at Vienna on 23 May 1969, opened for signature on the same date and entered into force on 27 January 1980. Article 27 of the Convention provides that a party may not invoke the provisions of its internal law as justification for its failure to perform a treaty.

37 See Liu (2009) pp. 86–88; Xuan and Wang (2012) p. 129; Research Group of Guangdong Higher People's Court (2013) p. 65.

specifically stipulates the priority of international treaties concluded or acceded to by China without mentioning whether the provisions therein are different from the Chinese domestic rules or not.[38] This approach is also adopted in the judicial direction issued by Guangdong Higher People's Court. Article 3(24) of its Notice of Issuance of the Guiding Opinions on Several Issues in Foreign-related Commercial Trials (2004 Guangdong Guiding Opinions)[39] provides that where a dispute falls within the scope of a treaty ratified or participated in by China (except for the provisions to which China has made a reservation), the treaty should apply unless the treaty permits the parties to exclude its application by agreement and such an agreement is made between the parties. Furthermore, Article 7 of the Law on the Conclusion of Treaties stipulates that the ratification of treaties and important agreements shall be decided by the NPCSC, and these treaties and important agreements include those which contain stipulations different from the laws of China. That is to say, the power to examine the provisions of a treaty and make a decision accordingly rests with the NPCSC, but not people's courts. Once a treaty is ratified or acceded to by China based on the decision of the NPCSC, it should be applied by people's courts in the adjudication of issues governed by it.

Fifth, China's Constitution does not adopt a clear-cut monist or dualist position concerning the status of international treaties. Nor are there such concepts as self-executing treaties or non-self-executing treaties in China.[40] Based on Article 142(2) of the Civil Law, the applicability of treaties in civil and commercial areas is not dependent on the adoption of supplementary statutes, or the issuance of a specific order from the NPCSC concerning the implementation of these treaties.[41]

Provisions similar to Article 142 of the Civil Law also exist in other domestic statutes concerning civil relations. Based on these provisions and the previous analysis, international treaties prevail over domestic laws in the relevant fields and can be applied directly by people's courts.[42] As Article 142 covers treaties dealing with foreign-related civil

[38] See Point 2 of the Notice (issued by the SPC on 17 April 2000).
[39] It was issued by the Guangdong Higher People's Court on 17 December 2004 and became effective on the same date.
[40] See Shao (2002) pp. 199–201; Tang (2012a) p. 614 and the references cited there.
[41] See Chen, Zhou and Jiang (2000) pp. 120–122; Shao (2002) p. 200; Zhao (2010) pp. 192–193.
[42] See Xue and Jin (2009) pp. 303–304, 310.

relations, it does not matter whether a treaty provides uniform substantive rules or conflicts rules: people's courts should first examine whether there is an international treaty concluded or acceded to by China that governs the dispute in question. For issues falling within the scope of such a treaty, the rules in the treaty override the relevant Chinese conflict of laws rules. The rules in the treaty either determine the law applicable to the issue concerned (if they are conflicts rules), or directly determine the rights and obligations of parties (if they are substantive rules).[43]

4.2.2 The Application of the CISG in China and Party Autonomy

The previous section analyses the status of international treaties in the Chinese legal system. This section further discusses whether a treaty providing uniform substantive rules is applied in people's courts as an *applicable law* in the sense of private international law. The application of the United Nations Convention on Contracts for the International Sale of Goods (CISG) in people's courts is taken as an example.

The CISG was ratified in China on 11 December 1986, and became effective on 1 January 1988.[44] Under Article 1(1), the CISG applies to contracts of sale of goods between parties whose places of business are in different states: (a) when the states are contracting states; or (b) when the rules of private international law lead to the application of the law of a contracting state, that is, when the applicable law is that of a contracting state. Based on Article 6, it is open to parties to expressly exclude or contract out of the operation of the convention. If parties do not exclude in whole or in part the application of the CISG, it directly applies to situations in which it provides express rules, and, according to Article 1 (1)(a), the need for conflicts law is obviated.[45]

In *The United States Joint Enterprises Ltd.* v. *Shandong Foreign Trade Corporation Yantai Branch*,[46] a dispute arose between the parties concerning the quality of garlic under their contract of sale. The places of business of the two parties were in the United States and China

[43] See Tang (2012a) pp. 610–619 and the cases cited there; Chen (2013) pp. 181–185.

[44] See Circular of the Supreme People's Court on Transmitting Certain Issues of the Ministry of Foreign Trade and Economic Cooperation in Connection with the Implementation of United Nations Convention on Contracts for the International Sale of Goods (Circular of the SPC Concerning the Implementation of the CISG, issued by the SPC on 10 December 1987).

[45] See Winship (1988) pp. 518–520.

[46] 8 August 2000, Supreme People's Court.

respectively, and both states are contracting states under Article 1(1)(a) of the CISG. As the dispute fell within the scope of the CISG, the Shandong Higher People's Court directly applied the relevant provisions of the convention and made a decision in favour of Shandong Foreign Trade Corporation Yantai Branch. The United States Joint Enterprises Ltd. then appealed to the SPC. One of its arguments was that the application of the CISG in the first trial was wrong. It argued that since the contract had the closest connection with the United States, American law should be applied. In the appellate judgment, the SPC rejected this argument. It ruled that as the parties did not choose the law governing their contract, and the requirements in Article 1(1)(a) of the CISG were met in this case, the convention should be applied. The SPC thus upheld the decision of first trial.

In the Circular concerning the Implementation of the CISG, the SPC pointed out that, according to Article 1(1)(a) of the convention, it automatically applies to contracts for sale of goods reached between parties with their places of business in contracting states, unless otherwise agreed. That is to say, the basis underlying the automatic application of the CISG is the provision stipulated in the convention: China must comply with its treaty obligation in good faith.[47]

Pursuant to Article 95, China made a reservation that it would not be bound by Article 1(1)(b) of the CISG. Accordingly, people's courts in China are under an obligation to apply the CISG *only if* the requirements of Article 1(1)(a) are met.[48] However, the effect of China's reservation under Article 95 is uncertain, particularly in situations where the requirements of Article 1(1)(a) are not met but where parties choose the law of a contracting state as the governing law of their contract. Article 1(1)(b) provides that the CISG applies to contracts of sale of goods between parties whose places of business are in different states when 'the rules of

[47] Therefore, when the requirements in Article 1(1)(a) are met, the application of the CISG is *not* dependent on parties' reference to the convention in contract. However, in two cases decided by the SPC and the Shandong Higher People's Court respectively, the courts determined the applicability of the CISG according to the parties' reference to the convention in their contracts even though the requirements in Article 1(1)(a) were met in these cases. This approach is not appropriate as it is not consistent with the one stipulated in Article 1(1)(a) of the CISG, which guarantees the autonomous application of the convention. J. Xu (2010) p. 146. Chen (2013) also argued (pp. 184–185) that before looking at parties' choice of law or other conflicts rules, a court should first examine whether an international substantive law treaty concluded or acceded to by China is applicable in a specific case.

[48] See Schwenzer (2010) p. 1190.

private international law' lead to the application of 'the law of a contracting state'. In Chinese courts, the outstanding questions are: whether the 'rules of private international law' in Article 95 includes the rule on parties' autonomy in choosing the law governing their contract, and whether parties' choice of the law of a contracting state should only be taken as referring to the domestic law of that state, excluding the CISG rules. Since the party autonomy principle has been adopted in China as the primary private international law rule concerning contracts,[49] it is not reasonable to exclude this rule in the context of Articles 1(1)(b) and 95 of the CISG. That is to say, based on the literal interpretation of these provisions, parties' choice of contracting states' laws in their sales contracts will not lead to the application of the CISG in Chinese courts.[50] However, in judicial practice, where parties have explicitly chosen Chinese law, which is the law of a contracting state of the CISG, people's courts have in some cases applied the CISG as part of Chinese law, while in others applied Chinese domestic law excluding the CISG.[51]

Chinese scholars are divided on this issue. Those who support the latter approach of excluding the CISG base their analysis on the interpretation of Article 1(1)(b), as has been given earlier.[52] Those who are in favour of the former approach argued that first, party autonomy is not included in, and should prevail over, the rules of private international law under Article 1(1)(b); second, CISG has obtained domestic legal effect under Article 142 of the Civil Law and thus should be taken as part of the domestic law of China; third, Chinese Contract Law lacks any specific provisions dealing with international sales contracts and the rules in it are not necessarily suited for cross-border sales transactions.[53]

In fact, China's reservation under Article 95 only excludes the obligation of people's courts to apply the CISG according to Article 1(1)(b), but does *not* prohibit the courts from applying the convention. Therefore, it is quite possible, and also within the discretionary power of a court, to apply the CISG where the applicable law of a sales contract is the law of a

[49] See Article 145 of the Civil Law, Article 126 of the Contract Law and Article 41 of the 2010 Conflicts Statute.

[50] See J. Xu (2010) pp. 153–154; Chen (2013) pp. 183–184.

[51] See the cases cited in Yang (2012) ¶20–223.

[52] See n 50 and the accompanying text.

[53] See Yang (2012) ¶20–223 (pp. 57–58); Xuan and Wang (2012) pp. 129–130. The uncertainties surrounding the effect of China's reservation under Article 95 not only exist in cases where parties have chosen Chinese law in sales contracts, but also in situations where the closest connection principle leads to the application of Chinese law. See Yang (2012) ¶20–224.

contracting state.[54] The reservation only creates uncertainties that cannot be ultimately resolved.[55] Therefore, some Chinese scholars have suggested that China should withdraw its Article 95 reservation.[56]

Moreover, the CISG is *not* taken as an independent applicable law in judicial practice, no matter whether it is applied on the basis of Article 1 (1)(a), or on the basis of the understanding of a court concerning Articles 1(1)(b) and 95 where parties have chosen Chinese law. On the one hand, the convention does not deal with all the issues arising from a sales contract: it does not address questions affecting the validity of the contract or any of its provisions, or the effect the contract may have on the property in the goods sold (Article 4),[57] nor does it deal with the liability of the seller for death or personal injury caused by the goods to any person (Article 5). These issues are to be settled in conformity with the law applicable by virtue of the rules of private international law. The CISG does not stipulate all the rules for the settlement of contractual disputes. The SPC thus suggested that Chinese companies should specify in contract the issues not covered by the convention, or select a local law of some country to govern the contract. On the other hand, international treaties concluded or acceded to by China obtain domestic legal effect by virtue of Article 142(2) of the Civil Law.[58] They are not, therefore, taken as independent applicable laws in the sense of private international law.

4.2.3 The Status of International Practice

Article 142(3) of the Civil Law provides that 'international practice' may be applied to resolve issues that are not specifically addressed either by

[54] See Schwenzer (2010) p. 1190; Yang (2012) p. 57.

[55] The reservation under Article 95 merely excludes the reserving state's duty under public international law to apply Article 1(1)(b) of the CISG. But Article 95 fails to specify what this means for courts and tribunals in practice. See Schroeter (2015) p. 245.

[56] For the effect of this reservation in Chinese courts and the suggestion that China should withdraw the reservation under Article 95, see further, Yang (2006) pp. 7–11; Yang (2012) ¶20–230; Li (2012).

[57] In *Sinochem International (Overseas) Pte. Ltd.* v. *ThyssenKrupp Metallurgical Products Gmbh* (30 June 2014, Supreme People's Court), the business locations of the parties in a dispute over their contract for sale of petrol coke were in Singapore and Germany respectively, and the parties chose American law as the governing law of the contract. The SPC held that since Singapore, Germany and America are all signatories of the CISG and the parties did not exclude the application of it, the CISG shall be applied in the trial of the case. But for the issues not covered by the CISG, such as the validity of the contract and the transfer of property, American law, as chosen by the parties, shall be applied.

[58] See the analysis in the previous section and also Xue and Jin (2009) p. 304.

Chinese law or by any international treaty to which China is a party. Accordingly, if international practice is applied under this provision, it only acts as a gap filler in the absence of relevant provisions in Chinese law or international treaties on the issues at stake,[59] but not as an independent applicable law. The term 'international practice' is taken from the English Database of Laws and Regulations of the NPC.[60] In the original Chinese text, the term *'guo ji guan li'* is used. This term, if literally translated into English, is 'international usage' or 'international customary practice'. In judicial practice, this term is consistently used by people's courts in foreign-related commercial cases and actually refers to a 'customary rule of international trade' or 'international trade custom'.[61]

International practice can also come into play when it is referred to by parties in contract. In Point 5(2) of Minutes of the National Conference on Foreign-, Hong Kong- and Macao-Related Economic Trials in Coastal Areas,[62] the SPC stipulated that parties' reference to such international practice as Incoterms, URC and UCP should be respected and the practice should be applied by people's courts. The remaining issue is whether international practice is applied as the governing law through parties' choice. This is addressed in the next section.

4.3 The Effect of Parties' Reference to Rules Other Than a Legal System of a State

This section analyses the effect of parties' reference in contract to: (a) international treaties that China has not concluded;[63] (b) rules contained in other international instruments dealing with commercial transactions, including parties' reference to the CISG when the requirements in Article 1(1)(a) of the convention are not met; and (c) a specific statute of a foreign jurisdiction.

59 Xiao and Long (2009) p. 201.

60 It is available at: www.npc.gov.cn/englishnpc/Law/2007-12/12/content_1383941.htm.

61 Xue and Jin (2009) p. 319, see also the cases cited at pp. 320–322. Xue and Jin argued that international practice such as UCP 500 and the Hague-Visby Rules could be chosen by parties as the applicable law of their contract. However, as is analysed shortly, international practice *cannot* be taken as applicable law and can only be incorporated by parties as contract terms. See Section 4.3.

62 It was issued by the SPC on 12 June 1989.

63 Only the international civil or commercial treaties that China has ratified or acceded to pursuant to a decision of the NPCSC can have the effect described in Article 142 of the Civil Law. See Section 4.2.1. This section discusses the effect of parties' reference to treaties that do not come under Article 142.

In the theory of private international law, it is generally accepted that when interpreting the parties' intention as to the selected law, it is important to distinguish carefully the express selection of the governing law from the quite different process of the incorporation in the contract of certain domestic provisions of a foreign law.[64] The distinction is considered to be unimportant or impractical by some Chinese scholars.[65] As is illustrated shortly, people's courts seldom make such a distinction either.[66] It is the failure to distinguish parties' choice of a governing law from their incorporation of some rules into their contract that makes the scholars and courts consider that parties can choose international treaties or practice as the law governing a contract.[67]

This section first discusses the inconsistent approaches adopted by Chinese courts in treating a paramount clause in maritime cases. Second, it analyses the function of paramount clause in maritime law. Third, it further illustrates the importance of making a distinction between incorporation by reference and choice of law in judicial practice. Fourth, it touches upon the requirement for certainty and clarity in parties' incorporation.

4.3.1 Inconsistent Approaches in Treating a Paramount Clause

In *American President Lines Ltd.* v. *Feida Appliance Company, Feili Industry Co. Ltd. & Changcheng Industry Company* (the *American President Lines* case),[68] GB Lighting Supplier of Singapore contracted for the purchase of lights with Feida Appliance Company (Feida). By two bills of lading, Feida, through its agents Feili Industry Co. Ltd. (Feili) and

64 See Kelly (1977); Mann (1937) pp. 101–102.

65 See, for example, J. Xu (2010) pp. 159–165; Tang (2012a) pp. 604–605. Tang argued (p. 605) that the distinction 'probably has only theoretic value', and 'may not be of great significance from a practical perspective'. However, the supporting evidence that she gave in the footnote (p. 605, n 41) was that she had interviewed ten arbitrators in China and the UK and all of them found no difference in terms of practice between incorporating treaties into a contract and applying the chosen treaties as applicable law. This point is unconvincing because the degree of judicial control in arbitration is substantially different from that in litigation in state courts. It is in relation to arbitration that the *lex mercatoria* has achieved its greatest significance so far, but that cannot be taken as a justification for the application of non-state rules as governing law. For the recognition of *lex mercatoria* in arbitration, see Nygh (1999) pp. 191–196; for the importance of the distinction in China, see the following analysis.

66 See the cases cited in Tang (2012a) pp. 624–628, and the cases to be discussed shortly.

67 See J. Xu (2010) pp. 159–165; Tang (2012a) pp. 604–605.

68 25 June 2002, Supreme People's Court.

Changcheng Industry Company (Changcheng), acknowledged with the carrier, American President Lines Ltd. (President Lines), shipment on board packages of lights and transformers for carriage to and delivery at Singapore for payment. The bills of lading specified President Lines as the carrier, Feili and Changcheng as the shipper and GB Lighting Supplier of Singapore as the consignee.

After the cargoes arrived in Singapore, the GB Lighting Supplier did not pay for the cargoes but instead issued two Letters of Indemnity to President Lines, asking them to release the cargoes and promised to be responsible for all the liabilities that might arise as a result. President Lines then released the cargoes without asking for the production of the original bills of lading. Feida could not receive the payment for goods and thus sued President Lines.

The Paramount Clause on the back of each of the bills of lading provided:

> The loading, handling, stowage, carriage and delivery of the goods should be governed by the terms and conditions of the contract for carriage as evidenced by this bill of lading, including: . . . (3) the provisions of the Carriage of Goods by Sea Act of United States, 1936 ('US COGSA') or national laws as applied by a competent court when adjudicating disputes arising from carriage contracts in a country where the International Convention for the unification of certain rules of law relating to Bills of lading signed at Brussels on 25th August 1924 (the Hague Rules) is applicable.

In the retrial of this case, President Lines argued that the COGSA or the Hague Rules, as referred to in the bills of lading, should be applied.[69] Concerning the effect of the reference to those rules in the bills, the SPC ruled that the bills of lading in question were used voluntarily by both parties, and thus the agreement on the application of the COGSA or Hague Rules reflected their mutual intentions. As the agreement was not contrary to the public interest of China, the Paramount Clause should be held effective and the laws chosen applicable according to Article 269 of

[69] Both the Guangzhou Maritime Court (in the first trial) and Guangdong Higher People's Court (in the appeal) characterized the disputed issue as one on tort, accordingly applied Chinese law as the governing law and made decisions for Feida. President Lines disagreed with the characterization of the disputed issue in the appellate judgment. It applied to the SPC for a retrial and also the suspension of the execution of the appellate judgment. For the discussion of characterization in this case, see Liang (2012) pp. 82–85. For the purpose of this section, the analysis here only focuses on how the SPC treated parties' reference to the COGSA in the bills of lading.

the Maritime Code. However, Article 1(b) of the Hague Rules stipulated that the Rules applied only to contracts of carriage covered by a bill of lading that could be taken as a document of title. The bills of lading in this case were straight consigned bills which were not transferable and did not have the effect of documents of title. Further, the Hague Rules did not contain any provisions concerning the carrier's delivery of goods under a straight consigned bill of lading. Therefore, the Hague Rules were not applicable in this case, and the COGSA should be applied.

As the provisions of §1303(4) and §1308 of the COGSA did not affect the rights and obligations of the carrier under the provisions of the 1916 Shipping Act, the SPC held that the rights and obligations of the parties could only be determined by applying both of the aforementioned two Acts. Reversing the judgments in both the first trial and appeal, the SPC decided in favour of President Lines.

The SPC considered the parties' reference to the COGSA and the Hague Rules as a choice of the applicable law. Although only the COGSA was referred to by the parties, the SPC also applied the Shipping Act, which was not mentioned in the bills of lading. The SPC obviously took the parties' reference to a specific foreign statute as the choice of the legal system of that foreign state. This approach was also adopted in two cases decided by the Guangdong Higher People's Court and Shanghai Higher People's Court respectively.[70]

In *Ningbo Market Union International Trade Company* v. *Tianjin Huafeng Transport Agency Shanghai Branch*,[71] the plaintiff shipper sued the defendant carrier for releasing cargoes without the production of the original bills of lading. Clause 2(a) of the bill stipulated that the responsibility of the carrier was governed by the Hague Rules and 'the corresponding legislation which are compulsorily applicable to the bill', including 'the 1936 US COGSA'. Clause 21 'Jurisdiction Clause' provided

[70] See *Guangzhou Zhaoying Metals Co. Ltd.* v. *Beijing Expeditors Transport Agency Guangzhou Branch, Beijing Expeditors Transport Agency and Jinda Transport Agency Co. Ltd.* (7 April 2005, Guangzhou Maritime Court; 9 October 2005, Guangdong Higher People's Court) and *Awell Logistics Group, Inc.* v. *Baron Motorcycles, Inc.* (20 September 2010, Shanghai Higher People's Court). These cases both involved a dispute concerning the release of cargoes without the presentation of original bills of lading and the bills concerned both referred to the COGSA. Both courts took this as a choice of the governing law and, instead of looking at this Act exclusively, they both applied another US statute (Guangdong Higher People's Court applied the 1916 Shipping Act, while the Shanghai Maritime Court applied the UCC).

[71] 2009, Shanghai Maritime Court (the specific date of the judgment not indicated), see Zhao (2015) pp. 391–396.

that any dispute arising under the bill of lading should be decided in the country where the carrier had his principal place of business and the law of such country should apply except as otherwise provided. The defendants argued that under the straight consigned bill of lading in this case, it should not be held responsible for releasing cargoes without the original bill according to the Hague Rules and the COGSA.

The Shanghai Maritime Court held that the Hague Rules were not applicable as the bill of lading concerned was not transferable. In accordance with Clause 2(a), the relevant provisions on carriers' rights and obligations in the COGSA should be taken as incorporated into the bill of lading, and constituted a term under the bill. Therefore, the validity of this term should be determined by the law governing the bill of lading. Since the carrier had its principal place of business in China, Chinese law should be the governing law of the bill based on Clause 21. The court considered that the responsibility of a carrier to release cargoes with the original bills of lading was of a mandatory nature in China's Maritime Code. Since the clause referring to the COGSA lessened the responsibility of the carrier, it was held invalid by the court.

The previous cases illustrate the inconsistent approaches adopted by people's courts in determining the effect of a paramount clause in a bill of lading.

4.3.2 *The Nature of the Paramount Clause*

A clause referring to the COGSA always exists in contracts for international carriage of goods by sea, and it is normally termed a 'Paramount Clause'. In *Marifortuna Naviera S.A.* v. *Government of Ceylon*,[72] Mocatta J. said:

> [The word 'Paramount'] is used in relation to the Hague Rules in two rather different senses. It is sometimes used as a form of shorthand to describe a clause in a bill of lading or in a charterparty making the whole or part of the Hague Rules applicable to those documents, but without any addition. On other occasions it has a wider meaning, in that it refers not only to a clause incorporating the Hague Rules in a bill of lading or charterparty, but to one going further and expressly providing that the provisions of the Hague Rules, where there is any conflict with the provisions of the bill of lading or charterparty, are to prevail, or in other words be paramount.

[72] [1970] 1 Lloyd's Rep. 247, 255.

A paramount clause may not only refer to the Hague Rules, but also to the relevant legislation that brings the Hague Rules into force. Therefore, it often happens that statutes governing the liability of a sea carrier, such as the former Harter Act in the US, or statutes implementing the Hague Rules, such as the COGSA or the United Kingdom Carriage of Goods by Sea Act 1971, are referred to in a paramount clause.[73] In such cases the foreign statute does not operate as a statute, but is treated as if it were a set of contractual terms agreed upon between the parties. In *Adamastos Shipping Co. Ltd.* v. *Anglo-Saxon Petroleum Co. Ltd.*,[74] the COGSA was referred to in the Paramount Clause. Concerning the effect of the Act, Viscount Simonds said:[75]

> The contract must be read as if the provisions of the Act were written out therein and thereby gained such contractual force as a proper construction of the document admits.

Accordingly, the foreign statute referred to in a paramount clause would only have effect as a matter of contract,[76] but is *not* taken as the governing law selected by parties. The reference to the foreign statute may be neither a choice of the foreign law nor an indication that the parties intended the foreign law to govern. This is particularly so where

[73] This method of securing conformity of contract became common after the passing of the Harter Act 1893, and the English courts, from the first, took the view that the terms of the Act should, as far as they are applicable, be read into the contract. That is to say, they should be applied contractually and not legislatively: see *G.E. Dobell & Co.* v. *S.S. Rossmore Co. Ltd.* [1895] 2 Q.B. 408 (McNair J.). This view has been adopted by the courts in similar cases coming within the Hague Rules: see *Golodetz* v. *Kersten, Hunik & Co.* (1926) 24 Ll. L. Rep. 374, particularly at 375 *per* Bankes L.J.; *Vita Food Products Inc.* v. *Unus Shipping Co. Ltd.* [1939] A.C. 277 (P.C.); *Ocean Steamship Co. Ltd.* v. *Queensland State Wheat Board* [1941] 1 K.B. 402 (C.A.); *Joseph Constantine Steamship Line Ltd.* v. *Imperial Smelting Corp. Ltd.* [1942] A.C. 154 (H.L.); *WR Varnish & Co. Ltd.* v. *Kheti (Owners)* (1949) 82 Ll. L. Rep. 525.

[74] [1959] A.C. 133 (H.L.).

[75] [1959] A.C. 133, 152 (H.L.). The result may be that the Hague Rules apply more widely in a particular case than they would have done if imposed by the legislation. Thus, in this case, the paramount clause was held to cover all voyages under the charterparty whether from United States ports or not. Conversely, when the Rules are applied in this way, the contract must, according to the usual rule of construction, be read as a whole, which may mean that some other clause may control their application: see *Vita Food Products Inc.* v. *Onus Shipping Co. Ltd.* [1939] A.C. 277 (P.C.) (bill of lading expressly made subject to English law). See also *Sabah Flour and Feedmills Sdn Bhd* v. *Comfez Ltd.* [1988] 2 Lloyd's Rep. 18 (C.A.).

[76] See also *Vita Food Products Inc.* v. *Unus Shipping Co. Ltd.* [1939] A.C. 277, 286 (P.C.); *The Stolt Sydness* [1997] 1 Lloyd's Rep. 273, 282.

the parties intend to incorporate the Hague Rules, which are international rules for the carriage of goods by sea, and which are frequently incorporated by reference to the COGSA: in such cases the fact that international rules are incorporated by reference to US legislation is of no or very limited guidance on the question of which law is applicable to the contract as a whole.[77]

Moreover, the legal effects of the application of a certain foreign code by virtue of a paramount clause are not in all aspects the same as when the code is applicable of its own force. Considering the historical background of the use of the paramount clause in international carriage of goods by sea,[78] courts of most countries have held that the provisions referred to in a paramount clause should not be regarded as statutory character, but merely as ordinary, contractual provisions, incorporated in the contract by the clause concerned. Consequently, they will be interpreted and construed in accordance with general principles of the law of contract, like any other provisions of a bill of lading. This point is important for the solutions to be applied to legal questions arising under a contract of carriage.[79]

Based on the analysis of the nature and function of a paramount clause, the approach adopted by the SPC in the *American President Lines* case was wrong.[80] In fact, the COGSA was a domestic enactment of the Hague Rules,[81] and the Hague Rules contained no provision which purported to regulate the responsibility of the carrier in relation to the delivery of goods at the end of the voyage.[82] Had the SPC determined the nature of the reference to the COGSA in the bills of lading as incorporation of foreign rules, it would have been able to find that the responsibility of the carrier President Lines was not covered by the terms of the contract, and thus should be decided according to the governing law, whose effects were further subject to China's mandatory rules.

77 See Dicey, Morris and Collins (2012) para. 32–057; *The Freights Queen* [1977] 2 Lloyd's Rep. 140, 143–145.

78 See Selvig (1961) pp. 205–213.

79 See Selvig (1961) p. 214; see also *The Stolt Sydness* [1997] 1 Lloyd's Rep. 273, where Rix J. held that when the Hague Rules are incorporated into a charterparty by reference to a foreign enactment they are interpreted by an English court as if they were contained in the English enactment, at any rate where the charterparty chose English law as the governing law.

80 See n 68 and the accompanying text.

81 See Sturley (1988) pp. 1–2.

82 See Williams (2010) pp. 194–195.

Although Guangdong Higher People's Court adopted the SPC's approach in a 2005 case,[83] in an earlier case, it rightly decided on the effect of parties' reference to the Hague Rules in bills of lading. In *PICC Property Insurance Company Zhanjiang Economic and Technological Development Zone Branch* v. *Cross Seas Shipping Corporation, Croatia Line and Lucky Seaway Service SPTE Ltd.*,[84] a dispute arose concerning whether the Cross Seas Shipping Corporation (Cross Seas), as the actual carrier, should be responsible for the loss and damages of the cargoes. The Paramount Clause on the back of the bills of lading concerned stipulated that the Hague Rules and the Hague-Visby Rules should be applied to the bills. In the first trial, the Guangzhou Maritime Court decided that, as the parties did not choose the law governing the bills of lading, the law having closest connection with the contract should be applied. The court thus applied Chinese law and made a decision that Cross Seas should also be responsible for the loss and damages.

Cross Seas appealed on the basis that the Hague Rules and the Hague-Visby Rules should be applied according to the Paramount Clause in the bills of lading. Since neither set of the Rules adopted the concept of 'actual carrier', Cross Seas argued that it should not be considered as a carrier and therefore was not responsible for the loss and damages of the cargoes. Guangdong Higher People's Court held as follows. First, although the Paramount Clause referred to the Hague and Hague-Visby Rules, it was not a choice of law clause, but only a clause making these rules part of the contract terms agreed upon by the parties. Therefore, the court of first trial was right in determining the governing law according to the closest connection principle. Second, the Paramount Clause should not be incompatible with the mandatory rules of the governing law, and the issues not covered by the contract terms should be determined by the governing law. As the parties did not stipulate the responsibility of an actual carrier, this issue should be decided according to Chinese law. The determination of the applicable law in the first trial was therefore confirmed.[85]

The decisions of both courts concerning the effect of the Paramount Clause in this case are consistent with the aforementioned international

[83] See n 70.

[84] 29 December 2000, Guangzhou Maritime Court; 9 July 2002, Guangdong Higher People's Court.

[85] But the judgment of first trial was reversed concerning the identification of the actual carrier and the responsibilities of Cross Seas, Seaway Service SPTE Ltd. and Croatia Line and Lucky.

practice of treating the rules or foreign statutes referred to in paramount clauses as incorporation of the relevant rules into a contract, but not a choice of the governing law. Article 3(29) of the 2004 Guangdong Guiding Opinions particularly stipulates: first, the foreign statute referred to in a paramount clause should be taken as a contract term incorporated into the contract and agreed upon by parties; second, under this circumstance, the parties should not be considered as having selected the governing law through the paramount clause; third, the law governing the contract should be determined according to the Chinese conflict of laws rules; and fourth, the disputed issues, including the validity of the paramount clause, should be determined by the governing law.[86]

4.3.3 *The Distinction between Incorporation by Reference and Choice of Law*

A The Importance of the Distinction in Theory and Practice

The previous analysis demonstrates that the failure to distinguish between incorporation by reference and choice of law results in inconsistent approaches in judicial practice, particularly in cases where the statute or set of rules referred to does not contain the relevant provisions dealing with the issue in dispute. The distinction is of significance both in the theory and in the practice of conflict of laws.

The first difference is concerned with the factor of time. When foreign law is applied as the governing law, it is applied as at the date of the event giving rise to the litigation in question, that is, as a 'living and changing body of law'.[87] When a foreign statute is applied by way of incorporation, its provisions become part of the contract, and it remains constant in the sense that it is unaffected by any change in the relevant foreign law occurring after the date of the contract.[88]

The second difference is concerned with construction. When foreign law is applied as the governing law of a contract, its substantive provisions are construed by reference to the constructional principles of the

[86] It is strange that the Guangdong Higher People's Court, after its issuance of the 2004 Guiding Opinions, still made a decision in 2005 which adopted the SPC's approach in the *American President Lines* case. See n 70. One possible reason may be that it tended to follow the 'precedent' of the SPC. See the discussion in Section 9.3 of Chapter 9.

[87] Wolff (1950) p. 424; McCartney (1960) p. 371; Dicey, Morris and Collins (2012) para. 32–058.

[88] Kelly (1977) pp. 858–859; Cheshire, North and Fawcett (2008) p. 701; Dicey, Morris and Collins (2012) para. 32–058.

system from which they are derived. When foreign law becomes applicable by incorporation, courts are not confined to expert evidence on that law, nor are they required to construe its provisions only by reference to the constructional principles of the system from which the law has been taken. Rather, they should construe the statute according to the constructional principles of the governing law.[89]

Third, greater restrictions are imposed on parties' freedom in choosing a governing law. Parties are free to incorporate rules from foreign statutes or international instruments to elaborate provisions in their contracts. The incorporation may be effected either by a verbatim transcription of the relevant provisions or by a general statement that the rights and liabilities shall in certain respects be subject to these provisions.[90] That parties are free to structure the terms of their contract is the essential principle in contract law.[91] For this reason, parties' freedom of incorporation is legally acceptable regardless of what law governs the validity of their contract.[92] However, parties' selection of the applicable law can be effective only if it is accepted by the conflicts rules of the forum.[93]

Fourth, in the judicial practice of China, the importance of the distinction can also be seen when the rules referred to by parties do not contain relevant provisions concerning the issue in dispute. When a foreign law, as the law governing a contract, does not contain the provisions dealing with the disputed issue, people's courts should decide that the applicable foreign law cannot be ascertained and therefore Chinese law should be applied.[94] Conversely, when the rules incorporated by parties into a contract do not address an issue, that issue should be determined according to the governing law of the contract, which is not necessarily Chinese law.

89 This assumes that the parties incorporate provisions of a system which is different from the governing law. See Kelly (1977) pp. 858–859; Dicey, Morris and Collins (2012) para. 32–058.

90 Cheshire, North and Fawcett (2008) p. 701.

91 Article 4 of the Chinese Contract Law provides: 'The parties shall, pursuant to law, have the right to enter into a contract on their own free will, and no unit or person may unlawfully interfere.'

92 See McCartney (1960) pp. 343, 359 and 378. The validity of the contract terms is, of course, subject to the governing law and also the mandatory rules and public policy of the forum.

93 The statutory restrictions on party autonomy are discussed in Chapters 5 and 6.

94 See Article 10 of the 2010 Conflicts Statute. Before the Statute, see Point 53 of the 2005 Minutes.

In *Lianyungang Koufu Food Co. Ltd.* v. *Industrial Bank of Korea Seoul (Head Office Seoul) and Bank of China (Lianyungang Nuclear Power Station Branch)*,[95] Lianyungang Koufu Food Co. Ltd. (Koufu) was the beneficiary under a letter of credit (L/C), and it sued the issuing bank, Industrial Bank of Korea Seoul (Head Office Seoul) (Industrial Bank), and the negotiating bank, Bank of China (Lianyungang Nuclear Power Station Branch), for their refusal to pay after it had submitted a full set of documents to the negotiating bank. The Industrial Bank answered that it refused to pay because the bill of lading submitted was an ante-dated bill and that Koufu committed a fraud under the L/C. The disputed issue in this case was whether Koufu committed a fraud and what should be the remedies for the two banks. In the first trial, the Nanjing Intermediate People's Court held that since all of the parties based their arguments on the UCP 500, and it represented the international practice on business involving a L/C, it should be applied according to Article 142 of the Civil Law. The court found that the Industrial Bank failed to prove Koufu had committed a fraud, and therefore decided in favour of Koufu. The Industrial Bank appealed to the Jiangsu Higher People's Court. Concerning the applicable law in this case, the appellate court decided as follows. First, since both parties referred to the UCP 500 in the first trial and did not raise any disagreement on the application of it in the appeal, the UCP 500 should be applied as the *governing law* to determine the rights and liabilities of the parties. Second, one of the disputed issues in the appeal was whether Koufu constituted a fraud under the L/C, but the UCP 500 did not deal with the issue of fraud and the relevant remedies. When the court enquired of the parties which law should be applied on this issue, Koufu and the negotiating bank pleaded Chinese law, while the Industrial Bank chose Korean law. Since all the documents under the L/C were issued in China, China was the place where the tort was committed. Chinese law should therefore be applied to determine the issue of fraud and the remedies according to Article 146(1) of the Civil Law.[96]

[95] 30 December 2002, Nanjing Intermediate People's Court; 23 December 2003, Jiangsu Higher People's Court. Although this is a case in tort, the analysis here focuses on the importance of the distinction between incorporation by reference and choice of law.

[96] Article 146(1) of the Civil Law provided: 'The law of the place where an infringing act is committed shall apply in handling compensation claims for any damage caused by the act. If both parties are citizens of the same country or have established domicile in another country, the law of their own country or the country of domicile may be applied.' According to Article 51 of the 2010 Conflicts Statute, this provision was superseded by the Statute as of 1 April 2011.

The court also found that the Industrial Bank could not prove Koufu's commission of fraud, and the first trial decision was confirmed.

In this case, while the Nanjing Intermediate People's Court did not specify whether the UCP 500 was applied as the governing law, the Jiangsu Higher People's Court clearly stated so. However, in this case, the UCP 500 was *not* applied as a governing law in the sense of private international law: if it had been applied as an independent governing law, the appellate court, concerning the issue of fraud which was not dealt with in the UCP 500, should *not* have determined the governing law according to the Chinese conflicts rule, but should have directly applied Chinese law since the 'governing law' did not contain the relevant provisions on the disputed issue.

In fact, when people's courts use the term 'governing law' (*zhun ju fa*), they do *not* necessarily mean the governing law of an issue in the sense of private international law, but may only use the term as a convenient reference to the rules that can be applied to determine an issue. In the previous case, the UCP 500 was applied because on the one hand, the parties referred to it in their arguments, and on the other hand, Chinese law does not contain specific rules on the relationship involving a L/C. According to Article 142(3) of the Civil Law, international practice can be applied when neither Chinese law nor the treaties concluded by China contain relevant provisions. The UCP 500 is actually applied as international practice in cases involving letters of credit.

In 2005, the SPC issued Provisions of the Supreme People's Court on Some Issues Concerning the Trial of Cases of Disputes over Letter of Credit.[97] Article 2 provides that in the adjudication of disputes over letters of credit, if parties have made any stipulation concerning the application of relevant international practice or other provisions that should be applied to such disputes, their stipulation shall prevail; if no such stipulation is made by the parties concerned, the UCP and other relevant international practice shall be applied. The SPC's provision confirms that parties are able to incorporate international practice into their contract. Moreover, it also clarifies that the UCP, as international practice in the field, is to be applied as a gap filler,[98] but not an

97 It was issued by the SPC on 14 November 2005 and became effective on 1 January 2006.

98 It is on this basis that people's courts have applied the UCP even in cases where one of the parties did not agree the application of it. In *Ningbo Congzhongxiao Gifts Co. Ltd.* v. *Banca Nazionale Del Lavoro S.P.A.* (11 January 2007, Zhejiang Higher People's Court), a dispute arose concerning whether the defendant, as the issuing bank, should pay the

independent governing law. Article 4 further stipulates that for issues not addressed in the UCP, the relevant governing law should be applied.[99]

Fifth, that the rules from international instruments referred to by parties can be applied by a court to solve an issue does *not* mean that parties are permitted to choose non-state norms as the governing law of a contract. On the one hand, in the circumstance envisaged in Article 142 (3) of the Civil Law, international practice can be applied as a 'gap filler', no matter whether it is referred to by parties or not.[100] On the other hand, when parties refer to a treaty that has been ratified or acceded to by China, the applicability of the treaty should be determined on the basis of its provisions, or of the regime of which it forms part, regardless of the parties' choice or agreement.

In *Societe Air France* v. *Geo Logistics Limited*,[101] a dispute arose concerning the contract for international carriage of goods by air between the parties. The place of departure was London and the destination was Shanghai. A clause on the back of the airway bill stipulated:

> If the carriage involves an ultimate destination or stop in a country other than the country of departure, the Warsaw Convention may be applicable ...
>
> WARSAW CONVENTION means the Convention for the Unification of Certain Rules Relating to International Carriage by Air, signed at Warsaw, October 12, 1929; or that Convention as amended at The Hague on September 28, 1955.

plaintiff, which was the beneficiary under the L/C concerned. The defendant argued that Italian law should be the governing law and the UCP should not be applied as the parties did not come to an agreement under the L/C concerning the application of the UCP. The Zhejiang Higher People's Court ruled that, as the parties did not choose the governing law, nor did they expressly exclude the UCP in the L/C, the UCP, as international practice, should be applied according to Article 142 of the Civil Law and Article 2 of the SPC's Provisions on Some Issues Concerning the Trial of Cases of Disputes over Letter of Credit.

99 Article 4 provides: 'Unless the parties to a foreign-related contract stipulate otherwise for the application of law, the relevant laws of the People's Republic of China shall apply to the arrearage disputes arising from the application for the issuance of a letter of credit, disputes arising from the entrustment to issue a letter of credit, disputes arising from the guaranty therefore as well as the disputes over the financing under the letter of credit.' It is not clear why Chinese law should be applied to these disputes in the absence of parties' choice of another law. But the provision at least demonstrates that parties are free to select the law governing the issues not addressed in the UCP.

100 See Xiao and Long (2009) p. 201.

101 12 March 2010, Shanghai First Intermediate People's Court.

Concerning the rules to be applied to solve the dispute, the Shanghai Pudong District People's Court held that for the unification and modernization of the Warsaw Convention and the relevant documents, on 28 May 1999, the Convention for the Unification of Certain Rules for International Carriage by Air was signed in Montreal (the Montreal Convention), and the aforementioned clause was old-fashioned after the Montreal Convention came into effect. Moreover, Article 55 of the Montreal Convention stipulated that the Convention shall prevail over any rules which apply to international carriage by air between States parties to the Convention, if those States are also parties to the Warsaw Convention and the Hague Protocol. Since both the place of departure, the United Kingdom, and the destination, China, are both parties to the Montreal Convention and also to the Warsaw regime, the court held that the Montreal Convention should prevail over the Warsaw Convention and the Hague Protocol in this case. The issues not covered in the Montreal Convention should be determined by Chinese law according to the closest connection principle. This decision was confirmed in the appeal.

As China is a state party to the Montreal Convention, Chinese courts should apply this treaty in accordance with its provisions. The previous case demonstrates that parties' reference to an international treaty ratified by China is not taken as a choice of the governing law, and is subject to the rule that Chinese courts are under an obligation to apply.

When parties refer to a treaty not concluded by China, the provisions of the treaty should be taken as contract terms. Article 9 of the Interpretation of the 2010 Conflicts Statute (1) stipulates:

> Where the parties concerned invoke in the contract any international treaty that has not yet been applicable to the People's Republic of China, people's courts may determine the rights and obligations between the parties concerned based on the content of that international treaty, unless such treaty goes against the social public interest of the People's Republic of China or violates the mandatory rules of the laws or administrative regulations of the People's Republic of China.

This provision was included in the Interpretation because in international carriage of goods by sea, parties commonly refer to the conventions containing the Hague Rules or Hague-Visby Rules, but China is not a state party to these conventions and people's courts have adopted inconsistent approaches in dealing with the effect of these conventions. The SPC finally adopted the approach of treating the conventions not concluded by China but referred to by parties in contract as contract terms agreed upon by parties. These rules therefore form the basis for the determination of parties' rights and obligations under their contract.[102]

In fact, international instruments do not necessarily deal with all the issues that may arise under a contract.[103] For issues not addressed in them, a court should determine the applicable law according to the conflicts rules of the forum.[104] This section illustrates the importance of the distinction between incorporation by reference and choice of law not only in theory, but also in judicial practice. People's courts should adopt a more consistent approach in dealing with parties' reference to international instruments in contract.

B The Requirement of Certainty of Terms in Incorporation

The doctrine of incorporation can only sensibly operate where the parties have sufficiently identified specific 'black letter' provisions of a foreign law or an international instrument or set of rules apt to be incorporated as terms of the relevant contract (such as articles of the French Civil Code or the Hague Rules).[105] In this regard, the incorporation of *lex mercatoria* or 'general principles of law' cannot meet the requirement of certainty of terms. On the one hand, their content is neither clear nor settled.[106] On the other hand, judges cannot be expected to use them as the template for resolving an argument, as the task of an appellate court would be practically impossible.[107] For these two reasons and on the basis of the meaning of 'law' in Article 41 of the 2010 Conflicts Statute,[108] parties wishing their contract to be governed by the *lex mercatoria* or 'general principles of law' cannot expect to have this choice given effect to

[102] See Gao (2013) p. 41.

[103] See, for example, Article 3.1.1 of the UNIDROIT Principles (2016) and Articles 4 and 5 of the CISG.

[104] See Article 7(2) of the CISG.

[105] Cheshire, North and Fawcett (2008) p. 701; Dicey, Morris and Collins (2012) para. 32–057; see *Shamil Bank of Bahrain EC* v. *Beximco Pharmaceuticals Ltd.* [2004] 1 W.L.R. 1784, at [51]; *Halpern* v. *Halpern (Nos. 1 and 2)* [2008] Q.B. 195, 213.

[106] See Briggs (2008) para. 10.06. *Lex mercatoria* may encompass different kinds of rules and therefore its content is not certain or predictable. See Nygh (1999) pp. 197–198; Flanagan (2004).

[107] Briggs (2008) para. 10.06. The situation may be different in international commercial arbitration.

[108] See Section 4.1.2.

by people's courts.[109] If they want adjudication in accordance with these rules, they may need to provide for arbitration before a tribunal of their designation.[110] Furthermore, when referring to international instruments such as the UCP or UNIDROIT Principles, parties should clearly indicate in contract which version of the set of rules they intend to incorporate.

4.4 Conclusion

Although the 2010 Conflicts Statute does not specify whether parties are permitted to choose non-state norms as the governing law of a contract, the analysis in this chapter indicates that non-state norms cannot be chosen as an independent governing law in current Chinese private international law. This does not mean that parties cannot make use of international instruments: they are free to incorporate those rules into their contract and the incorporated rules are normally applicable. However, the distinction between parties' incorporation of those rules and their choice of the governing law is still important because a consistent approach is required in judicial practice in treating parties' reference to non-state norms, particularly in cases where the incorporated rules do not address the issue in dispute. The cases just discussed reveal that, contrary to Tang's view,[111] the distinction between incorporation by reference and choice of law is a matter of great practical significance.

[109] There has been heated discussion among scholars as to the existence of 'global law', or the possibility of commercial parties' choosing the *lex mercatoria* as the law governing a contract. See, for example, Teubner (1997); Michaels (2005). However, the discussion seems to be more theoretical than real. In practice, the role for the *lex mercatoria* as an independent governing law before state courts is hardly recognized in regional instruments (such as the Rome I Regulation) or national conflict of laws. See Article 2 and Recital 13 of the Rome I Regulation; Symeonides (2006b) pp. 217, 227. Although Article 3 of the Hague Principles on Choice of Law in International Contracts allows explicitly for the choice of non-state law before state courts, this is a rather problematic provision. See Michaels (2014).

[110] For the recognition of the *lex mercatoria* in arbitration, see Nygh (1999) pp. 191–196.

[111] Tang (2012a) p. 605 considered that the distinction 'probably has only theoretic value'.

5

Statutory Restrictions on Party Autonomy (I)

According to Article 3 of Law on the Application of Laws to Foreign-related Civil Relationships (2010 Conflicts Statute),[1] parties to a foreign-related contract should exercise their freedom to choose the governing law *within the parameter provided by laws*. Several provisions in the Statute stipulate restrictions on party autonomy.

First, parties' freedom is restricted or even excluded in two contexts, namely, consumer contracts and labour contracts. According to Article 42, the laws at the habitual residence of consumers shall normally apply to consumer contracts. The laws at the locality of the provision of goods or services shall apply if the consumer chooses them or if a business operator does not engage in the relevant business activities at the habitual residence of the consumer. Pursuant to Article 43, parties are not allowed to select the governing law in labour contracts. Articles 42 and 43 are included in the Statute for the purpose of safeguarding the interests of consumers and labourers.[2]

Second, Article 4 of the Statute clearly specifies that the mandatory provisions on foreign-related civil relationships in the laws of China shall directly apply, and the law chosen by the parties will accordingly not be applied to determine the relevant issues covered by those provisions. This article, for the first time, specifies the effect of 'mandatory rules' for the purpose of private international law in China. However, it does not provide any definition of 'mandatory rules', nor does it clarify the distinction between domestic mandatory rules and those applicable in foreign-related cases.

[1] It was adopted at the 17th meeting of the Standing Committee of the 11th NPC on 28 October 2010 and became effective on 1 April 2011.

[2] See 'Report on the Main Issues concerning the Draft Law on the Application of Laws to Foreign-Related Civil Relationships of the PRC' (issued on the official website of the NPC on 28 August 2010).

Third, Article 5 provides for the reservation of social public interest: if the application of the selected foreign law infringes the social public interests of China, Chinese law will apply.

Chapters 5 and 6 analyse the statutory restrictions on parties' choice of law. Concerning the characterisation of consumer contracts and labour contracts, no clear guidance is provided in the 2010 Conflicts Statute or other laws, and the scope of protection provided by the Statute is therefore vague. This issue has been addressed elsewhere and thus is not included here.[3] Chapter 5 first deals with the scope of mandatory rules in China's legal system and illustrates the difficulties of identifying the rules in the context of private international law. Second, it analyses the definition of 'social public interest' reservation in contractual choice of law. Chapter 6 then touches upon the interrelationship between 'social public interest' and mandatory rules by looking at the relevant statutory provisions, administrative regulations and rules, and judicial interpretations on contracts involving foreign exchange and investment. Finally, it discusses how to identify the mandatory rules applicable in private international law and provides suggestions as to the use of social public interest reservation in contractual choice of law.

5.1 The Scope of Mandatory Rules

The term 'mandatory rules' was first referred to in China's private international law in Article 194 of Opinions on Several Issues Concerning the Implementation of the General Principles of Civil Law of the People's Republic of China (Provisional) (1988 Opinions)[4] issued by the Supreme People's Court (SPC): 'The foreign law shall not be applied where the parties evade the mandatory or prohibitive rules of law.' This rule was reiterated in Article 6 of the Provisions on Several Issues Concerning the Application of the Law in Trials of Foreign-related Civil and Commercial Contract Disputes (2007 Provisions).[5] However, the

[3] See Liang (2012) pp. 100–103.

[4] The 1988 Opinions was issued by the SPC on 2 April 1988. Several articles in it were invalidated by the SPC on 18 December 2008 because they contradicted the provisions in the Property Law (adopted at the 5th Session of the 10th NPC on 16 March 2007, effective on 1 October 2007). But the articles related to application of laws in foreign-related relations are not invalidated.

[5] It was issued by the SPC on 23 July 2007 and became effective on 8 August 2007. In The Catalogue of the Relevant Judicial Interpretations issued between 1 July 1997 and 31 December 2011 that would be Invalidated by the Supreme People's Court (the Tenth

scope of mandatory rules was not defined in these interpretations. Article 4 of the 2010 Conflicts Statute stipulates that if a law of China contains mandatory provisions on a foreign-related civil relationship, such mandatory provisions must be applied directly. This provision restricts the scope of mandatory rules: they should be governing *foreign-related* civil relations and provided in a *law* of China. However, it fails to provide guidance as to how to identify them in China's legal system. In domestic contract law, the effect and sources of 'mandatory rules' have been touched upon in several provisions.

5.1.1 Mandatory Rules in Chinese Domestic Contract Law

Article 52(1)(5) of the Contract Law provides that a contract is invalid if it violates the mandatory rules of any law or administrative regulation.[6] In Article 4 of Interpretation of the SPC Regarding Law Application Matters of the Contract Law (1) (Interpretation of Contract Law (1)), the SPC further specifies that the 'mandatory rules' are those contained in laws adopted by the National People's Congress (NPC) or its Standing Committee (NPCSC), or in administrative regulations adopted by the State Council, but not those provided in local regulations or administrative rules.[7] In 2009, the SPC issued two more judicial documents

Batch), the SPC has invalidated the 2007 Provisions and consequently it became void as of 8 April 2013. However, the rules provided therein and the notions underlying them concerning the identification of mandatory rules can still be found either in the SPC's interpretation of the 2010 Conflicts Statute or in judicial practice. Therefore, it is worthwhile to examine the relevant rules in the 2007 Provisions.

[6] Article 52 of the Contract Law reads: 'A contract is invalid in any of the following circumstances: (1) one party induced conclusion of the contract through fraud or duress, thereby harming the interests of the state; (2) the parties colluded in bad faith, thereby harming the interests of the state, the collective or any third party; (3) the parties intended to conceal an illegal purpose under the guise of a legitimate transaction; (4) the contract harms public interests; (5) the contract violates a mandatory rule of any law or administrative regulation.' The Law was adopted by the 2nd Session of the 9th NPC on 15 March 1999 and became effective on 1 October 1999.

[7] The Interpretation was issued by the SPC on 19 December 1999 and became effective on 29 December 1999. In China's legal system, 'laws (*falü*)' are enacted by the NPC or NPCSC. 'Administrative regulations (*xingzheng fagui*)' are enacted by the State Council and 'local regulations (*difangxing fagui*)' are formulated by the people's congresses and their standing committees of provinces, autonomous regions, directly administered municipalities or relatively large cities. 'Administrative rules (*xingzheng guizhang*)' are divided into 'departmental rules (*bumen guizhang*)', which are formulated by the various ministries and commissions under the State Council, the People's Bank of China, the Auditor-General and organs with administrative powers and functions directly under the

where it dealt with the categorization of mandatory rules. Article 14 of Interpretation of the SPC Regarding Law Application Matters of the Contract Law (2) (Interpretation of Contract Law (2))[8] provides that the 'mandatory rules' articulated in Article 52(1)(5) of the Contract Law means mandatory rules 'that affect validity'. Article 5(15) of Guiding Opinions on Several Issues Concerning the Trial of Civil and Commercial Contract Disputes under Current Circumstances (2009 Guiding Opinions)[9] further requires that people's courts should distinguish between mandatory rules 'that affect validity' and mandatory rules 'of an administrative nature' pursuant to Article 14 of the Interpretation of Contract Law (2). People's courts should invalidate those contracts which violate the mandatory rules *that affect validity*, and determine the validity of the contracts which are in violation of the mandatory rules *of an administrative nature* on a case-by-case basis.

These are the provisions on mandatory rules in domestic contract law. They should be distinguished from those in the sense of private international law since the definition and scope of mandatory rules in private international law should be narrower than those in domestic law.[10] Without further instructions, it is not clear whether the aforementioned provisions are also applicable in identifying 'mandatory rules' as referred to in Article 4 of the 2010 Conflicts Statute.

5.1.2 *Mandatory Rules in the 2010 Conflicts Statute*

In fact, Article 4 of the 2010 Conflicts Statute was inserted at the suggestion of the SPC. In the trial of cases involving foreign-related

State Council and 'government rules (*defang zhengfu guizhang*)', which are formulated by the people's governments of provinces, autonomous regions, directly administered municipalities and relatively large cities. See Articles 7, 65, 72, 80 and 82 of the Law on Legislation (adopted at the 3rd Session of the 9th NPC on 15 March 2000, and amended at the 3rd Session of the 12th NPC on 15 March 2015). According to Article 88 of this Law, the legal effects of laws is higher than that of administrative regulations, local regulations and administrative rules, and the legal effect of administrative regulations is higher than that of local regulations and administrative rules.

[8] It was issued by the SPC on 24 April 2009 and became effective on 13 May 2009.

[9] It was issued by the SPC on 7 July 2009.

[10] See Nygh (1999) p. 212; Schäfer (2010) pp. 31, 115. In this regard, a rule that is not mandatory in domestic sense cannot be categorized as mandatory in private international law.

guaranty contracts, people's courts considered that the registry rules on the provision of foreign guarantees by domestic institutions were of a mandatory nature and should be applied directly regardless of parties' choice of law in contract. However, before the 2010 Conflicts Statute, judges could not find a convincing legal basis for the direct application of those rules.[11] Therefore, the SPC suggested the Legislative Affairs Commission of the NPCSC when the Statute was being drafted that there should be a provision in the Statute specifying that mandatory rules should be directly applied, so that based on this provision, judges can apply the registry rules directly in foreign-related litigation.[12] This suggestion was accepted by the NPCSC.

Therefore, the original purpose of including Article 4 in the 2010 Conflicts Statute was to resolve the difficulty encountered by people's courts in applying the registry rules in foreign-related guaranty contracts. However, according to the provisions mentioned earlier on mandatory rules, the relevant registry rules are not mandatory even in domestic contract law.

The rules on the approval and registration procedures of guarantees were previously provided in the departmental rules entitled Procedures for the Administration of Guarantees Overseas by Institutions within the Chinese Territory[13] and Detailed Rules for the Implementation of the Administrative Measures for the Provision of Foreign Guarantees by Domestic

[11] In some cases, people's courts applied the evasion of law exception to exclude parties' choice of law clause, while in others they used the social public interest reservation. Both were unconvincing and have been criticized by scholars. In one case appealed to Guangdong Higher People's Court in 2004, the Court applied the concept of mandatory rules to exclude the law chosen by parties concerning the effect of a foreign-related guaranty contract. Even though the reasoning provided by the Court was convincing, it could not be justified by the existing laws at that time, because there was no provision on mandatory rules in the international sense before the 2010 Conflicts Statute. See Liang (2012) pp. 89–93; Xiao and Long (2009) pp. 204–207; Section 6.1.2 of Chapter 6.

[12] See G. Liu (2011) p. 41; Gao (2008) p. 130.

[13] Articles 12 and 17 (1) read:

Article 12 Guarantors can only provide guarantees overseas upon approvals by State Administration for Exchange Control.

Article 17 (1) If a guarantor provides guarantee overseas without approval, the foreign guaranty contract it concludes is invalid.

This document was issued by the People's Bank of China on 25 September 1996, and became effective on 1 October 1996. But it was repealed by the People's Bank of China on 8 June 2014. See 'Announcement No. 13 [2014] of the People's Bank of China – Announcement on Repealing Relevant Rules and Regulatory Documents'.

Institutions.[14] Their force is thus lower than both laws promulgated by the NPC and NPCSC and administrative regulations issued by the State Council. According to Article 52(1)(5) of the Contract Law, they do *not* even belong to the mandatory rules that can invalidate a *domestic* contract.

People's courts have actually taken those rules as a legal basis to render a foreign-related guaranty contract void in accordance with Article 6 of Judicial Interpretation of the SPC on Some Issues Regarding the Application of Security Law (Interpretation of Security Law).[15] However, the SPC's interpretation is problematic because it resorted to the departmental rules for the determination of the validity of a foreign-related security contract without regard to the governing law of the contract.[16] That is to say, even though Article 4 of the 2010 Conflicts Statute was originally included for the direct application of the approval and registry rules, those rules cannot be categorized as mandatory in private international law.

[14] Article 39 (1) and Article 48 read:

Article 39(1) A guarantor shall, after providing a foreign guarantee, handle the guaranty registration formalities with the local foreign exchange bureau.

Article 48 For a foreign guarantee subject to the approval of the foreign exchange bureau as required by these Detailed Rules, if the guarantor provides it without approval, the guarantee contract it concludes shall be invalidated.

This document was issued by the State Administration of Foreign Exchange on 11 December 1997, and repealed by it on 12 May 2014. See Annex 3 of Notice of the State Administration of Foreign Exchange on Issuing the Provisions on the Foreign Exchange Administration of Cross-Border Guarantees. The provisions therein supersede the previous rules issued by the same Administration which contradicted this Notice. But Article 39 was one of the bases upon which people's courts rendered a foreign-related guaranty contract void. See the analysis in Section 6.1.2.

[15] Article 6 of the Interpretation (issued by the SPC on 8 December 2000, effective on 13 December 2000) reads: 'A foreign security contract shall be invalid if: (1) the security is not approved or registered by relevant administration authorities; (2) the security is provided to domestic creditor for overseas organs without approval or registration by relevant administration authorities; (3) the security is created to secure registered capital or the foreign party's external debt of its investment in a foreign-invested enterprise; (4) a foreign exchange security is provided by a financial organ whose business scope does not include foreign exchange security, or a foreign exchange security offered by a non-financial enterprise legal person without foreign exchange income; (5) the security provider will not assume any obligation if the principal contract is altered or the creditor transfers the right of a foreign security contract without consent of the security provider or approval of relevant administration authorities, except as otherwise provided by laws and regulations.' This provision is considered to represent the mandatory rules on foreign exchange control. See L. Zhang (2012) p. 182.

[16] For a more detailed analysis of the Chinese rules on foreign-related guarantee, see Section 6.1.2 of Chapter 6.

5.1.3 Difficulties of Identifying Mandatory Rules after the 2010 Conflicts Statute

A Definition of Mandatory Rules in Private International Law

The genesis of 'mandatory rules' came from the category of 'exceptional laws' advocated by Savigny. According to him, these laws must reflect a public, rather than a private interest. That interest might be declared by the legislature, but this was rare. It was implicit in laws which sought to protect moral values, or they may 'rest on reasons of public interest, whether these relate to politics, police or political economy'.[17] In private international law, mandatory rules are the rules which override the normal conflicts rules, including the choice made by parties to an international contract. The scope of 'mandatory rules' in this sense is far narrower than that of the *jus cogens* or 'absolute laws', as Savigny called them, i.e., the rules in each legal system that the parties cannot by agreement alter or set aside, for they could still be replaced with the rules of another legal system through submission by the parties to that system. The background to the development of mandatory rules in contract cases is one of increasing state interference in contracts. A new species of contract rules has grown up which are not so much concerned with settling disputes between the parties but with protecting some group of persons or the national economic system.[18]

Under Article 7(2) of the 1980 Rome Convention on the Law Applicable to Contractual Obligations (Rome Convention), mandatory rules are applied in 'a situation where they are mandatory irrespective of the law otherwise applicable to the contract'.[19] Though this article refers to mandatory rules in the international sense, the same expression is also used in other articles in the Convention, where it refers to domestic mandatory rules.[20] The Regulation of the European Parliament and of the Council on the Law Applicable to Contractual Obligations (Rome

[17] See Nygh (1999) p. 199. The interrelationship between mandatory rules and social public interest is further discussed in Chapter 6.

[18] See Vischer (1974) chapter 2.

[19] See *Official Journal of the European Union* C 027, 26.01.1998, pp. 34–46; Giuliano and Lagarde (1980).

[20] See Articles 3(3), 5 and 6 of the Rome Convention. What Article 7(2) is concerned about is a far narrower subcategory of mandatory rules, namely rules which demand to be applied to the issue before the court regardless of any choice of law by the parties or any reference by a local choice of law rule to another legal system. See Nygh (1995) p. 377.

I Regulation) addresses the confusion by using the term 'overriding mandatory rules' when this term is being used in the Article 7 sense and by not using the term 'mandatory' at all when referring to provisions that cannot be derogated from by agreement.[21] Article 9(1) of the Rome I Regulation states:

> Overriding mandatory provisions are provisions the respect for which is regarded as crucial by a country for safeguarding its public interests, such as its political, social or economic organisation, to such an extent that they are applicable to any situation falling within their scope, irrespective of the law otherwise applicable to the contract under this Regulation.

The concept of overriding mandatory provisions is restricted in two different ways. First, there needs to be a legislative intent to make the norm applicable to any situation falling within their scope, irrespective of the law otherwise applicable to the contract under the Regulation. As with domestic mandatory norms, this intent must be established by way of statutory interpretation and with regard to the underlying policies and values. The norm should thus not be evaluated in an isolated manner but in accordance with the overall purpose of the legislative instrument of which it forms part. As a second requirement, the norm must also appertain to those provisions that are regarded as crucial by a country for safeguarding its public interests. Norms of such a nature are best described as serving a regulatory purpose and only the essential core norms of regulatory law are supposed to be overriding mandatory provisions.[22]

B Difficulties under the 2010 Conflicts Statute

a Identifying 'Mandatory Rules' as Defined in the 2010 Conflicts Statute The Interpretation of Contract Law (2) was issued for the proper trial of contractual cases and the application of the Contract Law in specific cases.[23] The provisions therein are thus for the purpose of domestic contract law. The 2009 Guiding Opinions were issued against the background that many new practical issues in civil and commercial trials have arisen because of the spread of the global financial crisis and

[21] See *Official Journal of the European Union* L 177, 4.7.2008, p. 13.

[22] See Calliess (2011) pp. 199–200.

[23] It is stated: 'In order to ensure proper trial of cases involving contract disputes, and in accordance with the Contract Law of the People's Republic of China, the following interpretations on certain issues concerning the application of the Contract Law are hereby issued.'

the change it has caused in the macroeconomic situation.[24] Article 5(15) and (16) of it further clarify the meaning of Article 14 of the Interpretation of Contract Law (2). That is to say, these provisions only deal with the identification of mandatory rules in domestic law. It is not certain whether the distinction between the two categories of mandatory rules provided in this sense, i.e., those 'that affect validity' and those 'of an administrative nature', also applies to the categorization of mandatory rules in the 2010 Conflicts Statute.[25]

In fact, this distinction looks more like an academic or theoretical construct that is difficult to understand and apply in the context of China's contemporary legal system. A more important difference should be made between mandatory rules in the sense of domestic substantive law and those in the sense of private international law. The prior category of rules would be applied in both purely domestic cases and foreign-related cases where Chinese law has been decided as the applicable law, whereas the latter should be applied in foreign-related cases where the people's courts have competent jurisdiction regardless of whether the governing law is Chinese law or not. In addition, the latter category should, no doubt, be narrowly defined.[26] Neither the Interpretation of Contract Law (2) nor the 2009 Guiding Opinions provides for the distinction between the two categories.

b 'Mandatory Rules' and the Use of Unilateral Choice of Law Rules What makes a law mandatory is an expression of policy which overrides bilateralism and, in effect, denies it.[27] In this regard, many mandatory rules have an attached unilateral choice of law rule, either express or implied.[28] This is understandable in view of the fact that they give effect to important policies and cannot be excluded by contract: it would not make sense if the parties could nevertheless exclude them by

[24] See the statement by the SPC at the beginning of the 2009 Guiding Opinions.

[25] Dr Gao Xiaoli, a judge of the SPC, argued that 'mandatory rules' in the 2010 Conflicts Statute is different from the 'mandatory rules' as mentioned in the Contract Law and thus the distinction is not applicable under the 2010 Conflicts Statute. But she did not analyse how to identify the 'mandatory rules' as referred to in the Statute. See Gao (2013) p. 42.

[26] The definition and scope of 'mandatory rules' should be narrower in private international law than in domestic law. See Nygh (1999) p. 212; Schäfer (2010) pp. 31, 115.

[27] Nygh (1995) p. 378.

[28] A unilateral choice of law rule is one that specifies the international application of the legal system of which it forms part of, without indicating what law will apply when it does not. See Hartley (1997) p. 347.

the use of a choice of law clause. Such rules are regarded as being internationally mandatory: they are applicable, in the situation described by their unilateral choice of law rule, irrespective of the normal rules of private international law.[29] However, an explicit statement about the immediate application by the legislator is rather the exception. Normally legislators abstain from expressing an opinion with regard to the international ambit of substantive rules. The identification of those laws which in view of their special nature claim application is the most difficult task for the courts.[30]

Article 145(1) of the General Principles of Civil Law (Civil Law),[31] Article 126(1) of the Contract Law and Article 3 of the 2010 Conflicts Statute all stipulate that parties should exercise their freedom in choosing a governing law within the scope provided by law. There is no express prohibition on parties' choice of law in contract, but there are unilateral choice of law rules and they actually exclude the application of party autonomy in the relevant contracts.

Article 126(2) of the Contract Law provides that Chinese law must be applied where contracts are to be performed in the territory of the PRC on Chinese-foreign equity joint ventures, on Chinese-foreign cooperative joint ventures and on Chinese-foreign cooperative arrangements involving the exploration and development of natural resources. Compared with Article 41 of the 2010 Conflicts Statute, Article 126(2) of the Contract Law excludes the application of the party autonomy principle in three categories of contracts. According to Article 2 of the Statute, if there are special provisions on the application of laws to foreign-related civil relationships in other laws, those provisions shall apply. Therefore, Article 126(2) of the Contract Law is still applicable after the 2010 Conflicts Statute enters into force.

Moreover, Article 8 of the 2007 Provisions included five additional categories of contracts in which only Chinese law should be applied and party autonomy is thus excluded.[32] These contracts were identified

[29] Hartley (1997) p. 348. [30] See Vischer (1992) p. 155.

[31] Article 145(1) reads: 'The parties to a foreign contract may choose the law applicable to the settlement of the disputes arising from the contract, unless the law provides otherwise.' The Civil Law was adopted at the 4th Session of the 6th NPC on 12 April 1986, became effective on 1 January 1987 and was amended at the 10th Session of the 11th NPC on 27 August 2009.

[32] They are: (1) contracts for the transfer of shares in Chinese-foreign equity joint ventures, Chinese-foreign cooperative joint ventures and wholly foreign-owned enterprises; (2) contracts under which foreign natural persons, legal persons or other organizations

because their validity is subject to the approval of the administrative authorities, and the relevant regulations were considered to be mandatory.[33] However, as discussed shortly,[34] the legal basis for providing unilateral choice of law rules and excluding party autonomy in those contracts is problematic.

As will be shown in Section 6.2, there is hardly any indication of the nature of the substantial rules in Chinese statutes. Even if unilateral choice of law rules are used, the provisions they refer to cannot be convincingly categorized as mandatory rules in the international sense. That leaves the problems for judges of identifying mandatory rules in China's private international law and of identifying a situation when such rules should be given the relevant effect.

5.1.4 The Evasion of Law Exception after the 2010 Conflicts Statute

The concept of 'mandatory rules' was used in Article 194 of the 1988 Opinions and then in Article 6 of the 2007 Provisions for the purpose of prohibiting parties' evasion of law. The 2007 Provisions has been invalidated, and the evasion of law exception is not repeated in the 2010 Conflicts Statute. The reason why the Legal Affairs Commission of the NPCSC did not include the evasion of law exception in the 2010 Conflicts Statute is that it considered the application of mandatory rules and the social public interest reservation sufficient for the protection of the national interest of China. Moreover, it recognized that in judicial practice, it was difficult to adjudicate whether a party 'deliberately' creates a connecting factor.[35] However, in Interpretation of the SPC on Certain Issues Concerning the Application of the Law of the PRC on the Application of Laws to Foreign-related Civil Relations (1) (Interpretation of

contract for the operations of Chinese-foreign equity joint ventures or cooperative joint ventures established within the territory of the PRC; (3) contracts for the purchase by foreign natural persons, legal persons or other organizations of equity from shareholders of non-foreign-invested enterprises within the territory of the PRC; (4) contracts for the subscription by foreign natural persons, legal persons or other organizations for capital increases of non-foreign-invested limited liability companies or companies limited by shares within the territory of the PRC; and (5) contracts for the purchase by foreign natural persons, legal persons or other organizations of assets of non-foreign-invested enterprises within the territory of the PRC.

[33] See Chen (2008) p. 264. [34] See Section 6.1.1 of Chapter 6.

[35] See Gao (2013) p. 42.

the 2010 Conflicts Statute (1)),[36] the evasion of law exception is reiterated by the SPC. Article 11 reads:

> Where one of the parties, in order to avoid the mandatory provisions of the laws and administrative regulations of the People's Republic of China, deliberately creates connecting factors in foreign-related civil relations, people's courts shall determine that the foreign law which is thus made applicable by the party shall not be applied.

The SPC deemed it necessary to include Article 11 because this provision protects the social public interest in a way different from the mandatory rules and the social public interest reservation.[37] Compared with Article 194 of the 1988 Opinions, Article 11 specifies that the exception can only be invoked in situations where a party 'deliberately creates connecting factors'. According to Article 21 of the Interpretation of the 2010 Conflicts Statute (1), Article 11 therein supersedes Article 194 of the 1988 Opinions.[38]

It is not clear whether a choice of a foreign law by both parties in contract can be considered as such a 'deliberate' creation. It is submitted that Article 11 should not be applied to invalidate parties' choice of foreign law in contract.

First, in a contractual dispute where all the other elements are located in mainland China except that the governing law selected by parties is a foreign law, the parties' choice of law is not effective. According to Article 3 of the 2010 Conflicts Statute, contractual parties can only choose the governing law in a *foreign-related* contract, and parties to a purely domestic contract are not permitted to choose a foreign governing law. That is to say, Article 3 excludes the foreign law chosen by parties when the only connecting factor of their contract with a foreign jurisdiction is their choice of law.[39] In this way, Article 3 guarantees that parties cannot

[36] It was issued by the SPC on 28 December 2012 and became effective on 7 January 2013.

[37] See Gao (2013) pp. 42–43.

[38] Article 21 reads: 'In case of discrepancy between the judicial interpretations issued previously by the Supreme People's Court and this Interpretation, this Interpretation shall prevail.'

[39] Both Article 126 of the Contract Law and Article 145 of the Civil Law provide for this restriction on the party autonomy principle in choice of law. For the criteria concerning the categorization of 'foreign-related contract' in judicial practice and the existing problems, see Liang (2012) pp. 86–88. Based on those criteria, only the choice of a foreign law, foreign court or foreign tribunal itself would not make a domestic contract become a foreign-related one.

evade the Chinese mandatory rules in domestic contract law if all the elements relevant to their contract are located in mainland China.

Second, in contractual cases where there are other elements located in foreign jurisdictions but parties choose a foreign law that has no connection with their relationship, their choice should not be held ineffective as they are *not* required to select a law that should have some connection with their transaction pursuant to Articles 3 and 41 of the 2010 Conflicts Statute.[40]

Third, even if parties' choice of foreign law might be taken as evasion of law, the legal effect of Article 11 of the Interpretation is substantially different from that of Article 4 of the 2010 Conflicts Statute. According to Article 11, parties' deliberate evasion of mandatory provisions of laws or administrative regulations of China would make the foreign law chosen by them not applicable and Chinese law would instead be applied to resolve disputes over the relevant contract.

Based on Article 4 of the Statute, only the mandatory rules concerning *foreign-related* civil relationships and provided in *laws* can be directly applied. Therefore, if parties avoid the application of rules that *do not* satisfy the criteria stipulated in Article 4 by choosing a foreign governing law, their choice of law clause is still *enforceable*. Even if the mandatory rules under Article 4 are applicable according to the facts of their dispute, the law selected by the parties is still applicable to determine the issues that are *not* governed by the mandatory rules. However, in this situation, Article 11 may *totally* exclude the choice of law clause itself.[41] That is to say, the legal effect of this provision is substantially different from that of Article 4, and a contradiction may thus exist.

Moreover, the application of the evasion of law exception in people's courts has been unsatisfactory. Judges have decided that parties have intentionally evaded the Chinese mandatory rules only on the basis of their choice of a foreign law. It remains to be seen how the courts will adjudicate whether parties 'deliberately' create a connecting factor after the Interpretation of the 2010 Conflicts Statute (1) takes effect. In the past, people's courts actually had difficulties in ascertaining the evasive intention of parties.[42]

40 Article 7 of the SPC's Interpretation of the 2010 Conflicts Statute (1) also stipulates that the lack of connection between the selected law and the case would not initiate parties' choice of law.

41 See Xiao and Long (2009) p. 206.

42 See the cases and analyses in Liang (2012) pp. 91–93. In *Tongchuan Xinguang Aluminum Ltd.* v. *Bank of China (Hong Kong) Ltd.* (8 May 2004, Guangdong Higher People's Court), the court rejected the evasion of law exception applied by the first trial court on the

In Notice on Seriously Studying and Implementing the Law on Application of Laws to Foreign-related Civil relationships of the PRC (2010 Notice) issued by the SPC on 2 December 2010, it is specifically provided that if the rules concerning the application of laws to foreign-related civil relationships in the previous judicial interpretations *contradict* the provisions in the 2010 Conflicts Statute, those rules shall not apply. In this regard, Article 11 of the Interpretation of the 2010 Conflicts Statute (1) should *not* be applied in a way that will contradict Article 4 of the Statute.[43]

Article 11 is unnecessary and provides a restriction that is beyond the scope of the 2010 Conflicts Statute. It is *not* an interpretation of any rule in the Statute at all.[44] In fact, the use of the concept of mandatory rules goes to the root of the problem of evasion, and makes it possible to stop the practice in those cases where the law which is being thwarted expresses a strong socioeconomic policy. If a rule is classified as a mandatory one it will still apply regardless of the choice of the parties. The concept of mandatory rules deals with a wider problem than that of evasion: mandatory rules even apply in situations where the applicable law is referred to by a conflicts rule in the absence of parties' choice of law.[45] Furthermore, by adopting the concept of mandatory rules it is possible to deal with the real evils of evasion of the law without actually having to go into the motives of the parties, which has to be done if one is looking for evasion. This is considered to be a 'distinct improvement in the law'.[46]

In summary, Articles 4 and 5 of the 2010 Conflicts Statue on mandatory rules and social public interest are sufficient to guarantee that the fundamental interest or policy of China would not be undermined by parties' choice of a foreign law.[47]

ground that the parties' evasive intention could not be proved. The relevant previous judicial interpretations are thus considered as unworkable. See Li (2004) p. 176.

43 Some Chinese scholars consider that Article 4 of the 2010 Conflicts Statute indicates that evasion of mandatory rules is prohibited in China. However, they do not clarify whether the evasion of law exception can be applied to invalidate parties' choice of law in contract. See Huang and Jiang (2011) p. 25.

44 To provide a rule that is wider in scope than the provisions of the 2010 Conflicts Statute is beyond the power of the SPC. See the relevant provisions cited in n 14 of Chapter 1; Liu (1997) p. 31.

45 See Fawcett (1990) p. 58. 46 Fawcett (1990) p. 59.

47 Some scholars argued that it may be necessary to apply the evasion of law exception to guarantee the application of the relevant rules because there was no provision on the effect of mandatory rules before the 2010 Conflicts Statute. See Xiao and Long (2009)

5.2 The 'Social Public Interest' Reservation in Contractual Choice of Law

5.2.1 Definitions and Expressions in Different Fields

Article 5 of the 2010 Conflicts Statute provides for the social public interest reservation: if the application of a foreign law violates the social public interest of China, Chinese law should be applied. This is in line with Article 150 of the Civil Law and Article 7 of the 2007 Provisions. The latter two articles both stipulate that if the application of foreign law infringes the social public interest of China, it should not be applied by people's courts.[48] The 'social public interest' is generally understood in China to mean fundamental legal principles and moral notions, state sovereignty and security, and public order.[49] It is an expression with Chinese characteristics of the more commonly used term 'public policy reservation' or *ordre public* in private international law. However, the boundary of 'social public interest', especially in the field of choice of law, is vague.[50] This reservation thus has an elastic nature and people's courts are provided with broad discretionary power to make decisions on an ad hoc basis.

The notion of *ordre public* is also reflected in other fields of Chinese private international law, but the relevant terminology used in the statutes is different. In Article 276 of the Civil Procedure Law, which

p. 206. Since Article 4 of the 2010 Conflicts Statute has provided for the application of mandatory rules, the evasion of law exception is no longer necessary. For the application of the social public interest reservation and its relationship with mandatory rules, see Chapter 6.

48 Article 150 of the Civil Law provides: 'The application of foreign laws or international practice in accordance with the provisions of this chapter shall not violate the public interest of the PRC.' Article 276 of the Maritime Code (adopted at the 28th Meeting of the Standing Committee of the 7th NPC on 7 November 1992, effective on 1 July 1993) and Article 190 of the Civil Aviation Law (adopted at the 6th Meeting of the Standing Committee of the 8th NPC on 30 October 1995; amended for the first time at the 10th meeting of the Standing Committee of the 11th NPC on 27 August 2009, amended for the second time at the 14th Meeting of the Standing Committee of the 12th NPC on 24 April 2015 and amended for the third time at the 30th Meeting of the Standing Committee of the 12th NPC on 4 November 2017.) are similar to the provision in the Civil Law. Article 7 of the 2007 Provisions reads: 'When the application of a foreign law violates the social public interest of the PRC, the foreign law shall not apply, and the law of the PRC shall apply.' There is a difference between the stipulations before 2007 and the articles in the 2007 Provisions and the 2010 Conflicts Statute: the latter two do not provide that the reservation also applies to international practice. Many Chinese scholars consider it unreasonable to include international practice in the reservation. See Huang (2011) p. 8.

49 See Zhang (2000) p. 94; Li, Ou, Jin and Zhang (2007) p. 181.

50 See Hu and Li (1992) p. 80.

addresses judicial assistance between China and foreign countries, the notion is defined as 'the sovereignty, security or social public interest of the PRC'.[51] In Article 282 of that Law, which deals with the recognition and enforcement of foreign judgments, its content is more specifically referred to as 'the fundamental principles of the laws of the PRC and the sovereignty, security and social public interest of the PRC'.[52] Concerning the recognition and enforcement of arbitral awards made by foreign institutions, the Convention on the Recognition and Enforcement of Foreign Arbitral Awards (New York Convention) should be applied since China is a party to it.[53] Article V(2)(b) of the Convention provides for the public policy reservation. As to arbitral awards made by an international arbitration institution in China, Article 274(2) of the Civil Procedure Law also stipulates the same reservation. Moreover, China has concluded treaties on mutual judicial assistance in commercial and/

[51] The Law was adopted at the 4th Session of the 7th NPC on 9 April 1991, amended for the first time at the 30th Meeting of the Standing Committee of the 10th NPC on 28 October 2007, amended for the second time at the 28th Meeting of the Standing Committee of the 11th NPC on 31 August 2012, and amended for the third time at the 28th Meeting of the Standing Committee of the 12th NPC on 27 June 2017. Article 276 reads:

> In accordance with an international treaty concluded or acceded to by the People's Republic of China or under the principle of reciprocity, a people's court and a foreign court may request each other to provide judicial assistance in service of process, investigation and collection of evidence and other litigation activities.
>
> If any matter requested by a foreign court for assistance is detrimental to the sovereignty, security or public interest of the People's Republic of China, the people's court shall not grant the request.

[52] Article 282 provides:

> After examining an application or request for recognition and enforcement of an effective judgment or ruling of a foreign court in accordance with an international treaty concluded or acceded to by the PRC or under the principle of reciprocity, a people's court shall issue a ruling to recognise the legal force of the judgment or ruling and issue an order for enforcement as needed to enforce the judgment or ruling according to the relevant provisions of this Law if the people's court deems that the judgment or ruling does not violate the basic principles of the laws of the PRC and the sovereignty, security and public interest of the PRC. If the judgment or ruling violates the basic principles of the laws of the People's Republic of China or the sovereignty, security or public interest of the PRC, the people's court shall not grant recognition and enforcement.

[53] See Notice of the SPC on the Implementation of the Convention on the Recognition and Enforcement of Foreign Arbitral Awards (issued on 10 April 1987).

or civil matters with more than twenty countries, and the social public interest reservation is provided in these treaties.[54]

This section first analyses the application of the reservation in these contexts in order to discover the meaning and content of 'social public interest'. It demonstrates that the vagueness of the scope of the reservation results in the inconsistency in judicial practice. The scope of the reservation in contractual choice of law will then be further explored.

A Service of Process and Taking Evidence for a Foreign Proceeding

In the context of service of process or taking evidence for a foreign proceeding, the relevant litigation is actually taking place in the requesting state according to its own law, but the request will have to be completed in the state addressed. The purpose of invoking the reservation is thus to protect the interest of the state requested. In this context, the content of 'social public interest' generally includes state sovereignty, security and political interest.[55] Chinese authorities have refused the request for assistance in this context because the PRC was listed as a defendant in the court of the requesting state, or the taking of evidence went against Chinese laws.

In *Miller* v. *Pyrodyne and Etaly*, the US Embassy in Beijing presented two diplomatic notes to the Foreign Ministry of China in 1991, seeking assistance in serving process on the PRC and the Local and Animal Products Import & Export Corporation of China respectively, two defendants among several.[56] In response, the Chinese authorities argued that since the court documents listed the PRC as a defendant, the service of it would violate the principle of sovereign immunity both in international law and the law of China. The Foreign Ministry then refused the request.

In 1988, the US District Court for the Central District of California entertained a petition in bankruptcy in which neither of the parties was Chinese. When preparing the case for trial, the debtor came to China to take the sworn testimony of certain Chinese corporations and nationals before a US consular officer. Since the depositions were taken without the prior knowledge or consent of Chinese authorities, the Foreign Ministry of China protested the conduct of the respondent to the

[54] For a more detail analysis of the legal basis regarding recognition and enforcement of foreign judgments and arbitral awards in mainland China, see Han (2005).

[55] Fei and Tang (1992) pp. 24–25.

[56] See Fei and Tang (1992) p. 90.

US Embassy in Beijing. Subsequently, the attorney for the creditor also came to China for the taking of evidence with the help of a Chinese lawyer. However, the Consular Department of the Foreign Ministry of China declined to authenticate the depositions since the way in which they had been collected violated the law of China. When those depositions were submitted to the District Court, the Court, through diplomatic channels, requested the Chinese Court to declare the testimony to the witness and to have the witness confirm it. The request was turned down once again as the Chinese Court considered that the taking of depositions had been conducted in violation of Chinese law.[57]

In the first case, the reservation was invoked because of sovereign immunity. This refusal can be justified in public international law. In the second case, the real reason for the Chinese Court's refusal of the request was not that the request infringed the sovereignty or security of China, but only that the evidence taken was not in accordance with the procedure stipulated in Chinese law.[58] However, as there was only one general provision in the 1982 Civil Procedure Law of the PRC (for Trial Implementation), scholars considered that the Court concerned refused the request on the basis of the social public interest reservation.[59] The conditions for service of process and taking evidence for foreign proceedings in China have been more specifically provided since the 1991 Civil Procedure Law. People's courts thus should no longer invoke the reservation on a basis similar to that of the second case.[60]

Some Chinese scholars have argued that infringement of sovereignty or security in the context of taking evidence takes on broader meaning than in the mere context of the service of process because state secrets

[57] See Xu (1996) pp. 241–242.

[58] Therefore in the second case the people's court concerned notified the District Court that it should put forward a fresh request for assistance in the taking of whatever evidence it deemed necessary to the case, and the competent Chinese court would then render assistance pursuant to Chinese law.

[59] See Xu (1996) pp. 241–242; Xiao and Huo (2005) p. 668. See also Article 202(2) of the then effective Civil Procedure Law of the PRC (for Trial Implementation, adopted at the 22nd Meeting of the Standing Committee of the 5th NPC on 8 March 1982 and effective on 1 October 1982). It provided: 'If the assistance requested by a foreign court violates the sovereignty or security of the People's Republic of China, the people's court shall turn down the request. If the request is out of the limits of the functions and powers of the people's court, the people's court shall return the request to the foreign court with explanations.'

[60] Article 279 of the current Civil Procedure Law clarify that people's courts should provide judicial assistance under the procedures prescribed by the laws of the PRC.

may be involved in the requested documents in the former situation.[61] This argument is unconvincing because if a request involves state secrets, people's court can clearly make this the basis for invoking social public interest reservation as it is related to state security, which is included in the scope of 'social public interest'. Moreover, under the current Civil Procedure Law, both the requests for taking evidence and service of process should be done in accordance with the law of the PRC. Therefore, there is no obvious reason why the social public interest reservation should have a broader meaning in the former situation.

B Recognition and Enforcement of Foreign Judgments

According to Article 282 of the Civil Procedure Law, people's courts should refuse to recognize or enforce a foreign judgment if it contravenes 'the fundamental principles of the laws of the PRC and the sovereignty, security and social public interest of the PRC'.

The meaning of these terms is not defined. The terminology is expansive and gives the court a considerable discretion in matters of this type. Grounds for concluding that a judgment ought not to be enforced under this head may include that the judgment of the foreign court was procured by fraud or that it did not observe due process or natural justice in its conduct of the case in question, or that enforcement of the judgment would involve enforcement of a foreign penal or taxation law, or would involve enforcement of the interest of a foreign government, or that enforcement would be against public policy. These are familiar grounds for refusing enforcement of foreign judgments in common law courts.[62]

Decisions of refusal to recognize or enforce foreign judgments on the basis of public policy reservation are few.[63] Han said that Chinese courts

[61] See Xiao and Huo (2005) p. 668; Xu (1996) pp. 241–242.

[62] See Blazey and Gillies (2008).

[63] Research has revealed no reported case on this topic up to now. See also Gao (2008) p. 192; Ye (2012) pp. 26–28; Tang, Xiao and Huo (2016) para. 6.74. The reason for this may be twofold. On the one hand, according to Article 282 of the Civil Procedure Law, people's courts should first examine the application for recognition and enforcement of a foreign judgment on the basis of an international treaty concluded or acceded to by the PRC or under the principle of reciprocity. If there is no international treaty concluded or acceded to between China and the rendering state concerning the recognition and enforcement of judgments made by each other's courts, or no relationship of reciprocity has been established between China and the rendering state, then people's court will simply refuse the application. For example, in *Case on the Application of Gomi Akira (A Japanese Citizen) to Chinese Court for Recognition and Enforcement of Japanese*

are generally reluctant to rely on public policy to deny recognition to a foreign judgment.[64] Without reported cases in this regard, it is not clear how the social public interest reservation will be applied by people's courts in recognition and enforcement of foreign judgments.[65]

C Recognition and Enforcement of Foreign Arbitral Awards

The New York Convention bound China from 1987. The recognition and enforcement of the party states' arbitral awards in China are governed by the Convention. In 1995, the SPC issued Notice on Several Issues Concerning People's Courts' Handling of Foreign-related and Foreign Arbitration (1995 Arbitration Notice).[66] It established a report and review system concerning the refusal to enforce foreign-related arbitral awards made in mainland China, as well as the refusal to recognize and enforce foreign arbitral awards made in a foreign country.[67] According to this

Judicial Decision (5 November 1994, Dalian Intermediate People's Court), the court rejected the applicant's request on this basis. On the other hand, most of the reported cases on foreign judgments involved foreign divorce proceedings between Chinese citizens, with one or both of them living overseas. According to Article 1 of the SPC's judicial interpretation in 1991, reciprocity is not a prerequisite for the recognition and enforcement of foreign divorce judgments. Moreover, in the reported cases in this field, the parties concerned only requested the Chinese courts to recognize the validity in China of the divorce decrees, and none of the cases actually required the courts to enforce anything. See Provisions on the Procedural Issues Concerning the Application of Chinese Citizens for the Recognition and Enforcement of Foreign Divorce Judgments (issued by the SPC on 13 August 1991). See also, for example, *Xue Yong's Application for Recognition of Foreign Judgment* (30 November 2009, Chengdu Intermediate People's Court), and *Shen Hua's Application for Recognition of Foreign Judgment* (27 July 2009, Chengdu Intermediate People's Court). In other reported cases where China has concluded bilateral treaties with the rendering state on judicial assistance, people's courts examined the applications according to the provisions of the treaties and did not invoke the social public interest reservation. See *The Application of B&T Ceramic Group s.r.1. Co. Ltd. for the Recognition and Enforcement of an Italian Bankruptcy Judgment* (application made on 18 December 2000 to Foshan Intermediate People's Court; the date of the judgment not clear).

64 Han (2005) p. 23.

65 It is said that the lack of specific guidelines for people's courts concerning the reservation may lead to arbitrary and (or) incoherent decisions. See Yuan (2004) pp. 766–767.

66 It was issued by the SPC on 28 August 1995. The sequential number of the relevant article of the Civil Procedure Law cited in it was revised by the SPC on 16 December 2008 after the NPCSC's Amendment of the Civil Procedure Law on 28 October 2007.

67 The SPC has thus established a so-called 'two track' system concerning the recognition and enforcement of arbitral awards: only foreign or foreign-related awards as referred to in the Notice are subject to the report and review system. According to the 1995 Arbitration Notice, a 'foreign-related arbitral award' means an award made by a foreign-related arbitration institution in mainland China, and a 'foreign' one made by a foreign

Notice, where a party submits an application for enforcement of a foreign arbitral award, the people's court concerned should report the application to its supervising higher people's court for re-examination if the former finds that the award falls under the circumstances stipulated in the Civil Procedure Law, or is not in conformity with the treaties to which China is a party or with the principle of reciprocity. If the higher people's court agrees with the reporting court and refuses to recognize and enforce the award, the former should then report to the SPC for re-examination and should not refuse to enforce a foreign arbitral award until receiving a reply from the SPC that decides the same. This reporting system endows the SPC with the final say over whether to decline the recognition and enforcement of foreign awards. This system is significant in practice for judicial review of foreign awards because it can find possible problems and mistakes, and avoid arbitrary and dogmatic refusal to recognize and enforce foreign arbitration awards at the level of lower courts.[68]

As just mentioned, violation of 'public policy' or 'social public interest' is one of the reasons for refusing recognition and enforcement of foreign (or foreign-related) arbitral awards in mainland China. People's courts invoked that reservation in three cases, and their rulings were confirmed by the SPC.

In *USA Productions and Tom Hulett & Associates* v. *China Women Travel Agency*,[69] the two applicants (American Companies) concluded a contract of performance with the China Women Travel Agency (Travel Agency) in 1992. Under this contract, the American Companies agreed to perform around twenty music shows in China, and that the music or songs they would play should be country music or other American popular songs that Chinese audiences would enjoy. They produced a

institution. The criteria provided in the Notice are different from those on the characterization of foreign-related cases, which are stipulated in Article 178 of the 1988 Opinions. A foreign-related arbitration institution in China can actually deal with purely domestic cases, while a domestic arbitration institution can also accept cases involving a foreign element. For the categorization of foreign-related and foreign awards in China, see Fei and Hill (2012) pp. 157–161. An award made by a foreign-related institution may not necessarily involve foreign elements. In this regard, the criteria in the 1995 Arbitration Notice are considered to be problematic, as they do not serve the original purpose of the Notice, that is, to guarantee the quality of decisions concerning the recognition and enforcement of international arbitral awards, no matter if they are made by a foreign institution or involve foreign elements. See Ouyang (2009).

68 See Han (2005) p. 25; Tang, Xiao and Huo (2016) section III.4 of chapter 7.

69 26 December 1997, Supreme People's Court. See Gao (2008) pp. 260–262.

sample video, and with that they obtained approval from the Ministry of Culture concerning the performance. However, the songs they actually performed in the shows were all heavy metal music, totally different from those in the sample video. The performers played crazily on the stage and the audiences felt highly uncomfortable with that. The audiences sought a refund of the price of the tickets, and the remaining shows were also stopped by the Ministry of Culture. The American Companies then applied for arbitration in the China International Economic and Trade Arbitration Commission (CIETAC) against the Travel Agency for the performance fee under the contract. An award was made for the American Companies, requiring the Travel Agency to pay 70 per cent of the total fee. The Companies then applied to the Beijing First Intermediate People's Court for the enforcement of the award. The Travel Agency raised the social public interest defence.

Both the Beijing First Intermediate People's Court and later the Beijing Higher People's Court considered that the enforcement of this award would be against the social public interest of China. They proposed to refuse the request and reported to the SPC for review. In its reply, the SPC mentioned that the Ministry of Culture considered that the performance of heavy metal music by the American Companies was not appropriate for the national conditions of China. The SPC said that the award had in fact confirmed the content of the performance and it overlooked the authority of approval of the Chinese Government. Considering that cases similar to this would have a negative effect on the cultural atmosphere and development of China, the SPC decided that the enforcement of this award was against the social public interest of China and thus the applicants' request should be refused.

The decision of the SPC was made in 1997, and it represented the Chinese courts' understanding of social public interest at that time. It was said that because the market for culture and performance was strictly controlled by government in the 1990s, the SPC's decision was reasonable.[70] However, the dispute involved in this case was a breach of contract. In fact, the arbitral tribunal in this case had considered the responsibility of the American Companies in their failure to perform as they had promised in the contract, and had made the award accordingly.[71] Since the Ministry of Culture had stopped the remaining

[70] See Gao (2008) p. 262.

[71] Based on the submitted evidence, the tribunal held that on the one hand, it was the Travel Agency that should be responsible for its failure to arrange the time and places for the

performances, the enforcement of the award would only resolve the dispute between the parties, and would in no way affect the public interest in China. Therefore, the SPC's reason for invoking the social public interest reservation is unconvincing.

In *Hemofarm D.D., MAG International Trade Ltd. and Sulame Media Ltd.* v. *Jinan Yongning Pharmaceutical Co. Ltd.*,[72] all of the parties jointly established an equity joint venture – the Jinan-Hemofarm Pharmaceutical Co. Ltd. (Jinan-Hemofarm). There was an arbitration clause in their joint venture agreement which provided that all the disputes related to their joint investment into the venture should be submitted to and resolved by the International Court of Arbitration under the International Chamber of Commerce (ICCA). Two disputes arose between Jinan Yongning Pharmaceutical Co. Ltd. (Jinan Company) and the joint venture, Jinan-Hemofarm, concerning some leased properties and the rent in 2003 and 2004 respectively. Since the Jinan Company considered that the arbitration clause only covered the disputes between the parties of the joint venture agreement, but not the disputes between the joint venture itself and other parties, it sued the joint venture in Jinan Intermediate People's Court. The Court decided that it had jurisdiction over those disputes and made decisions for the Jinan Company. Hemofarm D.D., MAG International Trade Ltd. and Sulame Media Ltd. thought that the Jinan Company was in breach of the joint venture agreement by bringing the disputes to litigation. The three applicants then applied for arbitration in the ICCA for damages caused by the Jinan Company's resort to litigation. The ICCA made an award for the applicants, which not only dealt with the disputes over the leased properties and the rent, but also held that the property preservation measure taken by the Jinan Intermediate People's Court could neither be justified legally nor commercially, and that the measure had directly caused the failure of the continual operation of the joint venture.[73] The applicants then applied to the Jinan Intermediate People's Court for the recognition and

remaining performance (from the 20th to the 23rd show); on the other hand, as to the quality of the performance, it was the American Companies' responsibility. Therefore, the tribunal held that the American Companies should share 30 per cent of the loss. See also Ye (2012) pp. 133–134.

72 See Reply of the Supreme People's Court to a Request for Instructions on the Non-Recognition and Non-Enforcement of an Arbitration Award of the ICC International Court of Arbitration (2 June 2008, Supreme People's Court).

73 During the litigation, the Jinan Intermediate People's Court impounded some bank savings and products of the joint venture.

enforcement of the award. The court and the Shandong Higher People's Court both decided that the award should not be enforced, and they reported to the SPC for review.

The SPC held that, the award dealt with disputes not falling within the arbitration clause concerned. Moreover, under the circumstances that the relevant Chinese courts had made judicial decisions on the same disputes, the tribunal still adjudicated the case and made an award. The SPC considered that this was an infringement of the judicial sovereignty of China and also the adjudication jurisdiction of Chinese courts. Based on Article V(1)(c) and Article V(2)(b) of the New York Convention, the SPC decided that the request should be refused.

The most important reason for the refusal in this case was that the award dealt with matters beyond the scope of the arbitration clause. Therefore, Article V(1)(c) of the New York Convention was a sufficient basis for the refusal. The only possible reason for the SPC's resort to the public policy reservation was that Chinese courts had already made decisions on those matters before the arbitral award.[74]

The social public interest reservation has also been applied in the enforcement of arbitral awards made in Hong Kong. In its reply to Jiangsu Higher People's Court concerning the refusal to enforce an arbitral award made by the ICC International Court of Arbitration in Hong Kong,[75] the SPC held that since the award contradicted the earlier decision of Jiangsu Higher People's Court on the effect of the arbitration clause between the parties,[76] the enforcement of the award would be

[74] Cf Ye (2012) p. 138; He (2013) pp. 1055–1056; Tang, Xiao and Huo (2016) para. 7.69. Ye considered that the reservation was invoked because of the non-arbitrability of the disputed issue in this case, as the arbitrability of an issue is involved in the enforcing state's public policy. He (2013) argued that the award violated the principle of *res judicata* and therefore it would have been much more persuasive had the SPC so held in its reply. He also suggested that *res judicata* constitutes a part of public policy. Tang, Xiao and Huo considered that holding the enforcement to be against public policy in this case was justifiable.

[75] See The SPC's Reply Concerning the Refusal to Enforce the Arbitral Award Made by the ICC International Court of Arbitration (No. 18295/CYK) (22 March 2016, Supreme People's Court). In this case, Wicor Holding A.G., a company incorporated in Switzerland, applied to Taizhou Intermediate People's Court for the enforcement of the award against Taizhou Haopu Investment Company. The award was made by the ICC International Court of Arbitration in 2014. The arbitration clause in the joint venture contract between the parties was held to be valid in the award.

[76] In December 2012, Jiangsu Higher People's Court made a decision that the arbitration clause in the joint venture contract between Wicor Holding A.G. and Taizhou Haopu Investment Company was invalid according to the law of mainland China, and thus the

against the social public interest of mainland China. Applying Article 7 (3) of the Arrangement of the Supreme People's Court on the Mutual Enforcement of Arbitral Awards between the Mainland and the Hong Kong Special Administrative Region,[77] the SPC confirmed that the application for the enforcement of the award should be refused.

In this case, the parties did not select the law applicable to the arbitration clause in their joint venture contract. According to Article 7 (1)(1) of the Arrangement,[78] the effect of the arbitration clause should be determined by the law of the place where the arbitral award was made, that is, Hong Kong law. The SPC's decision is controversial because it did not examine the effect of the arbitration clause on the basis of the Arrangement.

The previous three cases are the *only* reported cases where the SPC confirmed the application of the social public interest reservation in the recognition and enforcement of foreign awards. It should be noted that in other cases, the SPC overruled the decisions of the lower people's courts and held that the reservation should *not* be invoked for the refusal to recognize and enforce the foreign awards.[79] The report and review

Court had jurisdiction over the dispute arising from the contract. On the basis of that decision, both Taizhou Intermediate People's Court and Jiangsu Higher People's Court decided that the arbitral award should not be enforced. They reported to the SPC for review.

[77] The Arrangement was issued by the SPC on 24 January 2000 and effective on 1 February 2000. According to Article 1 of the Arrangement, if a party fails to comply with an arbitral award made in Hong Kong, the other party may apply to the relevant court in mainland China where the party against whom the application is filed is domiciled or where the property of the said party is situated to enforce the award. Since the arbitral award in this case was made in Hong Kong, the SPC applied the provisions in the Arrangement. Article 7(3) provides: 'The enforcement of the award may be refused if the court of the Mainland holds that the enforcement of the arbitral award in the Mainland would be contrary to the social public interests of the Mainland, or if the court of the HKSAR decides that the enforcement of the arbitral award in Hong Kong would be contrary to the public policy of the HKSAR.'

[78] Article 7(1)(1) provides: 'The party against whom an application is filed may, after receiving notice of an arbitral award, whether made in the Mainland or in the HKSAR, adduce evidence to show any of the situations set out shortly. Upon such evidence being examined and any of the said situations being found proved, the relevant court may refuse to enforce the arbitral award: (1) A party to the arbitration agreement was, under the law applicable to him, under some incapacity, or the arbitration agreement was not valid under the law to which the parties subjected it, or, failing any indication thereon, under the law of the place in which the arbitral award was made . . . '

[79] The SPC held that the violation of mandatory rules in China does not necessarily lead to the infringement of the Chinese social public interest. See the discussion in Section 6.1.3.

system set up by the SPC guarantees the consistency in the application of public policy reservation by people's courts: they generally apply the reservation with prudence and in accordance with the international trend of limiting the scope of judicial intervention in arbitration.[80]

5.2.2 *Meaning and Scope of 'Social Public Interest' in Contractual Choice of Law*

The term 'social public interest' is also used in Article 7 of the Civil Law and Article 7 of the Contract Law: it is a standard for the adjudication of the legality of civil activities and the validity of contracts in domestic law.[81] Though the same term is employed, Chinese scholars have argued for a distinction between social public interest in domestic cases and that in international conflicts cases: the scope of matters affected by the application of the two is different and the reservation should be applied with more restraint in the latter case.[82] Moreover, compared with the previous provisions, Article 5 of the 2010 Conflicts Statute more clearly refers to the 'application' of foreign law, which indicates that it is the result of the application of the foreign law that matters. Accordingly, the social public interest reservation should not be invoked simply because the content of the applicable foreign law is different from the relevant laws in China.[83]

In judicial practice, people's courts have invoked the social public interest reservation in cases involving foreign-related guaranty contracts.

In *Bank of China (Hong Kong) Co. Ltd.* v. *Shantou Hongye Co. Ltd. and Shantou Xinye Co. Ltd.* (the *Shantou Hongye* case),[84] the two

[80] See Han (2005) p. 25; Gao (2008) p. 253; Tang, Xiao and Huo (2016) para. 7.25.

[81] Article 7 of the Civil Law provides: 'Civil activities shall have respect for social ethics and shall not harm the social public interest or disrupt social economic order.' Article 7 of the Contract Law provides: 'The parties shall, in making and fulfilling the contract, abide by laws and administrative regulations and respect social ethics, and shall not disrupt the social economic order nor impair social public interest.'

[82] See Wan (2011a) p. 48.

[83] See Wan (2011a) pp. 45–46. Even before the 2010 Conflicts Statute, scholars have made similar arguments. See Li, Ou, Jin and Zhang (2007) pp. 184–185; Li (2004) p. 176; Chen (1987) p. 456.

[84] 9 July 2004, Supreme People's Court. The discussion of the Hong Kong-related cases mentioned in this chapter is for the purpose of analysing the nature of the Chinese rules on foreign exchange regulation and also the interrelationship between public policy and mandatory rules. The contractual choice of law issues under the 'One Country, Two Systems' regime are further addressed in Chapter 8.

defendants were Chinese companies in Shantou, Guangdong Province. They explicitly chose Hong Kong law in their guaranty contract with the Bank of China (Hong Kong) Co. Ltd., which was incorporated in Hong Kong, but they did not complete the registration procedures in the State Administration of Foreign Exchange. In the first trial of this case, the Guangdong Higher People's Court held that China is a state that implemented foreign exchange control, and Chinese law compulsorily required that a foreign-related guarantee should be subject to the approval of the administrative department of foreign exchange control. The Court then excluded the application of Hong Kong law according to Article 150 of Civil Law (which concerns the 'social public interest' exception) and Article 194 of the 1988 Opinions (which provided the 'evasion of law' exception). Further, based on Article 7 of the then Civil Law[85] and Article 6 of the Interpretation of Security Law,[86] the court decided that the failure of registration made the contract void under Chinese law. In the second and final trial of the case, the SPC held that that the regulations concerning the registration procedure of guarantee were mandatory, the selection of Hong Kong law was obviously an intentional evasion of these mandatory rules and thus the chosen Hong Kong law should not be applied. The governing law should be the law of mainland China.

The Guangdong Higher People's Court gave no detailed analysis of the reason why the application of Hong Kong law would be against the social public interest of China. In five cases adjudicated in 2003, where the Bank of China (Hong Kong) Co. Ltd. as the plaintiff sued the Mainland guarantors in Guangdong Province, the Guangdong Higher People's Court invoked the social public interest reservation to exclude parties' choice of Hong Kong law in the guaranty contracts.[87] As in the *Shantou Hongye* case, the Court considered that the parties' failure to follow the registration procedure in these cases was against the foreign exchange regulation system, and thus infringed on the economic order of China. However, as will be further analysed in Chapter 6, the provisions

[85] Article 7 of the then Civil Law provided: 'Civil activities must be in accordance with social morality. They must not harm the public interest, undermine the State economic plan, or disrupt the economic order.' This article was revised by the NPCSC in its amendment of the Civil Law on 27 August 2009.

[86] See n 15.

[87] See the five cases cited in Ouyang (2004) p. 14. The reservation was also invoked by the Guangdong Higher People's Court in *Foshan Chancheng District Government* v. *Bank of Communications (Hong Kong) Co. Ltd.* (22 January 2003, Guangdong Higher People's Court).

on foreign exchange control were only departmental rules and could not be applied to invalidate even a domestic contract according to the Contract Law.[88]

In the appellate decision of the *Shantou Hongye* case, the SPC did not resort to the social public interest reservation, but only invoked the evasion of law exception.[89] Although the SPC did not mention whether the Guangdong Court was right in applying the social public interest reservation in the first trial, it indicated its more cautious attitude towards the application of the reservation by refraining from using it.[90] After the *Shantou Hongye* case, the Guangdong Higher People's Court and other people's courts became more prudent in invoking the reservation: they generally did not invoke the social public interest reservation in similar cases, and applied the evasion of law exception or mandatory rules instead.[91] Even though the nature of the rules on foreign exchange control in China needs further investigation,[92] it is appropriate for people's courts to limit the application of the reservation to highly exceptional cases only.[93]

After the 2010 Conflicts Statute becomes effective, there is not much room for relying on 'social public interest', particularly in the area of contractual choice of law.

[88] See Section 6.1.2.

[89] The SPC's reasoning was unconvincing either, as it did not analyse how to identify the parties' evasive intention.

[90] See Ye (2012) pp. 41–42.

[91] For example, in *Bank of China (Hong Kong) Co. Ltd.* v. *Guangzhou Southern Steelworks* and *Bank of China (Hong Kong) Co. Ltd.* v. *Sonic Printing and Carton Co. Ltd. et al* (15 December 2008, Shenzhen Bao'an District People's Court), the courts concerned applied the evasion of law exception to exclude the parties' choice of Hong Kong law. For the former case, see Guangdong Higher People's Court (2006) pp. 117–127. In *Tongchuan Xinguang Aluminum Ltd.* v. *Bank of China (Hong Kong) Ltd.* (8 May 2004, Guangdong Higher People's Court), the court rejected Zhuhai Intermediate People's Court's application of the evasion of law exception in the first trial, and held that the registry rules on foreign-related guarantee were mandatory rules that should be directly applied in the case.

[92] See Section 6.1.2.

[93] In *Bank of China (Hong Kong) Co. Ltd.* v. *Fujian Longhai Power Co. and Fujian Longhai Government* (28 July 2005, Fujian Higher People's Court), which also involved a Hong Kong-related guaranty contract, the Fujian Higher People's Court rejected the social public interest reservation invoked by the court of first trial. The Court held that the reservation should not be taken as an arbitrary excuse for the exclusion of a foreign law, otherwise the value of conflict of laws would be undermined.

First, distinction should be made between the applications of the reservation in different areas of private international law.[94] The recognition and enforcement of foreign judgment is more intrusive and more directly related to state sovereignty. States traditionally adhere to the principle of sovereignty and are generally not willing to recognize the validity of any foreign judgment without at least some supervision or intervention by its own local courts.[95] The recognition and enforcement of foreign judgment are not only related to rights and obligations of the parties, and are more than the recognition of foreign law: the decision of a foreign state court is, through this procedure, put into the domestic legal order of the enforcing state. Therefore, the reservation is more forceful in the enforcement of foreign judgments for the protection of China's sovereignty and security. Moreover, there is only one provision in the Civil Procedure Law stipulating the conditions under which a Chinese court may grant recognition and enforcement to foreign judgments. Thus, the reservation provided in Article 282 looks more like an all-encompassing condition, which may not only relate to the substantive but also to the procedural issues of the judgment. In contractual choice of law, the reservation operates at an earlier stage of proceeding. It only aims at the court that has jurisdiction on the original case and relates only to the substantive law applicable by that court.[96]

Second, since the social public interest reservation is a ground for rejecting foreign law, it is clear that the judge must examine the foreign law before he rejects it.[97] In the *Shantou Hongye* case, the Guangdong Higher People's Court did not look at the content of Hong Kong law before they invoked the reservation: they actually started the choice of law process with the understanding that Chinese law should be applied. That is to say, the reservation was taken as a preliminary issue rather than a corrective device. In fact, it is the result of the application of a foreign law that matters. Judges should consider the circumstances of the case and provide in judgments detailed reasoning as to the legal solution of the dispute by the foreign rule when they invoke that reservation.[98]

Third, typical contract law cases are much less likely to raise issues of public policy than cases in more value-sensitive areas such as marriage

[94] Gao (2005) p. 221. [95] Caffrey (1985) p. 38.

[96] For a similar analysis in the context of the Rome I Regulation, see Calliess (2011) pp. 318–319.

[97] See Lagarde (1994) para. 5. [98] See Lagarde (1994) para. 24.

law and succession law.[99] Moreover, in contractual cases, the corrective and regulatory functions of public policy are, to a large part, fulfilled by way of applying mandatory rules. Since Article 4 of the 2010 Conflicts Statute has provided for the application of mandatory rules, the scope of the social public interest reservation in contractual conflicts cases should be further restricted.

99 In the discussion of the scope of the reservation in choice of law, scholars generally refer to marriage or succession law issues. See Ye (2012) pp. 219–226; Li, Ou, Jin and Zhang (2007) pp. 180–185; Chen (1987) pp. 455–456.

6

Statutory Restrictions on Party Autonomy (II)

Compared with the vague and expansive nature of the 'social public interest' reservation,[1] mandatory rules are the fruit of specific policies by definition, and those policies are regarded as being of such importance that they override the interests of the parties.[2] This chapter further analyses the interrelationship between mandatory rules and 'social public interest', and their application in judicial practice.

6.1 The Interrelationship between 'Social Public Interest' and Mandatory Rules

Mandatory rules comprise an element of social public interest and what makes a rule mandatory is that it involves social public interest.[3] Chinese scholars consider that the social public interest reservation has both a negative function and a positive one. Negatively, it can be applied to totally exclude the application of a foreign law and thus defend the forum's fundamental legal principles or moral values. Positively, it generates unilateral choice of law rules that require the application of Chinese law.[4]

According to Article 5 of the 2010 Conflicts Statute, the social public interest reservation can only be invoked to exclude a foreign law, but cannot be taken as a basis for the compulsory application of a Chinese substantive rule if that rule cannot be categorized as a 'mandatory rule' within the scope of Article 4. That is to say, at least after the 2010 Conflicts Statute, which contains a provision on mandatory rules, the social public interest reservation should no longer be used to justify the

1 See Chen (1987) p. 455; Li, Ou, Jin and Zhang (2007) p. 180.
2 Hartley (1997) p. 364.
3 Ever since the time of Savigny it has been recognized that mandatory rules comprise an element of public interest. See Nygh (1999) pp. 202–203.
4 See Li, Ou, Jin and Zhang (2007) pp. 179–182; Article 8 of the 2007 Provisions; see also Guedj (1991) p. 679.

argument that some of the departmental rules, even though they cannot be categorized as domestic mandatory rules under Article 52(1)(5) of the Contract Law, should be applied in foreign-related cases as they represent some important state policies. Before the Statute, this approach was actually applied by people's courts in cases involving a foreign-related guaranty contract.[5] Moreover, in the 2007 Provisions, the SPC provided that five additional categories of foreign-related contracts should be subject to Chinese law. According to the SPC's explanation, the rules on government approval or administrative supervision concerning foreign investment were deemed to be mandatory, and thus unilateral conflicts rules were added to assure that these rules can be applied.[6]

This section analyses, from the perspective of the interrelationship between the social public interest reservation and mandatory rules, the nature of the Chinese rules concerning foreign investment regulation and foreign exchange control, and their application in foreign-related contractual cases.

It should be noted at the outset that according to Article 3 of the 2010 Conflicts Statute, parties should exercise their freedom in accordance with *law*. Article 126(1) of the Contract Law and Article 145(1) of the Civil Law both provide that parties are free to select the governing law of their contract, unless stipulated otherwise by *law*. Concerning the statutory restrictions on party autonomy, the term 'law' (*falü*) in the 2010 Conflicts Statute, as well as in the Contract Law, should be interpreted as meaning the statutes enacted by the NPC or NPCSC.[7] That is to say, the scope of party autonomy in Chinese contractual conflict of laws should *only* be restricted by laws adopted by these authorities.

6.1.1 *Foreign Investment Regulation*

As to the scope of party autonomy, Article 126(2) of the Contract Law provides that Chinese law must be applied where contracts are to be performed within the territory of the PRC on Chinese-foreign equity joint ventures (EJVs), on Chinese-foreign cooperative joint ventures

[5] Based on that argument, the rules on foreign-related guarantees are deemed as mandatory. For further analysis on this issue, see Section 6.1.2.

[6] Although the 2007 Provisions was repealed by the SPC on 26 February 2013, it is important to analyse the notion underlying Article 8 of it, since that is also reflected in the Interpretation of the 2010 Conflicts Statute (1). See Section 6.2.3.

[7] See Liang (2012) pp. 104–106; Section 4.2.1 in Chapter 4.

(CJVs) and on Chinese-foreign cooperative arrangements involving the exploration and development of natural resources. This article remains effective after the 2010 Conflicts Statute.[8] In Article 8 of the 2007 Provisions, the SPC further excluded party autonomy in five additional categories of contracts performed within the territory of the PRC. They are: (1) contracts for the transfer of shares in EJVs, CJVs and wholly foreign-owned enterprises (WFOEs);[9] (2) contracts under which foreign natural persons, legal persons or other organizations contract for the operations of EJVs or CJVs established within the territory of the PRC; (3) contracts for the purchase by foreign natural persons, legal persons or other organizations of equity from shareholders of non-foreign-invested enterprises within the territory of the PRC; (4) contracts for the subscription by foreign natural persons, legal persons or other organizations to the increased registered capital of non-foreign-invested limited liability companies or companies limited by shares within the territory of the PRC; and (5) contracts for the purchase by foreign natural persons, legal persons or other organizations of assets of non-foreign-invested enterprises within the territory of the PRC.

The identified categories of contracts are all concerned with foreign investment in China. These transactions on the one hand affect the composition of the holders of equity and shares and are therefore closely related to the corporate structure of respective target companies.[10] On the other hand, they are also related to the economic security of the country since they may involve some industries which are sensitive or fundamental to the state interests of China.[11] Therefore, a certain extent of administrative supervision may be necessary in the relevant transactions. However, by making all the issues in these contracts subject to Chinese law, the SPC actually provided a unilateral choice of law rule that is both unnecessary and too broad.

First, the effect of administrative approval on the effectiveness of the relevant contracts is not clear. The rules deemed to be compulsorily applicable by the SPC in the 2007 Provisions are all rules which provide that the relevant transactions should be submitted to the competent

[8] See Liang (2012) p. 107.

[9] The EJVs, CJVs and WFOEs are hereafter referred to as foreign-invested enterprises (FIEs).

[10] Wolff (2008) p. 1061.

[11] See Gan (2012) pp. 52–56. The industries where foreign investment is allowed in China is indicated in Catalogue of Industries for Guiding Foreign Investment (2017 Revision) (issued by the National Development and Reform Commission and Ministry of Commerce on 28 June 2017, effective on 28 July 2017).

authorities for examination and approval, and should go through the registration procedures for changes with the registration and administration office.[12] According to Article 44 of the Contract Law, a contract normally becomes effective upon its conclusion; however, if laws or administrative regulations provide that a contract is required to be subject to approval or registration for its effectiveness, the effectiveness of the contract will not take place until and unless these requirements are met.[13]

The effect of the approval requirement is enlarged by the SPC in the Interpretation of Contract Law (1). Article 9(1) stipulates that where: (a) the relevant laws or administrative regulations specify that approval formalities are required for a contract, or (b) approval and registration formalities are required for the effectiveness of a contract; and the parties concerned fail to go through the relevant approval formalities or relevant approval and registration formalities before the completion of court hearings in the first trial, a people's court should rule that the contract has not taken effect. Based on Article 44(2) of the Contract Law, in situation (a), the parties' failure to obtain approval will not affect the effectiveness of a contract, since the relevant provisions do not specify so. But under the SPC's interpretation, the contract will not take effect in this situation. The reason behind Article 9(1) of the Interpretation of Contract Law (1) is that the provisions concerning the effectiveness of a contract which is required to be approved (or approved and registered) in Chinese laws and administrative regulations are not consistent. The SPC thus tried to provide a unified rule on this issue.[14]

Concerning the contracts identified earlier, the relevant provisions only provide that approval from the relevant authorities is required, but do not specify that this will affect the effectiveness of the contracts concerned. The SPC considered that based on the rules, those contracts

[12] For the specific provisions underlying Article 8 of the 2007 Provisions, see Chen (2008) pp. 264–265.

[13] In Chinese Contract Law, conclusion of a contract and effectiveness of a contract are deemed as two different matters that stand separately from each other. The effectiveness of a contract means a contract takes effect upon meeting all requirements set forth by law to be effective, while the conclusion of a contract only indicates that the parties have reached an agreement. For this reason, the conclusion of a contract and the effectiveness of a contract are provided in different chapters of the Contract Law, and the purpose is to differentiate one from the other. Zhang (2006a) p. 111.

[14] See Centre for Editing Legislative Regulations in the People's Court Press (2008) pp. 30–33 and the examples cited there.

will not take effect until they have been approved by the competent authorities. The rules are thus deemed to be mandatory by the SPC.[15] However, the SPC's understanding is unconvincing, and has been superseded by a subsequent interpretation issued by itself.

According to Article 9(1) of the Interpretation of Contract Law (1), if parties fail to obtain approval before the completion of court hearings in the first trial, their contract will be rendered invalid. That is to say, whether a contract within the scope of this article takes effect is determined by whether the obligation to seek approval is performed. Therefore, the party who bears this obligation under the contract can actually decide whether to make the contract effective or not. Article 9(1) is too favourable to the transferor and thus against the principle of fairness. For example, in the transfer of shares of FIEs, the transferor normally bears the responsibility of seeking the approval for transferring the shares he or she owns to the transferee. However, if, after the conclusion of the contract, he finds that the price of the shares is going up, he may not be willing to sell the shares at the price fixed in the contract. He can easily avoid the responsibility by simply not obtaining the approval so that the contract does not take effect.

This has happened in practice. It indicates that the system of administrative approval may encourage behaviour that is against the principle of good faith in the Contract Law.[16] The SPC therefore issued another interpretation in 2010. Article 1 of Provisions of the SPC on Several Issues concerning the Trial of Disputes Involving Foreign-invested Enterprises (1) (2010 Provisions on FIEs)[17] provides that where a contract concluded during the modification of a FIE does not take effect until it is approved by the FIE examination and approval organ in accordance with the laws and administrative regulations, and it is not approved, people's courts should determine that the contract is ineffective. If any party requests the court to determine the contract is void, that request should not be upheld by the court. Moreover, if a contract in this regard is determined as ineffective because it is not approved, this does not affect the effectiveness of the clauses on the parties' obligation to obtain approval. Compared with Article 9(1) of the Interpretation of Contract Law (1), this article does not provide that parties should seek approval

15 See Chen (2008) p. 265.

16 Article 6 of the Contract Law provides: 'The parties shall observe the principle of good faith in exercising their rights and fulfilling their obligations.'

17 It was issued by the SPC on 5 August 2010 and became effective on 16 August 2010.

before the court hearing of the first trial finishes. Moreover, it stipulates that the effectiveness of the clause on the obligation to obtain approval is separated from that of the contract, that is, even though the contract does not take effect, that clause is already binding on the parties. In the transfer of FIE shares, for example, if the transferee finds that making the contract take effect is more favourable to him, he may require the transferor to continue to perform the obligation.[18] Articles 5–9 of the 2010 Provisions on FIEs provide supportive rules concerning the pleadings on the obligation to seek approval under the contract which has not been approved.

The rules on administrative approval governing the contracts identified in Article 8 of the 2007 Provisions are only of an administrative nature. The underlying purpose of the rules is for the administrative authority to supervise the relevant transactions *afterwards*. In fact, the law does not prohibit parties' transactions.[19]

According to Article 14 of the Interpretation of Contract Law (2), the 'mandatory rules' articulated in Article 52(1)(5) of the Contract Law means mandatory rules 'that affect validity'. In Article 5(15) of the 2009 Guiding Opinions, the SPC requires people's courts to distinguish between mandatory rules 'that affect validity' and mandatory rules 'of an administrative nature' pursuant to Article 14 of the Interpretation of Contract Law (2). People's courts should invalidate those contracts which violate the mandatory rules *that affect validity*, and determine the validity of the contracts which are in violation of the mandatory rules *of an administrative nature* on a case-by-case basis.

Although the distinction between mandatory rules 'that affect validity' and mandatory rules 'of an administrative nature' is not clear,[20] judges in the SPC suggest that whether a provision prohibits the transaction itself should be taken as a criterion. If the provision provides that a certain kind of transaction is prohibited, then it is a mandatory rule that affects the validity of a contract.[21] In this regard, the rules underlying Article 8 of the 2007 Provisions are only regulatory rules, the purpose of which is not to render a contract void.

Second, it is not appropriate for the SPC to provide unilateral choice of law rules concerning the governing law of the identified foreign-related

[18] See Wan (2011b) pp. 29–30. [19] See Wan (2011b) pp. 43–45.
[20] See the analysis in Liang (2012) pp. 93–97; see also Section 6.2.
[21] Wan (2011b) pp. 19–20. Examples given include transactions of drugs and the abduction and sale of women or infants.

contracts. The purpose of the rules on administrative approval is to guarantee that foreign capital or assets are invested in China in the industries as listed in the Provisions on Guiding the Orientation of Foreign Investment by the State Council,[22] so that the national economic security of China can be maintained. On the one hand, the rules underlying Article 8 of the 2007 Provisions do not deal with the rights and obligations between private parties to the transactions concerned, but only address the relationship between the parties and the state: the state needs to have some supervision over those transactions. On the other hand, the Chinese rules on government regulation over foreign investments will definitely be applied by the administrative authorities even without the unilateral choice of law rules.

Article 31 of the Anti-Monopoly Law provides: 'Where a foreign investor participates in the concentration of business operators by merging or acquiring a domestic enterprise or by any other means and the national security is involved, besides the examination on the concentration of business operators according to this Law, the examination on the national security shall also be conducted according to the relevant provisions of the State.'[23] In 2011, the State Council established the security review system for mergers and acquisitions of domestic enterprises by foreign investors.[24] It identifies the situations where state security review is required and how the review should proceed. According to Article 4(1) of the Notice on Security Review, to merge or acquire a domestic enterprise, a foreign investor should file an application with the Ministry of Commerce according to the provisions therein. Even if an investor does not apply for a security review, other entities may also submit suggestion that a review should be conducted via the Ministry of Commerce, to the Joint Ministerial Meeting for the Security Review of Mergers and Acquisitions of Domestic Enterprises by Foreign Investors (Joint Meeting).[25] Moreover, where the merger or acquisition

[22] It was issued by the State Council on 11 February 2002 and became effective on 1 April 2002.

[23] It was adopted at the 29th meeting of the Standing Committee of the 10th NPC on 30 August 2007 and became effective on 1 August 2008.

[24] See Notice of the General Office of the State Council on the Establishment of the Security Review System for Mergers and Acquisitions of Domestic Enterprises by Foreign Investors (issued by the General Office of the State Council on 2 March 2011, effective on 3 March 2011) (hereinafter referred to as Notice on Security Review).

[25] The Joint Meeting is established according to Article 3 of the Notice, and it assumes the specific responsibility of security review of mergers and acquisitions. Article 4(2) provides

by a foreign investor has produced or may produce a material impact on the national security, members of the Joint Meeting should require the Ministry of Commerce to terminate the transaction between the parties concerned jointly with the relevant departments, or to transfer the relevant equities, assets or take other effective measures to eliminate the effect of such merger or acquisition on national security.

This analysis reveals that the rules on approval of contracts related to foreign investment are not mandatory rules that can affect the validity of contracts even in domestic law. They only deal with the relationship between the transactions of parties and the economic security of China. No matter whether unilateral choice of law rules are provided or not, they will be applied by the competent administrative authorities. Article 8 of the SPC's 2007 Provisions is therefore neither necessary nor appropriate.

6.1.2 *Foreign Exchange Regulation*

It has been mentioned that the social public interest reservation, evasion of law exception and mandatory rules were mostly applied by courts in cases involving foreign-related guaranty contracts, as parties' choice of foreign law was considered to be against the rules on administrative approval and registration of foreign guarantees.[26]

Pursuant to Article 19 of the Regulation on Foreign Exchange Administration (2008 Revision),[27] before concluding a foreign-related guaranty contract, an institution should apply to a foreign exchange administrative organ for approval. After the application is approved and the contract is concluded, the applicant should complete the registration formalities at the foreign exchange administrative organ. As analysed earlier, since it does not specify that such a contract does not take effect until it is approved or registered by the authorities, this provision does not affect the effectiveness of the contract concerned

that where the relevant department of the State Council, a national industrial association, an enterprise of the same profession, or an upstream or downstream enterprise deems it necessary to conduct a security review of the merger or acquisition of a domestic enterprise by a foreign investor, it may put forward suggestions on the security review of the merger or acquisition via the Ministry of Commerce. Members of the Joint Meeting may decide to conduct a security review if they do deem it necessary.

26 See Section 5.2.

27 It was issued by the State Council on 5 August 2008 and became effective on the same date.

according to Article 44 of the Contract Law. However, Article 17(1) of Procedures for the Administration of Guarantees Overseas by Institutions within the Chinese Territory and Article 48 of Detailed Rules for the Implementation of the Administrative Measures for the Provision of Foreign Guarantees by Domestic Institution both stipulated that if a guarantor provides a foreign-related guarantee without the approval from the competent authorities, the relevant contract is invalid.[28]

These two departmental rules thus provided further restriction on the effectiveness of foreign-related guaranty contracts which is beyond the scope of the relevant laws or administrative regulations.

Foreign exchange control is an important component of China's macroeconomic policies.[29] Up to now, there is no law adopted by the NPC or NPCSC concerning such control. According to Article 8(1)(8) of the Law on Legislation (2000), matters regarding basic systems of economy, treasury, customs, finance and foreign trade shall only be governed by law. Article 9 further provides that if no law has been enacted with regard to these matters, the NPC and NPCSC have the power to make decisions to authorize the State Council to formulate administrative regulations when necessary.[30] In 1985, the NPC adopted Decision of the NPC on Authorising the State Council to Formulate Interim Provisions or Regulations Concerning the Reform of the Economic Structure and the Open Policy.[31] The NPC decided to authorise the State Council to formulate, promulgate and implement, whenever necessary, interim provisions or regulations concerning the reform of the economic structure and the open policy in accordance with the Constitution without contravening the relevant laws and the basic principles of the relevant decisions of the NPC and its Standing Committee, and to report them to the NPCSC for record. Since then, the most authoritative legal document on foreign exchange control in China is the aforementioned Regulation on Foreign Exchange Administration.

Based on Article 71 of the Law on Legislation (2000), the departmental rules should be made in accordance with that Regulation and should only

[28] See nn 13 and 14 of Chapter 5.

[29] See Research Group of the SPC (2006) p. 231; Tu (2009) p. 16.

[30] The Law on Legislation (2000) is referred to in this section because the rules under discussion in relation to foreign exchange control were all issued before the Law on Legislation (2015 Amendment).

[31] It was adopted at the 3rd Session of the 6th NPC on 10 April 1985.

be related to its implementation.[32] Accordingly, neither the People's Bank of China nor the State Administration of Foreign Exchange[33] has the power to make rules beyond the scope of the Regulation. The rules they provided should not be applied to render a foreign-related guaranty contract void.

It has also been analysed elsewhere that the aforementioned two rules concerning foreign-related guarantees[34] were not even domestic mandatory rules that could invalidate a contract pursuant to Article 52(1)(5) of the Contract Law.[35] Therefore, they cannot be applied directly in foreign-related cases based on Article 4 of the 2010 Conflicts Statute.

Although the two departmental documents were both repealed in 2014,[36] they have been taken as the basis of excluding parties' choice of law in foreign-related guaranty contracts because of an interpretation by the SPC. Article 6 of the Interpretation of Security Law provides that a foreign security contract is invalid if the security is not approved or registered by relevant administration authorities.[37] This provision is still effective.[38] In fact, the SPC did realize that the two rules on the ineffectiveness of contracts were only departmental rules, and they could not be the legal basis for invalidating a contract. The basis for its interpretation was said to be the theory of public policy reservation and the relevant provisions in Chinese law, and also the principle that civil activities should have respect for social ethics and should not harm the public interest or disrupt social economic order, as is provided in Article 7 of the Civil Law. The SPC considered that, based on the nature of foreign-related guarantees and the effect they might have on society, the economic order regulated by the two departmental rules constituted part of

[32] Article 80(2) of the Law on Legislation (2015 Amendment) further stipulates that without any basis in laws or the administrative regulations, decisions and orders of the State Council, departmental rules shall not set out any requirements that impair the rights or increase the obligations of citizens, legal persons and other organizations, nor shall they increase the power or decrease the statutory duties of the issuing department.

[33] 'Procedures for the Administration of Guarantees Overseas by Institutions within the Chinese Territory' and 'Detailed Rules for the Implementation of the Administrative Measures for the Provision of Foreign Guarantees by Domestic Institution' were issued by them respectively.

[34] They are Article 17(1) of Procedures for the Administration of Guarantees Overseas by Institutions within the Chinese Territory and Article 48 of Detailed Rules for the Implementation of the Administrative Measures for the Provision of Foreign Guarantees by Domestic Institution.

[35] See Liang (2012) pp. 89–97. [36] See nn 13 and 14 of Chapter 5.

[37] See n 15 of Chapter 5. [38] It was applied in a recent case in 2015. See n 60.

the social public order, and the interest involved was thus part of the social public interest. By intertwining the two rules into its judicial interpretation, the SPC intended to make these rules become the legal basis upon which people's courts could invalidate a foreign-related guaranty contract.[39]

The SPC's explanation is unconvincing. It does not have the power to create any new laws, and it should limit itself to judicial interpretation of laws by interpreting their original meaning.[40] Therefore, it cannot provide interpretations that are wider in scope than the provisions of laws or administrative regulations.

6.1.3 Public Policy and Mandatory Rules in the Recognition and Enforcement of Foreign Arbitral Awards

Compared with people's courts' attitudes in the choice of law process, the courts, especially the SPC, seem to be more cautious in applying the public policy reservation in the recognition and enforcement of foreign arbitral awards in relation to foreign investment regulation and foreign exchange control. Even though the contracts concerned were deemed to be against the Chinese mandatory rules, the SPC did not consider that the recognition and enforcement of the relevant awards would be against the public policy of China according to Article V(2) of the New York Convention.

In its reply to Beijing Higher People's Court concerning the refusal to recognize and enforce an award made by London Sugar Association,[41] the SPC discussed the nature of Chinese mandatory rules on prohibiting FIEs registered in China from conducting futures transactions abroad without approval from the administrative authority.[42] The SPC held that those rules are mandatory and the parties' contract on futures transaction should be rendered void according to Chinese law.[43] However, the SPC said that breach of Chinese mandatory rules did not amount to infringement of Chinese public policy. The award was thus recognized and enforced.

39 See Li, Xi, Jin and Cao (2000) pp. 65–66.
40 See n 14 of Chapter 1; Liu (1997) p. 31.
41 See The SPC's Reply to the Request on the Application by ED&F (Hong Kong) Co. Ltd. for the Recognition and Enforcement of the Arbitral Award Made by London Sugar Association (1 July 2003, Supreme People's Court).
42 See Item 4 of Notice of the State Council on the Further Regulation of the Futures Market (issued by the State Council on 1 August 1998).
43 The contract was held to be effective in the award.

In the case from Hainan Higher People's Court concerning the refusal to recognize and enforce an award made by the Arbitration Institute of the Stockholm Chamber of Commerce in Sweden, a state-owned enterprise in Hainan, as the guarantor, made a guaranty contract with a Japanese company but did not obtain the approval from the foreign exchange administration authority. An award was made against the Hainan enterprise and it had to repay the debt.[44] The SPC decided that the breach of Chinese mandatory rules in administrative regulations and departmental rules did not necessarily infringe the public policy of China. Therefore, the award was held by the SPC to be enforceable.

The reason behind the SPC's prudent attitude to the public policy exception under the New York Convention may be that Article V must be construed narrowly: only violation of the enforcement state's public policy with respect to international relations is a valid defence.[45] Moreover, not every breach of a mandatory rule of the enforcing state can justify refusing recognition or enforcement of a foreign award. Such refusal is only justified where the award contravenes principles which are considered in the host country as reflecting its fundamental convictions, or as having an absolute, universal value.[46]

The SPC's rejection of the public policy reservation in the previous two cases indicates its prudent attitude in applying the reservation, as can also be seen in its determination of the law governing a foreign-related guarantee contract.[47] However, to enforce the arbitral awards which are in breach of the Chinese mandatory rules would be more intruding than the non-application of those rules in a foreign-related contract case at the stage of choice of law process. If the aforementioned foreign awards can be enforced in China, then the nature of the relevant administrative rules should be reassessed in the choice of law process. The two rules in relation to the invalidity of foreign-related guaranty contracts have now been repealed.[48] Article 29 of Provisions on the Foreign Exchange Administration of Cross-border Guarantees clearly stipulates that a

[44] See The SPC's Reply to Haikou Intermediate People's Court concerning the Non-Recognition and Non-Enforcement of the Award made by the Arbitration Institute of the Stockholm Chamber of Commerce in Sweden (13 July 2005, Supreme People's Court).

[45] See Lew, Mistelis and Kröll (2003) p. 721.

[46] Gaillard and Savage (1999) p. 996.

[47] The SPC prefers to use the evasion of law exception for the exclusion of parties' choice of foreign law in foreign-related guaranty contracts. See Section 5.2.2 of Chapter 5; see also Ye (2012) pp. 41–43.

[48] See nn 13 and 14 of Chapter 5.

foreign exchange authority's approval, registration or recording of a cross-border guaranty contract, or any other management matter or requirement as specified by the Provisions, does not constitute an essential element for the effectiveness of the contract.[49] Therefore, the rules on foreign exchange control in China should no longer be taken as mandatory rules in Chinese private international law.[50]

6.2 The Identification of Mandatory Rules and the Use of the 'Social Public Interest' Reservation in Contractual Choice of Law

6.2.1 State Policy and Its Representation in Legal Sources

Section 6.1 analyses how the SPC relates 'social public interest' to the identification of mandatory rules in foreign-related trials. In the field of foreign investment regulation, the SPC tried to advance the state interest of China by providing several unilateral choice of law rules in the 2007 Provisions. With regard to foreign exchange control, it absorbed the departmental rules into its Interpretation of the Security Law and stipulated that contracts in breach of the rules on administrative approval and registration should be rendered void.

It is generally admitted that the application of the *lex fori* is required for those legal rules and enactments which express a strong policy of the state. State interests are pertinent for instance when the issue concerns the regulation and control of the market and the national economy, the protection of national interest in landed property, the protection of monetary resources, the control of the securities market and so on. Regulations in the named areas are often enacted in the form of public law. But it should be noted that the focus in conflict of laws is on the consequences of those rules on private law relations which may be the civil liability of the offender or the nullity of contracts entered into in contravention of the relevant regulations. Penal or administrative sanctions are not the concern of private international law.[51] The SPC's interpretation in the aforementioned two fields has actually blended the

[49] It was issued by State Administration of Foreign Exchange on 12 May 2014 and became effective on 1 June 2014.

[50] However, the SPC provides another rule in Interpretation of the 2010 Conflicts Statute (1) for the purpose of making the rules on foreign exchange control mandatory. See Section 6.2.3.

[51] See Vischer (1992) p. 157.

administrative regulation with the commercial relationship between private parties. It is the latter that is the focus of private international law.

Foreign investment regulation and foreign exchange control are normally the fields where state interests are manifest.[52] In China, the purpose of regulating foreign investment is to keep the orientation of foreign investment in line with the national economy and social development plan of the country, and to satisfy the requirements of industrial policies of the State.[53] The objectives of foreign exchange control include: to maintain the strength of China's foreign currency reserves and to preserve a healthy international debt rating,[54] to ensure the stability of local currency exchange rate, to assure economic stability, and to strengthen the government's ability to regulate the economy.[55]

The intervention of the Chinese government in the previously mentioned two fields are mostly represented in departmental rules or other administrative documents of lower binding force. As has been analysed in Section 6.1, no matter whether the government approval is required before or after the parties' transaction, the rules do not prohibit the transaction itself. They are only of an administrative nature, but not rules that can render a contract void even in domestic law. Therefore, these rules cannot be categorized as 'mandatory rules' as provided in Article 4 of the 2010 Conflicts Statute.

Article 8 of the Law on Legislation (2015 Amendment) provides that matters related to basic economic, treasury and financial systems should only be governed by laws. Even though the State Council can be authorized to make preliminary administrative regulations on these matters, laws should be enacted by the NPC or NPCSC when experience has been gained from practice and when conditions are ripe.[56] In fact, the SPC's judicial interpretations in the aforementioned fields were issued because there were no corresponding laws or administrative regulations, or the most detailed and feasible rules are all of lower binding force, but the state interests were considered to be fundamental.[57] It is beyond

[52] See Vischer (1992) p. 157.

[53] See Article 1 of Provisions on Guiding the Orientation of Foreign Investment.

[54] Y. Shen (2000) p. 47. [55] Tu (2009) pp. 17–18.

[56] See Article 11 of the Law on Legislation (2015 Amendment) and Decision of the NPC on Authorising the State Council to Formulate Interim Provisions or Regulations Concerning the Reform of the Economic Structure and the Open Policy.

[57] In his speech on the national conference on civil trial, the then vice president of the SPC said that even though people's courts could not invalidate a contract on the basis of administrative rules according to Article 52(1)(5) of the Contract Law, in the fields such

the power of the SPC to make such interpretations. If the state policies or interest in these fields are really fundamental, they should be reflected in the statutes enacted by the NPC or NPCSC.

Furthermore, the identification of state policy should also be conducted against the background that state intervention in China into the economic development and transactions between private parties is being progressively relieved. In 2009, the NPCSC made a decision to amend some of the provisions in the laws which are not in line with the development of socialist market economy and the society. Based on this decision, Article 7 of the Civil Law was amended and the requirement that civil activities should not undermine state economic plans was deleted.[58] In its Opinions on Further Utilising Foreign Investment, the State Council also advocated that adjustments should be made to the contents of examination and approval – the relevant procedures should be simplified, the scope of examination and approval or verification and approval should be reduced to the greatest extent and the process should be more transparent.[59] In the 2010 Conflicts Statute, only the term 'law' is used, and no reference is made to other legal sources. Therefore, the mandatory rules applicable in foreign-related cases in China should only be identified in the statutes enacted by the NPC or NPCSC.

as foreign exchange and foreign trade administration, they should apply the departmental rules in the way that the SPC's judicial interpretations had provided. See G. Li (2000) pp. 32–34.

58 See Decision of the NPCSC on Amending Some Laws (issued by the NPCSC on 27 August 2009).

59 See Opinions of the State Council on Further Utilising Foreign Investment (issued by the State Council on 6 April 2010). On 19 January 2015, the Ministry of Commerce issued the Foreign Investment Law of the People's Republic of China (Draft for Comments) and sought public feedback on the Draft. The law is proposed to be uniformly applied to all foreign investment activities in China. According to the Draft, the case-by-case approval administration model prescribed in the existing laws will be transformed into the reconstructed 'limited approval and comprehensive reporting' foreign investment administration system. Under the negative listing administrative model, government approval will no longer be required for the majority of foreign investment. The Draft is available at http://tfs.mofcom.gov.cn/article/as/201501/20150100871010.shtml. It is not clear when the Draft will be developed into a legislative bill and submitted to the NPCSC, but it at least indicates that the Chinese government is increasingly open to foreign investment. According to Interim Measures for Record-filing Administration of the Establishment and Change of Foreign-invested Enterprises (2017 Revision, issued by the Ministry of Commerce on 30 July 2017), FIEs and their investors only need to complete the record-filing procedure for the establishment and change of FIEs so long as the special market entry management measures of China are not involved.

Although Article 52(1)(4) of the Contract Law provides that a contract should be invalidated if it is against 'social public interest', this article should only be applied in purely domestic cases, or to foreign-related contracts governed by Chinese law. The 'social public interest' reservation provided in Article 5 of the 2010 Conflicts Statute can only be invoked when the result of the application of a foreign law infringes the public interest of China. It should not be taken as a basis to directly apply a rule that cannot be categorized as a mandatory one pursuant to Article 4. In this regard, the SPC's explanation on Article 6 of the Interpretation of Security Law is problematic.[60]

The previous analysis reveals a dilemma in the identification of mandatory rules after the 2010 Conflicts Statute. On the one hand, state interest or policies in some fields are considered to be so important by the SPC that it has attempted to assure the corresponding rules can be applied in any foreign-related cases. On the other hand, the rules concerned are only provided in legal sources of low binding force, which cannot be categorized as mandatory rules even in domestic contract law. The next section illustrates another difficulty in the identification of mandatory rules in China's private international law.

6.2.2 Identification of Mandatory Rules and Statutory Interpretation

In Article 5(15) of the 2009 Guiding Opinions, the SPC requires people's courts to distinguish between mandatory rules 'that affect validity' and mandatory rules 'of an administrative nature' pursuant to Article 14 of the Interpretation of Contract Law (2). Regarding the criteria for the categorization of rules as mandatory, Article 5(16) of the 2009 Guiding Opinions states:

> People's courts should comprehensively consider the policy behind the laws and regulations and weigh mutually conflicting rights and interests, e.g., the types of rights and interests, the security of transactions and the objects regulated thereby, etc. to determine the type of the mandatory

[60] See n 39 and the accompanying text. However, in a recent case *OCBC Wing Hang Bank Limited* v. *Diyuan Trading Ltd.* (6 November 2015, Foshan Shunde People's Court), the court, on the basis of Article 6 of the Interpretation of Security Law, still held that the rules on foreign exchange control are mandatory rules under Article 4 of the 2010 Conflicts Statute and thus excluded the application of Hong Kong law, which was chosen by the parties in the Hong Kong-related guarantee contract.

> provision. If what is regulated by a mandatory provision is a contractual act itself and the interests of the state or the public interest would be harmed absolutely should such contractual act occur, the people's court shall hold the contract to be invalid. If what is regulated by the mandatory provision is the 'market entry' qualifications of a concerned party and not a certain type of contractual act, or what is regulated is an act of performance of a contract and not a certain type of contractual act, the people's court shall determine the validity of such contract with prudence and, where necessary, it shall seek the opinion of the relevant legislative authority or seek instructions from the people's court immediately above.

The 2009 Guiding Opinions was primarily issued for the trial of domestic cases. It refers to the policies underlying laws and regulations as the criteria for the identification of mandatory rules in domestic sense. When a domestic mandatory rule is involved in a foreign-related case, a court should further examine it to see whether the relevant statute also specifies its international reach: if it does, the court should apply it as specified and exclude the parties' chosen law on the issue governed by the rule, if it does not, a court has to determine the policies to which the statute seeks to give effect and try to fix its international scope on the basis of those policies.[61] If it is indicated in a statute that a rule therein is not subject to choice of law rules but should be applied regardless of the governing law in a foreign-related case, there is no problem of identifying such rules. However, statutes in China are rarely drafted with such clear indications of their purposes and scope, and their international reach will thus be a question depending on the true intention of the author of them.[62] Such intention is not easy to discover.[63] Determining the scope by interpreting a statute is extremely difficult and is described as being akin to the process of creating new legislation.[64]

The so-called mandatory rules that have been applied in people's courts in foreign-related cases, as analysed in the previous sections, are only departmental rules. As to the mandatory nature of a rule in a statute, Article 44 of the Maritime Code has been touched on in judicial practice.

In *Jiangsu Textile Import & Export Group Co. Ltd.* v. *Beijing Farenco Freight Services Co. Ltd. Shanghai Branch & Farenco Freight Services Ltd.*

[61] See Hartley (1997) p. 364; Guedj (1991) p. 667.
[62] The absence of an express legislative indication that a legal rule applies to foreign-related cases is often taken to indicate that the rule applies only to cases governed by the *lex fori*. See n 81 and the accompanying text.
[63] See Guedj (1991) p. 668. [64] Schäfer (2010) p. 98; Vischer (1992) p. 155.

(the *Farenco* case),[65] the plaintiff, as the shipper, did not receive the payment for the goods from the consignee. But it later found that the cargoes were released at the destination harbour without the presentation of the original bills of lading. It thus sued the two defendants for the loss.

Clause 33 of the bills of lading provided: 'No matter the Carriage includes Carriage to, from or through a port in the United States of America, the Carrier's responsibility under this Bill of Lading shall be subject to the United States Carriage of Goods by Sea Act 1936 (1936 US COGSA).' Clause 36 stated: 'The carriage of goods by sea contract, as is evidenced by this bill of lading, should be construed in accordance with Hong Kong law.'

Concerning the applicable law in this case, the Shanghai Higher People's Court decided as follows. First, according to Article 269 of China's Maritime Code,[66] the court confirmed that Clauses 33 and 36 in the bills of lading should be held effective.[67]

Second, in accordance with the choice of law clauses in the bills of lading, Hong Kong law should be applied. Based on Clause 33, the carrier's responsibility in this case should be determined by the 1936 US COGSA. Since the local clause was special agreements between the parties in respect of the applicable law as to the carrier's responsibility and the carriage in this case was to an American harbour, the US law, as referred to in Clause 33, should be applied.

However, it should be noted that Article 44 of China's Maritime Code provides: 'Any stipulation in a contract of carriage of goods by sea or a bill of lading or other similar documents evidencing such contract that derogates from the provisions of this Chapter shall be null and void.' Accordingly, if the choice of law as referred to in Clause 33 was contrary to China's mandatory rules, that law should not be applied. According to 1936 US COGSA and the 1916 US Shipping Act, the carrier would complete his obligations under a bill of lading once he delivered the

[65] 20 May 2004, Shanghai Maritime Court; 11 November 2004, Shanghai Higher People's Court. For the detailed facts of this case and the judgment of the first trial, see Section 3.1 of Chapter 3.

[66] It reads: 'The parties to a contract may choose the law applicable to such contract, unless stipulated otherwise by law. Where the parties to a contract have not made a choice, the law of the country having the closest connection with the contract shall apply.' The Maritime Code was adopted at the 28th Meeting of the Standing Committee of the 7th NPC on 7 November 1992 and became effective on 1 July 1993.

[67] For the identification of the existence of parties' choice of law in bills of lading, see the discussion in Chapter 3.

cargo to the named consignee, and he was not obliged to require the latter's presentation of the original bill of lading. But based on Article 71 of the China's Maritime Code, the carrier was required to deliver the cargo only upon production of the original bill of lading, no matter what category the bill of lading belonged to.[68]

The Shanghai Higher People's Court held that, compared with Article 71, the US law lessened the obligations and liabilities of the carrier and the application of it would be contrary to the Chinese mandatory rule. Therefore, Clause 33 was void. The responsibility of the carrier in this case was subject to China's Maritime Code.

The nature of Article 44 of China's Maritime Code and its relation with Article 269 are controversial. It is not clear whether Article 44 constitutes an exception under Article 269 and thus can exclude the foreign law chosen by parties if the content of that law is against the provisions in Chapter 4. There are three outstanding issues.

First, it is not specified which provisions in Chapter 4 are mandatory. Some scholars argue that all the provisions therein should be taken as mandatory, while others find that most of the provisions in Chapter 4 are only dispositive rules, and only Section 2 on carriers' responsibility is mandatory.[69]

Second, the scope of Chapter 4 is not defined in the Maritime Code. The Code was drafted on the basis of the Hague-Visby Rules,[70] and also with reference to some of the principles in the Hamburg Rules.[71] Article 2 of the Code provides:

> 'Carriage by sea' as referred to in this Code means the carriage of goods and passengers by sea, including the direct sea-river and river-sea transport.
>
> The provisions concerning contracts of carriage of goods by sea as contained in Chapter 4 of this Code should not be applicable to the maritime transport of goods between the ports of the People's Republic of China.

[68] Article 71 of the Maritime Code provides: 'A bill of lading is a document which serves as an evidence of the contract for carriage of goods by sea and the taking over or loading of the goods by the carrier, and based on which the carrier undertakes to deliver the goods against surrendering the same. A provision in the document stating that the goods are to be delivered to a named person, or to the order of a named person, or to a bearer, constitutes such an undertaking.'

[69] See Liu (2008) pp. 136–142.

[70] See Protocol to Amend the International Convention for the Unification of Certain Rules of Law Relating to Bills of Lading (Brussels, 23 February 1968).

[71] See United Nations Convention on the Carriage of Goods by Sea (Hamburg, 31 March 1978); Si (2002) pp. 298–299.

Compared with Article 10 of the Hague-Visby Rules and Article 2 of the Hamburg Rules, Article 2 of the Maritime Code only indicates that the rules in Chapter 4 may also be applied in international contracts, but does not clearly define the scope of Chapter 4. Therefore, it is not clear whether the rules in this chapter are compulsorily applicable to outward-bound or inward-bound international carriage of goods by sea, or even to both categories.[72]

Third, since the scope of Chapter 4 is not clearly defined, it is hard to determine whether the mandatory rules in it are only of a domestic nature, or should be directly applied in foreign-related cases. Some scholars argue that as the Maritime Code does not explicitly define the scope of Chapter 4, it should be presumed that this chapter can only be applied when Chinese law is determined as the governing law. Other scholars argue that Chapter 4 in fact sets out the maximum rights and minimum obligations of the carrier. Article 45 of the Code further stipulates that the provisions of Article 44 should not prejudice the increase of duties and obligations by the carrier besides those set out in chapter 4. Concerning the international scope of the Code as indicated in Article 2, Article 44 actually provides the restriction on parties' choice of law in contracts of international carriage of goods by sea or bills of lading or other similar documents evidencing such contracts.[73] While the Shanghai Higher People's Court adopted the latter approach, the former has also been applied in judicial practice.[74]

Article 2 of the Maritime Code indicates that the drafters of the Code did intend that it would also be applied in international carriages. The mandatory regime on the restriction of freedom of contract serves useful purposes for the common good in international trade.[75] The international instruments such as the Hague-Visby Rules and the Hamburg Rules, and the corresponding national laws[76] all represent the trend to

[72] See Liu (2008) p. 136; Si (2002) p. 300. [73] See Si and Li (2009) pp. 290–291, 342–343.

[74] For example, in *American President Lines Ltd.* v. *Feida Appliance Company, Feili Industry Co. Ltd. & Changcheng Industry Company* (25 June 2002, Supreme People's Court), the SPC applied the COGSA, as was stipulated in the Paramount Clause of the bills of lading concerned, in the determination of the carrier's liability in releasing the goods without the original bills of lading. The SPC did not discuss the nature of the provisions in Chapter 4 of the Maritime Code. For other outstanding issues involved in the SPC's judgment on this case, see the discussion in Section 4.2.3 of Chapter 4; see also Wang (2010) pp. 62 – 87.

[75] See Ramberg (1993) pp. 180, 183–185.

[76] For the approaches adopted in the United States and Australia, see Davies (2011).

unify the rules on the minimum responsibility of carriers, and the Chinese Maritime Code was also drafted in this context.[77] However, Chapter 4 of the Code covers a variety of issues under a contract of carriage of goods by sea. It is not reasonable to take all the rules therein as internationally mandatory: the wording of many articles indicate that they are not mandatory at all.[78] Without more specific provisions in the Code, it still cannot be convincingly justified that the rules referred to by Article 44 are mandatory rules in the international sense.[79]

The previous analysis illustrates the difficulty that may arise in identifying mandatory rules according to Article 4 of the 2010 Conflicts Statute through statutory interpretation: even though some rules may represent an important policy and are provided in a statute enacted by the NPC or NPCSC, normally there would hardly be sufficient evidence to justify the categorization.

In the theory of private international law, unless a clear intention of the author of the rules to the contrary is manifest, all internal substantive rules should remain subject to choice of law rules.[80] Under the legal system of China, this may mean that, only in rare cases can the rules provided in statutes be categorized as mandatory. This should not come as a surprise. As Nygh pointed out:[81]

> Mandatory rules should continue to be seen as 'exceptional laws'. The application of a mandatory law may operate to invalidate a contractual arrangement or, at the very least, substantially modify the obligations of the parties. Particularly, where the mandatory nature and the ambit of its application do not appear on the fact of the legislation, the invocation *ex post facto* of a 'mandatory provision' by a court adds to uncertainty and unpredictability in international commerce. It also provides a ready excuse for national courts to protect 'their own'.

[77] See Si (2002) p. 299.

[78] For examples, see Articles 43, 69, 83 and 90 of the Maritime Code.

[79] In his concluding speech at the National Conference on Maritime Trial, Judge Liu Guixiang, the then Director of the Fourth Civil Trial Division of the SPC (which is responsible for foreign-related trials), said that the provisions in Chapter 4 of the Maritime Code cannot be categorized as mandatory rules according to Article 4 of the 2010 Conflicts Statute. But he did not provide any analysis in his speech. See Liu (2013) pp. 23–24.

[80] Guedj (1991) p. 668, n 34.

[81] Nygh (1999) p. 211. In China, Professor Liu Renshan also suggested that the application of mandatory rules in international contracts should be limited to the areas that are fundamental to national economy. See Liu (2012) p. 439.

> The tendency of modern legislation is to specify its ambit where the legislature feels that its product should override the usual bilateral norms. It is therefore fair to presume that if recent legislation is silent on the point, it is not intended that it should be mandatory in the international sense.

The legislature in China should be aware of that when making new statutes or amending the existing laws.

6.2.3 Article 10 of the SPC's Interpretation of the 2010 Conflicts Statute (1)

In the Interpretation of the 2010 Conflicts Statute (1), the SPC provides a specific rule on the definition of mandatory rules. Article 10 reads:

> In any of the following situations, provisions of the laws and administrative regulations that involve the social public interest of the People's Republic of China, that parties cannot exclude their application through an agreement, and that are directly applicable to foreign-related civil relations without the direction from the conflicts rules, shall be recognised by people's courts as the mandatory rules specified in Article 4 of the Law on the Application of Laws to Foreign-Related Civil Relations:
>
> (1) Involving the protection of the interests of labourers;
> (2) Involving food or public health safety;
> (3) Involving environmental safety;
> (4) Involving financial safety such as foreign exchange administration;
> (5) Involving anti-monopoly or anti-dumping; or
> (6) Other situations where the rules concerned should be recognised as mandatory rules.

The purpose of this rule is to provide tangible guidance on the identification of mandatory rules in judicial practice. The order of the listed situations is arranged in accordance with their relevance to people's livelihood.[82] However, the rules stipulated in Article 10 do not necessarily deal with private relations, and thus may not satisfy the requirements as provided in Article 4 of the 2010 Conflicts Statute.

On the one hand, the source of mandatory rules is enlarged by the SPC: rules in administrative regulations can also be identified as mandatory according to Article 10. This is not in conformity with Article 4 of the Statute.[83]

On the other hand, it is not clear which rules are mandatory under the stipulated categories. As to the protection of labourers' interest, Article

[82] See Gao (2013) pp. 41–42. [83] See n 7 and the accompanying text.

43 of the 2010 Conflicts Statute has provided a particular rule for this purpose. Although the scope of protection under Article 43 is vague, it at least indicates that Chinese law does not directly apply to the relevant issues: Article 43 only excludes party autonomy in labour contracts, but not the application of foreign law.[84]

As to the rules involving food, public health or environmental safety, the relevant statutes mainly address how the legal rules in these fields are implemented by the competent administrative authorities, and do not focus on the relations between individuals. According to Article 1 of the Food Safety Law, it is enacted to ensure food safety and guarantee the safety of the lives and health of the general public, and to require the administrative authorities to be responsible for the food safety regulatory work.[85] Article 10 of the Environmental Protection Law stipulates that the competent department of environmental protection administration under the State Council shall conduct unified supervision and management of environmental protection throughout the country.[86]

Article 10(1)(4) of the Interpretation touches upon the laws and administrative regulations involving financial security, particularly foreign exchange control. The SPC wants to provide a legal basis upon which people's courts can determine that the rules concerning foreign exchange administration are mandatory rules in foreign-related litigation.[87] This provision has become the basis upon which the rules on foreign exchange control continue to be taken as mandatory rules in more recent judicial practice.[88] However, as has been analysed in Section 6.1.2, the rules in this

[84] See Liang (2012) pp. 100–103. Article 43 provides that a labour contract is governed by the law of the place where a labourer works, or the law of the place where the main business of the employer is located. In *Zhu Niankuan* v. *Dongguan Steel Structure Engineering Co. Ltd.* (19 September 2014, Dongguan Intermediate People's Court), a dispute arose concerning the labour contract between the parties. The court directly applied Chinese law on the basis of Article 4 of the 2010 Conflicts Statute and Article 10 of the SPC's Interpretation of the 2010 Conflicts Statute (1), but did not specify which rules were taken as mandatory.

[85] It was adopted at the 7th Meeting of the Standing Committee of the 11th NPC on 28 February 2009 and revised at the 14th Meeting of the Standing Committee of the 12th NPC on 24 April 2015.

[86] It was adopted at the 11th Meeting of the Standing Committee of the 7th NPC on 26 December 1989, and revised at the 8th Meeting of the Standing Committee of the 12th NPC on 24 April 2014.

[87] See Gao (2013) p. 42.

[88] See *Wing Hang Bank* v. *Hong Kong Yuan Feng Color Printing Limited* (18 December 2014, Fuzhou Intermediate People's Court) and *Baining Group* v. *Yangzhou Yongfengli Fashion Co. Ltd.* (17 June 2014, Yangzhou Intermediate People's Court).

field cannot be categorized as mandatory rules based on Article 4 of the 2010 Conflicts Statute. The SPC does not have the power to make those rules mandatory through a judicial interpretation.

Regarding foreign investment regulation, the unilateral choice of law rules provided in Article 8 of the 2007 Provisions have been invalidated. However, it remains to be seen whether people's courts in judicial practice will continue taking the relevant rules as mandatory on the basis that they are related to the financial security of China, as stipulated in Article 10(1)(4) of the Interpretation, or that these rules can be categorized as mandatory according to Article 10(1)(5) as they may be related to anti-monopoly or anti-dumping policy, or even that they belong to 'other situations' as provided in Article 10 (1)(6).

In *Sitic America Inc.* v. *Kunlun Properties Inc.*,[89] both parties were incorporated in the United States. They made a contract where Sitic America Inc. agreed to transfer the shares it held in Lunan Medicine Co. Ltd. to Kunlun Properties Inc. Lunan Medicine Co. Ltd. was a Chinese-foreign equity joint venture incorporated in China and Sitic America Inc. was the foreign investor. The parties selected Chinese law as the governing law. In the first trial, the Shandong Higher People's Court held that the parties' choice of law in contract was effective according to Article 145(1) of the Civil Law (which provides the party autonomy principle). In the appeal, the SPC held that, even though there was no particular choice of law rule for contracts on transfer of shares in Chinese-foreign equity joint ventures, Article 24 of the Regulations for the Implementation of the Law of the PRC on Chinese-Foreign Equity Joint Ventures stipulated that these contracts did not take effect until they were approved by the administrative authorities.[90] The SPC considered that the approval procedure was a substantial condition for the validity of those contracts. Consequently, the SPC decided that only Chinese law should be applied to the contracts on

[89] 16 May 2003, Shandong Higher People's Court; 20 October 2005, Supreme People's Court.

[90] The SPC quoted the Regulations as issued by the State Council on 20 September 1983. Article 24 provided: 'Any increase, reduction of the registered capital of a joint venture shall be approved by a meeting of the board of directors and submitted to the examination and approval authority for approval. Registration procedures for changes shall be dealt with at the registration and administration office.' It should be noted that the Regulations was revised on 15 January 1986, 21 December 1987, 22 July 2001, 8 January 2011 and 19 February 2014 by the State Council. Article 24 of the Regulations of 1983 was the same as Article 21 of it in its revised version of 2014.

transfer of shares in Chinese-foreign equity joint ventures and parties were not allowed to select a foreign law as the governing law. The SPC further pointed out that the parties' choice of Chinese law in contract was not against the aforementioned stipulation, but that did not mean that the determination of the governing law of the contract was based on the parties' choice.

This case was decided in 2005, that is, before the 2007 Provisions came into force. In fact, the approval or registration procedure in the administrative rules or regulations concerning foreign investment regulation was taken as the legal basis underlying Article 8 of the 2007 Provisions.[91] The reason provided by the SPC for the invalidation of the 2007 Provisions was simply that it 'contradicted' the 2010 Conflicts Statute.[92] The SPC did not specify which provisions therein were considered to be in contradiction with the Statute. As Articles 10(1)(4), 10(1)(5) and 10(1)(6) of the Interpretation of the 2010 Conflicts Statute (1) are rather open-ended, it is not clear whether the approach adopted by the SPC in the aforementioned case will be followed in judicial practice in the future.[93] Based on the analysis in Section 6.1.1, it is submitted that the governing laws of the contracts listed in Article 8 of the 2007 Provisions should now be determined according to Article 41 of the 2010 Conflicts Statute, and the rules on administrative approval or registration should not be taken as mandatory.[94]

Article 10 of the SPC's Interpretation of the Statute fails to provide useful instructions on the identification of mandatory rules. This again demonstrates that it is beyond the SPC's power to comprehensively resolve the issue.

[91] See Section 6.1.1.

[92] See The Catalogue of the Relevant Judicial Interpretations issued between 1 July 1997 and 31 December 2011 that would be Invalidated by the Supreme People's Court (the Tenth Batch) (issued on 26 February 2013 and effective on 8 April 2013).

[93] In *A Case concerning the Transfer of Shares between Zhang and A Company* (17 July 2013, Hubei Higher People's Court; the names of the parties not revealed in the judgment), the court still considered that the rules underlying Article 8 of the 2007 Provisions concerning the transfer of shares in FIEs were mandatory rules and Article 8 was still binding. It accordingly excluded Hong Kong law, which was chosen by the parties in their contract of shares transfer, and applied the law of mainland China.

[94] Cf Tu (2016), who believes (para. 132) that it will still be the 2007 Provisions that mainly govern the contractual conflicts issues in future for a while. He also argues (para. 132) that generally there are no essential conflicts between the 2010 Conflicts Statute and the 2007 Provisions.

6.2.4 The Application of the Social Public Interest Reservation in Contractual Choice of Law

Sections 5.2 and 6.1 have demonstrated that the 'social public interest' reservation should only be invoked in highly exceptional cases concerning choice of law in contracts. Two points need to be further addressed.

First, a distinction should be made between the resort to the reservation and the application of mandatory rules. Their functions are different in the choice of law process. For the identification of mandatory rules, the assessment of the forum's law operates prior to any rejection of a foreign law. The *lex causae* is not set aside because of the result of its application to the case at bar.[95] The 'social public interest' reservation is a mechanism which corrects the choice of law designation for substantive reasons, namely the defence of the forum's fundamental legal principles or moral values.[96] Therefore, it should only be invoked after a court has examined the content of a foreign law and the result it may bring about.[97]

Second, a court should also consider the extent of the forum contacts of the case when invoking the 'social public interest' reservation or identifying mandatory rules. Protective rules of the forum should be reserved only if the forum state has a dominant interest of application in view of all circumstances of the case, which include the importance of the substantive concern, the closeness of the transaction to the forum state and the justified expectation of the party in need of protection. The strength of the reservation, as well as the justification of categorizing a rule as mandatory, depends on the quality of the connection between the forum state and the case or dispute.[98]

Ultimately, the use of social public interest reservation in contractual choice of law is dependent on the extent to which a forum is willing to sacrifice domestic interests for the application of foreign law thereby achieving fairness and predictability of international transactions.[99]

[95] See Guedj (1991) p. 667. [96] Guedj (1991) p. 679. [97] See Lagarde (1994) para 5.

[98] See Vischer (1992) p. 160; Hay (2008) p. 99; Qin (2008) pp. 162–163; Mills (2008) pp. 210–212. This issue is further analysed in the context of the 'One Country, Two Systems' regime. See Section 8.2.2 of Chapter 8.

[99] See Chen (1987) p. 456.

7

Ascertainment of the Foreign Law Chosen by Parties

Chapters 3 and 4 address the issues preliminary to the operation of the party autonomy principle: (1) the existence of parties' choice of the governing law of their contract, (2) the validity of their choice, and (3) the 'law' that can be chosen by parties.

Once the issues in Chapters 3 and 4 are resolved and the parties appear to have agreed on a certain foreign law to govern their contract, three further issues remain to be solved: (1) whether the introduction of the selected foreign law is dependent on one (or both) of the parties' pleading it; (2) how the content of the selected foreign law is established; and (3) the effects of the failure to ascertain the selected foreign law. These issues are addressed in this chapter.

An analysis of these issues is essential to an understanding of the operation of party autonomy in Chinese law. The analysis reveals that in practice, the approach to these issues can hinder the effective operation of the party autonomy principle.

This chapter first analyses the provisions concerning the ascertainment of foreign law before the Law on the Application of Laws to Foreign-related Civil Relationships (2010 Conflicts Statute)[1] came into effect, and illustrates the problems existing in the cases where parties have made an effective choice of foreign law in their contract. It then looks at the new rule provided in the 2010 Conflicts Statute and the interpretations provided by the Supreme People's Court (SPC), and examines how they respond to the problems. In Sections 7.4 and 7.5, the chapter further analyses the remaining uncertainties in the greater context of civil litigation in China.

[1] It was adopted at the 17th meeting of the Standing Committee of the 11th NPC on 28 October 2010 and became effective on 1 April 2011.

7.1 Development of the Rules on Ascertainment of Foreign Law: Outstanding Issues

7.1.1 Article 193 of the 1988 Opinions

Before the 2010 Conflicts Statute, there was no provision in Chinese legislation concerning the ascertainment of foreign law. In October 1987, the SPC issued Response of the Supreme People's Court to Certain Questions Concerning the Application of the Foreign Economic Contract Law (1987 Response).[2] Article 2(11) stipulated:

> If a people's court is unable to determine the content of a foreign law in a case where that law should be applied, the court may ascertain the content via: (1) provision of the particulars by the parties concerned; (2) provision of the particulars by the Chinese embassy or consulate in the relevant country; (3) provision of the particulars by the embassy or consulate of the relevant country in China; or (4) provision of the particulars by a Chinese or foreign legal expert.[3]
>
> If details of the law in question are still unable to be ascertained after the use of the above-mentioned approaches, the case may be dealt with in accordance with the corresponding Chinese law.

The article specified that it was a court's responsibility to ascertain the content of an applicable foreign law by looking at certain forms of information. It listed the approaches by which the content of foreign law could be provided, and parties' provision of the information on the selected law was one of them. This article was later superseded by Article 193 of The Opinions Concerning Implementation and Application of the General Principles of the Civil Law of the People's Republic of China (Provisional) (1988 Opinions).[4] Article 193 provides:

> The applicable foreign law may be ascertained through the following ways: (1) provided by the parties; (2) provided by the central organ of the other state party who has concluded convention on judicial assistance with the People's Republic of China; (3) provided by China's embassy or consulate in the foreign country; (4) provided by the embassy of the

[2] It was issued by the SPC on 19 October 1987 and invalidated on 13 July 2000.

[3] The Chinese term of '*tigong*' is used in this article, which should be translated into 'provision' in English. But the meaning of this word seems to be 'submission' in the context. It means that the content of the applicable foreign law can be ascertained by a court through the submission of the relevant information by parties, legal experts or the entities mentioned in this article.

[4] It was issued by the SPC on 2 April 1988; Articles 88, 94, 115, 117, 118 and 177 therein were invalidated by the SPC on 18 December 2008.

> foreign country in China; and (5) provided by Chinese or foreign legal experts. If the applicable foreign law still cannot be ascertained through the above ways, the law of the People's Republic of China may apply.

Article 193 only listed the approaches. It failed to address four important issues: (1) how a foreign law should be introduced into court; (2) who should ultimately bear the responsibility of ascertaining the content of that law;[5] (3) as to the latter four approaches listed in Article 193, who should inform the relevant entities to provide the information on foreign law;[6] and (4) how a court should evaluate the information on the content of a foreign law and determine whether the law is successfully ascertained or not.

In cases where parties had effectively selected a foreign law to govern their contract, the first issue turned on the question whether the introduction of the selected foreign law was dependent on one (or both) of the parties' pleading it, or alternatively, a court should introduce the selected law *ex officio* according to Article 145 of the Civil Law and Article 126 of the Contract Law.[7] Since Article 193 of the 1988 Opinions provided that the content of a foreign law may be 'provided by parties', three further questions arose concerning the second and third issue. First, were parties under an obligation to provide the information of the foreign law that they have selected? Second, was it the responsibility of the parties alone to inform the other entities mentioned in Article 193 to provide information? Third, what would be the result of their failure to do so? These questions arose because Article 193 did not differentiate the issue of 'who bore the responsibility to ascertain a foreign law' from the issue 'what were the available approaches for establishing the content of a foreign

[5] Though this issue was specified in Article 2(11) of the 1987 Response, it was not addressed in Article 193 of the 1988 Opinions. After the 1987 Response was invalidated by the SPC, this issue remained unclear until the 2010 Conflicts Statute came into effect. See Section 7.2.1; see also Qi (2011) p. 136; Huang and Jiang (2011) p. 55.

[6] Article 2(11) of the 1987 Response specified that the approaches were to be used by a court. Article 193 of the 1988 Opinions did not clarify this point. It mixed two issues together: (1) who had the responsibility to supply the information on foreign law; and (2) what kind of information could be accepted by a court. Since the other entities listed in Article 193 normally were not parties in an international civil litigation, it was not clear who should seek the help from these entities in providing particulars of a foreign law.

[7] Both articles provide that parties to a foreign-related contract may choose the law applicable to their contract. The Civil Law was adopted on 12 April 1986 at the 4th Session of the 6th NPC and became effective on 1 January 1987; the Contract Law was adopted by the 2nd Session of the 9th NPC on 15 March 1999 and became effective on 1 October 1999.

law'. As a result, people's courts would not actively engage in ascertaining a foreign law as they did not consider they had such a responsibility. Requiring the parties to provide the content of a foreign law thus became the approach that was most frequently, or even solely, used by courts.[8]

Furthermore, as the criteria for determining whether the applicable foreign law could be ascertained were not clear, a court enjoyed very broad power in addressing the fourth issue and could easily come to the decision that Chinese law should be applied. These ambiguities have resulted in inconsistent judgments in practice.

In *Shenglun Import and Export Co. Ltd.* v. *Tianjin-Inchon International Passenger & Cargo Co. Ltd. and Tianjin-Inchon International Passenger & Cargo Co. Ltd. (Tianjin)*,[9] a dispute arose concerning the carrier's releasing cargoes without the original bills of lading. There was a clause in the bills providing that disputes that may arise concerning the bill should be resolved according to English law. The Tianjin Maritime Court decided that Chinese law was applicable because neither of the parties pleaded the law of other jurisdictions or submitted the evidence of foreign law to the court during the proceedings. The court obviously mixed two different issues: the need for the parties to plead the selected foreign law and the way in which that law could be ascertained. The latter issue would only arise after English law was introduced into court and the court determined that it should be applied. In this case, the court did not deny that the choice of English law in the bills was effective. If the court did assume that the introduction of English law was dependent on the parties' pleading, it should have directly decided that PRC law, as the forum law, should be applied because no other law was pleaded. However, it additionally based its decision on the parties' failure to prove the content of English law. But if English law was never introduced into court proceedings, the court did not need to consider whether English law was established at all.

In *German Reconstruction Bank* v. *Abu Dhabi Container Lines P.J.S.C.*,[10] the parties chose English law in their loan contract. The plaintiff pleaded Chinese law at trial without providing specific reasons

[8] See Xiao (2010) pp. 162–163.

[9] 30 July 2002, Tianjin Maritime Court. Tianjin-Inchon International Passenger & Cargo Co. Ltd. was incorporated in Korea.

[10] 21 June 2002, Shanghai Maritime Court. German Reconstruction Bank was incorporated in Germany and Abu Dhabi Container Lines P.J.S.C. was incorporated in the United Arab Emirates.

for its reliance on the law. The defendant did not appear in court proceedings. The Shanghai Maritime Court decided that the choice of law clause in the contract represented the parties' mutual intention and was not avoiding any mandatory rules of China. Therefore it should be held effective and English law was the governing law. The court said that the right to choose or change the governing law of a contract after a dispute arose was a right in civil law, not a procedural right. The defendant's failure to respond to the plaintiff's pleading in court hearings should not be taken as an acceptance of the plaintiff's change of the governing law. The governing law of the loan contract was still English law. But Chinese law was finally applied in the decision because neither of the parties provided the content of English law and the court found the law could not be ascertained. In this case, the court, on its own motion, examined the effect of the choice of law clause and the applicability of the selected English law, and distinguished these issues from how the content of English law should be established.

The previous two cases illustrate that people's courts had different understandings on how the foreign law selected by parties in contract should be introduced into court. As to the ascertainment of the content of foreign law, both courts considered the issue as one *totally* dependent on parties' provision of the relevant content of the selected law. They did not resort to the other approaches listed in Article 193 of the 1988 Opinions on Civil Law, but seemed to consider that only the parties were responsible for providing information on foreign law in cases where parties had chosen a foreign law.[11] The courts concerned might also have understood the latter

[11] This approach was adopted in other cases in ascertaining the content of the foreign law chosen by parties in contract. In *Kincheng-Tokyo Finance Company Ltd.* v. *Fullrate Enterprises Ltd.* (19 September 1991, Shenzhen Intermediate People's Court), both companies were incorporated in Hong Kong. The defendant could not repay the money it borrowed from the plaintiff and the latter sued the former in Shenzhen Intermediate People's Court as the estates which were owned by the defendant and mortgaged to the plaintiff was situate in Shenzhen. The court held that the parties had effectively selected Hong Kong law in their loan contract. Since neither of the parties could provide the Hong Kong statute or case law on loan and mortgage in the period stipulated by the court, the court held that Hong Kong law could not be ascertained and Chinese law should be applied according to Article 193 of the 1988 Opinions. In *Chongqing Lifan Industry Group and Chongqing Zhonglv Carriage and Trade Co. Ltd.* v. *Guangdong Yongbang Jingmao International Forwarding Co. Ltd., Maolin Express (Hong Kong) Co. Ltd. and Guangdong Zhongwaiyun Huangpu Storage and Forwarding Co. Ltd.* (20 May 2004, Guangzhou Maritime Court), Maolin Express (Hong Kong) Co. Ltd. was incorporated in Hong Kong and a dispute arose concerning the international carriage of goods by sea contract between the parties. Hong Kong law was selected as the governing law in the bills

four approaches in Article 193 as ones that should only be initiated by parties when the foreign law was chosen by them. But even though one of the parties provided evidence on the content of the selected law, the criteria by which a court evaluated the evidence were not clear.

In *Hong Kong Jingchuan International Shipping Group* v. *Huawei Offshore Shipping Ltd. and Rescue and Salvage Bureau of Ministry of Transport of PRC (Shanghai)*,[12] a dispute arose concerning the towage contract between the plaintiff and the first defendant. The plaintiff was incorporated in Hong Kong. The parties agreed in their contract that it should be interpreted in accordance with, and governed by, English law. The plaintiff did not provide evidence of English law. The first defendant submitted an opinion from an English lawyer concerning the relevant English law. The court held that the parties' choice of English law was effective, but that normally the opinions from a lawyer could not be accepted as sufficient evidence of foreign law. Since neither of the parties proved the content of English law to the satisfaction of the court and English law could not be ascertained through the other approaches stipulated in Article 193 of the 1988 Opinions, the court decided that Chinese law should be applied. In this case, the court did not analyse in detail why a legal opinion from an English lawyer was not sufficient. Nor did it indicate whether the other approaches had been tried by the court to ascertain the content of English law. The court's decision on this issue is not, therefore, very helpful.

The three cases in this section demonstrate how the lack of clear rules on the ascertainment of foreign law led to inconsistency in judicial practice. Obviously, this led, in turn, to uncertainty in the operation of the party autonomy principle in contractual choice of law.

7.1.2 *Article 9 of the 2007 Provisions*

The difficulties and ambiguities existing in the ascertainment of foreign law were brought to the attention of the SPC by lower people's courts. In

of lading concerned. Guangzhou Maritime Court held that the parties' choice of law was effective. However, since none of the parties submitted the content of Hong Kong law to the court, the law cannot be ascertained and Chinese law should be applied according to Article 193 of the 1988 Opinions.

12 See Jin (1998) pp. 466–472. This case was decided by the Guangzhou Maritime Court. From the available reports about this case on the Internet and in the book, no information is provided as to when the judgment was made. It was only mentioned in the reports that the plaintiff sued the defendants on 20 July 1997.

2007, the SPC issued Provisions on Several Issues Concerning the Application of the Law in Trials of Foreign-related Civil and Commercial Contract Disputes (2007 Provisions),[13] which contained two provisions on the ascertainment of foreign law. Article 9 of the 2007 Provisions provided:

> When parties select the law of a foreign country as the law applicable to a contractual dispute or change their selection of the applicable law into the law of a foreign country, they shall provide or prove the relevant content of the foreign law.
>
> When determining that the law of a foreign country is applicable to a contractual dispute pursuant to the principle of closest connection, a people's court may ascertain on its own motion, or require the parties to provide or prove, the relevant content of the foreign law.
>
> If neither the parties nor the people's court can ascertain the content of the foreign law through appropriate means, the people's court may apply the law of the People's Republic of China.

This provision only specified the role of parties and a court respectively in the ascertainment of foreign law, depending on how the governing law is determined in contractual cases. It did not respond to the problems outlined in the previous section. As is revealed in the analysis to come, this article further hindered the operation of the party autonomy principle.

A Ambiguity Concerning the Introduction of Foreign Law into Court

Article 9 did not clarify how a foreign law should be introduced into court, and, combined with Article 4(2) of the 2007 Provisions, it created a further ambiguity concerning the introduction of foreign law and the determination of parties' intention on choice of law. Article 4(2) provided:

> If the parties have not selected the law applicable to their contractual dispute but both cite the law of the same country or region and neither raises an objection to the application of that law, they shall be deemed to have selected that law as the law governing their contractual dispute.

This provision allowed parties to choose a foreign law after a dispute arose by both citing the same foreign law. It also encompassed the

[13] It was issued on 23 July 2007, became effective on 8 August 2007, and was invalidated by the SPC on 26 February 2013. See also Section 7.2.2.

situation where the parties did not choose the governing law in contract but both invoke Chinese law in court proceedings. Chinese law should thus be applied in this situation pursuant to Article 4(2). This rule was provided as the second sub-paragraph of Article 4, which permitted that parties can choose a law or alter a choice of law applicable to their contractual dispute by agreement.[14] That is to say, Article 4(2) only dealt with parties' freedom to choose the governing law. However, since Article 9 of the 2007 Provisions did not clarify whether the introduction of the selected foreign law was dependent on parties' pleading or not, it was not clear what was the true basis underlying the application of Chinese law pursuant to Article 4(2) in the situation where both parties relied on Chinese law. Consequently, Article 4(2) could be interpreted in two ways: (1) it could be read as indicating that the application of foreign law was dependent on parties' pleading and Chinese law should be applied in this circumstance since no party pleaded otherwise or (2) it only confirmed that parties could select the governing law after a dispute had been put before the court and Chinese law applied because the parties mutually chose it. In the latter regard, Article 4(2) was not different from Article 145(1) of the Civil Law and Article 126 of the Contract Law: both of these provisions allow parties to expressly agree on the governing law of their contract after a dispute arose. No matter which interpretation was adopted, the determination of the governing law would not be different in cases where parties both invoked Chinese law in the absence of a previous choice in contract. However, without a clear rule concerning the introduction of foreign law, the ambiguities of Article 4(2) created uncertainty and inconsistence in judicial practice.

In *Mediterranean Shipping Company S.A.* v. *Qingdao Jieyunda International Logistics Co. Ltd.*,[15] a dispute arose concerning a contract of international carriage of goods by sea between the parties. There was no choice of law clause in the bills of lading. In the first trial, the Tianjin Maritime Court held that since neither of the parties made any pleadings on the applicable law in this case, the Maritime Code of China should be applied. In the appeal, the Tianjin Higher People's Court decided that

[14] Article 4(1) of the 2007 Provisions read: 'If the parties reach a consensus through consultations on the selection or a change in the selection of the law applicable to their contract dispute prior to the conclusion of arguments in the court of first instance, the people's court should approve that.'

[15] 11 June 2010, Tianjin Higher People's Court. Mediterranean Shipping Company S.A. was incorporated in Switzerland.

since both parties invoked Chinese law in court proceedings, Chinese law should be the governing law as chosen by parties according to Article 145 (1) of the Civil Law.

This case was decided after the 2007 Provisions became effective. The main disputed issue in this case was the identification of the actual shipper and the obligation of the carrier to release cargo at the destination port in Shanghai harbour under the contract. The parties mainly disputed the facts of the case but not the legal issues. They debated whether the import custom clearance procedure was completed by referring to the Customs Law of China.[16] Neither of them made an argument as to the governing law of the contract. In its application for appeal, the Mediterranean Shipping Company claimed that the court's application of law at first instance was not right, but it did not argue which law should be applied. Although both courts applied Chinese law, the legal bases on which they relied were different. The Tianjin Maritime Court held that Chinese law was applied because no other laws were pleaded. Its analysis was based on its understanding of the procedural treatment of foreign law. The Tianjin Higher People's Court, by applying Article 145(1) of the Civil Law, clearly considered that the parties had made a choice of law agreement in court proceedings and Chinese law was selected as the governing law. Though it did not refer to Article 4(2) of the 2007 Provisions, its logic was the same as that of the article.[17]

This case reveals that a court may choose to take one of the two possible interpretations of Article 4(2) identified earlier. Moreover, it illustrates another ambiguity inherent in Article 4(2): by stipulating that 'both cite the law of the same country or region', it fails to differentiate the situations where the parties cite the law of the same country *as the governing law*, from those where the parties only refer to a national law for some other purpose.[18] In the aforementioned case, the Customs Law

[16] It was adopted at the 19th Meeting of the Standing Committee of the 6th NPC on 22 January 1987, amended for the first time on 8 July 2000, amended for the second time on 29 June 2013, amended for the third time on 28 December 2013, amended for the fourth time on 7 November 2016 and amended for the fifth time on 4 November 2017.

[17] The SPC considered that if, in the absence of a choice of law in contract, both parties relied on the law of the same jurisdiction and neither objected to the application of the law, they should be taken as having arrived at an agreement concerning the governing law. See Chen (2008) p. 262.

[18] Hook (2016) pp. 139–140 also considers whether exclusive reliance on forum law can be understood as an intention to choose the law of the forum as the governing law must depend on the facts of each case.

of China was referred to because the import custom clearance procedure could only be completed at the destination harbour in accordance with that law. The parties' reference to it did not necessarily mean that they selected Chinese law as the governing law.

Therefore, Article 4(2) of the 2007 Provisions not only increased the uncertainty surrounding the issue of how a foreign law should be introduced into court, but also blurred the determination of the parties' intention on choice of law. The purpose of the SPC in providing this rule was to help people's courts determine the governing law of a contract when both parties invoke the same law.[19] The provision was not necessary. Even before the 2010 Conflicts Statute became effective, the existing provisions on party autonomy in the Civil Law and Contract Law were sufficient to determine the governing law of a contract. Where both parties appear in court and rely on the same law, a court can easily verify the parties' intention by inquiring whether they agree to select the law of that same country as the governing law of their contract. Where one of the parties fails to appear in court, a court, in the absence of a previous choice of law in contract, should determine the governing law according to the closest connection principle. In cases where both parties rely on the same law that is different from the one they have chosen in contract, a court can interrogate the parties and determine whether they have agreed to change the governing law.[20] However, a rule similar to Article 4 (2) is adopted by the SPC in its interpretation of the 2010 Conflicts Statute.[21]

B The Responsibility to Ascertain the Selected Foreign Law

Compared with Article 2(11) of the 1987 Response, Article 9(1) of the 2007 Provisions did not specify who should ultimately bear the responsibility to ascertain the content of the foreign law selected by parties in

[19] See Chen (2008) p. 262.

[20] For example, in *The Oriental Scientific Instrument Zhejiang Import and Export Corporation* v. *Zim Israel Navigation Co. Ltd.* (16 July 2001, Ningbo Maritime Court), the defendant was incorporated in Israel and a dispute arose concerning the international carriage of goods by sea contract between the parties. Clause 24 of the bills of lading concerned selected the law of Israel as the governing law. But both parties invoked Chinese law in court and expressly agreed that Chinese law should be applied to solve their dispute. The Ningbo Maritime Court held that the parties should be taken as having changed their selection of the governing law into Chinese law. Chinese law was therefore applied in the judgment.

[21] See Section 7.2.2.

contract. Article 9(1) only provided that when parties choose a foreign law as the law governing their contractual dispute, they 'shall provide or prove the relevant content of the foreign law'. Moreover, it did not list the approaches through which the content of foreign law could be ascertained. Did it mean that under this circumstance, the *only* approach applicable to ascertain the content of foreign law was the provision of the relevant information by parties, and once the parties failed to do so, a court should determine that the content of the selected law could not be ascertained and Chinese law should be applied?

According to the SPC's explanation, Article 9 of the 2007 Provisions meant that the obligation to ascertain an applicable foreign law should be shared by people's court and parties. In cases where parties have chosen a foreign law in contract, the SPC assumed that parties must have estimated the legal risk in the context of the foreign law before their choice, and therefore they should be able to bear the burden of providing the content of the law they have voluntarily chosen.[22] In judicial practice, no matter who provides information on foreign law, it is ultimately a court that assesses the information, determines the content of the law and then applies it to solve the dispute between parties.[23] That is to say, what Article 9(1) required was that parties should *assist* the court in ascertaining the content of the law they have selected by providing the relevant content.[24] However, it was not clear how to interpret the parties' obligation to assist. Did it mean that a court, in cases where parties had chosen a foreign law in contract, was not under any obligation to resort to other approaches to ascertain the content of the law, but could just depend on the information provided by parties? Was there any exception to this rule?

The 2007 Provisions did not list the avenues through which the content of foreign law could be submitted. The SPC considered that in modern society, the avenues to obtaining information are not limited to those listed in Article 193 of the 1988 Opinions, and it was not necessary to list all the available avenues in the 2007 Provisions. Courts and parties are free to adopt the avenues they consider appropriate, including those provided in Article 193.[25]

[22] See Chen (2008) pp. 266–267.
[23] The role and power of a court in civil litigation in China are discussed in Sections 7.3 and 7.4.
[24] See Chen (2008) p. 266. [25] See Chen (2008) p. 267.

C The Evaluation of the Information on Foreign Law

Article 10 of the 2007 Provisions read:

> If the parties have no disagreements on the ascertained particulars of foreign law after cross-examination, people's court should confirm the content of the law accordingly. If disagreements exist, the court should examine the content and make a determination.

The SPC wanted to provide instructions to the lower courts on how to determine the content of a foreign law when faced with the information on the law. However, Article 10 failed to achieve this. First, it simply permitted a court to confirm the content of a foreign law that had been agreed upon by parties, without providing any exception to this rule. In this regard, the SPC failed to consider what would happen if a judge, based on his or her legal expertise, found that the uncontested information or evidence on foreign law was patently absurd.[26] Second, when a court is faced with conflicting evidence or parties have disagreements with each other on the content of foreign law, Article 10 only stated that a court should examine the evidence and make its own determination. It was said that the SPC purposed a 'simple and convenient' rule to deal with this complicated situation.[27] However, the rule provided no guidance at all. As has been illustrated in Section 7.1.1, in the absence of clear rules concerning the evaluation of the information on foreign law provided by parties, it is hard to predict how the information would be assessed and how the parties could be assured that the law they have selected can actually be applied.

In summary, the 2007 Provisions failed to respond to the existing problems and uncertainties in judicial practice, and left them to be solved by people's courts on a case-by-case basis. Consequently, a court had rather broad discretionary power in determining whether a foreign law could be ascertained.[28] That further hindered the operation of party autonomy.

7.2 Ascertainment of Foreign Law in the 2010 Conflicts Statute

7.2.1 Article 10 of the 2010 Conflicts Statute

A specific rule on the ascertainment of foreign law is included in the 2010 Conflicts Statute. Article 10 of the Statute provides:

26 See Xiao (2010) p. 175; Section 7.2.2.
27 See Chen (2008) p. 267.
28 See Zhang (2003) p. 97.

> The foreign law applicable to a foreign-related civil relation is ascertained by the people's court, arbitration institution or administrative authority. If parties choose a foreign law to be applied, they should provide that law [OR: If one of the parties chooses a foreign law to be applied, he or she should provide that law].[29]
>
> When a foreign law cannot be ascertained or it is silent on the relevant issues, the law of the People's Republic of China applies.

Compared with Article 193 of the 1988 Opinions and Article 9 of the 2007 Provisions, Article 10 clarifies that a court should ascertain the applicable foreign law in civil litigation, and it can require the parties to assist it under the stipulated circumstances.[30] When the Legislative Affairs Commission of the Standing Committee of the National People's Congress (NPCSC) was drafting the 2010 Conflicts Statute, some scholars suggested the Statute should provide that the parties bear the responsibility of proving a foreign law.[31] Most scholars did not agree, however, with that suggestion. They considered that the suggestion took foreign law as fact, which was against the prevailing principle in China that foreign law should be taken as law.[32] After debate, the scholarly consensus was that judges should bear the primary responsibility of ascertaining foreign law, while parties may be required to assist them under certain circumstances, resulting in Article 10 in its current form.[33]

According to the first sentence of Article 10(1), in a contractual litigation, it is a court that ascertains the foreign law applicable to a contract. The only exception is when the parties (or one of the parties) 'choose(s) a foreign law to be applied', they (or that party) should provide the content of the law. That is to say, in this situation, the parties (or one of them) bear(s) the responsibility of assisting the court in ascertaining

[29] The two possible translations are provided here because the meaning of the original Chinese is ambiguous and it is not clear whether the single or plural form of the word 'party / *dang shi ren*' should be used. See the analysis that immediately follows the quotation.

[30] See Xiao (2010) pp. 187–188; Wan (2011a) p. 78.

[31] Article 11 of the draft of the 2010 Conflicts Statute for the second reading stated: 'If the applicable foreign law is chosen by the parties, the parties shall provide that law; if it is not chosen by the parties, the court, arbitration tribunal, or administrative organ concerned can either ascertain *ex officio* or require the parties to provide the applicable foreign law ... ' The Draft is available at the official website of the NPC: www.npc.gov.cn/huiyi/cwh/1116/2010-08/28/content_1593162.htm.

[32] For the fact/law distinction concerning the nature of foreign law, see Section 7.3.

[33] See Qi (2011) pp. 137–138.

the selected foreign law by providing the content of the law. The problem is: when will this rule be applied?

In this regard, the wording of the second sentence of Article 10(1) is problematic.[34] First, it is not clear whether the word 'parties' means one of the parties in litigation, or both of the parties. Only the Chinese word '*dangshi ren*' (party) is used in the original Chinese text of this article. Nothing indicates whether the word is used in its single form or plural form. Second, the meaning of the phrase '*xuanze shiyong*' (choose a foreign law to be applied) is also ambiguous: does it mean that parties mutually choose a foreign law as the governing law of their contract, or that parties (or one of the parties) claim(s) that a foreign law should be applied in court proceedings?[35] Given the aforementioned two uncertainties, the second sentence of Article 10(1) is capable of encompassing five different situations in cases involving international contracts: (1) the parties have effectively chosen a foreign law to govern their contract but neither of them pleads that law in court proceedings; (2) the parties have effectively chosen a foreign governing law and one of them pleads that law in proceedings; (3) both parties plead the law that they have chosen in contract; (4) in the absence of an express choice of the governing law, one of the parties pleads a foreign law in accordance with the closest connection principle; and (5) in the absence of a previous choice of law, the parties plead two different foreign laws respectively according to the closest connection principle.[36]

[34] See Chen (2012) p. 238.

[35] Zhang (2011) p. 115 translated this phrase as 'choose to apply a foreign law', the meaning of which is also ambiguous. Compared with Article 9(1) of the 2007 Provisions, the wording of Article 10(1) is rather unclear. Article 9(1) clearly stipulated 'When parties select a foreign law *as the law applicable in a contract dispute* or change their selection of *the law applicable in a contract dispute* to a foreign law ...' (emphasis added). Chen (2012) p. 238 pointed out that Article 10(1) of the 2010 Conflicts Statute may only refer to the situation where both parties to a foreign-related relation select a foreign law *as the governing law* of their relation, but the wording of the provision was problematic and thus its meaning is not clear. Xiao (2010) pp. 188–189 also argued that 'choose a foreign law to be applied' meant the parties mutually chose the law as the governing law. However, since it was not clear whether 'party' means one or both of the parties, she also found this provision ambiguous.

[36] Therefore, it is not clear whether a party is required to provide the content of foreign law when, in the absence of a previous choice of law in contract, he or she pleads a foreign law in accordance with the closest connection principle. This issue is beyond the scope of this book. It may be helpful to mention that in *Fugong Tenghong Foreign Trade Co. Ltd.* v. *Li Changkui* (22 December 2015, Yunnan Higher People's Court), the courts of first trial and appeal both considered that when the defendant pleaded the law of the Republic of

Where parties have previously chosen a foreign governing law in their contract, does the provision mean that only the party who pleads the selected foreign law bears the responsibility of assisting the court to ascertain the law? If so, can parties avoid the obligation by not pleading the foreign law they have chosen in court proceedings? Alternatively, does it mean that both parties are under the obligation to assist the court once they have effectively agreed on a choice of foreign law in contract? As is analysed shortly, whether the parties are required to assist a court is of practical importance in the ascertainment of foreign law.[37]

Moreover, how should the parties' (or a party's) responsibility to assist the court be interpreted? How can a court determine whether that responsibility is discharged? Besides assistance from parties, does a court have any further responsibility to ascertain a selected foreign law by itself? Article 10 provides no answers to these questions.

7.2.2 *The SPC's Interpretation of the 2010 Conflicts Statute*

In December 2012, the SPC issued Interpretation of the Supreme People's Court on Certain Issues Concerning the Application of the Law on the Application of Laws to Foreign-related Civil Relations' (1) (Interpretation of the 2010 Conflicts Statute (1)).[38] There are three provisions relevant to the ascertainment of foreign law.

A A Further Ambiguity Concerning the Procedural Treatment of Foreign Law and Determination of Parties' Intention

Article 8 reads:

> People's courts should allow the parties to agree on the selection or change of the selection of the applicable laws before the end of the court debate at first instance.
>
> Where all the parties concerned invoke the laws of the same country and do not have any disagreement on the applicable laws, the people's

the Union of Myanmar on the basis of the closest connection principle but failed to provide the evidence on the law, it should be held that the law of Myanmar could not be ascertained according to Article 10(1) of the 2010 Conflicts Statute. Therefore, Chinese law was determined as the law governing the contract in this case. The courts' interpretation of Article 10(1) encompassed Situation (4) as mentioned in the text.

[37] See Part B of Section 7.2.2.

[38] It was issued by the SPC on 28 December 2012 and became effective on 7 January 2013.

court may determine that the parties concerned have chosen the law applicable to their foreign-related civil relation.

This provision is similar to Article 4 of the 2007 Provisions, which has been invalidated by the SPC. The only difference is that Article 8(2) does not involve the prerequisite 'in the absence of a previous choice of the governing law in contract'. As argued earlier, Article 4(2) of the 2007 Provisions not only increased the uncertainty on the issue of how a foreign law should be introduced into court, but also blurred the determination of parties' intention on the governing law.[39] The SPC's purpose in including Article 8 in the Interpretation of the 2010 Conflicts Statute (1) is the same as that behind Article 4(2) in the 2007 Provisions: to help the lower courts in determining the governing law in the situation where all the parties invoke the law of the same country in court proceedings.[40] However, Article 8(2) creates problems.

First, Article 8(2) again causes uncertainty with respect to the introduction of foreign law into court. Without the prerequisite in Article 4(2) of the 2007 Provisions, Article 8(2) of the Interpretation is applicable in cases where the parties have previously chosen the governing law in contract. It encompasses the situation where the parties both invoke the law of the same country which is different from the one they have selected in contract. Does Article 8(2) mean that in this situation, a court can directly decide that the law of that same country applies and ignore the law previously selected? If so, when parties both invoke Chinese law in court proceedings, is Chinese law applied as the forum law because neither of the parties pleads a foreign law, or is it applied as the governing law because the parties are taken to have changed their previous choice into Chinese law? Does it indicate that the introduction of foreign law is dependent on parties' pleading?

Even if Article 8(2) was originally designed to deal with parties' choice of the governing law but not to address the procedural treatment of foreign law in court, *Mediterranean Shipping Company S.A.* v. *Qingdao Jieyunda International Logistics Co. Ltd.* as discussed has demonstrated that parties' reference to the same law does *not* necessarily mean that they choose the law of the same country *as the governing law*.[41]

[39] See Part A of Section 7.1.2. [40] See Gao (2013) p. 41.

[41] See n 15 and the discussion of that case. Sometimes parties may even expressly point out that their invocation of Chinese law did not mean that they intended to choose Chinese law as the governing law. For example, in *PICC Property Insurance Company Zhanjiang Economic and Technological Development Zone Branch* v. *Cross Seas Shipping*

Moreover, Article 3 of the 2010 Conflicts Statute stipulates that parties' choice of the law governing their relation should be made *expressly*.[42] Article 8(2) of the SPC's Interpretation, however, allows parties to implicitly choose a law by both invoking it. This approach for determining parties' intention on choice of law is neither based upon the terms of the contract nor in accordance with the circumstances of the case.[43] It is therefore not appropriate to adopt this approach in the application of the party autonomy principle.

Second, while Article 4(2) of the 2007 Provisions was only applicable in contractual cases involving foreign elements,[44] the SPC does not specify the scope of Article 8(2). Does Article 8(2) indicate that even in cases where parties are *not* allowed to select the governing law, they can choose a law, particularly the forum law, by both invoking that law in court proceedings? In most if not all of the adjudicated cases where people's courts adopted the approach stipulated in Article 4(2) of the 2007 Provisions, the 'law of the same country or region' that the parties concerned relied on, was Chinese law.[45] The parties' freedom to choose

Corporation, Croatia Line and Lucky Seaway Service SPTE Ltd. (29 December 2000, Guangzhou Maritime Court; 9 July 2002, Guangdong Higher People's Court), Cross Seas Shipping Corporation cited Chinese law for its argument on the limitation period in the appeal, but stated that the citation did not mean that it had selected Chinese law as the governing law of the contract for carriage of goods by sea. Cross Seas Shipping Corporation and Croatia Line were incorporated in Panama and Croatia respectively.

42 Article 3 of the 2010 Conflicts Statute reads: 'Parties concerned may, in accordance with the law, expressly choose laws applicable to foreign-related civil relations.' See also Wan (2011a) pp. 31–32.

43 Both Article 3(1) of the 1980 Rome Convention on the Law Applicable to Contractual Obligations and Article 3(1) of the Regulation (EC) No 593/2008 of the European Parliament and of the Council of 17 June 2008 on the Law Applicable to Contractual Obligations (Rome I) stipulate that parties' choice of law in contract can be clearly demonstrated by the terms of the contract or the circumstances of the case. This is to recognize the possibility that a court may, in light of all the facts, find that the parties have made a real choice of law although this is not expressly stated in the contract. See Giuliano and Lagarde (1980) p. 17. For criticism on the approach as provided in Article 8(2) of the Interpretation of the 2010 Conflicts Statute (1), see also Song (2007) pp. 151–155.

44 The SPC stated in the 2007 Provisions: 'In order to correctly adjudicate cases involving foreign-related civil and commercial contracts, these Provisions have been formulated pursuant to the relevant provisions of the General Principles of Civil Law, the Contract Law, etc.'

45 Xu calculated that among the 282 foreign-related cases that he had examined, in more than thirty cases the courts adopted the approach provided in Article 4(2) of the 2007 Provisions. In all the cases cited by him, the law invoked by parties in court proceedings was Chinese law. See J. Xu (2010) pp. 95–102 and the cases cited there.

the governing law in categories of civil relations other than contract is beyond the scope of this book. However, if parties, in accordance with Article 8(2), can 'choose' Chinese law by both citing the law in court proceedings even though they are not allowed by the private international law rules to select the governing law in the relation concerned, then there is the possibility that Article 8(2) may enlarge the scope of party autonomy.[46] In this regard, the SPC may have provided an interpretation that is wider in scope than the law itself.[47] It remains to be seen whether Article 8(2) of the Interpretation of the 2010 Conflicts Statute (1) will encourage the application of Chinese law in judicial practice.

As has been pointed out in Section 7.1.2, Article 8(2) is not necessary as a court can interrogate the parties about their intention on the governing law in proceedings.[48] The rule therefore creates more problems than it solves.[49]

B Parties' Responsibility to Assist a Court in the Ascertainment of Foreign Law

Article 17 stipulates:

> Where a people's court fails to obtain the content of a foreign law[50] through channels such as parties' provision of the content, the approaches specified by the international treaty that has already been applicable to the People's Republic of China, or provision of the content by domestic or foreign legal experts, the court may determine that the foreign law concerned cannot be ascertained.

46 Whether parties can 'choose' the forum law by not pleading a foreign law in Chinese courts is further discussed in Section 7.4.

47 Article 3 of the 2010 Conflicts Statute provides that parties should choose the governing law 'in accordance with law'. That is to say, in the areas where parties' freedom to choose the governing law is not explicitly allowed by law, they are *not* permitted to select the applicable law. Article 6 of the Interpretation of the 2010 Conflicts Statute (1) confirms this point by stipulating that where the laws do not explicitly allow the parties to select the governing law of a foreign-related civil relation but the parties choose the applicable law, people's courts shall render their selection invalid. See Gao (2013) p. 40; Wan (2011a) pp. 30–31. However, the relationship between these rules and Article 8(2) is not clear.

48 See Part A of Section 7.1.2.

49 Cf Tang, Xiao and Huo (2016) para. 8.09. They argued that the scenario provided in Article 8(2) is a 'typical' one where the implied choice of law is 'approved by the parties' conduct', and that in this circumstance parties' implied choice of law 'will not give rise to many disputes or uncertainty and is accepted by Chinese courts'.

50 The original Chinese text states '*huode waiguo falü*' (obtain a foreign law), the meaning of which is not clear. Based on the subject of this provision and the issue it addresses, the author translates the phrase as 'obtain the content of a foreign law'.

> Where, in accordance with Article 10(1) of the Law on the Application of Laws to Foreign-related Civil Relations, the parties concerned should provide the content of a foreign law but fail to do so without legitimate grounds within the reasonable time limit specified by the people's court, the court may determine that the foreign law concerned cannot be ascertained.

Article 17(2) provides the criteria for determining that a foreign law cannot be ascertained under the circumstances stipulated in Article 10(1) of the 2010 Conflicts Statute: when the exception in Article 10(1) is triggered, parties are under an obligation to provide the content of a foreign law within the period specified by a court, and if they fail to do so without legitimate grounds, a court does not need to resort to other approaches but can directly decide that the foreign law cannot be ascertained. Article 17(2) clarifies the aforementioned uncertainty concerning a court's responsibility where parties are under an obligation to assist in ascertaining a foreign law: the court can specify a time limit and choose to rely solely on parties' provision of the content of the law. However, the question remains when the exception in Article 10(1) of the 2010 Conflicts Statute is triggered. Article 17(2) does not cure the problematic wording of Article 10(1). Furthermore, it involves two uncertainties.

First, the nature of the 'reasonable time limit specified by court' is not clear. Article 65 of the Civil Procedure Law provides:[51]

> A party shall provide evidence for his or her claims in a timely manner.
>
> A people's court shall, according to the claims of a party and the circumstances of the trial of a case, determine the evidence to be provided by a party and the time limit for the provision of evidence. Where it is difficult for a party to provide evidence within the time limit, the party may apply to the people's court for an extension, and the people's court may appropriately extend the time limit upon application of the party. Where a party provides any evidence beyond the time limit, the people's court shall order the party to provide an explanation, and if the party refuses to explain or the party's explanation is not acceptable, the people's court may, according to different circumstances, deem the evidence inadmissible or accept the evidence but impose an admonition or a fine on the party.

[51] It was adopted at the 4th Session of the 7th NPC on 9 April 1991, amended for the first time at the 30th Meeting of the Standing Committee of the 10th NPC on 28 October 2007, amended for the second time at the 28th Meeting of the Standing Committee of the 11th NPC on 31 August 2012 and amended for the third time at the 28th Meeting of the Standing Committee of the 12th NPC on 27 June 2017.

It is not clear whether the 'time limit' mentioned in Article 17(2) of the Interpretation should be determined according to the criteria in Article 65(2) of the Civil Procedure Law.[52]

Second, the SPC does not specify what can be considered as 'legitimate grounds'. Article 65(2) of the Civil Procedure Law allows a party to apply for an extension of the time limit when faced with difficulty, but such flexibility is not provided in Article 17(2). Article 17 only stipulates that if parties fail to provide the content of a foreign law without legitimate grounds, a court can determine that the law cannot be ascertained. But what if the parties have difficulties? Can that be taken as a 'legitimate ground'? In Minutes of the Second National Working Conference on the Trial of Foreign-related Commercial and Maritime Cases (2005 Minutes),[53] the SPC stated in Point 51(2) that where it is difficult for a party to provide the content of a foreign law, the party concerned may request the court to ascertain the foreign law *ex officio*. In fact, Article 10(1) of the 2010 Conflicts Statute does not explicitly exclude the possibility that a court may, upon the parties' request or on its own motion, resort to other approaches to ascertain a foreign law. Article 17(2) of the SPC's Interpretation therefore imposes a heavier burden on the parties.

C Assessment of the Information on Foreign Law

Article 18 of the Interpretation of the 2010 Conflicts Statute (1) reads:

> A court shall listen to the opinions of all the parties concerned on the content, interpretation and application of the applicable foreign law. Where the parties concerned do not raise any objection to the content, interpretation and application of such a law, the court may confirm the content. Where the parties concerned are in disagreement, the court shall determine the content through examination.

52 This issue is further discussed in Section 7.5.

53 It was issued by the SPC on 26 December 2005. The attendants of this conference included presidents and chief judges from higher people's courts who were in charge of the trial of foreign-related commercial and maritime cases, presidents of intermediate people's courts having jurisdiction over foreign-related commercial and maritime affairs who are in charge of the trial of foreign-related commercial and maritime cases, presidents of maritime courts and representatives of relevant departments under the Central Government. Although this document is not a judicial interpretation made by the SPC, it represented the consensus reached by the attendants concerning the solutions to the problems existing in judicial practice. It therefore provides some guidance in determining the issues that are not clearly resolved in legislation.

This provision is similar to Article 10 of the 2007 Provisions.[54] The only difference is that, while Article 10 provides that a court *should* confirm the content if parties have no disagreements, Article 18 of the Interpretation stipulates that a court *may* confirm the content if the parties do not raise any objection to that. Consequently, a court may refuse to recognize the content of a foreign law as agreed upon by parties if it finds that the uncontested information or evidence is patently absurd. However, Article 18 does not provide any guidance on how to evaluate the conflicting evidence on foreign law. It thus fails to provide helpful instructions on this issue.

7.3 Summary

Based on the analyses in Sections 7.1 and 7.2, it can be summarized that the fundamental uncertainties on the ascertainment of the foreign law chosen by parties mainly exist in two fields: the introduction of foreign law into court and the assessment of the information on foreign law. The former determines whether the foreign law selected by parties must be established at all. The latter is critical in a court's decision concerning whether the parties' obligation to assist is complete and whether a foreign law can be successfully ascertained.

Article 10 of the 2010 Conflicts Statute provides a particular rule on the ascertainment of foreign law, but its wording is problematic. The SPC has tried to provide some guidance in judicial practice through the Interpretation of the 2010 Conflicts Statute (1), but its attempt to do so brings about further uncertainties. Without clear rules on the introduction of foreign law into court and the assessment of information on foreign law, the heavy burden imposed on the parties becomes a substantial obstacle to the operation of the party autonomy principle. This is reinforced in the next two sections.

7.4 Introducing the Selected Foreign Law into Court

Article 10 of the 2010 Conflicts Statute stipulates how to ascertain an applicable foreign law, but not whether a foreign law should be applied or how it is introduced into court. The latter two issues concern whether a court should rule *ex officio* that foreign law is to be applied whenever this

[54] See Part C of Section 7.1.2.

is indicated by the relevant choice of law rule, or if it should apply foreign law only at the request of parties. As pointed out earlier, Article 8(2) of the Interpretation of the 2010 Conflicts Statute (1) creates a further ambiguity concerning the introduction of foreign law into court. In cases where parties have effectively chosen a foreign law to govern their contract, it is not clear whether the introduction of that law is dependent on one or both of the parties' pleading it.[55]

7.4.1 *The Fact/Law Distinction*

For the ascertainment of foreign law, it has been argued that the fundamental question to answer is whether foreign law is considered as law, proved and interpreted as such, or whether the law of another jurisdiction is merely a matter of fact.[56] The fact/law distinction concerning the nature and status of foreign law in national courts is also considered to be important and taken as a criterion in the analysis of the mechanism on ascertainment of foreign law by some Chinese scholars.[57] However, the distinction is not helpful in the analysis of whether a foreign law should be introduced into court.[58]

Even in common law, the distinction is not a matter of discerning the characteristics of foreign law to see whether they belong properly to the genus law, or the genus fact. On the contrary, in English law, issues tend to be placed in the category of fact or law because of the practical consequences of doing so. Historically, the reason why foreign laws came to be treated as fact was practical.[59] In *Mostyn* v. *Fabrigas*, Lord Mansfield said:[60]

> The way of knowing foreign laws is, by admitting them to be proved as facts . . .

This rationale for equating foreign law with fact indicates that foreign laws are fact because courts take the view that they cannot otherwise know their content. The fact doctrine in common law thus concerns how foreign law is established, but may have little or nothing to do with

[55] See Part A of Section 7.1.2 and Part A of Section 7.2.2. [56] See Dolinger (1995) p. 225.

[57] See Zhang (2003) p. 97; Liu (2007) chapter 2; Li, Ou, Jin and Zhang (2007) p. 189; Shen (2011) pp. 152–153. Both Zhang and Shen criticized that Article 193 of the 1988 Opinions failed to clarify whether the nature of foreign law should be categorized as fact or law.

[58] Nor is it applicable in China concerning the establishment of foreign law. See Sections 7.4.2 and 7.4.3.

[59] See Fentiman (2006) pp. 395–396. [60] (1774) 1 Cowp. 161, 174, per Lord Mansfield.

whether foreign law must be introduced in a given case. The latter issue is a private international law issue and should be determined according to the relevant choice of law rules of the forum.[61]

Once a choice of law rule indicates that a foreign law is applicable to a given case, a further issue arises as to whether a court, relying on the choice of law rule, should determine *ex officio* that the foreign law should be applied, or the applicability of the foreign law should depend on one or both of the parties' pleading of the law. This issue is related to the forum's tradition concerning the role of a judge.[62] Although the fact doctrine in English law does not deal with whether a foreign law must be established, it affects how a foreign law is introduced into court: being facts, foreign laws are subject to such principles of pleading as govern other facts.[63] The notion underlying the rule that foreign law must be pleaded is the adversarial principle in English civil litigation: courts are generally powerless to compel reliance upon foreign law.[64] Whether a foreign law should be applied in any case is still a matter for conflicts rules, not for the principles of pleading. The latter only determines *how* an applicable foreign law is introduced into court.

That is to say, whether a foreign law is applicable is related to the nature of conflict of laws rules. How the applicable law is introduced is dependent on the nature of the judicial process and the role of courts in a certain legal system.[65] What matters is not whether foreign law is taken as fact or law, but the mechanism for the application of private international law rules in civil litigation.

7.4.2 The Nature of Choice of Law Rules in China

Article 41 of the 2010 Conflicts Statute provides that parties may choose the laws applicable to their contract by agreement. Does it indicate that in

61 See Fentiman (1998) pp. 66–67.

62 See Hay, Borchers and Freer (2017) pp. 477–478.

63 See *King of Spain* v. *Machado* (1827) 4 Russ. 225, 239; *Ascherberg, Hopwood & Crew Ltd.* v. *Casa Musicale Sonzogno* [1971] 1 All ER 577, 579–580 (C.A.). There is, however, a statutory exception to this general rule. See Dicey, Morris and Collins (2012) para. 9–003.

64 See Fentiman (1998) pp. 64–65; Nishitani (2017) p. 15. The adversarial process in English civil procedure is subject to an increasing degree of judicial intervention, prompted by concerns over the system's protractedness and cost. But against the background of a changing legal framework, the orientation of English civil procedure remains adversarial and party-based, especially in connection with complex litigation. See Fentiman (1998) p. 174.

65 See Hartley (1996) p. 272.

a foreign-related case where parties have effectively chosen the law governing their contract, a court should determine the applicability of that law on its own motion, no matter whether that law is pleaded by one or both of the parties or not? This is related to the nature of private international law rules in China: are they mandatory in the sense that a court should apply them to determine the applicable law in a foreign-related case? Or is the application of these rules dependent on parties' pleading of a foreign law?

Article 7 of the Civil Procedure Law reads: 'People's courts must take the facts as the basis and the laws as the criterion when trying civil cases.' Accordingly, a court has a general duty to apply laws to the facts of a case. No distinction is made between different categories of legal rules in this provision. 'Laws' as mentioned in Article 7 thus encompasses substantive, procedural and also private international law rules in China's legal system.

Article 2 of the 2010 Conflicts Statute stipulates: 'Laws applicable to foreign-related civil relations *shall be determined in accordance with this Law*.' It indicates that whether a foreign law should be applied is determined by the choice of law rules contained in the Statute. Indeed, parties' pleading of foreign law is *not* a prerequisite for the applicability of foreign law in China, nor can parties avoid the conflicts rules by not pleading a foreign law.[66] Article 41 of the Statute is mandatory in the sense that no matter whether the foreign law chosen by parties is pleaded or not, a court should take that law as the governing law of their contract on condition that their choice is effective and no statutory restriction is triggered.

7.4.3 The Role and Power of a Court in International Civil Litigation

How a foreign law is introduced into court is also related to the role and power of a court in civil litigation. One of the fundamental tasks of China's Civil Procedure Law is to ensure that the courts establish the truth based on facts.[67] It is said that the Chinese civil procedural system

[66] See Guo (2007) pp. 4–5; Zheng and Zhang (2005).

[67] Article 2 of the Civil Procedure Law provides: 'The purposes of the Civil Procedure Law of the People's Republic of China are to protect the parties' exercise of procedural rights; ensure that a people's court finds facts, distinguishes right from wrong, applies law correctly and try civil cases in a timely manner; confirm civil rights and obligations; punish violations of civil law; protect the lawful rights and interests of the parties; educate citizens on consciously abiding by law; maintain the social and economic order; and guarantee smooth socialist development.'

is designed primarily to ascertain the truth.[68] For this purpose, Chinese law allows judges to play a more active role in adjudication than their counterparts in common law jurisdictions.[69] The characteristics of the judicial process in contemporary China may be traced back to the early 1950s, when the legal system of the PRC began to be established. The adjudication system and the style of work of Chinese courts were intended to be 'convenient to, maintain close ties with, and serve the masses'. It was said that only after a court had discovered the whole truth of a case and collected sufficient evidence could it make its judgment.[70]

Since the Civil Procedure Law in China was first adopted in 1982, it has been substantially amended four times, in 1991, 2007, 2012 and 2017 respectively. The purpose of the reform of the Civil Procedure Law since the 1990s has been to increase the burden of proof on the part of parties and weaken the power of judges in discovering the truth.[71] However, the Chinese civil litigation system remains a system based upon the inquisitorial model and the adversarial principle has not been used in China.[72]

First, while Article 64(1) of the Civil Procedure Law stipulates that a party shall bear the burden of providing evidence for his or her claims, Article 64(2) provides that a people's court shall investigate and collect evidence which a party and his or her litigation representative are unable to collect for some 'objective reasons'[73] and evidence which the people's court deems necessary for trying a case. Therefore, Chinese judges' determinations of facts are not restricted to the evidence presented at a hearing. They may conduct an independent investigation and collect evidence upon parties' request or on their own motion when necessary.

[68] Zhong and Yu (2004) p. 393.

[69] For the adversarial principle in English civil litigation, see n 64 and the accompanying text. For a comparative analysis between the Chinese and American systems, see Zhong and Yu (2004) p. 393.

[70] See the editorial published in People's Daily on 5 June 1951, quoted in He (1997) p. 121.

[71] See Zhong and Yu (2004) p. 400; Jiang and Wu (2002) pp. 25, 30.

[72] See Zhong and Yu (2004) p. 400; Jiang and Wu (2002) p. 30; Wan (2011a) pp. 78–79.

[73] The Civil Procedure Law does not define 'objective reasons'. Pursuant to Article 94 of Interpretation of the Supreme People's Court on the Application of Civil Procedure Law (issued by the SPC on 30 January 2015, effective on 4 February 2015), the following two types of evidence are those that a party may not be able to collect due to objective reasons: first, evidence that is 'kept by relevant organs of the state and a party or his representative does not have the access to it'; second, evidence that involves 'state secrets, commercial secrets or personal privacy'.

Second, before a court hearing begins, judges must carefully examine case materials and investigate and collect the necessary evidence.[74] People's courts have the power to investigate and collect evidence from the relevant entities and individuals, and the relevant entities and individuals cannot refuse such investigation and collection of evidence.[75] This power is considered to be inherent in the judicial power of people's courts.[76] A court may also entrust investigation to a court in a different place when necessary.[77] Moreover, if the evidence offered by the parties is conflicting and unascertainable, a court may investigate and collect evidence itself.[78]

Third, to achieve the goal of ascertaining the truth, appellate courts in China are also designed to be powerful and active.[79] Although the aforementioned provisions regarding evidence are found in Chapter 6 entitled 'Evidence' and Chapter 12 on 'First Trial Proceedings' of the Civil Procedure Law, they are also applicable in appeals according to Article 174.[80] That is to say, litigants may present new evidence before an appellate court. Furthermore, the litigants may request a new investigation or inspection. Since an appellate court must review the facts and application of law in relation to parties' claims in appeal,[81] it may question the parties, make additional investigation and consult the record of the proceedings at first trial.

The rules on evidence, first trial and appeal in domestic civil litigation are also applicable in foreign-related civil litigation in China.[82] Therefore, the role of a Chinese judge is not simply that of an umpire refereeing a contest between parties. He or she must play an active role even in civil litigation involving foreign elements. While courts in common law

74 See Article 129 of the Civil Procedure Law.

75 See Article 67(1) of the Civil Procedure Law.

76 See Civil Law Office of the Legislative Affairs Commission of the NPCSC (2012) p. 106.

77 See Article 131(1) of the Civil Procedure Law.

78 See Civil Law Office of the Legislative Affairs Commission of the NPCSC (2012) p. 101.

79 See Zhong and Yu (2004) pp. 417–421.

80 Article 174 reads: 'Subject to the provisions of this Chapter, a people's court of second instance shall try appeal cases under the formal procedure at first instance.'

81 See Article 168 of the Civil Procedure Law.

82 Article 259 of the Civil Procedure Law reads: 'The provisions of this Part shall apply to foreign-related civil actions within the territory of the People's Republic of China. Where this Part is silent, other relevant provisions of this Law shall apply.' This Part (Part 4 entitled 'Special Provisions on Foreign-related Civil Procedures') provides no special rules on evidence or court proceeding in foreign-related civil litigation. Therefore, the provisions mentioned earlier are applicable.

jurisdictions may have neither the power nor the duty to obtain evidence,[83] people's courts in China have the power, or are even required to collect evidence. Chinese courts not only decide issues of law, but also have their significant function in the finding and determination of facts.

The analysis in this section demonstrates that the fact/law distinction is *not* helpful concerning the introduction of foreign law into court in China. The application of private international law rules is not dependent on parties' pleading: the instructions provided by the legislature require their application in the determination of governing laws in foreign-related civil litigation. Moreover, the role and function of people's courts as stipulated in the Civil Procedure Law are *not* based on the fact/law distinction, but on the purposes of civil litigation in China. Courts have the duty to 'apply laws correctly'.[84]

In *ING Bank (Shanghai Branch)* v. *SIP Shell Gas Holland*,[85] the parties to a guaranty contract agreed that it should be governed by, and interpreted in accordance with, English Law. In litigation, neither of the parties pleaded English law. The Jiangsu Higher People's Court held that the choice of law clause was effective and required the parties to provide the relevant content of English law. However, both parties said they were not able to do so. The court, on its own motion and based on Article 193 (1)(5) of the 1988 Opinions,[86] entrusted Professor Chen Zhidong of the East China University of Political Science with the task of providing the relevant English law. Since neither of the parties objected to the content of Professor Chen's report, the court accepted his opinions on the content of English law.

In this case, the court *ex officio* examined the parties' choice of law clause in contract and determined that English law was applicable. Moreover, it tried to ascertain the content of the law even though neither of the parties could assist it.[87] This approach is appropriate: no matter

83 As Sir Frederick Pollock (1904) pp. 33–34 expressed it: '. . . the court will have nothing to do with making enquiries to find things out for itself. It is not there to inquire, or to do anything of its own motion, but to hear and determine between parties according to the proofs which the parties can bring forward.'

84 Article 2 of the Civil Procedure Law.

85 6 September 2000, Jiangsu Higher People's Court. ING Bank (Shanghai Branch) was a foreign-invested financial institution and SIP Shell Gas Holland was a foreign-invested company incorporated in China.

86 Article 193(1)(5) reads: 'The applicable foreign law may be ascertained through the following ways: . . . (5) provided by legal experts of China and foreign countries . . . '

87 For parties' obligation to assist a court in ascertaining the foreign law chosen by them, see Section 7.5.1.

whether parties make pleadings concerning the governing law of their contract or not, people's courts should determine the applicable law in accordance with the conflicts rules.[88]

7.5 Establishing the Content of the Selected Foreign Law

7.5.1 The Roles of Parties and Courts in Ascertaining the Selected Foreign Law

After a court determines that a foreign law should be applied, the next issue is how the content of the law can be established. As discussed, the wording of Article 10(1) of the 2010 Conflicts Statute is problematic.[89] Before the Statute, people's courts normally relied on parties to prove foreign law. Even though Article 193 of the 1988 Opinions provided five approaches through which a foreign law could be ascertained, the approach generally followed was that the information of foreign law should be submitted by parties.[90] It is very likely that a broader interpretation will now be adopted in judicial practice under Article 10(1) of the Statute. In contractual cases, courts may require parties to provide the content of the selected law no matter whether they have pleaded it or not.

However, this does *not* mean that parties are solely responsible for the ascertainment of foreign law. Section 7.4.3 demonstrates that people's courts are required to look into both factual and legal issues in civil litigation, the underlying notion being that a court shall make every effort to ensure errorless ascertainment of facts and application of law.[91] In this regard, the fact/law distinction is not helpful in analysing the establishment of foreign law in Chinese courts.[92] Foreign law is taken as law in the 2010 Conflicts Statute: it becomes applicable once the relevant choice of law rule so directs, and a court normally has the obligation to ascertain the content of it.[93]

Moreover, Article 10 of the 2010 Conflicts Statute does *not* stipulate that when parties are required to provide the content of a foreign law pursuant to this provision, a court is totally relieved from the obligation to ascertain the law. The provision only requires parties to assist the court. That parties should cooperate with people's courts in ascertaining

88 See Chen (1987) pp. 459–460; Zheng and Zhang (2005).
89 See Section 7.2.1.
90 See Kong and Hu (2002) p. 425; Huang and Li (2007) pp. 411–413; see also the cases cited in n 11.
91 See also Zhang (2002) p. 84.
92 See Lin (2011) p. 163.
93 See Wan (2011a) pp. 78–79.

the law they choose to be applied, and that a court does not totally shift the burden onto parties, are in line with the judicial process as set out in the Civil Procedure Law. According to Articles 64 and 65 of the Law, when faced with difficulties, parties can request a court to collect evidence, or to extend the time limit for the submission of evidence. The approaches listed in Article 193 of the 1988 Opinions and those in Point 51(1) of the 2005 Minutes are still applicable after the 2010 Conflicts Statute came into effect.[94] Therefore, even though a broader interpretation concerning the rule in Article 10(1) of the Statute is to be adopted in judicial practice, people's courts should not randomly decide that a foreign law cannot be ascertained.[95] They should provide positive guidance to parties and help them ascertain the content of foreign law.[96] Article 17(2) of the Interpretation of the 2010 Conflicts Statute (1) is, in this regard, inappropriate.[97]

7.5.2 Assessment of the Information on Foreign Law

A The Inconsistent Criteria Adopted by People's Courts

The admissible forms of evidence on foreign law are listed in Article 193 of the 1988 Opinions and Point 51(1) of the 2005 Minutes. The latter provides:

> Where the governing law of a foreign-related commercial case is foreign law, the parties concerned shall provide or prove the relevant content of the law. The parties may provide the relevant statutes or legal precedents of the foreign law through legal experts, legal service agencies, industrial associations, international organisations, or the Internet, and may also provide the relevant legal writings, legal introduction materials, and legal opinions by experts.

In judicial practice, the form of evidence that is most often used by litigants is the written legal opinions by experts or lawyers. However, the assessment of these legal opinions by people's courts has been inconsistent.

[94] See Wan (2011a) pp. 79–81; Section 7.5.2.

[95] However, in a recent speech made to the chief judges of people's courts' divisions responsible for foreign-related commercial and maritime trial, the Chief Judge of the Fourth Division of Civil Trial of the SPC said that, if both parties agree that a foreign law should be applied in their case but they fail to submit the evidence on that law without legitimate grounds within the reasonable time limit specified by the court, Chinese law should be applied. See Zhang (2017) p. 19.

[96] See Wan (2011a) p. 83. The assessment of evidence on foreign law is discussed in Section 7.5.2.

[97] See also Part B of Section 7.2.2.

First, courts have different approaches to the admissibility of legal opinions furnished by lawyers. Sometimes these are accepted; at other times not.

In *Hong Kong Jingchuan International Shipping Group* v. *Huawei Offshore Shipping Ltd. and Rescue and Salvage Bureau of Ministry of Transport of PRC (Shanghai)*, the court ruled that opinions furnished by lawyers concerning foreign law could not be used as effective proof of foreign law.[98] Similarly, in *Standard Chartered (Asia) Ltd.* v. *Guangxi Zhuang Autonomous Region Huajian Company*,[99] the parties agreed in the guaranty contract that Hong Kong law should govern the contract. The plaintiff submitted the legal opinions from Clifford Chance in Hong Kong to Nanning Intermediate People's Court. Nevertheless, the court held that the plaintiff only provided the opinions but had not proved whether the content therein was true and accurate. The court declined to adopt the opinions and applied Chinese law. In appeal, the Guangxi Zhuang Autonomous Region Higher People's Court confirmed this point.

In *China Ocean Shipping (Group) Company* v. *Ryoshin Lease International (Panama) S.A., Beijing Lucky Tower Co. Ltd. and Kingsun Holding Pte. Ltd.*,[100] the parties chose English law in the Loan Contract as well as the Subordination Agreement between them. Beijing Higher People's Court held that English law should be applied to the dispute arising from the two agreements. The main issue in contention was the validity of the Subordination Agreement pursuant to the principle of consideration in English contract law. China Ocean Shipping (Group) Company submitted the legal opinions furnished by the solicitors, Freshfields Bruckhaus Deringer, in which the relevant precedents and authoritative texts were set out concerning the principle. The opinions were also accredited by the Embassy of the PRC in the United Kingdom of Great Britain and Northern Ireland. The court simply ruled that it accepted the opinions concerning the content of English law and the relevant analysis, but did not further explain why.

[98] See n 12.

[99] 18 November 1992, Nanning Intermediate People's Court; 20 September 1993, Guangxi Zhuang Autonomous Region Higher People's Court. Standard Chartered (Asia) Ltd. was incorporated in Hong Kong.

[100] 18 December 2001, Beijing Higher People's Court. Ryoshin Lease International (Panama) S.A. and Kingsun Holding Pte. Ltd. were incorporated in Panama and Singapore respectively.

The courts in these cases did not provide the reasons for their decision on the effects of the legal opinions from foreign lawyers. It is not clear what criteria were adopted by people's courts. One possible explanation may be that, in *China Ocean Shipping (Group) Company* v. *Ryoshin Lease International (Panama) S.A., Beijing Lucky Tower Co. Ltd. and Kingsun Holding Pte. Ltd.*, more supporting materials were incorporated into the legal opinions concerning the content of English law.

Second, people's courts have used different approaches in determining the admissibility of legal opinions from the lawyer of one party if the other party takes issue with it. In *Japanese Pipe Centre Co. Ltd.* v. *Beijing Zhuangsheng Real Estate Development Co. Ltd.*,[101] the parties chose Hong Kong law in their contract of supply. Beijing Higher People's Court held that the choice was effective. Japanese Pipe Centre Co. Ltd. submitted a written legal opinion by a Hong Kong lawyer concerning the relevant content of Hong Kong law. Beijing Zhuangsheng Real Estate Development Co. Ltd. disagreed with the content of the opinion, and Japanese Pipe Centre Co. Ltd. did not provide further information on Hong Kong law. Accordingly, the court held that the approach adopted by the plaintiff for the proof of Hong Kong law did not conform to those stipulated in Article 193 of the 1988 Opinions, and that the legal opinion could not prove the content of Hong Kong law. As Hong Kong law could not be ascertained pursuant to Article 193, Chinese law should be applied.

In its judgment, the court did not mention in detail how the defendant disagreed with the legal opinions submitted by the plaintiff. Nor did it explain why the legal opinions furnished by a Hong Kong lawyer did not satisfy the requirements set out in Article 193. In fact, the written opinion in this case had been notarized and accredited. It provided analysis as to the content of the relevant Hong Kong law. Even if the court considered that the evidence was not sufficient, it should have given its view of the weight of the evidence.

In *Ping An Insurance (Group) Company of China Ltd. (Beijing Branch)* v. *Dongnama Shipping Co. Ltd.*,[102] the cargoes under the bill of lading issued by the defendant carrier were underwritten by the plaintiff, and the plaintiff was subrogated to the claims of the shipper under the bill

[101] 6 July 2009, Beijing Higher People's Court. Japanese Pipe Centre Co. Ltd. was incorporated in Japan.

[102] 24 March 2003, Tianjin Maritime Court. Both parties were incorporated in China, and the case involved a shipment of nitric acid for Indonesia.

after the plaintiff made payment for the loss of cargoes to the shipper. The Primary Clause on the bill said that disputes arising from it should be governed by the 1962 Commercial Code of Korea. The plaintiff pleaded Korean law and submitted to the court the Chinese translation of the relevant law contained in an official publication. The defendant argued that the submission of the plaintiff was only a translation, which was of no evidential effect. The Tianjin Maritime Court held that the choice of Korean law in the bill was effective and that the Chinese translation submitted by the plaintiff specified all the relevant content of Korean commercial law. Since the defendant could not provide evidence to prove that the translation of Korean law was not correct or was not in conformity with the original Korean text, the court ruled that the plaintiff had completed its obligation to prove the content of Korean law.

In this case, the court did not require the party who provided the evidence on foreign law to submit further information when the other party objected to the content as proved by the former. It may be because the Korean law concerned was statutory law, and it was easier for the court to examine its meaning and effect.

B A More Authentic Approach Is Needed for the Assessment

The decisions mentioned in Part A demonstrate that the approaches adopted by people's courts in the assessment of information on foreign law are neither consistent nor convincing. Article 64(3) of the Civil Procedure Law provides that people's courts should examine and verify evidence comprehensively and objectively pursuant to the statutory procedures. However, this provision is primarily designed for finding out the facts of a case, but not for the ascertainment of the content of foreign law. It cannot provide sufficient guidance to courts.[103]

On the one hand, as the forms of information on foreign law are similar to those listed as admissible in the Civil Procedure Law,[104] some of the principles concerning presentation and evaluation of evidence may also be helpful. On the other hand, since foreign law is taken as law in the 2010 Conflicts Statute,[105] the criteria for evaluating the information of foreign law may not be totally the same as those for the assessment of

[103] See Xiao (2010) pp. 166–167.

[104] Article 63(1) of the Civil Procedure Law provides: 'Evidence includes: (1) statement of a party; (2) documentary evidence; (3) physical evidence; (4) audio-visual recordings; (5) electronic data; (6) witness testimony; (7) expert opinion; and (8) records of inspection.'

[105] See Section 7.4.1.

evidence of facts. The legal character of foreign law should be taken into consideration. Three points should be noted.

First, according to Article 68 of the Civil Procedure Law, evidence on foreign law should be presented in court and be subject to cross-examination by parties. This is the most important vehicle through which a court can examine and verify the evidence.[106] Moreover, Article 79 stipulates that a party may request a court to notify a person with expertise to appear in court to offer an opinion regarding a specialized issue. Although this provision is primarily designed for dealing with the technical issues that are beyond the knowledge of a judge,[107] it should also be applicable where a party would like to invite a legal expert to provide the relevant content of foreign law in court. Proof of foreign law by legal experts is one of the approaches listed in Article 193 of the 1988 Opinions and Point 51 of the 2005 Minutes.

Second, people's courts should not set up a standard that is too high. In *Earl Nelson* v. *Lord Bridport*, Lord Langdale M. R. said:[108]

> If the utmost strictness were required in every case, justice might often have to stand still . . .

As pointed out, people's courts can still play an active role in the ascertainment of foreign law even when parties are required to assist them. Courts are not merely passive arbiters of the evidence put before them. Furthermore, judges should not ignore the legal character of

[106] See Civil Law Office of the Legislative Affairs Commission of the NPCSC (2012) p. 107. For example, in *United Overseas Bank (China) Shanghai Branch and The Hong Kong and Shanghai Banking Corporation Limited (Shanghai Branch)* v. *Shanghai Golden Real Estate Co. Ltd.* (7 June 2010, Shanghai Higher People's Court), the loan contract and other relevant agreements concerned were agreed to be governed by Hong Kong law. The original parties of those agreements were United Overseas Bank (Singapore), the Hong Kong and Shanghai Banking Corporation Limited (Hong Kong) and Shanghai Golden Real Estate Co. Ltd., but later the former two parties assigned their rights under the contracts to the two plaintiffs. The plaintiffs then confirmed with the defendant the content of the contracts, including the choice of law clause. Therefore, the Shanghai Higher People's Court held that the governing law of the contracts were still Hong Kong law. Furthermore, the court explained to the parties the choice of law issues in this case, and required them to provide expert opinions on Hong Kong law. Both parties submitted written reports from Hong Kong lawyers and the reports were cross-examined by the parties in court. Based on the parties' opinions on the evidence, the court assessed the evidence and determined the content of Hong Kong law.

[107] See Civil Law Office of the Legislative Affairs Commission of the NPCSC (2012) pp. 119–120.

[108] (1845) 8 Beavan 527, 537; see also *Parkasho* v. *Singh* [1968] P. 233, 251 (Cairns J.).

foreign law: to establish foreign law is to establish directly the parties' legal rights and duties. In this regard, a court's legal experience can and should be engaged in the process of evaluating the evidence. It necessarily has a legal input in this process that is absent in other situations involving expert evidence.[109] As Clark L. J. expressed it in *Morgan Grenfell Ltd.* v. *SACE*:[110]

> In assessing expert evidence of foreign law, the role of the judge is in one respect at least different from his role in assessing ordinary evidence of fact. It is that the judge is himself a lawyer.

People's court can even undertake further research on the relevant content of foreign law when necessary. In *SEoIL Shipping Co. Ltd.* v. *Tangshan Ganglu Iron & Steel Co. Ltd.*,[111] SEoIL Shipping Co. Ltd. (SEoIL) was the shipper and ship owner and Tangshan Ganglu Iron & Steel Co. Ltd. (Ganglu) held the bill of lading concerned. At the port of destination in China, SEoIL exercised its right of lien over the cargoes carried on board its ship because LMJ International Ltd. failed to pay the demurrage charges due under the charterparty between them. SEoIL refused to deliver the cargos to Ganglu at the port even though the latter held the original bill of lading. Ganglu then applied for a maritime injunction to the Tianjin Maritime Court. The court then made an order under which SEoIL was compelled to deliver the cargoes to Ganglu. Ganglu thus took the cargoes. SEoIL later sued Ganglu in Tianjin Maritime Court for the damages caused by Ganglu's application for an injunction.

In the proceedings of the first trial, both parties agreed to choose Chinese law to govern whether Ganglu's application for an injunction constituted tort and English law to govern whether SEoIL had the right of lien over the cargoes based on the demurrage charges. The Tianjin Maritime Court held that their choice was effective according to Article 44 of the 2010 Conflicts Statute.[112] Based on the English law 'as was

[109] See Fentiman (2006) pp. 395–396, 404–405.

[110] [2001] EWCA Civ 1932, at [49] (C.A.). This point was considered at length by Evans L.J. in *MCC Proceeds* v. *Bishopsgate* [1999] C.L.C. 417 (C.A.), at [12] – [13].

[111] 12 December 2012, Tianjin Higher People's Court. SEoIL Shipping Co. Ltd. was incorporated in Korea.

[112] Article 44 of the Statute provides: 'Tort liabilities shall be governed by *lex loci delicti*, provided that where the parties have a common habitual residence, laws of the common habitual residence shall apply. If parties reach an agreement on the governing law after the occurrence of tort, the law selected by them shall prevail.'

already ascertained',[113] the court decided that SEoIL did not have the right of lien over the cargos. Further, the court ruled that Ganglu's application did not constitute a tort under Chinese law and made a decision for Ganglu.

SEoIL then appealed to the Tianjin Higher People's Court. One of its arguments in the appeal was that the application of English law by the Tianjin Maritime Court was wrong. It said that the court only relied on the English law books provided by Ganglu. It pointed out that the English legal system is a common law system and the precedents were of binding force. It further argued that pursuant to the precedents it had collected on the Internet and submitted to the first trial court, it should have had the right of lien. SEoIL submitted an additional legal opinion furnished by an English lawyer in the appeal. Ganglu did not hand in any further evidence.

Concerning the additional evidence from SEoIL, the appellate court held that although the evidence was relevant to the case, its content did not support the arguments of SEoIL. The court thus declined to accept the legal opinion. As to the precedents submitted by SEoIL in the first trial, the appellate court determined that those cases only indicated that a ship owner had the right of lien when this was specified in the charterparty concerned, but they did not prove that a ship owner necessarily had the right of lien in English law. As to the evidence from Ganglu, the court held that the evidence was not sufficient for ascertaining the content of English law.

Because the evidence from the parties was deemed to be insufficient, the appellate court undertook its own research. It obtained from the Internet *Carriage of Goods by Sea* (7th edition) by Professor John F. Wilson.[114] It looked at *Carriage of Goods by Sea* by Stephen Girvin,[115] and also *Scrutton on Charterparties and Bills of Lading* by Alan Abraham Mocatta, Michael J. Mustill and Stewart C. Boyd[116] from the library of China University of Political Science and Law. After reading the three books, the court came to the conclusion that the right of lien with respect to demurrage charges did not exist in common law.

The court then listened to the opinions of both parties as to its findings on English law. SEoIL said that on the one hand, the court should look at the English precedents rather than law books, on the other hand, law books

[113] In the available appellate judgment of this case, how English law was ascertained in the first trial was only mentioned in SEoIL's application for appeal.

[114] See Wilson (2010). The information of the three books referred to in the judgment was verified by the author according to the ISBN code provided therein.

[115] See Girvin (2007). [116] See Mocatta, Mustill and Boyd (1984).

were not the admissible form of evidence concerning foreign law under Chinese law. Ganglu considered that the court's approach was legitimate and agreed on the content as had been ascertained. Tianjin Higher People's Court ruled that since the law books that had been examined were from the Internet and a university library, and they confirmed the situations where a ship owner could exercise the right of lien under English law, the rules therein could be taken as the content of English law and be applied to determine whether SEoIL had the right of lien over the cargoes. The court finally confirmed the judgment of first trial.

In this case, the appellate court not only played an active role in the ascertainment of English law, but also applied its skills in legal reasoning in the assessment of evidence. Although this was not a contractual case, English law was chosen by parties and the case demonstrated that a court had the ability to cooperate with parties in ascertaining the foreign law chosen by them.

The assessment of evidence on foreign law should also be conducted in accordance with the means by which the content of the law is provided, whether by oral examination in court, written reports, judicial assistance or a court-appointed expert.[117] It is not clear what qualifications an 'expert' should have in Chinese law: no specific rules are provided in the Civil Procedure Law. Whether a person is qualified to give evidence as to the particulars of a foreign law thus depends on the facts of a given case and the knowledge or experience of the person.[118] A flexible approach should be adopted which balances the desire to obtain the best possible evidence against the equally commendable desire not to involve the parties in unnecessary expense or delay.[119]

Moreover, the strength of expert legal evidence depends much on the logic and coherence of the arguments which supports it and its conformity with the written material which normally accompanies it.[120] Typically, where foreign law is concerned, this is in the form of legislation, decided cases and authoritative works. If the supporting materials are not

[117] See Fentiman (1998) p. 174.

[118] See Civil Law Office of the Legislative Affairs Commission of the NPCSC (2012) p. 120.

[119] Davies, Bell and Brereton (2014) para. 17.28, and also the cases cited in paras. 17.22–17.27; Fentiman (1998) pp. 178–182.

[120] For example, in *Delixy Energy Pte. Ltd.* v. *Dongming Zhongyou Petrochemical Co. Ltd.* (28 December 2016, Shandong Higher People's Court), the court held that whether the expert opinions on the content of English law could be accepted in this case was dependent on whether the opinions were accurate and complete, and whether they were helpful in resolving the disputed issues in the case.

provided, a court may even try to search the available resources and verify the content, as the Tianjin Higher People's Court had done in the aforementioned case.[121] Since a judge is a lawyer, skilled in legal reasoning, he or she may have an insight into the force and effectiveness of a legal expert's evidence which is less likely in cases involving, say, scientific evidence. In fact, the legal character of foreign law enables courts to test foreign legal evidence by deploying elementary standards of reasoning and coherence.[122] As Scott L. J. said in *A/S Tallinna Laevauhisus and Others* v. *Estonian State Steamship Line and Another*:[123]

> The witness, however expert in the foreign law, cannot prevent the court using its common sense; and the court can reject his evidence if he says something patently absurd, or something inconsistent with the rest of his evidence . . .

Third, people's courts should distinguish between the content of the evidence and its application in the particular case. In Australia, it is considered to be a general rule that an expert giving opinion evidence must confine his or her opinion to the content of the foreign law, and not its application to the particular case.[124] This approach is supported by Chinese scholars,[125] and has also been adopted by people's courts. In *ORIX Ship Resources Pte. Ltd.* v. *Shenzhen Huaxin Co. Ltd. and Shenzhen Xingpeng Shipping Industrial Company Ltd.*,[126] the parties chose English law to govern the contracts concerned. The Guangzhou Maritime Court held that the choice was effective and asked the parties to prove the content of English law. Both of the defendants pleaded Chinese law and

121 This approach was also adopted in *Jiangsu Light Industrial Products Import & Export Group Co. Ltd.* v. *Jiangsu Brilliant Globe Logistics & United States Brilliant Globe Logistics Inc.* (25 December 2001, Wuhan Maritime Court). In this case, the defendant submitted to the Wuhan Maritime Court the text of the UCC and the Attorney's Opinion Letter which were given by Professor John D. Kimball at New York University School of Law, notarized by an American notary public and certified by China's Consulate in New York. The plaintiff argued that the parties did not choose the UCC in the bills of lading concerned and thus denied its applicability in the case. The court then referred to the Database of The Collection of Laws and Regulations of the People's Republic of China and confirmed the content as provided in the Letter. The Database was examined and approved by the Office of the Legislative Affairs Commission under the Standing Committee of the NPC.

122 See Fentiman (1998) p. 177.

123 (1947) 80 Ll. L. R. 99, 108 (C.A.), per Scott L. J.

124 See *Allstate Life Insurance Co.* v. *Australia & New Zealand Banking Group Ltd. [No 6]* (1996) 64 FCR 79 at 83 per Lindgren J.; see also Tilbury, Davis and Opeskin (2002) p. 323; cf Davies, Bell and Brereton (2014) para. 17.30.

125 See Huang, Hu and Wang (2008) pp. 472–474.

126 2 July 2002, Guangzhou Maritime Court; 2 June 2003, Guangdong Higher People's Court. ORIX Ship Resources Pte. Ltd. was incorporated in Singapore.

therefore did not provide evidence. The plaintiff submitted the written legal opinions furnished by an English lawyer, whose signature on the opinions was notarized by a Hong Kong lawyer entrusted by the Ministry of Justice of the PRC. The opinions demonstrated that the English lawyer was appointed by the plaintiff. After the lawyer examined all the relevant contracts, he (or she) concluded: assuming that the conclusion of those contracts was in conformity with the laws of the jurisdictions where the contracts were concluded respectively, they were effective under English law. Accordingly, the lawyer stated that the claims of ORIX Ship Resources Pte. Ltd. could be supported by English law. He (or she) also listed some English precedents in the opinions.

The court ruled that the legal opinions only stated that the contracts concerned in this case were valid and that the plaintiff's claims could be supported, but contained no specific content of the relevant English law. Moreover, the opinions were not notarized by any notary in England. Therefore, the court decided that the opinions could not be taken as proof of the relevant English law. Nor could the precedents listed therein be verified. The court then applied Chinese law. The court's decision on governing law was confirmed in the appeal.

The purpose of this approach is not to make all the evidence on the application of foreign law to a given case inadmissible, but to assure that a court should not merely rely on the expert opinions when determining how a dispute should be resolved in accordance with the applicable foreign law. A court should focus on assessing whether the evidence can be taken to be proof of the relevant content. The need for application evidence may be apparent in those cases where the question of foreign law is novel or difficult, or in which there is no pattern of overseas decision-making that would assist a judge to determine how a power or discretion would be exercised by the foreign court.[127]

7.5.3 *Effects of the Failure to Ascertain the Selected Foreign Law*

Article 10(2) of the 2010 Conflicts Statute provides that if foreign laws cannot be ascertained or contain no relevant provisions, Chinese law should be applied. This rule is considered to be simple, convenient and feasible.[128] No exception is mentioned in it. However, given the aforementioned uncertainties in the ascertainment of foreign law,[129] a court

[127] McComish (2007) p. 421. McComish criticized the distinction between application and content evidence in Australian law on pp. 418–422.

[128] See Wan (2011a) p. 85. [129] See Sections 7.1 and 7.2.

enjoys a rather broad discretionary power in the determination of the ambiguities in judicial practice. The unexceptional application of Chinese law when proof of foreign law fails may further incline people's courts towards the application of forum law.

In English law, a court also normally applies forum law by default where foreign law is not proved. However, the recent practice of English courts suggests that the default application of English law is likely to be challenged where the English rule is statutory: the rule may appear to state a rule of purely domestic law; the wording of the statute may need to be adapted or changed in order to be made applicable to facts which do not otherwise fall within it; or, as Westlake had anticipated, the relevant statute may only exist as special institution with special machinery, and therefore it may be impossible to apply to foreign persons or events.[130] In fact, people's courts have also based their determination of the effect of failure to ascertain foreign law upon grounds that are more practical or convincing.

In *JP Morgan Chase Bank* v. *Seastream Shipping Inc.*,[131] Seastream Shipping Inc. failed to repay the money it borrowed from JP Morgan Chase Bank under a loan agreement. The ship 'M. T. Mariner' owned by the defendant was mortgaged to JP Morgan Chase Bank as guarantee for the payment. The plaintiff then applied to the Guangzhou Maritime Court for arresting the ship and the court so ordered. The plaintiff sued the defendant in the court.

According to Article 271 of the Chinese Maritime Code,[132] the law of the flag state of the ship shall apply to the mortgage of the ship. As the ship flew the flag of The Bahamas, Bahama law should be applied. In court proceedings, the plaintiff stated that it was difficult to ascertain the law of Bahamas in a timely manner. After the court enquired about the relevant situations, it directly made a phone call to the Embassy of the PRC in the Commonwealth of The Bahamas and requested the assistance from the Embassy. The Embassy sent the Bahamas Merchant Shipping Act, which had been notarized, to the court through express mail within ten days. The court decided the issues on mortgage accordingly.

[130] See Westlake and Bentwich (1922) p. 407, §353; Dicey, Morris and Collins (2012) paras. 9-025-9-028; Fentiman (2015) paras. 20.105-20.121.

[131] 25 July 2002, Guangzhou Maritime Court. JP Morgan Chase Bank was incorporated in the United States and Seastream Shipping Inc. was incorporated in Liberia.

[132] It was adopted at the 28th Meeting of the Standing Committee of the 7th NPC on 7 November 1992 and became effective on 1 July 1993.

As to the effect of the loan agreement, the parties agreed therein that it should be governed by English law. The court found that the relevant English precedents were rather difficult to ascertain. But the court also considered that the application of Chinese law to determine the effect of the agreement would also be inappropriate because on the one hand, the only connection of China with this case was that the ship was arrested in Guangzhou (all the other elements were located in foreign countries), on the other hand, to apply Chinese law would also be against the expectations of the parties. The court said that as both parties did not have disagreements upon the facts and the amount of the loan, it could determine the amount based on the evidence presented. Since the loan contract was not against the public interest of China, the court deemed it unnecessary to further examine the effect of the contract.

In this case, the court adopted different approaches in the ascertainment of the law of The Bahamas and of English law. It may be more active in ascertaining the former because the relevant law was a statute. Although it did not explain whether it had tried to search the content of English law,[133] it did not simply apply Chinese law instead: it used a more practical approach and respected the parties' intention.

Chinese law should normally be applied when the applicable foreign law cannot be ascertained. But people's courts should also be permitted to take exceptional situations into consideration.

7.6 Conclusion

This chapter analyses the current mechanism for ascertainment of foreign law in China. It illustrates how the uncertainties in legal rules have resulted in inconsistency in the resolution of outstanding issues in judicial practice that seriously hinder the operation of the party autonomy principle. It is true that to ascertain a foreign law may not be an easy task.[134] We should not expect more of the proof of foreign law than of the determination of issues of domestic law. Nor should we expect the

[133] It is submitted that a court should not simply determine that a foreign law cannot be ascertained without providing detailed and convincing legal reasoning. See Sections 7.5.1 and 7.5.2. However, the focus of the analysis of this case here is the court's determination concerning the effects of the failure to ascertain English law.

[134] This view is echoed by Zweigert (1973), p. 293: 'The judge applying foreign law is a dilettante, a beginner; he is timid. The judge applying the lex fori is a learned expert; he is a sovereign, superior judge ... On the whole the judicial process has a lower quality when the judge applies foreign law than when he applies lex fori.'

proof of foreign law to produce a correct result or to excavate objective legal truth, any more than the process of adjudication ever does so.[135] But we may insist that the process should be authentic, convincing and predictable for parties in international litigation. If no adequate regime is available to ensure the desired application of foreign law, the autonomy of parties to structure their legal relationships is meaningless.[136]

[135] See Fentiman (1998) pp. 20–21. [136] See Geeroms (2004) p. 1.

8

Contractual Choice of Law under the 'One Country, Two Systems' Regime

The previous chapters have dealt with the contentious issues involved in the operation of the party autonomy principle. The discussions and analyses therein all concern commercial contracts with *foreign* elements. In the conflict of laws, a 'foreign element' means a contact with some system of law other than that of the forum, that is, the country whose courts are seized of the case.[1] In this sense, the word 'country' was defined by Dicey as 'the whole of a territory subject under one sovereign to one body of law'. Although he suggested that a better expression might be 'law district', this phrase has never found much favour with English-speaking writers, and the more familiar word 'country' has from long usage become almost a term of art among those writers.[2]

After the People's Republic of China (PRC) resumed sovereignty over Hong Kong and Macao, each became a Special Administrative Region (SAR) of the PRC. According to the Basic Laws establishing these two SARs, they enjoy a high degree of autonomy and their own legal systems, particularly their civil and commercial laws, remain basically unchanged after 1 July 1997 and 20 December 1999 respectively.[3] Moreover, although Taiwan[4] is still separated from mainland China for various reasons, the civil and commercial contacts between people from the Mainland and Taiwan are developing rapidly, and it is inevitable that

[1] See Morris (2009) para. 1-002; Dicey, Morris and Collins (2012) para. 1-001.

[2] See Morris (2009) para. 1-004; Dicey, Morris and Collins (2012) para. 1-065.

[3] See Article 8 of The Basic Law of the Hong Kong Special Administrative Region (hereinafter the Hong Kong Basic Law, adopted at the 3rd Session of the 7th NPC on 4 April 1990, effective on 1 July 1997); Article 8 of The Basic Law of the Macao Special Administrative Region (hereinafter the Macao Basic Law, adopted at the 1st Session of the 8th NPC on 31 March 1993, effective on 20 December 1999).

[4] The Taiwan region includes Taiwan Island, the Pescadores Islands (or Penghu) and the islands of Matsu and Kinmen. For its status, see Section 8.1.2.

the laws of the Taiwan region often come into play in the resolution of Taiwan-related disputes. Since the PRC Constitution provides that Hong Kong, Macao and Taiwan are all under the sovereignty of the PRC[5] while each has a separate system of law which is different from that of the Mainland,[6] they can each be defined as a 'country' in the sense of the conflict of laws.

The establishment of the Hong Kong and Macao SARs was based on the fundamental principle of 'One Country, Two Systems', which was originally formulated by senior Chinese statesman Deng Xiaoping in the late 1970s to entice Taiwan into reunification with the Mainland.[7] Under this principle, 'one country' means that the PRC is a country of single unity, and that the SARs are local administrative regions under the unified central leadership.[8] In order to avoid confusion, Hong Kong, Macao and Taiwan are referred to as 'law districts' in this book. With the addition of these three law districts, there are four law districts in the PRC (the Mainland, Hong Kong, Macao and Taiwan).

This chapter considers, from the perspective of people's courts sitting in the Mainland, the impact that the 'One Country, Two Systems' principle may have upon the treatment of the issues addressed in Chapters 5, 6 and 7. It discusses the constraints that should be imposed on the application of the 'social public interest' reservation in cases

[5] See the Preamble of the Constitution of the PRC (adopted at the 5th Session of the 5th NPC and promulgated for implementation by the Announcement of the NPC on 4 December 1982, amended in accordance with the Amendments to the Constitution of the People's Republic of China adopted respectively at the 1st Session of the 7th NPC on 12 April 1988, the 1st Session of the 8th NPC on 29 March 1993, the 2nd Session of the 9th NPC on 15 March 1999 and the 2nd Session of the 10th NPC on 14 March 2004) and the Preambles and the first articles of the Hong Kong Basic Law and the Macao Basic Law. As to the status of Taiwan, see further, Sections 8.1.2 and 8.1.3.

[6] Hong Kong retains a legal system deeply influenced by British common law, Macao retains a legal system influenced by Portuguese civil law, and the legal system in Taiwan has historically been influenced by Japanese and European civil law traditions. See Wang (1992) chapter 2; Huang and Qian (1995) pp. 294–295.

[7] The principle of 'One Country, Two Systems' emerged when Deng Xiaoping formulated his policy for the peaceful settlement of the Taiwan Issue. For the evolution of this principle, see Cooney (1997) pp. 501–507; Wang and Leung (1998) pp. 280–293; Chen (2003).

[8] See Article 12 of the Hong Kong Basic Law and Article 12 of the Macao Basic Law. This principle is also of fundamental importance to the resolution of the Taiwan issue. See further, Sections 8.1.2 and 8.1.3.

involving two (or more) law districts within the PRC, and also the approaches that may be helpful in ascertaining the laws of Hong Kong, Macao and Taiwan.

8.1 One Country, Two Systems and Four Law Districts

8.1.1 The High Degree of Autonomy of Hong Kong and Macao

In accordance with Article 31 of the PRC Constitution, the Hong Kong and Macao SARs are governed by their own Basic Laws, which provide for their own social and economic systems, the systems for safeguarding the fundamental rights and freedoms of their residents, the executive, legislative and judicial systems and the relevant policies.[9] Article 2 of both Basic Laws stipulates that the NPC authorizes the SARs to exercise 'a high degree of autonomy and enjoy executive, legislative and independent judicial power, including that of final adjudication'. All laws previously in force in the SARs have been maintained except those inconsistent with the Basic Laws.[10] Most significantly, based on Article 18(2) of both Basic Laws, national laws simply do not apply to the SARs except those few explicitly listed in Annex III of the Basic Laws. There is no reference to the PRC Constitution, save that the SARs are established in accordance with Article 31 of the Constitution and that the socialist system and policies will not be practised in the SARs.[11] As both SARs are inalienable parts of the PRC, logic suggests that the PRC Constitution must apply to them. On the other hand, it seems at least some parts of the Constitution, such as those relating to socialist policies, are excluded by Article 31, which authorizes the establishment of the SARs.[12] It has therefore been argued that the Constitution itself does not apply to the SARs, except Articles 31 and 62(1)(13), the latter providing for the NPC's power to decide the establishment of SARs and the systems to be instituted therein.[13] In this regard, the degree of

[9] See Article 11 of the Hong Kong Basic Law and Article 11 of the Macao Basic Law.
[10] See Article 8 of the Hong Kong Basic Law and Article 8 of the Macao Basic Law.
[11] See the Preambles to both Basic Laws. [12] Lim and Chan (2015) para. 2.033.
[13] See Q. Zhang (2012) p. 109. During the drafting of the Hong Kong Basic Law, some attempts had been made to identify the provisions of the PRC Constitution that apply to Hong Kong. These attempts were eventually abandoned as it was found that it would be impossible to identify such provisions at an abstract level. In the years after the establishment of the Hong Kong SAR, it is said that the PRC Constitution has not played any significant role in the legal system of Hong Kong. See Lim and Chan (2015) para. 2.033. It

autonomy enjoyed by the Hong Kong and Macao SARs seems to exceed that of a state or province in federal jurisdictions, where federal powers granted by a constitution apply uniformly and supersede any local laws in conflict.[14]

The return of Hong Kong and Macao might be considered to have introduced 'certain elements of federalism' to the political structure of the PRC.[15] However, in contrast with other federal systems where general principles are provided in federal constitutions or formulated by the supreme court concerning the constitutional limitations on intrastate or interprovincial conflict of laws issues,[16] there is no equivalent provision in the PRC Constitution. Moreover, in spite of the 'high degree of autonomy' granted by the Basic Laws, the Hong Kong and Macao SARs are subject to 'potentially far-reaching political control by the PRC central government in a number of ways'.[17] Therefore, the relationship between the SARs and the Central People's Government (CPG) has some substantial differences from that between a state or province and the federal government in a federal system. It is necessary to discuss the differences before further analysis of interregional conflict of laws issues within the PRC.

First, according to Articles 2 and 12 of both Basic Laws, the powers and jurisdictions of the SARs are derived from the authorization of the

should however be noted that certain articles of the Hong Kong Basic Law reflect principles present in the PRC Constitution and hence suggest a broader applicability of the PRC Constitution to the Hong Kong SAR than is evident by looking at Articles 31 and 62(1)(13). For example, Articles 1, 12, 17, 20, 23, 158 and 160 of the Basic Law appear to reflect the Chinese principles of 'unitary state', 'democratic centralism', 'legislative supremacy of the NPC and its Standing Committee' and 'legislative interpretation' as enshrined respectively in the Preamble, Article 3, Articles 57 and 58, and Articles 62 and 67 of the PRC Constitution. See the analysis in Cheung (1999) pp. 190–193.

14 See, for example, the 'Supremacy Clause' in Article 6 of the United States Constitution. See also Huang and Qian (1995) pp. 303–304; Q. Zhang (2012) p. 113.

15 See Huang and Qian (1995) p. 293, n 18.

16 See the Full Faith and Credit Clause in the United States Constitution (Article IV, Section 1) and in the Constitution of Australia (Section 118). For further analysis of the constitutional limitations on conflict of laws issues in the United States and Australia, see Hay, Borchers and Symeonides (2010) chapter 3; Tilbury, Davis and Opeskin (2002) Chapter 16. Despite the lack of explicit provisions directed at the conflict of laws in the Constitution of Canada, in a series of cases beginning in 1990, the Supreme Court of Canada held that the nature of the Canadian Constitutional arrangements established certain fundamental requirements for conflict of laws rules, which the Court described as the principles of order and fairness. See Castel and Walker (2002) chapter 2.

17 Q. Zhang (2012) p. 113.

NPC and the SARs are local administrative regions of the PRC. Therefore, any residual power that is not expressly or impliedly granted to the SARs must be reserved to the sovereign. This is not a situation such as that under a federal system where the power rests with the states who have decided to join themselves together to form a federal government. Article 20 of both Laws further stipulates that the SARs may enjoy other powers *granted to them* by the NPC, the Standing Committee of the NPC (NPCSC) or the CPG, thereby confirming that the SARs are merely exercising a delegated power.[18]

Second, the principal officials of the SAR administrations, including the Chief Executive (CE), are 'appointed' by the State Council, even though the CE is elected according to Annex I of the Basic Laws and other principal officials are appointed upon his or her nomination.[19] Whether the nature of the final appointment procedure is substantive or not is unclear, but it obviously gives the CPG power to influence the CE elections since the result of any election would not be formally effective without central approval.[20] In a formal sense, the SARs may be even less politically autonomous than ordinary local governments in the Mainland, since the principal officials there are supposed to be elected by and directly accountable to the local people's congress rather than appointed by any superior government.[21] Moreover, although the members of a SAR's Legislative Council (LegCo) are elected according to Annex II of the Basic Laws, the method of the LegCo elections, like the method of the CE elections, is decided as a part of the Basic Laws by the NPC rather than by a majority of the SAR residents themselves or legislators

[18] An important legal distinction should be drawn between incidental and necessary powers on the one hand, and residual powers on the other. It would be an oversimplification to suggest that whatever that is not provided for in the Basic Laws falls within the category of residual powers. See Lim and Chan (2015) para. 2.032.

[19] See Articles 15, 45 and 48 of the Hong Kong Basic Law and Articles 15, 47 and 50 of the Macao Basic Law.

[20] One important question for the Hong Kong SAR is whether the CPG's power of appointment includes the substantive power to reject Hong Kong's chosen CE. The CPG has repeatedly asserted that its power to appoint the CE is a substantive power. See Lim and Chan (2015) section 16 and further, Chen (2015), Lim (2015) and Tai (2015). Traces of central guidance are said to have been quite evident in the running of CE elections in each SAR. See Q. Zhang (2012) p. 113.

[21] Article 101 of the PRC Constitution provides: 'Local people's congresses at their respective levels elect and have the power to recall governors and deputy governors, or mayors and deputy mayors, or heads and deputy heads of counties, districts, townships and towns.'

accountable to them.[22] So far only half of the LegCo members in Hong Kong are elected directly by the residents there, the other half are elected by functional constituencies, comprising representation from business,

[22] See Article 68 and Annex II of the Hong Kong Basic Law and Article 68 and Annex II of the Macao Basic Law. Under the pressure from Hong Kong residents, the CPG has announced a timetable for democratic reform and has promised to implement direct elections for the CE and the full LegCo by 2017–18. See Decision of the Standing Committee of the National People's Congress on the Methods for Selecting the Chief Executive and Forming the Legislative Council of the Hong Kong Special Administrative Region in 2012 and Issues on Universal Suffrage (adopted at the 31st Meeting of the Standing Committee of the 10th NPC on 29 December 2007). However, the Decision had not resolved the most controversial issues regarding Hong Kong's political development. Particularly, there were concerns about whether the universal suffrage promised with regard to the election of the CE in 2017 and LegCo thereafter was genuine or 'fake' universal suffrage, as the issues of the nomination threshold and the 'screening mechanism' for candidates for the CE had not been resolved, nor had the issue of whether universal suffrage for the election of all legislators meant the abolition of functional constituencies. See Chen (2015) para. 8.264.

From 4 December 2013 to 3 May 2014, the Government of the Hong Kong SAR conducted a public consultation exercise on the electoral reforms for the LegCo and the CE to be elected in 2016 and 2017 respectively. During the consultation period, many political parties and civil society groups, including those which are 'pro-China' and those which are 'pro-democracy', put forward their proposed models for the nomination and election of the CE in 2017. On 15 July 2014, the then CE submitted to the NPCSC a report on the issue concerning amending the methods for selecting the CE in 2017 and for forming the LegCo in 2016. On 31 August 2014, the NPCSC adopted Decision of the Standing Committee of the National People's Congress on Issues concerning the Selection of the Chief Executive of the Hong Kong Special Administrative Region by Universal Suffrage and on the Method for the Formation of the Legislative Council of the Hong Kong Special Administrative Region in 2016 (adopted at the 10th Meeting of the Standing Committee of the 12th NPC on 31 August 2014). The NPCSC decided that, from 2017, the CE of the Hong Kong SAR may be selected by universal suffrage. The specific method for selecting the CE by universal suffrage shall be prescribed by amending the Annex I Method for the Selection of the Chief Executive of the Hong Kong SAR to the Hong Kong Basic Law under lawful procedures. The bills on amendments and the amendments to such bills shall be proposed by the Government of the Hong Kong SAR to the LegCo in accordance with the Hong Kong Basic Law and should be adopted with the endorsement of a two-thirds majority of all the LegCo members and the consent of the CE, and reported to the NPCSC for approval.

The NPCSC's Decision of 31 August 2014 was met by strong protest from pro-democracy forces in Hong Kong, which launched the 'Occupy Central' Movement (also known as the 'Umbrella Movement'). Several key government and business districts in Hong Kong were occupied by protesters for as long as seventy-nine days. For the history and orientation of the 'pro-democracy' politicians as a political force in Hong Kong, and comments on the 'Occupy Central' Movement, see Chen (2015) paras. 8.090 – 8.106. For a review of the evolution of Hong Kong's political system and investigation into the different understanding and interpretations of the Hong Kong Basic Law on the part of the Chinese regime and on the part of democracy activists in Hong Kong, see Chen (2017).

the professions and other sectors.[23] This system has been a domestically contentious issue in Hong Kong.[24]

Third, though the judiciaries in the SARs are accorded extraordinary autonomy, in particular the power of final adjudication and a judicial selection mechanism free from central control,[25] encroachments by the CPG are made possible by provisions within the Basic Laws. Fundamentally, the ultimate power to interpret the Basic Laws is, as with every other piece of national legislation enacted by the NPC, vested in the NPCSC rather than in the SAR courts of final appeal.[26] The NPCSC does 'authorize' the SAR courts in adjudication 'to interpret on their own' the provisions in the Basic Laws that are 'within the limits of the autonomy of the Region' as well as other provisions, but if interpretation touches upon affairs regulated by the CPG or 'concerning the relationship between the Central Authorities and the Region', the Court of Final Appeal is obliged to seek from the NPCSC an interpretation of the relevant provisions and follow such interpretation in deciding those cases.[27] Two difficult issues have arisen concerning Article 158 of the Hong Kong Basic Law. The first has to do with the NPCSC's power of final interpretation in relation to the interpretation of the Basic Law. At

On 7 January 2015, the Hong Kong Government launched the 'second round consultation' on political reform. On 22 April 2015, the Government published a policy document on the basis of the NPCSC's Decision, proposing a concrete model for nominating candidates for and electing the CE in 2017, including proposed amendments to Annex I to the Hong Kong Basic Law. The proposed model was subsequently introduced in the LegCo and put to a vote on 18 June 2015. With twenty-eight of the seventy-member Council voting against the proposal, it failed to secure the requisite two-thirds majority for amendment of Annex I to the Basic Law. Consequently, the existing system of the election of the CE would continue in force in the foreseeable future. See Chen (2015) paras. 8.088–8.089.

23 See Annex II of the Hong Kong Basic Law. The number of LegCo members has increased to seventy in 2012, with thirty-five members returned by geographical election and thirty-five members returned by functional constituencies. See further, Lim (2015).

24 While the people of Hong Kong have a right to vote, they are not equally treated as voters so long as the present arrangements for the selection of the members of LegCo remain. Instead, members of functional constituencies who exercise a further right to return functional constituency Legislative Councilors have an additional vote to the geographical constituency vote that they already enjoy. Thus this system violates voter equality. See Lim (2015) paras. 29.003–29.004. For the residents' right to vote and right to political participation in Hong Kong, see further, Chen (2015) and Lim (2015).

25 See Articles 88 – 93 of the Hong Kong Basic Law and Articles 87–91 of the Macao Basic Law.

26 According to Article 67(1)(4) of the PRC Constitution, one of the functions of the NPCSC is to interpret laws.

27 See Article 158 of the Hong Kong Basic Law and Article 143 of the Macao Basic Law.

heart lies the question of who should decide when such a final, authoritative interpretation should be given. This was one of the issues that arose in the right of abode controversy in Hong Kong. As the Hong Kong Court of Final Appeal (HKCFA) explained in *Democratic Republic of the Congo* v. *FG Hemisphere Associates LLC (No. 1)*,[28] the Court in *Ng Ka Ling* v. *Director of Immigration* had adopted this approach towards the final power of interpretation of the Hong Kong Basic Law: if both 'the classification condition' and 'the necessity condition' are satisfied, then the court has a duty to make a reference to the NPCSC. In determining whether the classification condition had been met, the HKCFA adopted the predominant provision test under Article 158 of the Hong Kong Basic Law, namely: 'As a matter of substance what predominately is the provision that has to be interpreted in the adjudication of the case?'[29] The continued validity of this test, however, needs to be further determined by the HKCFA after the NPCSC's Interpretation of 26 June 1999,[30] which was given in response to *Ng Ka Ling* v. *Director of Immigration*.[31]

The second issue was the claim by the HKCFA in *Ng Ka Ling* v. *Director of Immigration* that it could 'examine whether any legislative acts of the NPC or its Standing Committee . . . are consistent with the Basic Law and to declare them to be invalid if found to be inconsistent'.[32] This statement of jurisdiction 'got the CFA into trouble with those who thought that it had defied the authority of the NPC and set itself above the "sovereign"'.[33] In *Ng Ka Ling* v. *Director of Immigration (No. 2)*, the HKCFA put its unanimous clarification in these terms:[34]

> The court's judgment on 29 January 1999 did not question the authority of the Standing Committee to make an interpretation under art. 158 which would have to be followed by the courts of the Region. The Court

[28] (2011) 14 HKCFAR 95, [396]. [29] *Ibid*, [397].

[30] See the Interpretation of Articles 22(4) and 24(2)(3) of the Basic Law of the Hong Kong Special Administrative Region of the People's Republic of China by the Standing Committee of the National People's Congress (adopted at the 10th Meeting of the Standing Committee of the 9th NPC on 26 June 1999).

[31] [1999] 1 HKC 291. As for the classification and necessity conditions in this case, the HKCFA in *Lau Kong Yung* v. *Director of Immigration* [1999] 4 HKC 731 accepted that these conditions 'may' have to be revisited in a future case. The recent decision of the HKCFA in *Vallejos* v. *Commissioner of Registration* (2013) 16 HKCFAR 45 has secured the continued application of the classification and necessity conditions as a matter of Hong Kong law. See further, Lim and Chan (2015) paras. 2.089–2.093.

[32] [1999] 1 HKC 291, 323–324.

[33] See Ghai (2000) pp. 3 and 18. See further, Chen (2006) p. 636.

[34] [1999] 1 HKC 425, 427.

accepts that it cannot question that authority. Nor did the Court's judgment question, and the Court accepts that it cannot question, the authority of the National People's Congress or the Standing Committee to do any act which is in accordance with the provisions of the Basic Law and the procedure therein.

The legal significance of the NPCSC's Interpretation of 26 June 1999, namely, whether the NPCSC is confined to act within the scope of Hong Kong's autonomy in exercising its power of interpretation under Article 67(1)(4) of the PRC Constitution and Article 158 of the Hong Kong Basic Law, arose later as the central issue in *Lau Kong Yung* v. *Director of Immigration*.[35] The HKCFA answered this question in the negative. According to the Court, the NPCSC's power flows from the aforementioned provisions and 'is in general and unqualified terms'. Under Article 158(1) of the Basic Law, the power to interpret the Basic Law is vested in the NPCSC, and this power is not limited by Articles 158(2) and 158(3). The Court also cited Ghai's view that the NPCSC enjoys a 'plenary power', that is, its power of interpretation extends to any provision of the Basic Law and may be exercised in the absence of litigation.[36] The question raised in the right of abode affair concerned not only the power of final interpretation of the Basic Law, but also the question of the Basic Law's 'entrenchment' as well as the degree to which the NPCSC may bypass the Basic Law's amendment procedure.

Fourth, the 'high degree of autonomy' of the SARs is 'fatally deficient' in making and revising the Basic Laws themselves, and the process for amendment of the Basic Laws is extremely difficult.[37] The Basic Laws are nothing but national laws enacted by the NPC, over which the residents in the SARs have no control except through a handful of deputies assigned to the SARs, who seem to play little role in NPC lawmaking.[38] Moreover, part of the controversy over the NPCSC's Interpretation of the Hong Kong Basic Law in the right of abode affair has been the manner in which such interpretations might bypass the amendment procedure under Article 159 of the Hong Kong Basic Law. In *Lau Kong Yung* v. *Director of Immigration*, Sir Anthony Mason NPJ and Ching PJ considered that an interpretation by the NPCSC is not merely interpretative in nature, but expresses the intent of the Legislature.[39] Thus, the question

[35] [1999] 4 HKC 731. [36] [1999] 4 HKC 731, 756.

[37] For the amendment process of both Basic Laws, see Article 159 of the Hong Kong Basic Law and Article 144 of the Macao Basic Law.

[38] See Q. Zhang (2012) p. 114. [39] [1999] 4 HKC 731.

that arises is whether Article 158 acts to limit the full scope of Article 159 of the Hong Kong Basic Law where an NPCSC Interpretation may obviate the need to formally amend the Basic Law in certain cases where the meaning of the Basic Law is called into question. The prospect is that of an abuse of Article 158 assuming that the NPCSC would determine for itself both the need for an interpretation and its scope. It is here that the question of entrenchment has arisen in practice, following the right of abode affair.[40] Furthermore, Article 159(4) of the Hong Kong Basic Law provides that no amendment of the Law shall contravene the established basic policies of the PRC regarding Hong Kong. A further question thus arises concerning which authority is to determine that this requirement has been met. It is not clear whether the HKCFA may claim the power to do so.[41]

According to Chen:[42]

> When we turn from the breadth of autonomy to the legal security of autonomy however, Hong Kong under ... [the 'One Country, Two Systems' principle, or 'OCTS'] ... does not compare as favourably with states or provinces of the United States, Canada or Australia. This is because the formula for division of power between the central government and the SAR is not entrenched in the PRC Constitution itself. The formula is provided for instead in the Basic Law of the Hong Kong SAR ... a law made, and amended unilaterally by, the National People's Congress ... which is the supreme legislative organ of the PRC ... furthermore, unlike in the United States, Canada and Australia, there is no national Supreme Court in OCTS that arbitrates and resolves jurisdictional disputes between the national government and the regional government. Instead, the highest authority for the interpretation of the Basic Law, including the formula for division of power embodied in the Basic Law, is the ... NPCSC ... a political or parliamentary institution rather than a Supreme Court ...

The 'One Country, Two Systems' principle is not prescribed in the PRC Constitution. Nor is there any provision concerning the division of power between the SARs and the CPG. According to the late Professor

40 Lim and Chan (2015) para. 2.096. The Interpretation of Article 104 of the Basic Law of the Hong Kong Special Administrative Region of the People's Republic of China by the Standing Committee of the National People's Congress (adopted at the 24th Meeting of the Standing Committee of the 12th NPC on 7 November 2016), which stipulates the way that oath should be taken when the Chief Executive, principal officials, members of the Executive Council and of the Legco, judges of the courts at all levels and other members of the judiciary in the Hong Kong SAR assume office, also raised this issue. See Chan (2016).

41 See Lim and Chan (2015) para. 2.103.

42 Chen (2006) p. 631. Cf Lim and Chan (2015) para. 2.104.

Xu Chongde, who had participated in the drafting of the PRC Constitution and had been a member in the drafting committees for the Hong Kong and Macao Basic Laws, that is because the current Constitution was drafted during the period from September 1980 to November 1982, well before the Sino-British negotiations concerning China's resumption of sovereignty over Hong Kong began. Although the 'One Country, Two Systems' principle and the basic policies to maintain Hong Kong's stability and prosperity had been formed at that time, the ultimate result of the negotiations were uncertain. Therefore, it was considered not appropriate to put that principle in the Constitution.[43] Instead, Article 31 was formulated, which stipulates:

> The State may establish special administrative regions when necessary. The systems to be instituted in special administrative regions shall be prescribed by law enacted by the National People's Congress in the light of specific conditions.

Fifth, Article 95 of the Hong Kong Basic Law and Article 93 of the Macao Basic Law both provide that the SARs may, through consultations and in accordance with law, maintain *juridical (judicial)*[44] relations with the judicial organs of other parts of the country, and they may render assistance to each other. Some important developments in the field of cross-border cooperation have appeared since the handover of Hong Kong and Macao.[45] Although the previous two articles touch upon conflict of laws issues, there is no formal dispute settlement mechanism which exists independently of the ordinary operation of the PRC Constitution and that under the Constitution, no national court is granted the independent power of applying and enforcing the Constitution, or supervising the implementation of the Basic Laws, or resolving the legal conflicts between the SARs' autonomy and certain elements of the PRC legal system.[46] Consequently, in contrast to other compound legal systems, the PRC has no supreme judicial organ to coordinate and to

[43] See C. Xu (2010) p. 21. For the history of Hong Kong from a colony to a special administrative region, see Chan (2015).

[44] The word 'juridical' is used in the Hong Kong Basic Law, while the word 'judicial' is employed in the Macao Basic Law. As Ghai has observed, it is unclear whether the use of the word 'juridical' in the English version of the former is meant to distinguish it from 'judicial'. In the Chinese versions of both laws, the same word '*sifa*' is adopted. See Ghai (1999) p. 351.

[45] See the relevant documents contained in Office of Hong Kong-, Macao- and Taiwan-related Judicial Issues of the SPC (2013) and n 96.

[46] See C. Xu (2010) p. 77; Lim and Chan (2015) paras. 2.023–2.025.

resolve conflict of laws issues among the independent courts of the SARs and the people's courts in the Mainland. Uncertainties have thus emerged.[47]

The earlier analysis illustrates the differences between the Hong Kong and Macao SARs in the PRC and states or provinces under a federal system. Although the boundary of the autonomy of the SARs is not clear in certain areas, with respect to civil and commercial law, the two law districts may enjoy complete legislative independence. The particular choice of law issues as a result of the arrangements made for the SARs' autonomy under the Basic Laws are discussed in Section 8.2.

8.1.2 The Taiwan Region

The island of Taiwan was ceded to Japan in 1895 after China's defeat in the First Sino-Japanese War.[48] Japanese colonial rule in Taiwan ended in 1945 with Japan's defeat in the Second World War. On 1 October 1949, the PRC was established and the CPG became the sole legal government of China. The Kuomintang (Nationalist Party) Government of the Republic of China then retreated from the Mainland and established its rule over Taiwan in confrontation with the CPG. Since the founding of the PRC, the CPG has persistently worked towards the reunification of Taiwan with the Mainland.

The CPG's basic position regarding settlement of the Taiwan issue is: peaceful reunification and one country, two systems. According to the plan proposed by Deng Xiaoping in 1983, the terms offered to Taiwan were even more favourable than those devised for Hong Kong and

[47] For the use of the public policy exception in contracts and the ascertainment of Hong Kong, Macao and Taiwan laws, see Sections 8.2 and 8.3.

[48] In ancient times, Chinese governments of different periods set up administrative bodies to exercise jurisdiction over Taiwan. 'In order to upgrade the administration of Taiwan, the Qing government created Taibei Prefecture, Jilong Canton and three counties of Danshui, Xinzhu and Yilan in 1875 (1st year of the reign of Emperor Guangxu). In 1885 (11th year of the reign of Emperor Guangxu), the government formally made Taiwan a full province covering three prefectures and one sub prefecture and incorporating 11 counties and 5 cantons. Liu Mingchuan was appointed first Governor of Taiwan. During his tenure of office, railways were laid, mines opened, telegraph service installed, merchant ships built, industries started and new-style schools set up. Considerable social, economic and cultural advancement in Taiwan was achieved as a result.' See *The Taiwan Issue and Reunification of China* (White Paper on Taiwan Issue issued by the Taiwan Affairs Office of the State Council of the PRC on 1 September 1993), available at the official website of the Taiwan Affairs Office of the State Council www.gwytb.gov.cn/en/Special/WhitePapers/201103/t20110316_1789216.htm.

Macao.[49] Under this plan, the PRC would recognize Taiwan as a special administrative region with its own government, with its own domestic laws, with an independent judicial system, and with independent armed forces. In return, the government in Taiwan would be required to abandon its claim to authority over the Mainland and to recognize the PRC as its sole international representative. In the event, this 'One Country, Two Systems' concept proved to be totally unattractive to Taiwan.[50] Until now, the debate about reunification or independence still tears the people of Taiwan apart, and Taiwan is still separated from the Mainland. Although political disputes remain an obstacle between the Mainland and Taiwan, social, cultural and economic contacts across the Taiwan Strait have developed rapidly since the end of 1987, when the state of isolation between two sides was terminated. On the economic plane, doors have been opened to facilitate the flow of goods, capital and people. Businessmen from Taiwan are accorded preferential treatment and legal safeguards,[51] and are welcome to invest or trade on the Mainland. The Chinese Government has also adopted a positive attitude and taken measures to encourage bilateral exchanges and cooperation in various areas. A non-governmental Association for Relations Across the Taiwan Straits has been set up. It is authorized by the CPG to liaise with the Straits Exchange Foundation and other relevant non-governmental bodies in Taiwan for the purpose of maintaining the legitimate rights and interests of people on both sides and promoting inter-Straits relations.

Notwithstanding the possibility of reunification,[52] the increasing number of interactions between the Mainland and Taiwan has resulted in more cross-border legal issues in judicial practice. As Taiwan can maintain its own domestic laws even after reunification, it should be treated as a law district in the sense of conflict of laws.

[49] This proposal first became known in a discussion between Deng Xiaoping and Professor Yang Liyu of Seton Hall University. For an account of the discussion and for a summary of the proposal, see Deng (2009) pp. 193–194.

[50] See Ma (1993).

[51] They can enjoy preferential treatment that is offered to 'foreign investors'. See Section 8.2.

[52] The possible reunification of Taiwan is especially contentious in Taiwan. In response to the Mainland's proposal of 'one country, two systems', there have been contentious and sometimes fierce arguments in Taiwan and elsewhere for either 'one China, one Taiwan (*yizhong yitai*)', 'two Chinas (*liang'ge zhongguo*)' or alternatively 'Taiwan independence (*taidu*)' and 'an independent Taiwan (*dutai*)'. Taiwan's response has invited strong criticism from the Mainland. See *The Taiwan Issue and Reunification of China*, n 48.

8.1.3 The Relevant Provisions in Judicial Documents Concerning the Application of Hong Kong, Macao and Taiwan Laws

A Characteristics of Conflict of Laws among the Four Law Districts

The previous section has analysed the relation between the Mainland and Hong Kong, Macao and Taiwan. Under the 'One Country, Two Systems' regime, the latter three law districts all retain their own distinctive legal systems. In the private law context, the Mainland's legal system is not superior to any of the other legal systems. The Mainland, Hong Kong, Macao and Taiwan are therefore equal and independent law districts.[53] Taking into account the historical development of the four law districts, the conflicts of their laws have some characteristics that may distinguish them from those that arise in other compound legal systems.

First, the conflicts involve not only different socio-economic systems, but also legal systems of different traditions. While the socialist system (with Chinese characteristics) is practised in mainland China, the capitalist system and way of life in Hong Kong and Macao shall remain unchanged for at least fifty years.[54] Moreover, the legal system in each of the law districts has been shaped by different legal doctrines and heritages. The legal systems in Macao and Taiwan have been profoundly influenced by the continental European civil law system.[55] The legal system in Hong Kong was derived from the English common law system,[56] and the external influences that have contributed to shaping the contemporary legal system in mainland China include Soviet law, civil law and common law.[57]

[53] See Huang and Qian (1995) p. 303.

[54] See the Preamble of the PRC Constitution; Article 5 of the Hong Kong Basic Law and Article 5 of the Macao Basic Law. According to Deng Xiaoping, '50 years' is only a vivid expression: the capitalist system in the SARs will not be changed even after fifty years. See C. Xu (2010) pp. 14–16.

[55] See Wang (2006) chapter 2. [56] See Wesley-Smith (1998) p. 13.

[57] See Chen (2000). Chen also argued (pp. 68–69) that the classification of different legal systems is already out of date. Cf Huang and Qian (1995) pp. 294–303. Huang and Qian argued that since the legal system in mainland China belongs to the socialist law family, the whole landscape of legal systems of the Mainland, Hong Kong, Macao and Taiwan could be characterized by '1–2–3–4', that is, one country (the PRC), two systems (the capitalist and socialist systems), three law families (Chinese socialist law, common law and civil law) and four law districts. The author's analysis here is not to make a clear classification of different law families, but to demonstrate that difference does exist among the four law districts. The effect that such difference may have upon the treatment of choice of law issues in contract is further analysed in Section 8.2.

Second, the PRC Constitution has no unified binding force over the Mainland and the other three law districts. Even for the Mainland, there is no provision therein concerning the treatment of Hong Kong, Macao and Taiwan laws.

Third, as already mentioned, each law district enjoys independent judicial power, including the power of final adjudication. There is no supreme judicial organ to deal with conflict of laws issues among the four law districts.

These characteristics demonstrate the complexity of the conflicts. Chinese scholars often use the term 'interregional conflict of laws' to describe the phenomenon of conflict of laws among the four law districts within the PRC.[58] Before analysing the relevant provisions concerning choice of law in Hong Kong-, Macao- and Taiwan-related cases, two general points should be made.

On the one hand, Hong Kong, Macao and Taiwan elements cannot be defined as 'foreign elements' in litigation in the Mainland. Chinese scholars consider that interregional conflict of laws is different from private international law. Besides the characteristics just given, the most substantial difference, according to them, is that, while the conflict of laws to be resolved in private international law is that among different sovereign states, the interregional conflict of laws within the PRC is among different law districts *under the same sovereignty*.[59] As was mentioned, in the theory of conflict of laws, a contact with some system of law other than that of the forum can be taken as a 'foreign element', no matter whether that system is under the same sovereignty as the forum or not.[60] That is to say, the word 'foreign' or 'international' in conflict of laws or private international law is *not* indicative of the sovereignty to which a law district is subject. In fact, the fundamental reason underlying the conceptual distinction made by the Chinese scholars between interregional conflict of laws and private international law is the notion of sovereignty, which is always treated as a matter that cannot be compromised in China.[61] Since Hong Kong, Macao and Taiwan are all part of the territory of the PRC, Hong Kong-, Macao- and Taiwan-related cases are, in judicial practice, treated as being different from 'foreign-related'

[58] For the concept and the theory relevant to 'interregional conflict of laws', see Huang and Qian (1995) pp. 292–294; Zhu (2002) pp. 618–629.

[59] See Huang (1989) p. 66; Han (2003) pp. 322–327.

[60] See n 1.

[61] For the importance of sovereignty in the long history of China, and also the evolution of the 'One Country, Two Systems' policy, see Wang and Leung (1998) pp. 280–293.

cases, which involve contacts with other jurisdictions under different sovereignty.[62] Moreover, the adjudication of the civil and commercial cases involving contacts with those three law districts is considered to be of great significance to both the unification of the whole country and the implementation of the 'One Country, Two Systems' principle.[63]

On the other hand, the wholly-owned enterprises, equity joint ventures and contractual joint ventures funded and run by Hong Kong, Macao and Taiwan compatriots are entitled to enjoy the same preferential treatments as those accorded to foreign-invested enterprises in the Mainland.[64] That is to say, investors from these three districts are actually treated as 'foreign' investors.

In the Chinese statutes, there is no provision that particularly deals with the choice of law issues among the four law districts in the PRC. Although Hong Kong-, Macao- and Taiwan-related cases cannot be classified as foreign-related cases, the SPC has issued judicial documents stipulating that people's courts in the Mainland, when adjudicating cases involving those three law districts, should determine the applicable law 'by reference to' the ordinary private international law rules provided in statutes or judicial interpretations by the SPC.[65] As is further discussed shortly,[66] at least in the field of choice of law,[67] the distinction between the expressions 'foreign-related' and 'Hong Kong-, Macao- and Taiwan-related' cases only serves the purpose of emphasizing the principle of 'One Country, Two Systems' and that the PRC has the sovereign control over the three territories.[68]

62 See Yan and Liang (1992) p. 1; Yang and Zhang (1993) Preface, p. 1.

63 See Yang and Zhang (1993) Preface, p. 1; Han (2003) pp. 324–326.

64 See Article 5 of Regulations on Encouragement of Investments from Overseas Chinese and Hong Kong and Macao Compatriots (promulgated by the State Council on 19 August 1990) and Article 5 of Provisions of the State Council of the People's Republic of China for Encouraging Taiwan Compatriots to Invest in the Mainland (promulgated by the State Council on 3 July 1988).

65 See Parts B and C of this Section.

66 See Section 8.2.

67 Special arrangements between the Mainland and the other three law districts have appeared in fields such as recognition and enforcement of judgments, service of judicial documents and judicial cooperation. But the discussion of these issues is beyond the scope of this book.

68 A special rule on limitation period was provided by the SPC concerning Taiwan-related cases in order to protect the rights of Taiwan residents, and thus the classification of Taiwan-related cases had been important as that would determine whether the rule could be applied (see Part B of this Section). However, the rule is only applicable to obligations that were created in a particular period, and is thus of no significance in the adjudication of Taiwan-related cases now. See Zhang (2009) pp. 39–40.

B Provisions Concerning Hong Kong- and Macao-Related Cases

Before October 1987, there were no particular rules guiding the adjudication of Hong Kong- and Macao-related cases in the Mainland. When faced with a case involving Hong Kong or Macao elements, people's courts would have to seek guidance from the SPC. An example is that in 1957, the Higher People's Court of Liaoning Province received a case concerning a loan between a Hong Kong resident and a Mainland citizen. The defendant, when doing business in Hong Kong in 1949, borrowed 200 US dollars from the plaintiff there, but did not return the money until he was sued by the plaintiff in 1957. Not sure about whether to protect the obligation created in Hong Kong, the Higher People's Court of Liaoning Province sought guidance from the SPC. The SPC replied that since the obligation was between two private persons and had been proved to be a fact, the legal right of the plaintiff should be recognized and protected.[69]

On 19 October 1987, the SPC issued two judicial documents, both of which contained rules dealing with Hong Kong- and Macao-related cases. Article 2 of the Foreign Economic Contract Law[70] provided that the law applied to economic contracts concluded between enterprises or other economic organizations of the Mainland and foreign enterprises, other economic organizations or individuals. In Response of the Supreme People's Court to Certain Questions Concerning the Application of the Foreign Economic Contract Law,[71] the SPC stipulated that this law may also apply to economic contracts involving Hong Kong or Macao enterprises or other economic organizations or individuals. Hong Kong- or Macao-related economic contracts were therefore treated as foreign contracts, and the choice of law rule provided in Article 5 of the Foreign Economic Contract Law was applicable to them. On the same date, the SPC issued Response of the Supreme People's Court to Certain Questions Concerning the Adjudication of Cases involving Hong Kong- and

[69] See The Reply of the Supreme People's Court Regarding Whether to Protect the Obligation Created in Hong Kong between Xia Qinrui and Wu Zhixiang, in Research Office of the SPC (1997) pp. 574–575.

[70] It was adopted at the 10th meeting of the Standing Committee of the 6th NPC on 21 March 1985, became effective on 1 July 1985, and was invalidated from 1 October 1999 when the Contract Law entered into force.

[71] See Article 1(2). The Response was issued on 19 October 1987 by the SPC and invalidated on 13 July 2000.

Macao-related Economic Disputes.[72] Article 3(3) stipulated that if, according to the rules in Chapter 8 of the General Principles of the Civil Law entitled 'The Application of Laws in Foreign-related Civil Relations'[73] and Article 5 of the Foreign Economic Contract Law, Hong Kong, Macao or foreign laws should be applied in a case, these laws could be applied on condition that their application would not infringe the social public interest of China.

After the previous two judicial interpretations, the SPC has, in the subsequent documents, repeatedly stipulated that the choice of law rules provided for foreign-related cases 'shall be applied as a reference (*canzhao shiyong*)' in Hong Kong- or Macao-related cases.[74]

In Minutes of the Second National Working Conference on the Trial of Foreign-related Commercial and Maritime Cases (2005 Minutes),[75] there is no special choice of law rule for Hong Kong- or Macao-related cases. According to Article 153, the provisions for foreign-related cases shall apply. In 2007, the SPC issued Provisions on Several Issues Concerning the Application of the Law in Trials of Foreign-related Civil and Commercial Contract Disputes (2007 Provisions),[76] which contained particular choice of law rules in foreign-related commercial contracts. Article 11 provided that reference shall be made to the Provisions with respect to the law governing Hong Kong- and Macao-related contracts. A more recent provision is in Interpretation of the Supreme People's Court on Certain Issues Concerning the Application of the 'Law on the Application of Laws to Foreign-related Civil Relations' (1) (Interpretation of the 2010 Conflicts Statute (1)).[77] As the Law on the Application of Laws to Foreign-related Civil Relations (2010 Conflicts Statute)[78] does not specify whether the rules therein are also applicable to Hong Kong- and Macao-related cases, the SPC in this Interpretation clarifies this issue by providing that the rules in the 2010 Conflicts Statute as well as in the

[72] This interpretation was invalidated by the SPC on 13 July 2000.

[73] The General Principles of Civil Law was adopted at the 4th Session of the 6th NPC on 12 April 1986, became effective on 1 January 1987 and was amended at the 10th Meeting of the Standing Committee of the 11th NPC on 27 August 2009.

[74] The purpose of using 'as a reference' is to differentiate the Hong Kong- and Macao-related cases from other foreign-related cases.

[75] It was issued by the SPC on 26 December 2005.

[76] It was issued by the SPC on 23 July 2007, became effective on 8 August 2007, and was invalidated on 26 February 2013.

[77] It was issued by the SPC on 28 December 2012 and became effective on 7 January 2013.

[78] It was adopted at the 17th meeting of the Standing Committee of the 11th NPC on 28 October 2010 and became effective on 1 April 2011.

Interpretation shall apply as a reference to issues concerning the application of laws in cases involving Hong Kong and Macao elements.

The SPC's interpretations mentioned previously are the legal source for people's courts in the determination of the governing law in Hong Kong- and Macao-related cases.[79]

C Provisions Concerning Taiwan-Related Cases

Compared with the application of Hong Kong and Macao laws in people's courts, the status of Taiwan law has been a rather sensitive issue. It remained an obstacle in the adjudication of Taiwan-related cases until the SPC resolved it in a 2010 judicial interpretation.

Ever since the relaxation of tension between the two sides of the Taiwan Strait in 1987,[80] the SPC in mainland China has taken initial steps toward the creation of legal rules dealing with Taiwan-related issues in judicial practice. On 9 August 1988, the then vice president of the SPC, Ma Yuan, outlined the policy of the court toward a selected series of substantive issues of civil law relations between individuals from the two sides of the Taiwan Strait, including marriage, matrimonial property relationship, succession, adoption and guardianship, debts, real property rights and limitation.[81] The occasion was an address at the first press conference held by the SPC, and the statement represented the general policy of protecting the legitimate interests of parties from both sides of the Taiwan Strait and thus advancing the normal interactions of people and also the peaceful unification of the whole nation.[82] In The Report of the Work of the SPC, which was passed at the Fourth Session of the Seventh NPC in 1991,[83] the President of the SPC stated that the effects of the civil actions by Taiwan residents in Taiwan and of the civil rights that

[79] See Gao (2013) p. 45.

[80] For the situation of people to people contact between the two sides from 1949 to the end of 1987, see *The One-China Principle and the Taiwan Issue* (White Paper on the Taiwan Issue issued by the Taiwan Affairs Office of the State Council of the PRC on 21 February 2000), available at the official website of the Taiwan Affairs Office www.gwytb.gov.cn/en/Special/WhitePapers/201103/t20110316_1789217.htm; Tsai (1998) pp. 10–16.

[81] See 'Some Legal Issues concerning People's Courts' Dealing With Taiwan-related Civil Cases (Address by the Vice President Ma Yuan at the First News Conference Held by the SPC)', in Office of Hong Kong-, Macao- and Taiwan-related Judicial Issues of the SPC (2013) pp. 343–346.

[82] See *ibid.*

[83] See The Report on the Work of the SPC at the 4th Session of the 7th NPC in 1991 (passed on 9 April 1991), in Office of Hong Kong-, Macao- and Taiwan-related Judicial Issues of the SPC (2013) p. 178.

they acquired there according to the laws in the Taiwan Region could be recognized in the Mainland on condition that such actions or rights were not against the fundamental principles of the laws in mainland China. Moreover, the effect of the civil judgments rendered by Taiwan courts could also be recognized in accordance with the specific circumstances of a case. The rules on the recognition of Taiwan civil judgments in the Mainland are specified in 1998 in Provisions of the SPC on the People's Courts' Recognition of the Civil Judgments Made by Courts of the Taiwan Region.[84] In its Supplementary Provisions in 2009, the SPC further extended the scope of recognition to include civil rulings, mediation records and payment orders made by the courts of the Taiwan Region as well as awards made by the arbitral institutions of the Taiwan Region.[85] The SPC also stipulated that a civil judgment of a court of the Taiwan Region which is recognized upon a ruling of the people's court shall be of equal effect as an effective judgment of the people's court in the Mainland.[86] In 2015, the SPC issued Provisions on Recognition and Enforcement of the Civil Judgments of Courts of the Taiwan Region,[87] which superseded the aforementioned documents. Article 15(2) of it stipulates that if the recognition of a civil judgment from a court in Taiwan would violate the principle of 'One China', the fundamental principles of national laws or the social public interest of China, then people's courts should not recognize it.

In Provisions of the SPC on the Application of Law in the Trial of Taiwan-related Civil and Commercial Cases (Provisions on the Application of Law in Taiwan-Related Cases),[88] Article 1 provides:

> A people's court, when trying a Taiwan-related civil or commercial case, shall apply the relevant provisions of laws and judicial interpretations.
>
> Where, according to the choice of law rules as specified in laws and judicial interpretations, the civil laws of the Taiwan region are determined as applicable laws, the people's court shall apply these laws.

[84] It was issued by the SPC on 22 May 1998, became effective on 26 May 1998, and was invalidated on 29 June 2015.

[85] See Article 2 of Supplementary Provisions of the Supreme People's Court on the People's Courts' Recognition of Civil Judgments Made by the Courts of the Taiwan Region (issued on 24 April 2009 by the SPC, effective on 14 May 2009, invalidated on 29 June 2015).

[86] Article 1(2), *ibid.*

[87] It was issued by the SPC on 29 June 2015 and became effective on 1 July 2015.

[88] It was issued by the SPC on 27 December 2010 and became effective on 1 January 2011.

The 'choice of law rules' referred to in Article 1 include the rules provided in Chapter 8 of the Civil Law and also in the 2010 Conflicts Statute. In contrast with the aforementioned judicial interpretations concerning Hong Kong- and Macao-related cases, the SPC does not expressly mention that the governing law in Taiwan-related cases should be determined 'with reference to' the choice of laws rules applicable in foreign-related cases, although the same choice of law rules actually apply to both Taiwan-related and foreign-related cases. As is pointed out earlier, that is because the issue of sovereignty is of fundamental importance and the SPC must not create any confusion concerning the status of the Taiwan region.[89]

8.2 The Scope of the 'Social Public Interest' Reservation under the 'One Country, Two Systems' Regime

In the absence of any choice of law rules that particularly deal with the interregional conflict of laws within the PRC, the statutory restrictions on party autonomy, which have been discussed in Chapters 5 and 6, are also applicable in Hong Kong-, Macao- and Taiwan-related contractual cases. As the identification of mandatory rules should be conducted by interpreting the relevant statutes of the forum, the 'One Country, Two Systems' principle would not have much effect upon this issue.[90] This section thus focuses on the scope of the 'social public interest' reservation under the principle.

8.2.1 Applicability of the Reservation in Hong Kong-, Macao- and Taiwan-Related Cases

Some Chinese scholars have argued that the social public interest exception should *not* be upheld in interregional conflicts.[91] They considered that *ordre public* is a principle for the exclusion of foreign law in international litigation, and its purpose is to protect state sovereignty and interest. However, in an interregional context, the different law districts should respect each other, and recognize and enforce the decisions rendered in the other districts. Moreover, the substantial differences in political, economic and legal systems between the Mainland and

[89] See the discussion in Part A.
[90] For the identification of mandatory rules, see Section 6.2 of Chapter 6.
[91] See Guo (2002) pp. 50–51.

the SARs should have been recognized and accepted by the other law districts under the 'One Country, Two Systems' principle. If *ordre public* continues to be applied in interregional conflicts, then the relationship between the four law districts may become similar to that between different sovereign states, which is against the purpose underlying the principle and also harmful to the long-term development of the Mainland as well as the SARs.

Other scholars, however, insisted that the application of public policy may in fact be beneficial to the SARs. They concluded that, to uphold the exception of *ordre public* would, on the one hand, guarantee the implementation of the 'One Country, Two Systems' policy as far as the interregional conflict of laws is concerned, and it would be beneficial to the co-existence of all legal systems in a relatively long time. On the other hand, it would provide a 'safety valve' for all regions concerned to prevent their respective basic interests from any infringement, so as to dispel the fear and suspicion of the people in the SARs about the socialist legal system (of the Mainland), and to increase their confidence in the success of 'One Country, Two Systems'.[92]

The statement looked at interregional conflict of laws from a broader perspective. It should be noted that, under the 'One Country, Two Systems' principle, whether *ordre public* is applicable or not in the conflict of laws rules of each law district is to be determined by the legislature and courts of that district. Moreover, no matter whether the *ordre public* exception is applied or not, the PRC Constitution and the Basic Laws have already guaranteed the co-existence of the legal systems of the four law districts.[93] Therefore, the statement is not very convincing as it did not provide sufficient analysis on why the social public interest reservation should be upheld.

In judicial practice, clauses on social public interest are included in the arrangements between the Mainland and the SARs on judicial assistance and also the SPC's judicial interpretation on the application of Taiwan law.

In Arrangement of the SPC for Mutual Authorisation between Courts in Mainland and Macao SAR for Service of Judicial Documents and Obtainment of Evidence in Civil And Commercial Cases,[94] Article 8(2) states:

> In the process of fulfilling an authorisation, where the authorised courts hold that the fulfilment of the authorisation does not fall under the

[92] Han and Huang (1989) p. 128. [93] See Section 8.1.
[94] It was issued by the SPC on 27 August 2001 and became effective on 25 September 2001.

> jurisdiction of courts, where the authorised People's Courts based in the Mainland hold that the fulfilment of the authorisation in the Mainland goes against its basic legal principles or social public interests, or where courts based in the Macao SAR hold that the fulfilment of the authorisation in the Macao SAR goes against its basic legal principles or public order, they can reject the authorisation. However, under such a circumstance, they shall explain to the authorising courts the reason for the rejection in written form and in a timely manner.

The judges from the SPC explained how this article was conceived:[95]

> The wording of public order is mainly applied in documents concerning international relations. Initially, we considered that Macao is a part of China after its return to China, and that in documents related to private rights of the parties concerned, the wording of public order may not necessarily be used. But in the ensuing consultation, the two sides felt that there are differences in the legal systems of the two sides. Therefore, proceeding from the principle of mutual respect, the Arrangement applies the wording of public order in Clause 2 of Article 8 in accordance with the relevant legal provisions of both sides.

But the judges do not reveal to which existing legal sources 'the relevant legal provisions of both sides' relate. Social public interest provisions are also included in the agreements on recognition and enforcement of judgments or arbitral awards between the Mainland and Hong Kong or Macao SAR.[96] For Taiwan-related cases, Article 3 of the Provisions on the Application of Law in Taiwan-Related Cases stipulates:

[95] See Shao and Yu (2013) pp. 17–18.

[96] See Article 11 of Arrangement between the Mainland and the Macao Special Administrative Region on the Mutual Recognition and Enforcement of Civil and Commercial Judgments (issued by the SPC on 21 March 2006, effective on 1 April 2006), Article 7 of Arrangement between the Mainland and the Macao SAR on Reciprocal Recognition and Enforcement of Arbitration Awards (issued by the SPC on 12 December 2007, effective on 1 January 2008), Article 7 of Arrangements of the Supreme People's Court on the Mutual Enforcement of Arbitral Awards between the Mainland and the Hong Kong Special Administrative Region (issued by the SPC on 24 January 2000, effective on 1 February 2000), Article 9 of Arrangement of the Supreme People's Court between the Mainland and the HKSAR on Reciprocal Recognition and Enforcement of the Decisions of Civil and Commercial Cases under Consensual Jurisdiction (issued by the SPC on 3 July 2008, effective on 1 August 2008) and Article 9(2) of Arrangement on Reciprocal Recognition and Enforcement of Civil Judgments in Matrimonial and Family Cases by the Courts of the Mainland and of the Hong Kong Special Administrative Region (issued by the SPC on 20 June 2017, to be effective after both sides have completed their respective internal procedures).

> The relevant laws determined according to these provisions as applicable may not be applied when such laws are in violation of the basic principles of national law or the social public interest.

Therefore, based on the above judicial documents issued by the SPC, the social public interest reservation can also be invoked by people's courts when the application of Hong Kong, Macao or Taiwan laws are found to be against the social public interest of the Mainland. It has been mentioned in Chapters 5 and 6 that people's courts have already applied this reservation in Hong Kong-related cases involving guaranty contracts. Their approach is unconvincing as the provisions on foreign exchange control in the Mainland cannot be categorized as mandatory rules even in domestic contract law.[97] Besides guaranty contracts, there is another category of contract, which is easily considered to attract the reservation. That is loan contracts for the purpose of gambling. The next section analyses whether the social public interest exception should be invoked in this kind of contract.[98]

8.2.2 Analysis of 'Social Public Interest': Taking Gambling Debt as an Example

A Application of the Social Public Interest Reservation in Gambling Debts

With a gaming history stretching back for more than three centuries, Macao was renowned as the 'Las Vegas of the East', and gambling is now the pillar industry of Macao. It is said that around 60 to 70 per cent of revenue or even more in the gambling industry in Macao is generated from VIP rooms in the casinos, which mostly do business by way of offering casino credit, that is, lending money to the gamblers first and getting repaid afterwards.[99] Nowadays, many gamblers in VIP rooms are

[97] See Sections 5.2.2 and 6.1.2 of Chapters 5 and 6. However, in a more recent case, the SPC still considered that the Chinese provisions on foreign exchange control should be taken as mandatory rules in the sense of Article 4 of the 2010 Conflicts Statute. Therefore, it disregarded the choice of Hong Kong law by the parties in the three guaranty contracts and directly applied the law of the Mainland. See *Shantou Ocean Enterprise Group Co.* v. *Bank of China (Hong Kong) Co. Ltd.* (17 January 2012, Supreme People's Court).

[98] Although people's courts normally determine the governing law of such cases according to the closest connection principle but not the party autonomy principle, the analysis to come indicates the scope of the social public interest exception in contractual choice of law and how it should be invoked in judicial practice.

[99] See Wang (2011) p. 47.

from mainland China.[100] Mainlanders may also participate in gambling by going on cruise ships in Hong Kong, which will later travel to the high seas. Lenders normally advance an amount of money to gamblers in the form of gambling chips, with which gamblers from the Mainland play at casinos.[101] If the Mainland gamblers lose, which is the normal case, and they fail to repay the money advanced to them by the lenders, claims will probably be made against the gamblers in a Macao or Hong Kong court, or, where the gamblers have no or not enough property in Macao or Hong Kong, in people's courts in the Mainland. Chinese scholars and judges have argued that if Mainland gamblers are sued in people's courts for the money they borrowed in Macao for gambling purpose, the debts thus incurred should not be recognized and protected because they are against the social public interest of mainland China.[102] People's courts have also invoked the reservation in judicial practice.

In *Yu Jinhong* v. *Liang Yangjiao*,[103] Liang Yangjiao was a resident of the city of Foshan in the Mainland and Yu Jinhong was an employee working in the casino on the cruise ship named 'Metropolis'. Liang played at the gambling table with the chips provided by Yu when the ship was travelling on the high seas. Liang lost all the chips advanced to her in gambling. After the cruise came back to a Hong Kong harbour, she signed on the receipt of the loan prepared by Yu, which recorded that Liang owed HKD 80,000 to Yu. Yu then sued Liang in Foshan for the money. In the first trial, the Nanhai District People's Court determined that as the parties did not choose the applicable law, Hong Kong law should be applied as the residence of the lender was in Hong Kong. However, the gambling debt was against the provisions in the Mainland prohibiting gambling. The application of Hong Kong law would therefore infringe the social public interest of the Mainland. The court accordingly held that the law of mainland China should be applied and dismissed Yu's claims. Yu then appealed to Foshan Intermediate People's Court. Yu argued that his provision of gambling chips to Liang was

[100] Gamblers from the Mainland bet on credit also because of the cash regulations in mainland China. The laws restrict to RMB 20,000 yuan the amount a citizen may take across the border, and a maximum of RMB 10,000 yuan from a cash machine in a day. See *Macau Casinos Cut Out Middlemen and Recruit Gamblers Directly from Mainland China*, available on the website of South China Morning Post: www.scmp.com/news/china/article/1438209/macau-casinos-cut-out-middlemen-and-recruit-gamblers-directly-mainland accessed on 4 July 2017.

[101] See *ibid.* [102] See Sun (2005) pp. 81–82; Yan (2006) p. 158; Ye (2012) pp. 167–168.

[103] 13 November 2013, Foshan Intermediate People's Court.

lawful in Hong Kong, and that whether Liang gambled with the chips or not was none of his business. He thus considered that the debt was not a gambling debt as he did not gamble with Liang. Moreover, he insisted that the loan receipt was signed in Hong Kong and Hong Kong law should be applied. The appellate court also decided that Hong Kong law should be the governing law concerning the loan relationship between the parties. But the court held that, since the debt was incurred as a result of Yu's providing gambling chips to Liang for her participation in gambling, the formation of the debt was against the provisions in mainland China prohibiting gambling and the application of Hong Kong law would infringe the social public interest of the Mainland. The appeal was thus dismissed.

In *Xu Wen* v. *Hu Guisheng*,[104] Xu and Hu made a cooperation agreement for the purpose of investing in the business of chips turnover at casinos in Macao. Xu then transferred the amount of money specified in the agreement to Hu's bank account and they then began conducting the business together. However, Xu later found that Hu did not allow him to participate in the business, and did not share the profits with him. Xu then sued Hu in Guiyang Intermediate People's Court for the money that he had transferred to Hu and for compensation for his losses. The court held that the key issue in this case was whether the claims of Xu were based on lawful civil rights. Since the agreement was made in Macao and the business was conducted in Macao, the court considered that the contract was a Macao-related one, and Macao had the closest connection with the contract. Thus, the court determined that Macao Law should be the governing law. According to the relevant laws of Macao, the business of chips turnover was lawful. However, the court held that the application of Macao law would be against the social public interest of mainland China, and on the basis of Article 150 of the Civil Law (on social public interest), the court applied the law of the Mainland. Because Xu knew that the money that he transferred to Hu would be used to provide loans to patrons at casinos, the court decided that Xu's claims were illegal civil rights and could not be protected according to Article 5 of the Civil Law.[105]

[104] 15 December 2014, Guiyang Intermediate People's Court; 15 June 2016, Guizhou Higher People's Court.

[105] Article 5 of the Civil Law reads: 'The lawful civil Rights and interests of citizens and legal persons shall be protected by law and should not be infringed by any organization or individual.'

Xu then appealed to Guizhou Higher People's Court. The appellate court confirmed that Macao law should be the law governing the agreement. As to the business conducted by the parties, the court held that chips turnover was one of the services provided for the purpose of gambling. Although it was legal in Macao, to recognize its legality and protect the debts that arose from it would undermine the social public interest and good morals of the Mainland. Therefore, according to Article 5 of the 2010 Conflicts Statute (on social public interest), the law of mainland China should be applied in this case. On the basis of Article 52(1)(4) of the Contract Law,[106] the court decided that the agreement between the parties was void, and that Hu should return the money to Xu according to Article 58 of the Contract Law.[107]

In other cases, people's courts either invoked the reservation to exclude Macao or Hong Kong laws,[108] or alternatively, simply held that, since the creditors chose to sue the debtors in people's courts in the Mainland, the law of mainland China should be applied.[109] The relevant gambling debts were not protected as they were found to be against the Mainland provisions prohibiting gambling.

[106] Article 52(1)(4) reads: 'A contract shall be null and void under any of the following circumstances: . . . (4) undermining social public interest . . . '

[107] Article 58 reads: 'After a contract becomes invalid or is rescinded, any property obtained under the contract shall be returned. If it is impossible or unnecessary to return the property, compensation shall be made at an estimated price. The party at fault shall compensate the other party for the loss caused by the fault. If both parties have faults, they shall bear their respective responsibilities.'

[108] For example, in *Lai* v. *Li* (Nanwan Circuit Tribunal of Xiangzhou People's Court in Zhuhai, reported in *People's Court Daily*, 13 May 2012), Lai was domiciled in Macao and worked at a casino, and Li was a resident in Zhuhai, Guangdong Province. They entered into a contract in Zhuhai for the purpose of conducting business by providing loans for gambling in Macao. Lai and Li both agreed that they should have equal share of profits and loss. After their relationship broke down, Lai sued Li in Zhuhai for the money that he claimed Li had owed him. Since the parties did not choose the law governing the contract, the court held that the contract should be governed by the law of the place with the closest connection to the dispute, that is, Macao law. Although the contract was not a gambling contract in a strict sense (because it was not between a patron and an operator or lender to enable the patron to engage in gambling activities), the court held that, the prohibition of gambling represented the public policy of the Mainland, and the application of Macao law, under which gambling was legal, would violate the social public interest of mainland China. On that basis, the court excluded Macao law and applied the law of the Mainland. Since gambling debts were not protected under the law of the Mainland, the court finally dismissed the action.

[109] See *Zhu Guiqing* v. *Fan Huiqiang* (23 July 2013, Nanning Intermediate People's Court of Guangxi Zhuang Autonomous Region).

In the previously mentioned sources, scholars or judges have only made the general argument that gambling is prohibited in the Mainland. They have not analysed how the enforcement of gambling debts would infringe social public interest. Nor have they provided detailed legal reasoning concerning the public policy in mainland China in relation to gambling. As analysed in Chapters 5 and 6, the social public interest reservation should be invoked at the end of the choice of law process and after a court has examined the content of a foreign law and the result it may bring about. Moreover, the strength of the reservation depends on the quality of connection between the forum and the case or dispute.[110] The following sections address these issues.

B The Public Policy in Mainland China in Relation to Gambling

On 2 December 2011, the SPC issued Notice on Legally and Properly Hearing Cases on Disputes over Private Lending to Promote Economic Development and Maintain Social Stability (Notice on Private Lending).[111] Point 4 states:

> People's courts shall confirm the validity of a private lending contract according to law, protect the legal creditor-debtor relationship, effectively protect the lawful rights and interests of the parties, and ensure that the handling of the case can achieve positive legal and social effects. The creditor-debtor relationship formed by illegal and criminal activities such as gambling and drug abuse, or under the circumstance that the lender has knowledge that the borrower borrows the money for engaging in the said illegal and criminal activities, shall not be, in accordance with law, provided protection.

This statement is relied on by people's courts and is taken to be indicative of the public policy in the Mainland concerning gambling.[112] In 2015, the SPC further issued Provisions on Several Issues concerning the Application of Law in the Trial of Private Lending Cases.[113] Article 14 provides that if the lender provides the loan although he or she knows in advance or should have known that the borrower borrowed the money

[110] See Section 6.2.4 of Chapter 6. [111] It was effective on 2 December 2011.

[112] See *Zhu Guiqing* v. *Fan Huiqiang* (23 July 2013, Nanning Intermediate People's Court of Guangxi Zhuang Autonomous Region) and *Yu Jinhong* v. *Liang Yangjiao* (13 November 2013, Foshan Intermediate People's Court).

[113] It was issued by the SPC on 6 August 2015 and became effective on 1 September 2015.

for illegal and criminal activities, then people's courts shall determine that the private lending contract between them is null and void.

The gambling debts that are rendered unenforceable by the aforementioned provisions are only those involving *illegal and criminal activities*. Whether the activities involved in a debt are 'illegal and criminal' should generally be determined according to the laws of the jurisdiction where such activities take place.[114] Even within the territory of the Mainland, not all forms of gambling are illegal or criminal.

Article 303 of the Criminal Law of the PRC[115] provides:

> Whoever, for the purpose of making profits, gathers people to engage in gambling or makes gambling his profession shall be sentenced to fixed-term imprisonment of not more than three years, criminal detention or public surveillance and shall, in addition, be fined.
>
> Whoever runs a gambling house shall be sentenced to fixed-term imprisonment of not more than three years, criminal detention or public surveillance and shall, in addition, be fined; and if the circumstances are serious, he shall be sentenced to fixed-term imprisonment of not less than three years but not more than ten years and shall, in addition, be fined.

The elements to be considered when deciding whether a person has committed the criminal offence of gambling include the purpose *and* the forms of his or her conduct. If a person is not engaging in gambling for the purpose of making profits, or if he or she did not conduct one of the three forms of behaviour in Article 303, then the behaviour does not constitute a criminal offence. That is to say, participation in gambling for high stakes, even regularly, does not necessarily constitute a criminal offence on condition that the person does not make gambling his or her occupation or as the main source of his or her daily life.[116]

[114] The gambling activities of Mainland citizens outside the territory of the Mainland may also be criminalized under the Criminal Law of the PRC. But whether those activities are criminal should be determined on the basis of the criteria provided by the law.

[115] It was adopted by the 2nd Session of the 5th NPC on 1 July 1979, revised at the 5th Session of the 8th NPC on 14 March 1997, amended for the first time on 25 December 1999, for the second time on 31 August 2001, for the third time on 29 December 2001, for the fourth time on 28 December 2002, for the fifth time on 28 February 2005, for the sixth time on 29 June 2006, for the seventh time on 28 February 2009, for the eighth time on 1 May 2011, for the ninth time on 29 August 2015 and for the tenth time on 4 November 2017.

[116] See Jia and You (1997) pp. 521–522; Chen and Huang (2000) pp. 419–420.

As to illegal gambling that does not constitute a criminal offence, Article 70 of the Public Security Administration Punishments Law of the PRC provides:[117]

> Anyone who facilitates gambling for the purpose of making profits, or participates in any gambling activity on a relatively large sum of gambling stakes shall be detained for not more than 5 days or shall be fined not more than 500 yuan. If the circumstances are serious, he (she) shall be detained for not less than 10 days but not more than 15 days, and shall be concurrently fined not less than 500 yuan but not more than 3,000 yuan.

This article does not prohibit people from participating in gambling, but only those on a 'relatively large sum of gambling stakes' should be punished. It is not clear how to determine whether a certain amount of money is 'relatively large' or not. In fact, in an interpretation issued in 2005, the SPC specified that those who engage in win-or-loss entertainments involving a small amount of property but not for the purpose of making profits, or provide chess and cards rooms or other entertainment places and only charge normal place and service fees will not be punished as gambling.[118]

The above provisions demonstrate that not all forms of gambling constitute criminal offences or should be punished in mainland China. Furthermore, these provisions are mainly applicable to activities within the territory of the Mainland.[119] For Mainland citizens' participation in gambling in Macao or Hong Kong SARs, none of those provisions applies to them if their behaviour does not constitute an offence according to the Criminal Law.[120]

[117] It was adopted at the 17th Meeting of the Standing Committee of the 10th NPC on 28 August 2005, became effective on 1 March 2006, and was amended at the 29th Meeting of the Standing Committee of the 11th NPC on 26 October 2012.

[118] See Article 9 of Interpretation of the Supreme People's Court and Supreme People's Procuratorate about Some Issues Concerning the Application of Law in Gambling Criminal Cases (issued by the SPC and the Supreme People's Procuratorate on 11 May 2005, effective on 13 May 2005).

[119] Article 4 of the Public Security Administration Punishments Law provides that the law only applies to acts within the territory of the Mainland. Articles 6 and 7 of the Criminal Law stipulates that the Law applies to all who commit crimes within the territory of the Mainland, and also to mainland citizens who commit the crimes specified in the Law outside the territory of the Mainland; but those who commit the crimes may not be dealt with in the Mainland provided that the Law stipulates a maximum sentence of less than a three-year fixed-term imprisonment for such crimes.

[120] Article 7 of the PRC Criminal Law criminalizes the gambling activities of Mainland citizens outside the territory of the Mainland only when such activities constitute an offence under Article 303 of the Law. See n 119.

Not only are certain forms of gambling not prohibited in the Mainland, but certain forms of gambling or gaming are encouraged or even promoted. It is a matter of common knowledge to people living in the Mainland that there are many varieties of welfare lottery and sports lottery tickets that can be purchased by individuals voluntarily at lottery sellers. Those tickets are franchised, issued and sold by the state for the purpose of raising public welfare funds and promoting the development of public welfare establishments.[121] Many people take part in frequent lawful lotteries and they can win prizes out of them according to the relevant rules. The public purse benefits from this widespread gambling in the Mainland: the lottery public welfare fund is used particularly for public welfare, sports and other public welfare establishments that benefit Mainland citizens.[122] The state policy towards gambling can also be seen in the development of the tourism industry in Hainan Province, particularly the city of Sanya. In Several Opinions of the State Council on Promoting the Construction and Development of the Hainan International Tourism Island, the State Council mentioned that some internationally popular tourist sports and entertainment projects should be tried, and guess-type sports lotteries and instant ticket lotteries for large international events should be developed gradually.[123]

From the above, it can be understood that the public policy of mainland China as reflected in the laws and state policy is not against gambling *per se*. The public policy in relation to gambling is that gambling should be strictly controlled by law and directed by the government so that it can be developed in a way that is beneficial to the whole community, not only to the private interests of casino owners.

C Social Public Interest, the Connection of the Case to the Forum and the Control of Gambling in the Mainland

Besides analysing the public policy in the Mainland relating to gambling, it is also necessary to examine the connection of a specific case to the forum[124] and the role of people's courts in controlling gambling.

[121] For the purpose and administration of lawful lotteries in the Mainland, see Lottery Regulations (issued by the State Council on 4 May 2009, effective on 1 July 2009).

[122] For details of the distribution of the lottery public welfare fund in the Mainland, see, for example, Report of the Financial Ministry concerning the Distribution and Use of the Lottery Public Welfare Fund in 2014 (issued by the Ministry of Finance on 26 August 2015).

[123] It was issued by the State Council on 31 December 2009.

[124] See Section 6.2.4 of Chapter 6.

On the one hand, the application of the social public interest reservation should involve the examination of the connection between the forum and the case. In *Yu Jinhong* v. *Liang Yangjiao*,[125] the only connection of the case with the Mainland was that the debtor's habitual residence was in mainland China. Hong Kong was the place of performance of the contract and where the loan contract was signed, and also the residence of the creditor. In *Xu Wen* v. *Hu Guisheng*,[126] the agreement between the parties was signed and performed in Macao. Although both parties were residents of the Mainland, the business of chips turnover was conducted in Macao. In the other cases cited above,[127] Macao was also the place where the loan contracts were signed and performed. The creditors sued the debtors in the Mainland only because the debtors had property in the Mainland. Since the gambling activities involved in these cases did not take place in the Mainland, to enforce the debts thus incurred would not be against the provisions of mainland China prohibiting illegal and criminal gambling.[128]

On the other hand, the social public interest reservation should not extend to the protection of people incapable of making rational decisions regarding their financial affairs. The giving of credit for gambling in Hong Kong or Macao might be alleged to encourage or assist people from the Mainland to gamble,[129] but that should not be the legal basis according to which a court invokes the reservation and renders a loan contract void. In the unreported judgment of *Las Vegas Hilton Corporation* v. *Lo Yuk Leung*,[130] Findlay J. said this in relation to public policy, the law and gambling in Hong Kong:[131]

> We have, in Hong Kong, plenty of addictive gamblers, drinkers and shoppers, and those that supply the facilities to gamble, drink and shop provide plenty of encouragement and assistance to these people to indulge their addictions. It is not conceivable that any court in Hong Kong would find it contrary to public policy or morality to allow the recovery of debts

[125] See n 103. [126] See n 104. [127] See nn 108 and 109.

[128] See the discussion of the relevant provisions in Part B.

[129] In the first trial of *Yu Jinhong* v. *Liang Yangjiao*, the People's Court of Nanhai District in Foshan held that Yu's lending of chips to Liang actually provided assistance to her participation in gambling and therefore, the debt should not be protected by law. The judgment of first trial was confirmed in the appeal.

[130] [1998] HKCU 33 (1997, No. A8739, 19 January 1998). The analysis in this judgment of the public policy in Hong Kong in relation to gambling is very instructive for the author's discussion in this section.

[131] [1998] HKCU 33 at 11–12.

incurred by such persons in the pursuit of their addictions. That may be desirable in a Utopia, but we do not live in such a society. If a person is incapable of making rational decisions regarding his financial affairs, that is something that he, his family, his friends or the public authorities should do something about; it is not a situation in which the Hong Kong Jockey Club, or any other supplier of goods or services, should be expected to protect that person against his own inclinations that may be detrimental to his welfare and that of his family.

These remarks are also helpful and instructive for the situation in the Mainland. Under Mainland and Hong Kong Closer Economic Partnership Arrangement and Mainland and Macao Closer Economic Partnership Arrangement (CEPA),[132] Mainland residents in Guangdong Province are permitted to visit Hong Kong and Macao individually. They thus have the freedom to participate in any activities that are legal under the laws of Hong Kong or Macao when visiting. This has caused concern in the Mainland. Editorials in the Mainland state press, such as *Beijing Youth Daily*, have described casinos in Macao as bringing an 'epidemic' to mainland China because reckless gambling by Mainland government officials and entrepreneurs in Macao threaten the national treasury of the Mainland and have 'led to countless losses of family savings' and bankruptcy of many enterprises in mainland China.[133] Although the concern may not be groundless, it cannot justify people's courts playing a role in controlling gambling through refusing the enforcement of gambling debts in civil litigation. That is something that state authorities should deal with. In fact, the Mainland government has taken steps to strengthen the regulation of money flows in order to control gambling more and alert people, telling them to behave. Moreover, Macao is an obvious focus as the government tightens oversight of civil servants and keeps an ever closer watch on flamboyant luxury spending.[134] If a debt is not incurred in the Mainland from illegal or criminal gambling, the enforcement of it will not infringe on the social order of the Mainland. On the contrary, if people's courts insist that to enforce a gambling debt valid under its governing law is against the public policy of the Mainland, that will actually provide much

[132] See Article 14 of both Arrangements. The former was signed in Hong Kong on 29 June 2003 and became effective on the same date; the latter was signed in Macao on 17 October 2003 and became effective on the same date.

[133] See Huang (2010) p. 124, n 76 and the articles cited there.

[134] See Oswald Chen, *Macao-related Gambling Shares Dip on Central Govt. Clampdown*, available at the website of China Daily: www.chinadaily.com.cn/hkedition/2012-12/05/content_15986335.htm accessed on 4 July 2017.

more encouragement and assistance to addictive gamblers to indulge their additions: by going back to the Mainland, they can be relieved from their debts as the creditor from Macao or Hong Kong will not be able to collect the debt through litigation in the Mainland.[135] Furthermore, the non-enforcement of gambling debts will also create an imbalance: if Mainland gamblers win, money can be taken there from Macao; if they lose and return, gambling debts would not be collectable from there back to Macao. The latter situation could even instigate the collectors of gambling debts to resort to violence, which is of course undesirable.[136] Enforcing a loan contract for gambling which is valid under the governing law will further force a gambler to make rational decisions concerning his or her financial situation and this, to some extent, will help control irrational gambling.

D The 'One Country, Two Systems' Principle and Social Public Interest

The different legal provisions concerning gambling between the SARs and the Mainland is the inevitable result of the 'One Country, Two Systems' principle.[137] According to the Basic Laws, Hong Kong and Macao both enjoy a high degree of autonomy, including the legislative power and the power of final adjudication.[138] They are thus free to develop their tourism and recreation industries. Article 118 of the Macao Basic Law particularly stipulates that Macao shall, on its own, make policies on tourism and recreation in the light of its overall interests. Certain categories of gambling debts are legal and can be collected through lawsuits according to Macao Law. Article 1171(1) of Macao Civil Code provides:[139]

> Gaming and betting are sources of civil obligations when special laws so provide; gaming and betting in sports competitions in relation to the persons taking part in them are also sources of civil obligations; otherwise, lawful gaming and betting are a mere source of natural obligations.

Casino credits were formally legalized in Macao in 2004. Article 4 of the Regulation on Gambling or Betting Credits in Casinos stipulates:[140]

> Credits offered in accordance with this law shall incur legal obligations.

[135] This will also cause injustice – the defendant will benefit by escaping liability which he or she freely entered into. See Anagnost (1968) p. 855.

[136] See Tu (2013) pp. 372–373; Tang (2014) p. 12.

[137] See Zhu (2013) pp. 62–63.

[138] See Section 8.1.1.

[139] See Macao Civil Code, Law No.33/99/M. The translation is by the author.

[140] See Regulation on Gambling or Betting Credit in Casinos, Law No.5/2004.

Based on the provisions in the Regulation, natural persons who are gambling agents working in casinos are also permitted to give credits to gamblers.[141] Gambling in Hong Kong is governed by the Gambling Ordinance (Cap. 148). Generally, gambling is unlawful in Hong Kong, but this is subject to the broad exception that it 'is lawful if the game is played on a social occasion in private premises and is not promoted or conducted by way of trade or business or for the private gain of any person otherwise than to the extent of a person's winnings as a player of or at the game'.[142]

The effectiveness of those laws in the SARs is guaranteed by the Basic Laws adopted by the NPC, which are binding over all the organs in the PRC, including people's courts in the Mainland.[143] Therefore, people's courts should be aware of the difference and should not invoke the social public interest reservation at random simply because the laws in the SARs are different from the relevant laws in the Mainland.[144]

E Summary

The previous analysis does not suggest that the statutory rules relating to gambling in mainland China do not have any role to play in a conflict of laws context. According to ordinary conflicts rules, they should be regarded as applicable to all contracts which are either governed by the law of the Mainland, or entered into for the purpose of activities to be carried out within the territory of mainland China.[145] The above sections demonstrate that there should not be a social public interest objection to the enforcement through people's courts of a contract which is governed by non-Mainland law and relating to activities outside the territory of the Mainland even though the contract would have been unenforceable had

[141] See Wang (2011) pp. 44–45.

[142] Gambling in a casino in Hong Kong is also unlawful, and a criminal offence. For the law and public policy in Hong Kong in relation to gambling, see *Las Vegas Hilton Corporation* v. *Lo Yuk Leung* [1998] HKCU 33.

[143] See Article 17 of both Basic Laws. For the binding force of the Hong Kong Basic Law, see C. Xu (2010) pp. 35–38; Lim and Chan (2015) para. 2.040.

[144] Judges in Guangdong Higher People' Court have also suggested that if the relevant Hong Kong and Macao laws applicable in a case are not against the PRC Constitution or the principles set out in the two Basic Laws, they should not be excluded on the basis of the social public interest reservation. See Research Group of Guangdong Higher People's Court (2013) p. 64.

[145] The Criminal Law and Public Security Administration Punishments Law govern the activities within the Mainland. See Part B of this Section.

the relevant activities occurred in the Mainland or had the contract been governed by the laws of mainland China.[146]

8.2.3 Dimensions of the Reservation under the 'One Country, Two Systems' Regime

Sections 8.2.1 and 8.2.2 discuss the application of the social public interest reservation in choice of law in Hong Kong- and Macao-related cases. When people's courts invoke the reservation, they should pay due regard to the 'One Country, Two Systems' regime and the autonomy of the SARs under it. Moreover, they should provide detailed analysis as to the result of the application of Hong Kong or Macao law and how the result infringes the social public interest of the Mainland. In the adjudication of Taiwan-related cases, Article 3 of the SPC's Provisions on the Application of Law in Taiwan-Related Cases provides:

> If the application of the relevant laws determined as applicable according to these provisions is against the basic principles of national law or the social public interest, such laws shall not be applied.

Although the content of the 'basic principles of national law' or the 'social public interest' as stipulated in Article 3 is not specified, two fundamental elements should be involved in the application of this provision. The Preamble of the PRC Constitution declares:

[146] In *Song Kai* v. *Li Shilong* (1 November 2015, Shanxi Higher People's Court; 28 March 2016, Supreme People's Court), a dispute arose concerning the shares transfer agreement between the parties. Song claimed that he had transferred his shares in a company (incorporated in mainland China) to Li, but Li did not make the payment. In the first trial, the Shanxi Higher People's Court held that both parties had performed their obligations under the agreement and dismissed the action. Song then appealed to the SPC. In the appeal, Song claimed that the agreement was made on the basis of a gambling debt that arose in Macao, which, he argued, should not be protected under the law of mainland China. The SPC held that, *even if* the agreement had been based on a gambling debt, since Song claimed that the debt had arisen in Macao, Macao law should have been the law governing the validity of the debt according to Article 41 of the 2010 Conflicts Statute. Consequently, Song's argument that the relevant debt and the shares transfer agreement were void under Chinese law was not supported by the SPC. The judgment of first trial was confirmed. In this case, Song only mentioned the so-called 'gambling debt' in the appeal. From the SPC's judgment, no further details were provided concerning the debt. Therefore, the SPC's ruling on the validity of the debt was only based on a hypothesis. It remains to be seen whether the SPC would adopt a similar approach in cases involving foreign-related gambling debts.

> Taiwan is part of the sacred territory of the People's Republic of China. It is the lofty duty of all Chinese people, including the compatriots in Taiwan, to accomplish the great task of reunifying the motherland.

On the one hand, the principle of 'One China' should be put as a priority.[147] Normally, civil and commercial cases are only related to private relations between individuals and do not have a connection to political issues. On the other hand, the advancement of the lofty duty of reunifying the motherland should also be a significant element of the 'social public interest'. Reunification will tend to be promoted rather than impeded if the law of the Taiwan region can be applied based on the ordinary choice of law rules and also the protection of the legitimate expectations of parties.

Chinese scholars usually put the principle of 'One Country, Two Systems' as the one of priority in dealing with interregional conflict of laws issues within the PRC.[148] In the application of this principle, people's courts should be aware that the twin facets of the principle consist of both 'one country' and 'two systems'. Therefore, there should be no over-stressing of one aspect in disregard of the other: there should not be a mere emphasis on the sovereignty of the state and the integrity and unity of its territory alone, without paying due regard to a 'high degree of autonomy' of the SARs; conversely, nor should there be a simple emphasis on the 'high degree of autonomy' alone, without paying due regard to the sovereignty and unity of the PRC. On the precondition that there must be a firm insistence on 'one country', the co-existence of 'two systems' shall be maintained.[149] Judges in the Mainland should be guided by the two objectives of the principle, that is, to maintain the unity of the country and promote normal civil and commercial intercourse between mainland China and the SARs.[150]

Furthermore, in considering whether the social public interest reservation should be used, people's courts should not have too much regard to the nature and content of the relevant Hong Kong, Macao or Taiwan rules, but should carefully examine the consequences which are likely to result from the application of those rules. This examination is mostly

147 See also Article 15 of Provisions of the SPC on Recognition and Enforcement of the Civil Judgments of Courts of the Taiwan Region and the discussion in Part C of Section 8.1.3.

148 See Huang and Qian (1995) p. 307; Gao (2005) p. 220; Ye (2012) pp. 218–219; Feng (2012) p. 154.

149 For the interrelationship between 'one country' and 'two systems', see Xiao (1995) pp. 87–88.

150 Huang and Qian (1995) p. 307.

dependent on the weighing of the contacts of a specific case with the territory of the forum.[151] In contractual conflict of laws, it is obviously important to see whether the contract involves or contemplates any activity within the Mainland. The policy considerations may be different in a case where the contract itself is entirely unconnected with the Mainland and in one where the contract is made or involves the effecting of its purpose within mainland China.[152] In the cases cited above where the social public interest reservation was applied, the courts did not analyse why the reservation was invoked at all, but only stated that gambling was illegal in the Mainland. If the reservation is understood to be a concept that provides a substitute for analysis or an excuse to apply the law of the forum, then it will stand in the way of careful thought, of detailed legal reasoning, and of true policy development in conflict of laws.[153] Even worse, in the interregional conflict of laws of the PRC, the misuse of the reservation would be harmful to the normal civil exchanges among people from different law districts, and would thus jeopardize the realization of 'One Country, Two Systems'.[154]

Lord Cooke of Thorndon, formerly a non-permanent judge of the HKCFA, speaking of whether the bankruptcy order made in Taiwan should be enforced in Hong Kong in *Chen Li Hung and Another* v. *Ting Lei Miao and Others*, said:[155]

> [National politics] should not be allowed to obtrude into or overshadow a question of the private rights and day-to-day affairs of ordinary people. The ordinary principles of private international law should be applied without importing extraneous high-level public controversy.

These remarks are insightful. The scope of the social public interest reservation in interregional conflict of laws should be narrowly confined so that fairness and predictability in cross-border transactions can be achieved.

8.3 The Ascertainment of Hong Kong, Macao and Taiwan Laws

Chapter 7 has analysed the current mechanism for ascertainment of foreign law in mainland China and addressed the outstanding issues in

151 See Paulsen and Sovern (1956) pp. 980–981.

152 For the application of the doctrine of *ordre public* in contract and a comparative analysis of French and English laws on this issue, see Lloyd (1953) pp. 83–96.

153 See Paulsen and Sovern (1956) p. 1016. The authors urged that courts should make the proper distinctions and restrict the use of public policy.

154 See Han and Huang (1989) pp, 128–129.

155 [2000] 1 HKC 461, 478.

judicial practice.[156] As no particular rules are provided concerning the proof of Hong Kong, Macao and Taiwan laws, the existing rules in the 2010 Conflicts Statute and the interpretations by the SPC,[157] as well as the approaches suggested in Chapter 7, are also applicable to the proof of the laws of those districts.[158] The only difference between the ascertainment of the laws of the three districts and that of other foreign laws is that, according to Article 95 of the Hong Kong Basic Law and Article 93 of the Macao Basic Law, the Hong Kong and Macao SARs can make special arrangements with the judicial organs of the Mainland concerning judicial assistance and cooperation.

The Mainland and Macao have accordingly concluded Arrangement for Mutual Authorisation between Courts in Mainland and Macao SAR for Service of Judicial Documents and Obtainment of Evidence in Civil and Commercial Cases (Arrangement between the Mainland and Macao on Judicial Assistance).[159] Article 2 provides that the mutual entrustment of service of judicial documents and investigation and evidence obtainment shall be conducted through the higher people's courts in the Mainland and the Court of Final Appeal of Macao SAR (Macao CFA). The SPC and the Macao CFA may entrust each other with the service of judicial documents and investigation and evidence obtainment directly. According to Article 17, the scope of authorization for investigation and evidence obtainment includes: inquiring of a party, witness and expert witness, identification and on-site investigation, and obtainment of other evidence relevant to the litigation. The evidence on the content of Macao laws determined to be applicable in a case should be included in the scope stipulated in Article 17.

156 The cases cited there also include cases involving the ascertainment of Hong Kong law. See Section 7.4.2 of Chapter 7.

157 See the rules discussed in Sections 7.1 and 7.2 of Chapter 7. However, since Hong Kong, Macao and Taiwan are all part of the territory of the PRC, the provision of the content of their laws cannot be made through embassy or consulate as stipulated in Article 193 of The Opinions Concerning Implementation and Application of the General Principles of the Civil Law of the People's Republic of China (Provisional) (issued by the SPC on 2 April 1988; Articles 88, 94, 115, 117, 118 and 177 therein were invalidated by the SPC on 18 December 2008). The proof of the laws of these districts can be facilitated through the making of judicial cooperation arrangements between them and the Mainland.

158 For the ascertainment of Hong Kong and Macao laws in judicial practice, see Shanghai Higher People's Court (2008) pp. 152–153; Guangdong Higher People's Court (2008) pp. 164–165; Shenzhen Intermediate People's Court (2008) pp. 194–195.

159 It was issued by the SPC on 27 August 2001 and became effective on 15 September 2001.

On 26 April 2009, the Association for Relations Across the Taiwan Straits of the Mainland concluded an agreement with the Straits Exchange Foundation of the Taiwan region entitled Agreement on Joint Cross-Strait Crime-Fighting and Mutual Judicial Assistance.[160] Based on this Agreement, the SPC issued Provisions of the Supreme People's Court on People's Courts' Handling of Cases of Mutual Judicial Assistance in Terms of Serving Legal Documents, Investigation and Evidence Collection between Both Sides of the Taiwan Strait (Provisions on Cross-Straits Judicial Assistance).[161] Article 15 stipulates that people's courts' handling of mutual judicial assistance in the investigation and evidence collection between both sides of Taiwan Strait is limited to the mutual assistance with the courts of Taiwan in investigation and the collection of evidence related to lawsuits, including obtaining testimony and statements, providing documentary evidence, physical evidence and audio-visual materials, determining the locality of the relevant parties or determining their identity, criminal records, etc. and conducting an investigation, inspection, detention, authentication, inquiry, etc. Article 24 further states that no notarization, authentication or other formal proof needs to be handled for the evidence, judicial documents and other materials obtained from the Taiwan region pursuant to the Agreement and these Provisions.

People's courts have made use of the Provisions in the ascertainment of Taiwan law. In *Xiamen Branch of Industry and Commercial Bank of China* v. *Liao Jinghui, Zeng Baiqi and Zeng Baixiong*,[162] the plaintiff Bank sued the defendants for the credits that the former had advanced to Zeng Jin'an. Liao Jinghui was Zeng Jin'an's wife and the other two defendants were his children. Zeng Jin'an passed away in 2011. The credit card contract between the Bank and Zeng Jin'an referred to the law of mainland China as the governing law of the contract. The court thus held that Chinese law should be applied to the contractual relationship between the Bank and Zeng Jin'an. However, as Zeng Jin'an had died without a will, the responsibility of his legal heirs towards the debt he owed to the Bank should be determined according to the law applicable to succession. Based on Article 31 of the 2010 Conflicts Statute,[163]

[160] It was signed on 26 April 2009 and became effective on 25 June 2009.

[161] It was issued by the SPC on 14 June 2011 and became effective on 25 June 2011.

[162] 12 March 2013, Haicang District People's Court of the Xiamen City, Fujian Province.

[163] Article 31 of the 2010 Conflicts Statute stipulates: 'Statutory succession shall be governed by laws of the habitual residence of the decedent at the time of death, however, statutory succession to real properties shall be governed by *lex situs* of the properties.'

the court decided that the heirs' statutory succession to Zeng's real properties in Taiwan should be governed by *lex situs*, that is, the law of the Taiwan region. As to the content of the relevant Taiwan laws, the court needed assistance from the Taiwan region.[164] The court filed its request to the Xiamen Intermediate People's Court, the latter delivered it to the Fujian Higher People's Court and the request was finally forwarded to the SPC. After examining the materials, the contact person in the SPC mailed the request to the contact person in the Taiwan region. Taichung District Court of the Taiwan region then mailed the relevant provisions of the Taiwan Civil Code to the SPC. Based on those provisions, the Haicang District People's Court confirmed that the content of Taiwan law had been ascertained, and made a decision accordingly. Before the Provisions on Cross-Straits Judicial Assistance, people's courts would not positively ascertain Taiwan law. For example, in *Shanghai Gramter Shipping Co. Ltd.* v. *China Oriental Local Products and Livestock Import and Export Co. Ltd. and Others*,[165] the court simply held that, although Taiwan law should be applied based on the choice of law clause on the bill of lading, it could not be ascertained as none of the parties submitted the content of the law. The court then applied the law of the Mainland.

The arrangements on judicial assistance between the Mainland and Macao and Taiwan region provide a useful and reliable way through which people's courts as well as litigants can obtain the content of Macao or Taiwan law. In December 2016, the Mainland and Hong Kong concluded Arrangement on Mutual Taking of Evidence in Civil and Commercial Matters between the Courts of the Mainland and the Hong Kong Special Administrative Region.[166] Article 6(1) stipulates that the scope of assistance that may be requested by a people's court of the Mainland in requesting the taking of evidence by the courts of the Hong Kong SAR under the Arrangement includes: (1) examination of witnesses; (2) obtaining of documents; (3) inspection, photographing, preservation, custody or detention of any property; (4) taking of samples of any property or carrying out of any experiments on any property; and (5) medical examination of any person. It is not clear whether the 'obtaining of documents' mentioned in Article 6 includes the obtaining of evidence on Hong Kong law. If the Arrangement is not applicable, people's courts

[164] For the procedure of mutual assistance in evidence collection, see Articles 15–21 of the Provisions on Cross-Straits Judicial Assistance.

[165] 27 May 2009, Shandong Higher People's Court.

[166] It was issued by the SPC on 27 February 2017 and effective on 1 March 2017.

actually lack any efficient means of ascertaining Hong Kong law.[167] Since the legal system in Hong Kong is greatly influenced by the common law tradition, people's courts are not very confident in verifying the content of Hong Kong law. In practice, people's courts may have to entrust an expert or a lawyer with the task of providing written legal opinions on Hong Kong law when neither of the parties submit the relevant content of the law, inconsistency exists between the materials provided by the parties or one of the parties disagrees with the content provided by the other party. The fees for such service are normally high. If both parties refuse to prepay the fees, it is not clear whether a court should decide that the applicable Hong Kong law cannot be ascertained. Xiamen Intermediate People's Court in Fujian Province has in one case met with such a situation, and in the end, had to decide that both parties had given up the application of Hong Kong law.[168]

The 'One Country, Two Systems' principle does not render the ascertainment of Hong Kong, Macao and Taiwan laws substantially different from the proof of laws of other jurisdictions. As is argued in Chapter 7, people's courts should adopt an approach that is authentic, convincing and predictable, making use of the arrangements between the Mainland and the other three law districts on judicial assistance.

[167] For the difficulties in the ascertainment of Hong Kong law, see Shanghai Higher People's Court (2008) p. 153.

[168] See Fujian Higher People's Court (2008) p. 159.

9

The Party Autonomy Principle in the Context of the Chinese Legal System

The previous chapters have focused on unresolved issues in China's legislation and judicial interpretations in relation to the operation of the party autonomy principle in contractual choice of law. Through the analysis of cases, they have also illustrated how those issues have been dealt with by people's courts in judicial practice. The book has demonstrated that the ambiguities and difficulties relating to the operation of the party autonomy principle in China's private international law of contract arise principally at two levels: the substance of the relevant legal rules and their application in people's courts.

9.1 The Indeterminacy of Chinese Legal Rules

Loose drafting has long marked Chinese legislation and contributed to its lack of precision.[1] The prevailing principle of Chinese legislative drafting has been that laws should be both 'general' (*yuanze xing*) and 'flexible' (*linghuo xing*). These qualities are sometimes referred to by Chinese law drafters as the policy of 'preferring the coarse to the fine' (*yicu bu yixi*).[2] This practice is understandable in the early period when China has begun to establish a system of law: the implementing provisions and interpretations, which are intended to supplement the laws, can be changed much more easily than laws. In this way, the laws that are drafted in broad language can be adapted to new circumstances without the need for amendment.[3]

However, the general language in legislation also inevitably sacrifices a degree of certainty and clarity.[4] As the analyses in this book indicate, the provisions in laws adopted by the National People's Congress (NPC) or its Standing Committee (NPCSC) concerning the party autonomy principle in contractual choice of law are, generally, rigid, concept-ridden and

[1] Lubman (2006) p. 36.

[2] For the principle of Chinese legislative drafting, see Guo (1987).

[3] See Keller (2000) p. 81. [4] See Keller (2000) p. 81; Lubman (2006) p. 36.

dogma-ridden, evidencing little insight into the real nature of the problems that they are attempting to solve. It is true that some degree of vagueness in complex statutes is inevitable because no legislature during the drafting process can formulate a rule of general application that can match legislative intent to all specific situations.[5] But the degree of vagueness is greater in China because of a number of factors: the drafting process is relatively closed, the legislators lack legal experience and there is a paucity of institutional means to identify and remedy such problems in the drafting process.[6] As the NPC is only in session for about two weeks each year, it has little time to adopt more sophisticated statutes or to review problems associated with the application of existing statutes.[7] Although the NPCSC enjoys the authority to interpret laws,[8] it lacks capacity to perform this duty adequately because of a lack of professional legal staff.[9] It is also impractical for the NPCSC, which convenes bimonthly, to carry out the task of interpretation when it is already overloaded with legislative tasks.[10]

In fact, the purpose of the NPCSC's drafting and enacting the Law on the Application of Laws to Foreign-related Civil Relationships (2010 Conflicts Statute)[11] is *not* to resolve all the practical issues that are bound to arise in foreign-related relationships, but to address the issues which arise quite often in judicial practice, and on which there has been a general consensus as to their resolution. The technique of the drafting was to absorb the provisions or approaches that have been adopted for years by people's courts, and at the same time, to reflect international developments in the relevant fields so as to improve the foreign-related legal system in China.[12] Consequently, as has been illustrated in this

[5] Ross and Ross (2000) p. 222. [6] Ross and Ross (2000) p. 223.

[7] Wei (1997) p. 104.

[8] See Article 67(1)(4) of the Constitution (adopted at the 5th Session of the 5th NPC and promulgated for implementation by the Announcement of the NPC on 4 December 1982, amended in accordance with the Amendments to the Constitution of the People's Republic of China adopted respectively at the 1st Session of the 7th NPC on 12 April 1988, the 1st Session of the 8th NPC on 29 March 1993, the 2nd Session of the 9th NPC on 15 March 1999 and the 2nd Session of the 10th NPC on 14 March 2004).

[9] See Li (2009) p. 66. Only a very small portion of the members of the NPCSC are legal professionals. The information of the 161 members of the 12th NPCSC is available at the official website of the NPC: www.npc.gov.cn/npc/cwhhy/12jcwh/node_24674.htm.

[10] See Cai and Liu (1993) p. 39; Shen (1993) pp. 61–62; Chen (2016) p. 268.

[11] It was adopted at the 17th meeting of the Standing Committee of the 11th NPC on 28 October 2010 and became effective on 1 April 2011.

[12] See 'Report on the Main Issues concerning the Draft Law on the Application of Laws to Foreign-related Civil Relationships of the PRC' (issued on the official website of the NPC on 28 August 2010).

book, although the 2010 Conflicts Statute clarifies some ambiguities existing in the previous rules, it also creates further uncertainties and fails to respond to more fundamental issues.

Under these circumstances, the Supreme People's Court (SPC), in order to provide more specific guidance to lower people's courts, has stepped into the vacuum left by the legislature, and issued judicial interpretations or other forms of instructions. After the 2010 Conflicts Statute, the SPC issued Interpretation on Certain Issues Concerning the Application of the 'Law on the Application of Laws to Foreign-related Civil Relations' (1) (Interpretation of the 2010 Conflicts Statute (1)),[13] where it comprehensively reviewed the general provisions in the Statute. The SPC not only interpreted vague provisions in the Statute,[14] but also provided rules on issues that are *not* touched upon in the Statute.[15] The SPC has justified its expansive judicial interpretations on the grounds that they are more helpful than vague statutes in guiding higher people's courts in settling major controversies, promoting consistency of legal principles and structuring lower court discretion.[16] The SPC does provide more specific rules on the issues surrounding the party autonomy principle, but it cannot resolve all the ambiguities and difficulties that are bound to arise in practice. It is beyond the SPC's power to ultimately solve such critical uncertainties as the identification of mandatory rules in private international law, or the ascertainment of the foreign law chosen by parties. The former issue is related to the effects of different legal sources under China's legal system and also the relationship between parties and the state,[17] while the latter is more relevant to the mode of civil litigation in China.[18]

Indeed, not all conflict of laws issues can be solved in advance by prescribed legal rules. The principle of *ordre public* is an obvious example. One of the principal functions of courts in private international law is to determine the content, scope and application of *ordre public* in specific cases.[19] As Chapters 5, 6 and 8 demonstrate, the application of the social public interest reservation is dependent on a court's analysis of the result of the application of the chosen foreign law and also the consequent effect on the fundamental policies of the state.[20] Moreover,

[13] It was issued by the SPC on 28 December 2012 and became effective on 7 January 2013.

[14] See, for example, Articles 10, 15–17 of the Interpretation of the 2010 Conflicts Statute (1).

[15] See, for example, Article 11 (the evasion of law exception) and Article 18 (the assessment of evidence on foreign law) of the Interpretation of the 2010 Conflicts Statute (1).

[16] See Wu (2007). [17] See Chapter 6. [18] See Sections 7.4 and 7.5 of Chapter 7.

[19] See Kahn-Freund (1976) pp. 110–111.

[20] See Section 6.2 of Chapter 6 and Section 8.2 of Chapter 8.

the operation of the party autonomy principle in contractual choice of law also involves issues that are to be determined by the particular facts of a case. The existence of parties' choice of law, as has been discussed in Chapter 3, cannot be resolved by the exhaustive listing in legal rules of all the relevant factors: it can only be determined by a court on a case-by-case basis, taking into account trade practice and commercial reality.[21]

Therefore, besides the making of coherent conflict of laws rules, the resolution of the issues identified in this book is also dependent on judges: it is their exercise of discretionary power that finally determines the outcome of parties' choice of law in contracts.

9.2 Judicial Quality and Institutional Constraints on Chinese Judges

9.2.1 The Centralized Jurisdiction System

After the reform and opening-up policy was initiated in China in 1978, judicial reforms were adopted for the institutionalization and professionalization of the Chinese judiciary. The judiciary increasingly emphasizes the importance of formal judicial education in its hiring process and intensified professional training for judges.[22] Consequently, the education levels of judges have improved greatly.[23]

Despite the major efforts to improve the quality of the Chinese judiciary, the widening inequality in Chinese society is also reflected in the courts. Many courts in the underdeveloped areas in China are finding it difficult to attract qualified personnel and are losing existing judges to higher paying jobs as lawyers, in particular in more developed areas.[24]

[21] See Section 3.1 of Chapter 3.

[22] The enactment of the Law on Judges (adopted at the 12th meeting of the Standing Committee of the 8th NPC on 28 February 1995, amended for the first time at the 22nd Meeting of the Standing Committee of the 9th NPC on 30 June 2001 and amended for the second time at the 29th Meeting of the Standing Committee of the 12th NPC on 1 September 2017) was a major step taken. This is the first law in the history of China that attempts to make provisions for the judiciary in a comprehensive and systematic manner. The Law was amended in 2001 and 2017 respectively. The principal amendments include the introduction of a unified judicial examination (the 2001 amendment), which was later amended to be a unified legal profession qualification examination (the 2017 amendment, effective as of 1 January 2018) for intending judges. See Articles 9, 12, 21–28 of the Law; see further, Chen (2011) pp. 176–178; Chen (2016) pp. 191–194, 218–220.

[23] See Liebman (2007) pp. 12–13.

[24] See Liebman (2007) pp. 28–30. With regard to the unequal development of courts in China, Article 9(3) of the Law on Judges as amended in 2017 also provides that in regions

Moreover, after China became a member of the World Trade Organization in 2001, it was expected that the number of foreign-related cases would increase rapidly. Under these circumstances, the SPC established the system of centralized jurisdiction (*jizhong guanxia zhidu*) over foreign-related civil and commercial cases in order to guarantee that these cases are adjudicated in courts which are more capable of dealing with them. Although Articles 18 and 19(1) of the 1991 Civil Procedure Law[25] provided that basic-level people's courts[26] shall have jurisdiction as courts of first instance over civil cases, including those involving foreign elements, and only the 'major' foreign-related cases shall be tried at intermediate people's courts, in Provisions of the SPC on Certain Issues concerning Jurisdiction over Foreign-related Civil and Commercial Cases (Provisions on Jurisdiction over Foreign-related Cases),[27] the SPC stipulated that only the listed intermediate people's courts can have the first instance jurisdiction over foreign-related civil and commercial cases. Article 1 reads:

> The following people's courts shall have the first instance jurisdiction over the civil and commercial cases involving foreign elements:
>
> (1) People's courts established in the economic and technological development zones upon the approval of the State Council;
> (2) Intermediate people's courts in the capital cities of provinces and autonomous regions as well as the municipalities directly under the control of the Central Government;

which have difficulties in meeting the minimum eligibility criteria of Article 9(1)(6) that judges should have a bachelor's degree, the minimum qualification may be that of a higher diploma.

25 It was adopted at the 4th Session of the 7th NPC on 9 April 1991 and became effective on the same date. This Law was amended for the first time at the 30th Meeting of the Standing Committee of the 10th NPC on 28 October 2007, amended for the second time at the 28th Meeting of the Standing Committee of the 11th NPC on 31 August 2012 and amended for the third time at the 28th Meeting of the Standing Committee of the 12th NPC on 27 June 2017. Even after the 2017 Amendment, Articles 17 and 18(1) of the Civil Procedure Law are the same as Articles 18 and 19(1) of its 1991 version.

26 The design of the court system in China is based on the principle of 'four levels of courts and at most two trials to conclude a case' (one trial at first instance, one trial on appeal). The four levels of courts are composed of thousands of basic-level people's courts at county level (with many divisions known as people's tribunals in towns and villages), hundreds of intermediate people's courts in cities and prefectures within provinces, thirty-one higher people's courts at provincial level and the Supreme People's Court. See Chen (2011) p. 180. There are also specialized courts, such as military courts, railway transport courts and maritime courts, and the specialized tribunals established in recent years within the general courts at different levels. See Chen (2016) pp. 188–189.

27 It was issued by the SPC on 25 February 2002 and became effective on 1 March 2002.

(3) Intermediate people's courts in the special economic regions and specially designated cities in the State plan;
(4) Other intermediate people's courts designated by the Supreme People's Court; and
(5) Higher people's courts.

The scope of the jurisdiction of each of the abovementioned intermediate people's courts shall be determined by the higher people's court in the area concerned.

Accordingly, most of the basic-level people's courts are deprived of first instance jurisdiction over foreign-related civil or commercial cases, which they normally have under the Civil Procedure Law.[28] In the Notice on Strengthening the Work of Jurisdiction over Foreign-related Commercial Cases,[29] the SPC authorized the higher people's courts of Guangdong Province and the municipalities directly under the control of the Central Government to designate the basic-level people's courts within the relevant areas that have first instance jurisdiction over foreign-related (including Hong Kong-, Macao- and Taiwan-related) cases and to determine the scope of the jurisdiction of each basic-level court. The SPC emphasized that the judges responsible for adjudicating foreign-related cases must have sufficient knowledge of law, international trade and foreign languages, and should receive regular training concerning foreign-related trials[30] and that only those basic-level people's courts that have sufficient resources and capable judges can be designated.[31] With regard to the unequal development in and staffing of the courts in China's interior, the system is designed to avoid the situation that foreign-related cases are adjudicated in courts that do not have judges capable of, or experienced in, dealing with the complicated issues that would always arise in those cases.[32]

[28] Therefore, this interpretation has invoked heated criticism among Chinese scholars concerning its legality. See Ding (2009) pp. 78–81. For a more detailed discussion of the centralized jurisdiction system, see Du (2009) pp. 73–76.

[29] It was issued by the SPC on 29 December 2004.

[30] See Notice of the Supreme People's Court on Earnestly Studying and Implementing 'Provisions of the Supreme People's Court on Certain Issues Concerning Jurisdiction over Civil and Commercial Cases Involving Foreign Elements' (issued by the SPC on 1 March 2002).

[31] See Notice on Strengthening the Work of Jurisdiction over Foreign-related Commercial Cases, n 29.

[32] See Ding (2009) pp. 76–78; The Fourth Division of Civil Trial of the SPC (2011) pp. 216–217.

People's courts' jurisdiction over foreign-related contractual cases is also determined on the basis of the centralized jurisdiction system.[33] However, the system can only assure that those cases are adjudicated by courts that are *comparatively* more qualified. It cannot respond to the problems leading to the unsatisfactory resolution of the issues concerning the operation of the party autonomy principle. The analysis in the previous chapters reveals that people's courts' application of the legal rules and their treatment of the issues unresolved in the rules are often far from convincing for three principal reasons. First, they do not have an appropriate understanding of the essence of the party autonomy principle or the relevant theories in conflict of laws. Second, their interpretation of the applicable legal rules is not consistent. Third, they seldom provide detailed and logical reasoning in their judgments.[34]

Liebman has pointed out that Chinese courts may in some ways enjoy both too little and too much autonomy. 'Too little' refers to the fact that courts are still sometimes subject to external interference and pressure. Yet 'too much' refers to the fact that absent such external pressure courts often have large amounts of discretion.[35] In the field of foreign-related commercial trials, there is, on the one hand, really broad scope for judges to 'play' with the rules in the determination of the governing law of an issue, as neither statutes nor judicial interpretations provide clear rules or instructions. On the other hand, judges are also subject to the institutional constraints that commonly exist in China's judicial system.

9.2.2 *Institutional Constraints on Judges*

Although Article 126 of China's Constitution stipulates that people's courts exercise judicial power independently and are not subject to interference by any administrative organ, public organization or individual, Chinese judges have less authority than their counterparts in Western countries. Under the concept of '*youji zhengti*' (court as an organic whole), the Chinese legal system treats individual judges less as an individual entity empowered to adjudicate and more as one component of the judicial system.[36] The independent exercise of adjudicative power does not

[33] See Article 3 of the Provisions on Jurisdiction over Foreign-related Cases.

[34] The typical judgment of a Chinese court is short and does not set out lines or steps of legal reasoning and logical analysis in a way as detailed as in the judgments in common law courts. See Chen (2011) p. 196.

[35] Liebman (2009) p. 29. [36] Liang (1993) p. 249.

mean the independence of individual judges or of a panel, but means only the independence of the court as a collective entity vis-à-vis other state organs and outside pressures.[37] Inside the court system, individual Chinese judges are subject to several forms of supervision or administration.

First, except for minor cases, judges preside in panels of three, not alone. By and large, judges follow the lead of the presiding judge of the panel. All of the important judicial decisions must also be examined and approved by the court president, the administrative head of the court.[38] Although there is no express provision in law to this effect, a long-standing practice has been that a judgment of the court is not normally valid unless and until it has been approved and signed by the president or a chief judge of a division of the court.[39] Therefore, besides the judge(s) who hear(s) a case, there are other possible participants in the decision-making process of a court.

On 26 February 2015, the SPC issued Opinion of the Supreme People's Court on Deepening Reform of the People's Courts Comprehensively: Outline of the Fourth Five-Year Reform of the People's Courts (2014–2018) (Fourth Five-Year Reform Outline). One of the specific objectives under the current reform is to 'improve the functional mechanism of adjudicative power'. Items 27 and 28 of the Outline stipulate that the signature mechanism of judgments shall be reformed and the judicial accountability system should be improved. In Opinions of the Supreme People's Court on Improving the Judicial Accountability System of People's Courts,[40] the SPC makes it clear (in Item 6) that except for the cases discussed and decided by the adjudicative committee, the president, vice presidents and divisional chiefs shall not approve, verify, sign or issue judgments for cases in which they are not directly involved. Item 25 further emphasizes that judges are liable for their conduct in the performance of their adjudicative duties and must take responsibility for the quality of their adjudications. Judges are required to bear 'lifelong liability' (*zhongshen fuze*) for cases decided wrongly.[41]

[37] See Chen (2011) pp. 186–187. [38] See Woo (2000) pp. 178–179.

[39] See Koguchi (1987) p. 206.

[40] It was issued by the SPC on 21 September 2015 and became effective on the same date.

[41] There are, however, no clear criteria to determine whether a judgment is correct or wrong. According to Items 26–28 of Opinions of the Supreme People's Court on Improving the Judicial Accountability System of People's Courts, the relevant rules can be summarized as follows. First, a judge will only be held liable if he either 'intentionally violates the laws during adjudicative procedure or renders erroneous ruling by gross negligence which causes serious consequences'. Second, a judge shall 'assume full liabilities for the fact finding and the law application of the cases'. Third, a judge will be

These measures are further elaborated in the Whitepaper on Judicial Reform in China.[42]

While the reform of the signature mechanism of judgments may reduce the interference from judges in the same court,[43] the judicial accountability system, together with the case quality evaluation system to be discussed shortly, will bring pressure to bear on judges.

Second, Chinese judges are recruited, administered and promoted almost the same as functionaries in other bureaucratic institutions.[44] The assessment of judges, which is directly linked to their salary increases and promotions, is thus based upon many quantified administrative criteria. Based on the Guiding Opinions of the Supreme People's Court on Carrying out the Case Quality Evaluation Work (for Trial Implementation) (Opinions on Case Quality Evaluation Work),[45] for the purpose of the administration of trial work, a case quality evaluation system (*anjian zhiliang pinggu zhidu*) has been established. The evaluation index system is composed of different indices. The main indices include the ratio of cases whose first judgments are reversed in appeal, the ratio of cases remanded by the appellate court to the court of first instance for retrial, the ratio of cases whose effective judgments are changed, the ratio of effective cases remanded for retrial, the ratio of appeal cases and the ratio of cases where disputes are settled by the judgment of first instance.[46] The SPC considers that the evaluation results can comprehensively reflect the trial work of the people's courts and takes them as an important basis for conducting trial administration and the making of relevant decisions, and also for evaluating the performance of the people's courts at all levels.[47] That is to say, the results will affect the

exempt from liabilities: (1) when 'there are discrepancies of understanding and knowledge of the specific provisions of the laws, regulations, rules and judicial interpretations, but reasonable explanation could be given within the scope of professional knowledge'; (2) when 'there are disputes or doubts on the fact finding of the cases, but reasonable explanation could be given according to the rules of evidence'; and (3) when 'the party concerned waives his claims'. See also Lin (2016) pp. 14–15.

42 It was issued by the SPC on 29 February 2016.

43 The establishment of the specialized judges' council system will however affect the independence of individual judges.

44 See He and Ng (2013) pp. 311–312.

45 It was issued by the SPC on 11 January 2008 and became effective on the same date.

46 See Items 8–10 of the Opinions on Case Quality Evaluation Work.

47 According to Article 127 of the Constitution, the SPC is the highest judicial organ in China, and it supervises the administration of justice by people's courts at various local levels and by the specialized people's courts.

career prospects of judges and also court administrators.[48] Naturally, this institutional environment generates certain incentives, alongside disincentives, for judges.[49]

Previously, when faced with a significant or complicated case without a clear-cut answer from the legal rules, Chinese judges would seek instruction from upper level courts.[50] A lower court may seek directions from the next higher court on how to deal with a particular case, or it may seek the higher court's approval regarding a proposed way of deciding the case.[51] One of the reasons for these practices is that the lower courts want to avoid potential liability for answering legally difficult questions.[52] These practices have been criticized for lack of transparency and for rendering nugatory the right of parties to appeal. Recently, upper level courts have become reluctant to offer opinions,[53] and individual judges have been authorized to handle cases more independently.[54]

48 Items 21 and 51 of the Fourth Five-Year Outline also emphasize the importance of improving the case quality evaluation system and judges' performance system, and the results of the evaluation will be the critical reference for the promotion of judges.

49 He and Ng (2013) p. 312.

50 See He (2009) pp. 103–104; Li (2014) pp. 25–27.

51 Chen (2011) p. 188.

52 He (2009) p. 104.

53 See He (2009) p. 104; Chen (2011) pp. 188–189. The promulgation by the SPC in 2010 of Several Opinions Regulating the Relationship between Higher and Lower Courts in Adjudicative Work (issued by the SPC on 28 December 2010, effective on the same day) is apparently a step towards the practice of lower courts seeking directions from higher courts. The Opinions transformed the system of request for instruction into a system of the transfer of jurisdiction to the next higher-level court. The Opinions stipulate the types of first instance cases which a basic-level or intermediate court may transfer to the court of a level immediately above it for trial. The court above may also on its own initiative decide to try such a case itself. The Opinions also provide for the means by which a higher court may provide guidance for lower courts, and giving instructions on how the court should decide a particular case is *not* mentioned as one of such means. See also Li (2014) p. 27.

54 See the discussion of the reform of signature mechanism of judgments. In 2015, the SPC promulgated Measures for the People's Courts' Implementation of the Provisions on the Recording and Accountability of Staff Members of Judicial Organs for Their Intervention in Case Handling (issued by the SPC on 19 August 2015, effective on 20 August 2015). Article 5(2) provides that staff members of people's courts shall not intervene in a case being handled by a case handling entity or case-handling personnel, or approve and forward, or transfer to the case-handing entity or case handling personnel the case-related materials for any reason other than performance of his or her statutory duties or without following the statutory procedures or relevant working procedures. See also the relevant provisions in Opinions of the Supreme People's Court on Improving the Judicial Accountability System of People's Courts and Opinions of the Supreme People's Court on Enforcing the Judicial Accountability System and Improving the Adjudication Supervision and Administration Mechanism (for Trial Implementation) (issued by the SPC on 12 April 2017, effective on 1 May 2017). Item 1 of the latter Opinions emphasizes that the

However, subject to the constraints imposed by the case quality evaluation system and the judicial accountability system just mentioned, judges still have the incentive to employ self-protective measures. They may refer to internal directives, speeches of court leaders and minutes of meetings in which higher-ranking judicial officials have participated as the basis for deciding legally difficult questions.[55] When these resources are not available, judges may try to rely on the 'precedents' of upper level courts, even though they know these 'precedents' are not legally binding.[56] They do so because the 'precedents', particularly those adjudicated by the SPC, provide some shelter for avoiding potential criticism and scrutiny.

While the current judicial reform adopts measures to enhance the independence of individual judges to exercise their adjudicative power, it also strengthens the administration and supervision of judicial work. Item 23 of the Fourth Five-Year Outline points out that the guiding cases system should be further improved to ensure the unified application of laws in judicial practice. The guiding cases system was established in 2010.[57] Under this system, the SPC shall determine and uniformly publish guiding cases that can provide guidance for trial and enforcement work by people's courts throughout the country. When trying similar cases, people's courts at all levels are required to use the guiding cases issued by the SPC as a reference. After the establishment of the judicial accountability system, the SPC even requires people's courts at all levels to establish a 'mandatory mechanism' for the searching of similar cases and affiliated cases (*leian ji guanlian anjian qiangzhi jiansuo jizhi*), so as to guarantee the unification of ruling criteria and application of law in the adjudication of similar cases.[58] Furthermore, courts at all levels are required to establish

presidents and chief judges of a people's court shall not examine and approve cases by disguised means such as giving oral instructions, sitting in during collegiate discussions, reviewing the instruments submitted thereto, etc.

55 See He (2009) p. 104. 56 See Cao (2006) p. 178.

57 See Provisions on Case Guidance (issued by the SPC on 26 November 2010, effective on the same date) and Detailed Rules for the Implementation of the Provisions of the Supreme People's Court on Case Guidance (issued by the SPC on 13 May 2015, effective on the same date). Article 2 of the latter provides that a guiding case shall be a case in which the judgment has become effective, the determination of facts is clear, the application of law is correct and the reasoning is sufficient, and which has positive legal and social effects and can provide guidance in the trial of similar cases. As of 15 November 2017, the SPC has published ninety-two guiding cases in seventeen batches successively.

58 See Item 6 of Opinions of the Supreme People's Court on Enforcing the Judicial Accountability System and Improving the Adjudication Supervision and Administration Mechanism (for Trial Implementation).

specialized judges' councils (*zhuanye faguan huiyi*) to provide advisory opinions for the reference of the panels so that they can 'correctly understand and apply laws'.[59] These mechanisms, together with the case quality evaluation system, all encourage judges to follow 'precedents' or 'instructions' in judicial practice, rather than adjudicating cases according to law.

The main reason for the existence of the aforementioned constraints is the shortage of qualified and experienced judges in China and the sometimes unsatisfactory quality of those who occupy judicial offices.[60] In these circumstances, supervision by the higher courts or higher-ranking judicial officials inside a court can be seen as a device for quality control.[61] While the various forms of control may have been helpful in improving the judicial quality in China, they have, at the same time, created problems.

9.3 Institutional Constraints and Foreign-Related Commercial Trial in China

This book has revealed that judicial supervision (particularly that of the SPC) and institutional constraints on people's courts have had a twofold effect upon the foreign-related commercial trial in China.

59 See Item 8 of Opinions of the Supreme People's Court on Improving the Judicial Accountability System of People's Courts.

60 In order to improve the professionalism of court personnel, the SPC also adopts measures in pilot areas for the reform of the selection and appointment system of judges, and for the establishment of the quota system for judges (*faguan yuan e zhi*). According to Part VIII of the Whitepaper on Judicial Reform in China, the pilot areas will set up judges selection committees consisting of judge representatives and other social members at provincial level in order to ensure only those excellent legal talents with good personal integrity, abundant experience and high professional expertise become judge candidates. As to the quota system for judges, the quota set by the Central Political Legal Committee (which is the highest committee within the Chinese Communist Party in charge of coordination of legal matters of courts, procuracy and public security) is that maximum 39 per cent of court personnel can be quota judges. But each province is given some flexibility to adjust the quota within its jurisdiction in order to allocate more quota to those courts which have more cases to handle. The actual effect of the quota system is hard to predict. The number of quota judges will definitely be less than the number of incumbent judges in most courts. But the number of cases handled by courts is increasing year by year. The consequence is that fewer judges will handle more cases and quota judges will bear a much heavier workload. Moreover, although the intention underlying the reform is to give substantial increment of salary to quota judges, the actual increment may turn out to be much less. It remains doubtful whether such small increment will be attractive enough to keep good judges within the judiciary. For an analysis of the measures to improve the professionalism of court personnel and their effects, see Lin (2016) pp. 6–8.

61 See Chen (2011) p. 188.

On the one hand, by issuing judicial interpretations and publishing its decisions, the SPC can clarify the ambiguities in statutory rules and set up standards in the application of legal rules or principles. This is helpful in unifying the approaches to the resolution of the practical issues that are not specifically addressed in legislation. For example, in *Bank of China (Hong Kong) Co. Ltd.* v. *Shantou Hongye Co. Ltd. and Shantou Xinye Co. Ltd.* (the *Shantou Hongye* case),[62] the SPC has shown its more cautious attitude towards the application of the social public interest reservation in cases concerning foreign-related guaranty contracts. After this case, the lower people's courts became more prudent in invoking the reservation in similar cases.[63]

On the other hand, when the SPC fails to solve a legal issue appropriately, or in the absence of its 'precedents' or specific directions concerning a particular issue, lower people's courts will tend to follow the inappropriate solution of the SPC, or adopt inconsistent approaches when dealing with unresolved issues.

In the *Shantou Hongye* case, the SPC invoked the evasion of law exception as it held that the rules on foreign exchange control in China were mandatory rules in the sense of private international law. Its analysis was unconvincing. After the 2010 Conflicts Statute, that approach should no longer be adopted in the identification of mandatory rules.[64] However, in a more recent case in 2012, the SPC still considered those rules to be mandatory.[65] If this is taken as a 'precedent' and followed by lower courts, the inconsistency mentioned in Chapters 5 and 6 will not be reduced.

In *American President Lines Ltd.* v. *Feida Appliance Company, Feili Industry Co. Ltd. & Changcheng Industry Company* (the *American President Lines* case),[66] the SPC considered parties' reference to the Carriage of Goods by Sea Act of the United States (COGSA) and the Hague Rules in the Paramount Clause of the bill of lading concerned as a choice of the

62 9 July 2004, Supreme People's Court.

63 See Section 5.2.2 of Chapter 5. Although it provided guidance on the application of the reservation, the SPC's analysis of the nature of the rules on foreign exchange control and its invocation of the evasion of law exception in this case were both problematic. This typically reveals the negative effects of the supervision and institutional constraints, which are discussed shortly.

64 See the discussion in Sections 5.2.2 and 6.1.2 of Chapters 5 and 6.

65 See *Shantou Ocean Enterprise Group Co.* v. *Bank of China (Hong Kong) Co. Ltd.* (17 January 2012, Supreme People's Court).

66 25 June 2002, Supreme People's Court.

applicable law. It thus failed to make the distinction between the incorporation of rules into a contract and the choice of its governing law.[67] Although the Guangdong Higher People's court had, in an earlier case and also in its guiding opinions, rightly analysed the nature of a paramount clause and made that distinction,[68] it followed the SPC's decision in the *American President Lines* case in a later case concerning the parties' reference to the COGSA in a bill of lading.[69] The judges in the first trial of this case decided that since the *American President Lines* case was published in the Gazette of the SPC, it should be referred to in similar cases.[70] Their judgment was confirmed in the appeal by the Guangdong Higher People's Court. As the distinction between incorporation of rules by reference and choice of a governing law is a principle in the conflict of laws but is not clearly provided in Chinese legal rules,[71] lower people's courts may continue to follow the SPC's determination of the nature of a paramount clause in the *American President Lines* case if they want to avoid potential criticism.

In the adjudication of cases involving foreign-related gambling contracts, the SPC's Notice issued in 2011[72] has been relied on by lower courts and taken to be indicative of the public policy in the Mainland concerning gambling. In the absence of 'precedents' from the SPC on the issue, people's courts only rigidly interpreted and applied the rules in the Notice regardless of their scope and the circumstances of the case at hand. They generally invoked the social public interest reservation without further analysing the result of the application of the governing law, or the policy in the Mainland towards gambling.[73]

Regarding the ascertainment of the foreign law chosen by parties, neither the rules in statutes nor the SPC's interpretations are helpful in clarifying the uncertainties. Whether the selected law can be ascertained is thus ultimately dependent on the decision of judges. Inconsistent

[67] See the analysis in Section 4.3.1 of Chapter 4. [68] See the discussion in Section 4.3.2.

[69] See *Guangzhou Zhaoying Metals Co. Ltd.* v. *Beijing Expeditors Transport Agency Guangzhou Branch, Beijing Expeditors Transport Agency and Jinda Transport Agency Co. Ltd.* (7 April 2005, Guangzhou Maritime Court; 9 October 2005, Guangdong Higher People's Court); see also the discussion in Section 4.3.1 of Chapter 4.

[70] See the analysis of this case by the two judges of Guangzhou Maritime Court, n 69.

[71] See Section 4.3 of Chapter 4.

[72] See Notice of the Supreme People's Court on Legally and Properly Hearing Cases on Disputes over Private Lending to Promote Economic Development and Maintain Social Stability (issued by the SPC on 2 December 2011, effective on the same date).

[73] See the cases discussed in Part A of Section 8.2.2 in Chapter 8.

approaches have been adopted that have, generally, resulted in the application of the law of the forum. The reason for this may be that foreign laws have seldom been applied in Chinese judicial practice.[74] Judges tend to avoid the potential censure involved in being found to have wrongly applied foreign laws.

Therefore, the previously mentioned institutional constraints may change the focus of judges in foreign-related commercial trials from the appropriate treatment of the legal issues to measures that can help them avoid potential scrutiny. When judges succumb to the pressures of the assessment criteria, the quality of their decisions, as well as the predictability and certainty in foreign-related trials, will definitely be undermined. In this regard, the system of centralized jurisdiction over foreign-related cases in China may only serve to cure the problem of unequal development and staffing in courts among different districts, but cannot respond to the negative effects generated by the institutional constraints on people's courts.

9.4 Concluding Remarks

The purpose underlying the party autonomy principle is to protect the legitimate expectations of the parties and promote the predictability of outcomes in transnational commercial litigation.[75] Regarding the vagueness and flexibility of the statutory rules in China, it has been argued that a system for ensuring standardized decisions and outcomes is much needed.[76] However, standardization does not necessarily mean predictability. Based on the earlier analysis, two important points should be made.

First, consistency in the determination of legal issues is significant, but the precondition for the consistency should be that the analysis of facts and application of rules and principles in the judgments of upper-level courts are appropriate and supported by convincing legal reasoning. Only if this condition is satisfied can the judgments of higher courts or the SPC serve the purpose of improving the predictability of outcomes in foreign-related trials.

[74] According to the statistics provided by J. Xu (2010) pp. 33–35, among the 1000 foreign-related cases collected by him, foreign laws were applied in only 2.9 per cent of the cases, and Hong Kong or Macao law was applied in 1.5 per cent of the cases.

[75] See Reese (1960) pp. 50–51; O'Hara and Ribstein (2009) p. 37.

[76] See Liebman (2009) p. 29.

Second, the space for individual judges to exercise their discretionary power should be maintained. As has been demonstrated in this book, the instructions, guidance or 'precedents' of higher courts do not always provide convincing solutions to legal issues. Therefore, it is necessary to leave individual judges to exercise their judicial power independently and base their judgments on their professional analysis of facts and legal rules.[77] The assessment of judicial quality should not be conducted on the basis of rigid and quantified administrative criteria. Judicial quality can be improved, rather than impeded, if judges can be freed from inappropriate institutional constraints, can receive professional training on foreign-related trials[78] and can have sufficient scope to really exercise their discretionary power independently.

Foreign-related trials are regarded as 'a window' of China's judicial system to the outside world.[79] The SPC has issued several circulars and the leaders of the SPC have delivered important speeches in order to urge the people's courts to conduct reforms to further improve the quality of foreign-related judgments: to guarantee the correctness in the determination of applicable law, as well as strengthen the legal reasoning in the judgments.[80] As to the application of the party autonomy principle, the SPC has also called for a more serious attitude towards the principle: once the parties have chosen a foreign law and are able to provide proof of its content, or the foreign law can be ascertained by other legitimate

[77] As in *Shenzhen Yihe Import & Export Co. Ltd.* v. *MSC Mediterranean Shipping Company S.A., Go-Trans (Hong Kong) Co. Ltd. and Go-Trans Express Co. Ltd.* (25 December 2003, Guangzhou Maritime Court) where the Guangzhou Maritime Court, taking into account the practice in international trade, rightly decided that the choice of law clause on the back of the bill of lading also bound the shipper. See also the discussion in Section 3.1.4 of Chapter 3.

[78] Based on the statistics of the distribution of credits among different legal subject areas in the unified national judicial examination in China, private international law only occupies 2.8 per cent of all the credits. The questions are relatively simple and in the form of multiple choice. Therefore, the analytical abilities necessary to interpret and apply legal rules, as well as independent decision-making and thinking in resolving complicated legal issues, are not among the technical skills needed to pass the judicial examination. See Ahl (2006) pp. 189, 199–200. Consequently, judges responsible for foreign-related trials need further professional training in the field.

[79] See Zhou (2014).

[80] See Wan (2006) pp. 15–17; He (2015) p. 28; Items 4 and 5 of Opinions of the Supreme People's Court on Comprehensively Carrying Forward the Strategy of Producing Fine Works on the Trial of Foreign-related Commercial and Maritime Cases to Provide Effective Judicial Safeguard for Establishing an Open Economic System and Building up a Maritime Power (issued by the SPC on 14 July 2015).

means, that foreign law should be applied, except as otherwise provided by law or judicial interpretations. Moreover, people's court should endeavour to clear the obstacles in the ascertainment of foreign law and improve the methods of proving its content.[81]

Based on the analysis in this book, a choice of law clause in a foreign-related commercial contract should only be interfered with or overridden by the law of the forum when it is necessary to secure a broader public interest, the justification of which should be formed in statutes adopted by the NPC or NPCSC. The resolution of the identified problems concerning the party autonomy principle is dependent both on the reform of the legislative drafting process in China, and on the reform in people's courts. The drafting of choice of law rules should not solely address the issues surrounding the determination of governing law, but also be based on the whole Chinese legal system, taking into account the fundamental policies of the state, the effects that the rules will have upon future transactions and the guidance they will provide for parties' behaviour.[82] In this way, private international law rules can function well with other substantive rules and respond to practical issues. More importantly, judges in foreign-related trials should interpret and apply the relevant rules consistently, respecting the intent of parties, engaging conflict of laws theories and principles and providing logical and detailed legal reasoning in judgments.[83] The improvement of judicial quality in China should be conducted with due regard to the inherent requirements of the judicial function, and towards the 'return' of judicial power to judges. The effect of the current reform upon judicial quality in China remains to be seen in the years to come.

81 See Wan (2006) p. 17.

82 Private international law, like any area of law, shapes the expectations and also decisions of parties, and parties look at legal obligations prospectively. For the prophylactic function of private international law rules, see North (1993) p. 183; Mills (2009) pp. 8–11.

83 Item 34 of the Fourth Five-Year Reform Outline stipulates that whether logical and detailed reasoning is provided in judgments should also be taken as a criterion in the promotion of judges.

BIBLIOGRAPHY

Books and Articles

In order to preserve alphabetical order, where Chinese names are given in traditional style, that is, family name first (e.g., Wan E'xiang) in the source document, the bibliography preserves the name in that form. However, if the name is rearranged in the source to conform to the Western style, that is, the family name comes last (e.g., Tung-Pi Chen), the bibliography presents the entry using the family name first followed by a comma (e.g., Chen, Tung-Pi) to indicate the editorial change.

Ahl, Björn, 'Advancing the Rule of Law through Education? An Analysis of the Chinese National Judicial Examination' (2006) 42 *Issues & Studies* 171.

Anagnost, Timolean, 'Conflicts – Enforceability of Foreign Gambling Contracts' (1968) 22 *University of Miami Law Review* 853.

Anton, A. E., *Private International Law: A Treatise from the Standpoint of Scots Law* (Edinburgh: Green, 1967).

Armfelt, Andrew, 'Foreign Economic Contract Law of the People's Republic of China' (1987) 36 *International and Comparative Law Quarterly* 151.

Atiyah, P. S., *The Rise and Fall of Freedom of Contract* (Oxford: Clarendon Press, 1979).

von Bar, Christian and Clive, Eric (eds), *Principles, Definitions and Model Rules of European Private Law: Draft Common Frame of Reference (DCFR)* (Oxford: Oxford University Press, 2010).

Bederman, David J., *Custom as a Source of Law* (New York: Cambridge University Press, 2010).

Bennett, W. P., *The History and Present Position of the Bill of Lading as a Document of Title to Goods* (Cambridge: Cambridge University Press, 1914).

Blackstone, William, *Commentaries on the Laws of England, Book the Second* (Oxford, Printed at Clarendon Press. M.DCC.LXVIII. 3rd edn, 1768).

Blazey, Patricia and Gillies, Peter, 'Recognition and Enforcement of Foreign Judgments in China', *Macquarie Law Working Paper No. 2008–5*, March 2008.

Boer, Th. M. de, 'Facultative Choice of Law: The Procedural Status of Choice-of-Law Rules and Foreign Law' (1996) 257 *Recueil des Cours* 223.

Brand, Ronald A., 'Sovereignty: The State, the Individual, and the International Legal System in the Twenty First Century' (2002) 25 *Hastings International & Comparative Law Review* 279.

'Balancing Sovereignty and Party Autonomy in Private International Law', in Erauw, J., Tomljenović, V. and Volken, P. (eds), *Liber Memorialis Petar Šarčević: Universalism, Tradition and the Individual* (Munich: Sellier, 2006) pp. 35–52.

Briggs, Adrian, 'Wider Still and Wider: The Bounds of Australian Exorbitant Jurisdiction' (1989) 1 *Lloyd's Maritime and Commercial Law Quarterly* 216.

Agreements on Jurisdiction and Choice of Law (New York: Oxford University Press, 2008).

'The Subtle Variety of Jurisdiction Agreements' (2012) 3 *Lloyd's Maritime and Commercial Law Quarterly* 364.

The Conflict of Laws (Oxford: Oxford University Press, 3rd edn, 2013).

Caffrey, Bradford A., *International Jurisdiction and the Recognition and Enforcement of Foreign Judgments in the LAWASIA Region: A Comparative Study of the Laws of Eleven Asian Countries Inter-se and with the E.E.C. Countries* (Sydney: CCH Australia, 1985).

Cai Dingjian and Liu Xinghong, 'Legislative Interpretation' (1993) 6 *China Legal Science* 36. 蔡定剑, 刘星红. 论立法解释[J]. 中国法学, 1993 (6): 36.

Calliess, Gralf-Peter (ed), *Rome Regulations: Commentary on the European Rules of the Conflict of Laws* (Alphen aan den Rijn: Kluwer Law International, 2011).

Cao Shibing, 'The Legal Status of the Decisions and Judicial Interpretations of the Supreme People's Court' (2006) 3 *China Legal Science* 175. 曹士兵. 最高人民法院裁判、司法解释的法律地位[J]. 中国法学, 2006(3): 175.

Castel, Jean-Gabriel and Walker, Janet, *Canadian Conflict of Laws* (Toronto: Butterworths, 5th edn, 2002).

Centre for Editing Legislative Regulations of the People's Court Press (ed), *Collection of Judicial Interpretations on the Contract Law* (Beijing: People's Court Press, 2008). 人民法院出版社法规编辑中心. 合同司法解释小文库[M]. 北京: 人民法院出版社, 2008.

Chan, Cora, *The Legal Limits on Beijing's Powers to Interpret Hong Kong's Basic Law*, published on HKU Legal Scholarship Blog (http://researchblog.law.hku.hk/) on 3 November 2016.

Chan, Johannes, 'From Colony to Special Administrative Region', in Chan and Lim (2015) Chapter 1.

Chan, Johannes SC (Hon) and Lim, C. L. (eds), *Law of the Hong Kong Constitution* (Hong Kong: Sweet & Maxwell Hong Kong, 2nd edn, 2015).

Chan, Johannes M. M., Fu, H. L. and Ghai, Yash (eds), *Hong Kong's Constitutional Debate: Conflict over Interpretation* (Hong Kong: Hong Kong University Press, 2000).

Chen, Albert H. Y., 'The Developing Theory of Law and Market Economy in Contemporary China', in Wang Guiguo and Wei Zhenying (eds), *Legal*

Developments in China: Market Economy and Law (Hong Kong: Sweet & Maxwell Asia, 1996, reprinted 1997), pp. 3–20.

'Socialist Law, Civil Law, Common Law, and the Classification of Contemporary Chinese Law', in Otto, Polak, Chen and Li (2000) pp. 55–74.

'The Concept of "One Country, Two Systems" and Its Application to Hong Kong', in Hsu, C. Stephen (ed), *Understanding China's Legal System* (New York: New York University Press, 2003) Chapter 9.

'Constitutional Adjudication in Post-1997 Hong Kong' (2006) 15 *Pacific Rim Law & Policy Journal* 627.

An Introduction to the Legal System of the People's Republic of China (Hong Kong: LexisNexis, 4th edn, 2011).

'Development of Representative Government', in Chan and Lim (2015) Chapter 8.

Chen Albert, 'The Law and Politics of Constitutional Reform and Democratisation in Hong Kong', in Jones, Brian Christopher (ed), *Law and Politics of the Taiwan Sunflower and Hong Kong Umbrella Movements* (New York: Routledge, 2017) Chapter 4.

Chen Hanfeng, Zhou Weiguo and Jiang Hao, 'The Relationship between International Treaties and National Law and the Chinese Practice' (2000) 2 *Tribune of Political Science and Law* 117. 陈寒枫, 周卫国, 蒋豪. 国际条约与国内法的关系及中国的实践[J]. 政法论坛, 2000(2): 117.

Chen, Jianfu, *From Administrative Authorisation to Private Law: A Comparative Perspective of the Developing Civil Law in the PRC* (Dordrecht: Martinus Nijhoff Publishers, 1995).

Chinese Law: Context and Transformation (Leiden, The Netherlands: Brill Nijhoff, Revised and Expanded edn, 2016).

Chen, Jianfu, Li, Yuwen, and Otto, Jan Michiel (eds), *Implementation of Law in the People's Republic of China* (The Hague: Kluwer Law International, 2002).

Chen Jizhong, 'On the Understanding and Application of the "Provisions on Several Issues Concerning the Application of the Law in Trials of Foreign-related Civil and Commercial Contract Disputes"', in The Fourth Division of Civil Case Trial of the SPC (ed), (2007) 2 *Guide on Foreign-Related Commercial and Maritime Trial* (Beijing: People's Court Press, 2008) pp. 259–277. 陈纪忠. 《最高人民法院关于审理涉外民事或商事合同纠纷案件法律适用若干问题的规定》的理解与适用[M]// 最高人民法院民事审判第四庭. (2007) 2 涉外商事海事审判指导. 北京: 人民法院出版社, 2008: 259–277.

Chen Li and Huang Yongsheng (eds), *The Criminal Law of China* (Xiamen: Xiamen University Press, 2000). 陈立, 黄永盛. 中国刑法[M]// 厦门: 厦门大学出版社, 2000.

Chen, Tung-Pi, 'Private International Law of the People's Republic of China: An Overview' (1987) 35 (3) *American Journal of Comparative Law* 445.

Chen Weizuo, 'Thoughts on the Codification of the Law on Application of Laws in Foreign-Related Civil Matters' (2010) 4 (3) *Tsinghua Law Journal* 110. 陈卫佐. 涉外民事法律适用法的立法思考[J]. 清华法学, 2010, 4(3): 110.

Comparative Private International Law (Beijing: Law Press, 2012). 陈卫佐. 比较国际私法：涉外民事关系法律适用法的立法、规则和原理的比较研究[M]. 北京: 法律出版社, 2012.

'The Relationship between the Conflicts Rules of the Forum and International Treaties' (2013) 2 *Chinese Journal of Law* 173. 陈卫佐. 法院地国家国内法中的冲突规则与国际条约的关系[J]. 法学研究, 2013(2): 173.

Cheung, Heng Loong, 'Hong Kong SAR: Autonomy within Integration?' (1999) 4 *UCLA Journal of International Law and Foreign Affairs* 181.

Civil Law Office of the Legislative Affairs Commission of the Standing Committee of the National People's Congress (ed), *Interpretation and Application of the Civil Procedure Law of the People's Republic of China* (Beijing: People's Court Press, 2012). 全国人大常委会法制工作委员会民法室. 《中华人民共和国民事诉讼法》解释与适用[M]. 北京: 人民法院出版社, 2012.

Cohen, Jerome Alan, 'The Role of Arbitration in Economic Co-Operation with China', in Moser, Michael J. (ed), *Foreign Trade, Investment and the Law in the People's Republic of China* (Oxford: Oxford University Press, 1984) Chapter 11.

Committee of Civil and Commercial Matters under the Society of Chinese Trial Theories (ed), *Understanding and Judicial Application of the Articles in 'General Provisions of Civil Law'* (Beijing: Law Press, 2017). 中国审判理论研究会民商事专业委员会. 《民法总则》条文理解与司法适用[M]. 北京: 法律出版社, 2017.

Cooney, Sean, 'Why Taiwan Is Not Hong Kong: A Review of the PRC's "One Country, Two Systems" Model for Reunification with Taiwan' (1997) 6 *Pacific Rim Law & Policy Journal* 497.

Cox, Raymond, Merrett, Louise and Smith, Marcus, *Private International Law of Reinsurance and Insurance* (London: Informa, 2006).

Davies, Martin, 'Forum Selection, Choice of Law and Mandatory Rules' (2011) 2 *Lloyd's Maritime and Commercial Law Quarterly* 237.

Bell, Andrew and Brereton, Paul Le Gay, *Nygh's Conflict of Laws in Australia* (Chatswood: LexisNexis Butterworths, 9th edn, 2014).

Deng Jilian (ed), *Commentary on the Selected Cases from Shenzhen Courts (2006 Volume)* (Beijing: People's Court Press, 2008). 邓基联. 深圳法院精选案例评析(2006年卷)[M]. 北京: 人民法院出版社, 2008.

Deng Xiaoping, 'An Idea for the Peaceful Reunification of the Chinese Mainland and Taiwan', reprinted in Zhang Wanming, *An Overview of Taiwan-related Issues* (Beijing: Law Press, 2nd edn, 2009) pp. 193–194. 邓小平. 中国大陆和台湾和平统一的设想[M]// 张万明. 涉台法律问题总论. 北京: 法律出版社, 2009: 193–194.

Collins, Lawrence (ed), *Dicey and Morris on The Conflict of Laws* (London: Stevens & Sons, 11th edn, 1987).

Lord Collins of Mapesbury (ed), *Dicey, Morris and Collins on the Conflict of Laws* (London: Sweet & Maxwell, 15th edn, 2012).

Dickinson, Andrew, 'Back to the Future: the UK's EU Exit and the Conflict of Laws' (2016) 12 (2) *Journal of Private International Law* 195.

Ding Wei (ed), *Private International Law* (Shanghai: Shanghai People's Press, 2004). 丁伟. 国际私法学[M]. 上海: 上海人民出版社, 2004.

The Harmonious Development of China's Private International Law (Shanghai: Shanghai Social Sciences Academy Press, 2009). 丁伟. 中国国际私法和谐发展研究[M]. 上海: 上海社会科学院出版社, 2009.

Dolinger, Jacob, 'Application, Proof, and Interpretation of Foreign Law: A Comparative Study in Private International Law' (1995) 12 *Arizona Journal of International and Comparative Law* 225.

Du Huanfang, 'An Overview of Choice of Jurisdiction and Law of Foreign-Related Cases in China' (2009) 4(4) *Journal of Cambridge Studies* 72.

Economic Case Trial Division of the SPC (ed), *Explanation and Application of the Contract Law* (Beijing: Xinhua Press, 1999). 最高人民法院经济审判庭. 合同法解释与适用[M]. 北京: 新华出版社, 1999.

Ehrenzweig, Albert Armin, *Private International Law* (Leiden: Sijthoff, 1972) Vol. I.

Fawcett, J. J., 'Evasion of Law and Mandatory Rules in Private International Law' (1990) 49 *Cambridge Law Journal* 44.

Fawcett, J. J. and Carruthers, J. M. (eds), *Cheshire, North and Fawcett: Private International Law* (Oxford: Oxford University Press, 14th edn, 2008).

Fei, Jia (Jessica) and Hill, Richard, 'Enforcement of Arbitral Awards in the PRC', in Moser, Michael J. (ed), *Dispute Resolution in China* (New York: Juris, 2012) Chapter 4.

Fei Zongyi and Tang Chengyuan (eds), *The Theory and Practice of Judicial Assistance in China* (Beijing: People's Court Press, 1992). 费宗祎, 唐承元. 中国司法协助的理论与实践[M]. 北京: 人民法院出版社, 1992.

Feng Wensheng (ed), *Interpretation of the Supreme People's Court on Several Issues Concerning the Application of the Contract Law of the People's Republic of China (2): Principles, Cases and Application* (Beijing: China Legal Publishing House, 2010). 冯文生. 最高人民法院关于适用《中华人民共和国合同法》若干问题的解释（二）原理精解·案例与适用[M]. 北京: 中国法制出版社, 2010.

Feng Xia, *Hong Kong-, Macao- and Taiwan-related Inter-regional Conflict of Laws* (Beijing: Chinese University of Political Science and Law Press, 2012). 冯霞. 涉港澳台区际私法[M]. 北京: 中国政法大学出版社, 2012.

Fentiman, Richard, *Foreign Law in English Courts: Pleading, Proof and Choice of Law* (Oxford: Oxford University Press, 1998).

'Laws, Foreign Laws, and Facts' (2006) 59 (1) *Current Legal Problems* 391.

International Commercial Litigation (New York: Oxford University Press, 2nd edn, 2015).

Finder, Susan, 'The Supreme People's Court of the People's Republic of China' (1993) 7 *Journal of Chinese Law* 145.

Flanagan, Peter M., 'Demythologising the Law Merchant: The Impropriety of the Lex Mercatoria as a Choice of Law' (2004) 15 *International Company and Commercial Law Review* 297.

The Fourth Division of Civil Trial of the SPC, 'Report on the Implementation of the System of Centralised Jurisdiction over Foreign-Related Commercial Cases and Improvement Policies', in The Fourth Division of Civil Trial of the SPC (ed), (2010) 2 *Guide on Foreign-Related Commercial and Maritime Trial* (Beijing: People's Court Press, 2011) pp. 216–230. 最高人民法院民四庭. 关于涉外商事案件集中管辖制度的实施情况及完善对策的调研报告[M]// 最高人民法院民事审判第四庭. (2007) 2 涉外商事海事审判指导. 北京: 人民法院出版社, 2011: 216–230.

Fujian Higher People's Court, 'Work Hard to Promote Hong Kong-, Macao- and Taiwan-related Commercial Trial', in The Fourth Division of Civil Case Trial of the SPC (ed), (2007) 2/*Guide on Foreign-Related Commercial and Maritime Trial* (Beijing: People's Court Press, 2008) pp. 155–159. 福建省高级人民法院. 积极探索 勇于创新 努力提升涉港澳台商事审判工作水平[M]// 最高人民法院民事审判第四庭. (2007) 2 涉外商事海事审判指导. 北京: 人民法院出版社, 2008: 155–159.

Gaillard, Emmanual and Savage, John (eds), *Fouchard, Gaillard, Goldman on International Commercial Arbitration* (The Hague: Kluwer Law International, 1999).

Gan Peizhong (ed), *Legal Protection of National Economic Safety* (Beijing: Law Press, 2012). 甘培忠. 国家经济安全法律保障制度研究[M]. 北京: 法律出版社, 2012.

Gao Xiaoli, 'Analysis of, and Suggested Approaches to, the Application of Public Policy in China's Private International Law', in The Fourth Division of Civil Case Trial of the SPC (ed), (2005) 1 *Guide on Foreign-Related Commercial and Maritime Trial* (Beijing: People's Court Press, 2005) pp. 197–221. 高晓力. 目前我国国际私法上的公共政策运用状况分析及应具有的思路[M]// 最高人民法院民事审判第四庭. (2005) 1 涉外商事海事审判指导. 北京: 人民法院出版社, 2005: 197–221

The Application of Public Policy in Private International Law (Beijing: China Press on Democracy and Legal System, 2008). 高晓力. 国际私法上公共政策的运用[M]// 北京: 中国民主法制出版社, 2008.

'Understanding "Interpretation of the Supreme People's Court on Certain Issues Concerning the Application of the Law of the People's Republic of China on the Application of Laws to Foreign-Related Civil Relations (1)' (2013) 3 *Journal of Law Application* 38. 高晓力. 最高人民法院《关于适用〈中华人民共和国涉外民事关系法律适用法〉若干问题的解释（一）》解读[J]. 法律适用, 2013(3): 38.

Gaskell, Nicholas, Asariotis, Regina and Baatz, Yvonne, *Bills of Lading: Law and Contracts* (London: LLP, 2000).

Geeroms, Sofie, *Foreign Law in Civil Litigation: A Comparative and Functional Analysis* (New York: Oxford University Press, 2004).

Ghai, Yash, *Hong Kong's New Constitutional Order: The Resumption of Chinese Sovereignty and the Basic Law* (Hong Kong: Hong Kong University Press, 2nd edn, 1999).

'Litigating the Basic Law: Jurisdiction, Interpretation and Procedure', in Chan, Fu and Ghai (2000) pp. 3–52.

Gilmore, Grant and Black, Charles L., *The Law of Admiralty* (New York: The Foundation Press, 2nd edn, 1975).

Girvin, Stephen, *Carriage of Goods by Sea* (Oxford: Oxford University Press, 2007).

Giuliano, Mario and Lagarde, Paul, *Report on the Convention on the Law Applicable to Contractual Obligations* (Official Journal C 282, 31/10/1980, P. 0001–0050), available at: http://eur-lex.europa.eu/LexUriServ/LexUriServ.do?uri=CELEX:31980Y1031(01):EN:HTML

Gottschalk, Eckart, Michaels, Ralf, Rühl, Giesela and von Hein, Jan (eds), *Conflict of Laws in a Globalized World* (New York: Cambridge University Press, 2007).

Graveson, Ronald H., 'Problems of Private International Law in Non-Unified Legal Systems' (1974a) 141 *Recueil des Cours* 187.

Conflict of Laws: Private International Law (London: Sweet & Maxwell, 7th edn., 1974b).

Guangdong Higher People's Court (ed), *Guide on China's Foreign-Related Commercial Trials* (Beijing: Law Press, 2004). 广东省高级人民法院. 中国涉外商事审判实务[M]. 北京: 法律出版社, 2004.

(ed), *Selected Cases and Analysis on Hong Kong- and Macao-related Commercial Matters* (Beijing: Law Press, 2006). 广东省高级人民法院. 涉港澳商事案例精选精析[M]. 北京: 法律出版社, 2006.

'Insisting on the Principles and Grasping the Law in Order to Promote the Development of Hong Kong- and Macao-related Commercial Trial', in The Fourth Division of Civil Case Trial of the SPC (ed), (2007) 2 *Guide on Foreign-Related Commercial and Maritime Trial* (Beijing: People's Court Press, 2008) pp. 160–165. 广东省高级人民法院. 坚持原则 把握规律 推进涉港澳商事审判工作新发展[M]// 最高人民法院民事审判第四庭. 涉外商事海事审判指导. 北京: 人民法院出版社, 2008: 160–165.

Guedj, Thomas G., 'The Theory of the Lois de Police, A Functional Trend in Continental Private International Law – A Comparative Analysis with Modern American Theories' (1991) 36 *The American Journal of Comparative Law* 661.

Guo Daohui, 'On the Conjunction of Generality and Flexibility in Legislation' (1987) 1 *Law Review* 15. 郭道晖. 论立法中原则性与灵活性结合[J]. 法学评论, 1987(1): 15.

Guo Yanzhi, 'On the Inter-regional Judicial Assistance between the Mainland and Hong Kong' (2002) 11 *Journal of Law Application* 50. 郭燕枝. 对内地与香港间区际民商事司法协助的探讨[J]. 法律适用, 2002(11): 50.

Guo Yujun, 'The Chinese Theory and Practice concerning Ascertainment of Foreign Law in Recent Years' (2007) 2 *International Law Review of Wuhan University* 1. 郭玉军. 近年中国有关外国法查明与适用的理论与实践[J]. 武大国际法评论, 2007(2): 1.

Guo Yujun and Xu Jintang, 'On the Development of China's Foreign-Related Civil and Commercial Trial Practice from Statistical Analysis', in Huang Jin, Xiao Yongping and Liu Renshan (eds), *Chinese Yearbook of Private International Law and Comparative Law (Eleventh Volume)* (Beijing: Peking University Press, 2008) pp. 122–155. 郭玉军, 徐锦堂. 从统计分析看我国涉外民商审判实践的发展[M]// 黄进, 肖永平, 刘仁山. 中国国际私法与比较法年刊(第十一卷). 北京: 北京大学出版社, 2008: 122–155.

Han Depei (ed), *Private International Law* (Wuhan: Wuhan University Press, 2003). 韩德培. 国际私法新论[M]. 武汉: 武汉大学出版社, 2003.

Han Depei and Huang Jin, 'Inter-Regional Conflict of Laws in China' (1989) 1 *Social Sciences in China* 117. 韩德培, 黄进. 中国区际法律冲突问题研究[J]. 中国社会科学, 1989(1): 117.

Han Jian, 'Recognition and Enforcement of Foreign Judgments and Awards in Mainland China' (2005) 2 *US-China Law Review* 20.

Hartley, Trevor C., 'Pleading and Proof of Foreign Law: The Major European Systems Compared' (1996) 45 *International and Comparative Law Quarterly* 271.

'Mandatory Rules in International Contracts: The Common Law Approach' (1997) 266 *Recueil des Cours* 337.

Hay, Peter, 'Comments on Public Policy in Current American Conflicts Law', in Baetge, Dietmar, von Hein, Jan and von Hinden, Michael (eds), *Die richtige Ordnung: Festschrift für Jan Kropholler zum 70. Geburtstag* (Tübingen: Mohr Siebeck, 2008) pp. 89–103.

Hay, Peter, Borchers, Patrick J. and Freer, Richard D., *Conflict of Laws: Private International Law, Cases and Materials* (St. Paul: Foundation Press, 15th edn, 2017)

Hay, Peter, Borchers, Patrick J. and Symeonides, Symeon C., *Conflict of Laws* (St. Paul: West, 5th edn, 2010).

He, Qisheng, 'Public Policy in Enforcement of Foreign Arbitral Awards in the Supreme People's Court of China' (2013) 43 *Hong Kong Law Journal* 1037.

He Rong, 'Speech at the Fourth National Conference on the Trial of Foreign-Related Commercial and Maritime Cases', in The Fourth Division of Civil Trial of the SPC (ed), (2014) 2 *Guide on Foreign-Related Commercial and Maritime Trial* (Beijing: People's Court Press, 2015) pp. 20–33. 贺荣. 深入学习贯彻党的十八届四中全会精神 全面推进涉外商事海事审判工作 为开放型经济新体制和海洋强国战略提供坚实司法保障——在第四次全国涉外商事海事审判工作会议上的讲话[M]// 最高人民法院民事审判第四庭. (2014) 2 涉外商事海事审判指导. 北京: 人民法院出版社, 2015: 20–33.

He Weifang, 'Two Issues in the Judicial Administration in China' (1997) 6 *Social Sciences in China* 117. 贺卫方. 中国司法管理制度的两个问题[J]. 中国社会科学, 1997(6): 117.

He, Xin, 'Routinization of Divorce Law Practice in China: Institutional Constraints' Influence on Judicial Behaviour' (2009) 23 *International Journal of Law, Policy and the Family* 83.

He, Xin and Ng, Kwai Hang, 'Inquisitorial Adjudication and Institutional Constraints in Chinese Civil Justice' (2013) 35 *Law & Policy* 290.

Henkin, Louis, *How Nations Behave: Law and Foreign Policy* (New York: Columbia University Press, 2nd edn, 1979).

Henkin, Louis, 'Human Rights and State "Sovereignty"(1995) 25 *Georgia Journal of International and Comparative Law* 31.

Hook, Maria, *The Choice of Law Contract* (Oxford: Hart Publishing, 2016).

Hu Henan, *Re-Examining Territorial Sovereignty in International Law: A New Perspective of the Settlement of the China Seas Disputes* (PhD Thesis submitted to the University of Hong Kong in 2015).

'The Doctrine of Occupation: An Analysis of Its Invalidity under the Framework of International Legal Positivism' (2016) 15 *Chinese Journal of International Law* 75.

Hu Zhenjie and Li Shuangyuan, 'On the Proper Application of Ordre Public in Private International Law from Several Cases Adjudicated by Chinese Courts' (1992) 5 *Tribune of Political Science and Law* 77. 胡振杰, 李双元. 从我国法院的几个案例谈国际私法上公共秩序保留制度的正确运用[J]. 政法论坛, 1992(5): 77.

Huang Jin, 'Several Basic Issues Regarding Inter-Regional Conflict of Laws' (1989) 4 *Studies in Law and Business* 65. 黄进. 区际冲突法的几个基本问题[J]. 中南政法学院学报, 1989(4): 65.

(ed), *Private International Law* (Beijing: Law Press, 1999). 黄进. 国际私法[M]. 北京：法律出版社, 1999.

'On the Codification and Improvement of the Law on the Application of Laws to Foreign-Related Civil Relationships' (2011) 3 *Tribune of Political Science and Law* 3. 黄进. 中国涉外民事关系法律适用法的制定与完善[J]. 政法论坛, 2011(3): 3.

Huang, Jie, 'Direct Application of International Commercial Law in Chinese Courts: Intellectual Property, Trade, and International Transportation' (2008) 5 (3) *Manchester Journal of International Economic Law* 105.

'Interregional Recognition and Enforcement of Civil and Commercial Judgments: Lessons for China from US and EU Laws' (2010) 6 *Journal of Private International Law* 109.

Huang Jin and Jiang Rujiao (eds), *Interpretation and Analysis of 'Law on Application of Laws to Foreign-Related Civil Relationships of the People's Republic of China'* (Beijing: Law Press, 2011). 黄进, 姜茹娇. 《中华人民共和国涉外民事关系法律适用法》释义与分析[M]. 北京: 法律出版社, 2011.

Huang Jin and Li Qingming, 'Private International Law in the Chinese Courts in 2006', in Huang Jin, Xiao Yongping and Liu Renshan (eds), *Chinese Yearbook of Private International Law and Comparative Law (10th Volume)* (Beijing: Peking University Press, 2007) pp. 371–414. 黄进, 李庆明. 2006年中国国际私法司法实践述评[M]// 黄进,肖永平, 刘仁山. 中国国际私法与比较法年刊（第十卷）. 北京: 北京大学出版社, 2007: 371–414.

Huang, Jin and Qian, Andrew Xuefeng, '"One Country, Two Systems", Three Law Families, and Four Legal Regions: The Emerging Inter-Regional Conflicts of Law in China', (1995) 5 *Duke Journal of Comparative & International Law* 289.

Huang Jin, Hu Wei and Wang Qingsong, 'Private International Law Practice in Chinese Courts in 2007', in Huang Jin, Xiao Yongping and Liu Renshan (eds), *Chinese Yearbook of Private International Law and Comparative Law (11th Volume)* (Beijing: Peking University Press, 2008) pp. 433–481. 黄进, 胡炜, 王青松. 2007年中国国际私法司法实践述评[M]//黄进, 肖永平, 刘仁山. 中国国际私法与比较法年刊（第十一卷）. 北京: 北京大学出版社, 2008: 433–481.

Institute of Chinese Law of the Supreme People's Court (ed), 1996 (3) *Selected Cases of People's Court* (Beijing: People's Court Press, 1996). 最高人民法院中国应用法学研究所. (1996) 3 人民法院案例选[M]. 北京: 人民法院出版社, 1996.

Ip, Eric C., 'The Supreme People's Court and the Political Economy of Judicial Empowerment in Contemporary China' (2011) 24 *Columbia Journal of Asian Law* 367.

Jayme, Erik, 'Identité Culturelle et Intégration: Le Droit International Privé Postmoderne' (1995) 251 *Recueil des Cours* (cited at Nygh [1999] p. 36).

Jennings, R. Y., 'Extraterritorial Jurisdiction and the United States' Anti-Trust Laws' (1957) 33 *British Yearbook of International Law* 146.

Jia Yu and You Wei (eds), *The Criminal Law of China* (Beijing: China University of Political Science and Law Press, 1997). 贾宇, 游伟. 中国刑法[M]. 北京: 中国政法大学出版社, 1997.

Jiang Wei and Wu Zeyong, 'Jurisprudential Analysis of Several Fundamental Issues in Evidence Law' (2002) 1 *China Legal Science* 24. 江伟, 吴泽勇. 证据法若干基本问题的法哲学分析[J]. 中国法学, 2002(1): 24.

Jin Zhengjia (ed), *Analyses of Typical Maritime Cases in China* (Beijing: Law Press, 1998). 金正佳. 中国典型海事案例评析[M]. 北京: 法律出版社, 1998.

Juenger, Friedrich K., 'General Course on Private International Law' (1983) 193 *Recueil des Cours* 123.

Choice of Law and Multistate Justice (Dordrecht: Martinus Nijhoff, 1992).

'The Need for a Comparative Approach to Choice-of-Law Problems' (1999) 73 *Tulane Law Review* 1309.

Kahn-Freund, O., *General Problems of Private International Law* (Leiden: A. W. Sijthoff, 1976).

Kalenský, Pavel, *Trends in Private International Law* (Prague: Academia, 1971).

Kalmo, Hent and Skinner, Quentin (eds.), *Sovereignty in Fragments: The Past, Present and Future of a Contested Concept* (Cambridge: Cambridge University Press, 2010).

Keller, Perry, 'The National People's Congress and the Making of National Law', in Otto, Polak, Chen and Li (2000) pp. 75–90.

Kelly, D. St. L., 'Reference, Choice, Restriction and Prohibition' (1977) 26 *International and Comparative Law Quarterly* 857.

Kelly, J. M., *A Short History of Western Legal Theory* (Oxford: Clarendon Press, 1992).

Knauth, Arnold Whitman, *The American Law of Ocean Bills of Lading* (Baltimore: American Maritime Cases Inc., 1953).

Knight, CJS, 'Book Review of The Confluence of Public and Private International Law: Justice, Pluralism and Subsidiarity in the International Constitutional Ordering of Private Law' (2010) *Lloyd's Maritime and Commercial Law Quarterly* 349.

Koguchi, Hikota, 'Some Observations about "Judicial Independence" in Post-Mao China' (1987) 7 *Boston College Third World Law Journal* 195.

Kong, Qingjiang and Hu Minfei, 'The Chinese Practice of Private International Law' (2002) 3 *Melbourne Journal of International Law* 414.

Lagarde, Paul, 'Public Policy', in Kurt Lipstein (ed), *International Encyclopedia of Comparative Law* (Tübingen: J. C. B. Mohr (Paul Siebeck), 1994) Volume III Chapter 11.

Lando, Ole, 'Contracts', in Kurt Lipstein (ed), *International Encyclopedia of Comparative Law* (Tübingen: J. C. B. Mohr [Paul Siebeck], 1976) Volume III Chapter 24.

Laski, Harold J., *The Foundations of Sovereignty and Other Essays* (London: Allen & Unwin, 1921).

Lauterpacht, Hersch, *International Law and Human Rights* (London: Stevens & Sons, 1950).

Lew, Julian D. M., Mistelis, Loukas A. and Kröll, Stefan M., *Comparative International Commercial Arbitration* (The Hague: Kluwer Law International, 2003).

Li Guoguang, 'Speech of Li Guoguang on the National Conference on Civil Trial', in Tang Dehua (ed), (2000) 4 *Guide and Reference on Civil Trial* (Beijing: Law Press, 2000) pp. 32–34. 李国光. 最高人民法院副院长李国光在全国民事审判工作会议上的讲话（2000年10月28日）[M]// 唐德华. 民事审判指导与参考. 北京: 法律出版社, 2000: 32–34.

Li Guoguang, Xi Xiaoming, Jin Jianfeng and Cao Shibing, *Understanding and Application of 'Interpretation of the SPC on Some Issues Regarding the Application of Security Law'* (Changchun: Jilin People's Press, 2000). 李国光, 奚晓明, 金剑峰, 曹士兵. 最高人民法院《关于适用〈中华人民共和国担保法〉若干问题的解释》理解与适用[M]. 长春: 吉林人民出版社, 2000.

Li Haopei, *Selection of Li Haopei's Articles* (Beijing: Law Press, 2000). 李浩培. 李浩培文选[M]. 北京: 法律出版社, 2000.

Li Ji, 'Application of Mandatory Rules in Foreign-Related Civil Relationships', in The Fourth Division of Civil Case Trial of the SPC (ed), (2004) 1 *Guide on Foreign-Related Commercial and Maritime Trial* (Beijing: People's Court Press, 2004) p. 169–177. 李继. 试论强制性规范在涉外民事法律关系中的适用[M]// 最高人民法院民事审判第四庭. (2004) 1 涉外商事海事审判指导. 北京: 人民法院出版社, 2004: 169–177.

Li Jianguo, 'Report on the Draft of General Provisions of the Civil Law of the People's Republic of China – at the Fifth Session of the Twelfth National People's Congress on 8 March 2017', in Editorial Group for the Book 'Legislation Background and Point on General Provisions of the Civil Law' (ed), *Legislation Background and Point on General Provisions of the Civil Law* (Beijing: Law Press, 2017), pp. 3–10. 李建国. 关于《中华人民共和国民法总则（草案）》的说明——2017年3月8日在第十二届全国人民代表大会第五次会议上[M]//《民法总则立法背景与观点全集》编写组. 民法总则立法背景与观点全集. 北京: 法律出版社, 2017: 3–10

Li Shichun, 'Another Path for the Case Guidance System – Restraint Application of Judicial Activism in China' (2009) 6 *Legal Science* 59. 李仕春. 案例指导制度的另一条思路——司法能动主义在中国的有限适用[J]. 法学, 2009(6): 59.

Li Shuangyuan, Ou Fuyong, Jin Pengnian and Zhang Mao, *General Private International Law of China* (Beijing: Law Press, 3rd edn, 2007). 李双元, 欧福永, 金彭年, 张茂. 中国国际私法通论[M]. 北京:法律出版社, 2007.

Li Wei, 'On the Positive Meanings of China's Withdrawing Its Reservation to Article 1(1)(b) CISG' (2012) 5 *The Jurist* 93. 李巍. 论中国撤回对于《联合国国际货物销售合同公约》第一条b项的保留[J]. 法学家, 2012(5): 93.

Li, Yuwen, *The Judicial System and Reform in Post-Mao China: Stumbling towards Justice* (Farnham: Ashgate, 2014).

Liang, Jieying, 'Statutory Restrictions on Party Autonomy in China's Private International Law of Contract: How Far Does the 2010 Codification Go?' (2012) 8 *Journal of Private International Law* 77.

Liang Shuwen (ed), *Collection of Civil and Procedure Laws* (Shijiazhuang: Hebei People's Press, 1993). 梁书文. 民事诉讼实用大全[M]. 石家庄: 河北人民出版社, 1993.

Libling, D. F., 'Formation of International Contracts' (1979) 42 *The Modern Law Review* 169.

Liebman, Benjamin L., 'Assessing China's Legal Reforms' (2009) 23 *Columbia Journal of Asian Law* 17.

'China's Courts: Restricted Reform' (2007) 21 *Columbia Journal of Asian Law* 1.

Lim, C. L., 'Right to Vote and Right to Political Participation', in Chan and Lim (2015) Chapter 29.

Lim, C. L. and Chan, Johannes, 'Autonomy and Central-Local Relations', in Chan and Lim (2015) Chapter 2.

Lin Feng, 'The Future of Judicial Independence in China', Working Paper Series No.2, Centre for Judicial Education and Research, City University of Hong Kong (May 2016).

Lin Huachang, *Change and Reflection: Study on the Legal System of China's Foreign Exchange Administration* (Beijing: Law Press, 2010). 林华昌. 变革与反思：中国外汇管理法律制度研究[M]. 北京:法律出版社, 2010.

Lin Li, 'On Ascertainment of Foreign Law', in Zheng E (ed), *Research on Foreign-related Commercial Trial (Volume 2)* (Beijing: Law Press, 2011) pp. 159–175. 林立. 域外法查明制度研究[M]// 郑鄂. 中国涉外商事审判研究（第二辑）. 北京: 法律出版社, 2011: 159–175.

Lin Yanping, 'Legal Analysis of the Judicial Interpretation on Private International Law in China' (2000) 5 *Legal Science* 27. 林燕平. 对我国国际私法司法解释现象的法理分析[J]. 法学, 2000, 5: 27.

Lipstein, K., 'The General Principles of Private International Law' (1972) 135 *Recueil des Cours* 96

Liu Guixiang, 'Several Issues Concerning the Law on the Application of Laws to Foreign-related Civil Relationships in Judicial Practice' (2011) 11 *The People's Judicature* 37. 刘贵祥. 涉外民事关系法律适用法在审判实践中的几个问题[J]. 人民司法, 2011(11): 37.

'Concluding Speech at the National Conference on Maritime Trial', in The Fourth Division of Civil Case Trial of the SPC (ed), (2012) 2 *Guide on Foreign-Related Commercial and Maritime Trial* (Beijing: People's Court Press, 2013) pp. 16–31. 刘贵祥. 在全国海事审判工作会议上的总结讲话[M]// 最高人民法院民事审判第四庭. (2012) 2涉外商事海事审判指导. 北京: 人民法院出版社, 2013: 16–31.

Liu Laiping, *Proof of Foreign Law* (Beijing: Law Press, 2007). 刘来平. 外国法的查明[M]. 北京: 法律出版社, 2007.

Liu, Nanping, *Judicial Interpretation in China: Opinions of the Supreme People's Court* (Hong Kong: Sweet & Maxwell, 1997).

Liu Ping, *A Study on PIL Problems in Delivery of Cargo without B/L: Based on China's Theoretic Analysis and Practical Inspection* (Beijing: Law Press, 2008). 刘萍. 无单放货中国际私法问题研究: 基于中国的理论分析与实证考察[M]. 北京: 法律出版社, 2008.

Liu Renshan, 'The Theory and Practice concerning "Loi application Immediate": A Commentary on Article 4 of "Law on the Application of Laws to Foreign-related Civil Relations" of China', in Chinese Society of International Law (ed), *Chinese Yearbook of International Law* (Beijing: World Affairs Press, 2012) pp. 410–440. 刘仁山. "直接适用的法" 之理论与实践问题——兼评中国《涉外民事关系法律适用法》第4条[M]// 中国国际法学会. 中国国际法年刊. 北京: 世界知识出版社, 2012: 410–440.

Liu Xiangshu, *Fundamental Issues of Private International Law* (Beijing: Law Press, 2001). 刘想树. 国际私法基本问题研究[M]. 北京: 法律出版社, 2001.

Liu Xingli, *Choice of Jurisdiction on International Marine Cargo Claims: Competing Court and Appropriate Forum* (Beijing: Peking University Press, 2011). 刘兴莉. 国际海事货物索赔管辖权的选择[M]. 北京: 北京大学出版社, 2011.

Liu Ying, 'The Direct Application of the CISG in Chinese Courts' (2009) 5 *Law Review* 83. 刘瑛. 论《联合国国际货物销售合同公约》在中国法院的直接适用[J]. 法学评论, 2009(5): 83.

Lloyd, Dennis, *Public Policy: A Comparative Study in English and French Law* (London: The Athlone Press, 1953).

Lowenfeld, Andreas F., *International Litigation and the Quest for Reasonableness: Essays in Private International Law* (Oxford: Clarendon Press, 1996).

Lubman, Stanley, 'Looking for Law in China' (2006) 20 *Columbia Journal of Asian Law* 1.

Ma, Ying-jeou, 'Policy towards the Chinese Mainland: Taipei's View', in Tsang, Steve (ed), *In the Shadow of China: Political Developments in Taiwan Since 1949* (Hong Kong: Hong Kong University Press, 1993) Chapter 8.

Mann, F. A., 'Proper Law and Illegality in Private International Law' (1937) 18 *British Yearbook of International Law* 97.

McCartney, Robert C., 'The Use of Choice-of-Law Clauses in International Commercial Contracts' (1960) 6 *Wayne Law Review* 340.

McClean, David, 'A Common Heritance? An Examination of the Private International Law Tradition of the Commonwealth' (1996) 260 *Recueil des Cours* 9.

McComish, James, 'Pleading and Proving Foreign Law in Australia' (2007) 31 *Melbourne University Law Review* 400.

Michaels, Ralf, 'The Re-state-ment of Non-State Law: The State, Choice of Law, and the Challenge from Global Legal Pluralism' (2005) 51 *The Wayne Law Review* 1209.

'Non-State Law in the Hague Principles on Choice of Law in International Commercial Contracts', in Purnhagen, Kai and Rott, Peter (eds), *Varieties of European Economic Law and Regulation: Liber Amicorum for Hans Micklitz* (Heidelberg: Springer International Publishing, 2014) pp. 43–69.

Mills, Alex, 'The Dimensions of Public Policy in Private International Law' (2008) 4(2) *Journal of Private International Law* 201.

The Confluence of Public and Private International Law: Justice, Pluralism and Subsidiarity in the International Constitutional Ordering of Private Law (New York: Cambridge University Press, 2009).

Mocatta, Sir Alan Abraham, Mustill, Sir Michael J. and Boyd, Stewart C., *Scrutton on Charterparties and Bills of Lading* (London: Sweet & Maxwell, 19th edn, 1984).

McClean, David and Beevers, Kisch, *Morris: The Conflict of Laws* (London: Sweet & Maxwell, 7th edn, 2009).

Moyle, J. B., *The Institutes of Justinian* (Oxford: Clarendon Press, 5th edn, 1913).

Muir Watt, Horatia, 'Party Autonomy in Global Context: The Political Economy of a Self-Constituting Regime' (2015) 58 *Japanese Yearbook of International Law* 175.

Muir Watt, Horatia and Fernández Arroyo, Diego P, *Private International Law and Global Governance* (Oxford: Oxford University Press, 2014).

Neff, S., 'A Short History of International Law', in Evans, M. D. (ed), *International Law* (Oxford: Oxford University Press, 2nd edn, 2006).

Newton, Justin, *The Uniform Interpretation of the Brussels and Lugano Conventions* (Oxford: Hart Publishing, 2002).

Nishitani, Yuko, 'Treatment of Foreign Law: Dynamics Towards Convergence? – General Report', in Nishitani, Yuko (ed), *Treatment of Foreign Law – Dynamics Towards Convergence?* (Cham: Springer International Publishing, 2017) pp. 3 – 60.

North, Peter Machin, 'Jurisdiction Clauses in Bills of Lading and the European Judgments Convention' (1985) *Lloyd's Maritime and Commercial Law Quarterly* 177.

'Choice in Choice of Law', in *Essays in Private International Law* (Oxford: Clarendon Press, 1993) pp. 171–200.

Nygh, Peter, 'The Reasonable Expectations of the Parties as A Guide to the Choice of Law in Contract and in Tort' (1995) 251 *Recueil des Cours* 269.

Autonomy in International Contracts (New York: Oxford University Press, 1999).

Office of Hong Kong-, Macao- and Taiwan-related Judicial Issues of the SPC (ed), *Handbook on Hong Kong-, Macao- and Taiwan-related Judicial Practice*

(Beijing: People's Court Press, 2013). 最高人民法院港澳台司法事务办公室. 涉港澳台司法实务手册[M]. 北京: 人民法院出版社, 2013.

O'Hara, Erin Ann, 'Opting out of Regulation: A Public Choice Analysis of Contractual Choice of Law' (2000) 53 *Vanderbilt Law Review* 1551.

O'Hara, Erin Ann and Ribstein, Larry E., *The Law Market* (New York: Oxford University Press, 2009).

Otto, Jan Michiel, Polak, Maurice V., Chen, Jianfu and Li, Yuwen (eds), *Law-making in the People's Republic of China* (The Hague: Kluwer Law International, 2000).

Ouyang Zhenyuan, 'On the Problems and Solutions in Choice of Law in the Foreign- and Hong Kong–related Commercial Trials' (2004) 9 *Application of Law* 14. 欧阳振远. 涉外和涉港商事审判法律适用存在的问题与对策[J]. 法律适用, 2004(9): 14.

'Judicial Support and Supervision over International Commercial Arbitration in China', in Chen An (ed), (2009) 16(1) *Journal of International Economic Law* (Beijing: Peking University Press, 2009). 欧阳振远. 中国司法对国际商事仲裁的支持和监督——兼评济南市中级人民法院不予承认与执行ICC第13464/MS/JB/JEM号仲裁裁决案[M]// 陈安. (2009) 16(1) 国际经济法学刊. 北京: 北京大学出版社, 2009.

Paulsen, Monrad G. and Sovern, Michael I., '"Public Policy" in the Conflict of Laws' (1956) 56 *Columbia Law Review* 969.

Peerenboom, Randall, *China's Long March toward Rule of Law* (Cambridge: Cambridge University Press, 2002).

Pendleton, Michael, 'Non-empirical Discovery in Legal Scholarship – Choosing, Researching and Writing a Scholarly Article', in McConville, Mike and Chui, Wing Hong (eds), *Research Methods for Law* (Edinburgh: Edinburgh University Press, 2007) pp. 159–180.

Pollock, Sir Frederick, *The Expansion of the Common Law* (London: Stevens and Sons, 1904).

Potter, Pitman B., 'Law-making in the People's Republic of China: The Case of Contracts', in Otto, Polack, Chen and Li (2000) pp. 189–203.

Prausnitz, O., *The Standardization of Commercial Contracts in English and Continental Law* (London: Sweet & Maxwell, 1937).

Qi Xiangquan, *Principles and Essentials of Law of Law Application of Foreign Civil Relations* (Beijing: Law Press, 2011). 齐湘泉.《涉外民事关系法律适用法》原理与精要[M]. 北京:法律出版社, 2011.

Qin Ruiting (ed), *Private International Law* (Tianjin: Nankai University Press, 2008). 秦瑞亭. 国际私法[M]. 天津: 南开大学出版社, 2008.

'Theory and Practice of China's Contractual Conflict of Laws', in *The Collection of Papers for the 2010 Annual Conference of the Chinese Academy of Private International Law (I)* pp. 227–245. 秦瑞亭. 中国合同冲突法的理论与实践

[C]// 中国国际私法学会2010年年会暨涉外民事关系法律适用法研讨会论文集(上). 天津: [出版者不详], 2010: 227–245.

Qu Guangqing and Zhang Xinying, 'Conflict of Laws in International Insurance Contracts' (2006) 4 *Journal of Shandong Police College* 36. 屈广清,张新颖. 国际保险合同的法律冲突与法律适用[J]. 山东警察学院学报, 2006(4): 36.

Radon, J., 'Sovereignty: A Political Emotion, Not a Concept' (2004) 40 *Stanford Journal of International Law* 195.

Ramberg, Jan, 'Freedom of Contract in Maritime Law' (1993) *Lloyd's Maritime and Commercial Law Quarterly* 178.

Reese, Willis L. M., 'Power of Parties to Choose Law Governing Their Contract' (1960) 54 *American Society of International Law Proceedings* 49.

Research Group of Guangdong Higher People's Court, 'Several Issues concerning the Law on Application of Laws to Foreign-Related Civil Relations and Suggestions on Drafting a Judicial Interpretation' (2013) 1 *People's Judicature•Application* 59. 广东省高级人民法院课题组. 关于涉外民事关系法律适用法的若干问题及起草司法解释的建议[J]. 人民司法•应用, 2013(1): 59.

Research Group (compromised of Wang Yun, Chen Jizhong and Zhou Xiang in the Fourth Division of Civil Trial of the SPC), 'The Development of Foreign-invested Financial Services and Foreign-Related Civil Trial', in The Fourth Division of Civil Case Trial of the SPC (ed), (2005) 2 *Guide on Foreign-related Commercial and Maritime Trial* (Beijing: People's Court Press, 2006) pp. 226–235. 课题调研组 (由最高人民法院民四庭王玧、陈纪忠、周翔组成). 中国外资金融服务的发展与涉外民商事审判[M]// 最高人民法院民事审判第四庭. (2005) 2 涉外商事海事审判指导. 北京: 人民法院出版社, 2006: 226–235.

The Research Office of the Supreme People's Court (ed), *Selected Judicial Documents (The Volume on Civil Law)* (Beijing: Economic Daily Press, 1997). 最高人民法院研究室. 精选司法文件(民法卷)[M]. 北京: 经济日报出版社, 1997.

Ribstein, Larry E., 'From Efficiency to Politics in Contractual Choice of Law' (2003) 37 *Georgia Law Review* 363.

Ross, Claudia and Ross, Lester, 'Language and Law: Sources of Systemic Vagueness and Ambiguous Authority in Chinese Statutory Language', in Turner, Feinerman and Guy (2000) pp. 221–270.

Rudolph, Christopher, 'Sovereignty and Territorial Borders in a Global Age' (2005) 7 *International Studies Review* 1.

Rühl, Giesela, 'Party Autonomy in Private International Law of Contracts – Transatlantic Convergence and Economic Efficiency', in Gottschalk, Michaels, Rühl, and von Hein (2007) pp. 153–183.

Sadat, L. N., 'An American Vision for Global Justice: Taking the Rule of (International) Law Seriously' (2005) 4 *Washington University Global Studies Law Review* 329.

Salmond, John W., *Jurisprudence or The Theory of the Law* (London: Stevens and Haynes, 2nd edn, 1907).

Schäfer, Kerstin Ann-Susann, *Application of Mandatory Rules in the Private International Law of Contracts* (Frankfurt: Peter Lang, 2010).

Schmitthoff, Clive M., *International Trade Usages* (Paris: Institute of International Business Law and Practice, 1987).

Schoenbaum, Thomas J., *Admiralty and Maritime Law* (4th edn, St. Paul: Thomson/West, 2004).

Schroeter, Ulrich G., 'Reservations and the CISG: The Borderland of Uniform International Sales Law and Treaty Law after Thirty-Five Years' (2015) 41(1) *Brooklyn Journal of International Law* 203.

Schwenzer, Ingeborg (ed), *Commentary on the UN Convention on the International Sale of Goods (CISG)* (New York: Oxford University Press, 2010).

Selvig, Erling, 'The Paramount Clause' (1961) 10 *The American Journal of Comparative Law* 205.

Von Senger, Harro, 'Ideology and Law-Making', in Otto, Polak, Chen and Li (2000) pp. 41–54.

Shanghai Higher People's Court, 'Report on the General Approaches, Outstanding Issues and Suggested Solutions in the Trial of Hong Kong-, Macao- and Taiwan-related Commercial Cases', in The Fourth Division of Civil Case Trial of the SPC (ed), (2007) 2 *Guide on Foreign-Related Commercial and Maritime Trial* (Beijing: People's Court Press, 2008) pp. 145–154. 上海高级人民法院. 关于审理涉港澳台商事案件中主要做法、发现问题以及应对建议的报告[M]// 最高人民法院民事审判第四庭. (2007) 2 涉外商事海事审判指导. 北京: 人民法院出版社, 2008: 145–154.

Shao, Shaping, 'The Theory and Practice of the Implementation of International Law in China', in Chen, Li and Otto (2002) pp. 197–212.

Shao Wenhong and Yu Xiaobai, 'Understanding and the Implementation of "Arrangement for Mutual Entrustment in Civil and Commercial Matters for the Service of Judicial Documents and Investigation and Evidence Obtainment between the Mainland and Macao Special Administrative Region"', in Office of Hong Kong-, Macao- and Taiwan-related Judicial Issues of the SPC (ed), *Handbook on Hong Kong-, Macao- and Taiwan-related Judicial Practice* (Beijing: People's Court Press, 2013) pp. 15–18. 邵文虹, 于晓白. 《最高人民法院〈关于内地与澳门特别行政区就民商事案件司法文书送达与调取证据的安排〉》的理解与适用[M]// 最高人民法院港澳台司法事务办公室. 涉港澳台司法实务手册. 北京: 人民法院出版社, 2013: 15–18.

Shen Deyong, 'Speech at the Fourth National Conference on the Trial of Foreign-related Commercial and Maritime Cases', in The Fourth Division of Civil Case Trial of the SPC (ed), (2014) 2 *Guide on Foreign-Related Commercial and Maritime Trial* (Beijing: People's Court Press, 2015) pp. 12–19. 沈德咏. 在第四次全国涉外商事海事审判工作会议上的讲话[M]// 最高人民法院民事审判第四庭. (2014) 2 涉外商事海事审判指导与研究. 北京：人民法院出版社, 2015: 12–19.

Shen Deyong and Xi Xiaoming (eds), *On the Understanding and Application of the Interpretation of the Supreme People's Court on the Contract Law (2)* (Beijing: People's Court Press, 2009). 沈德咏, 奚晓明. 最高人民法院关于合同法司法解释（二）理解与适用[M]. 北京: 人民法院出版社, 2009.

Shen Juan, *Interpretation on the Theory of Applicable Law of Contract* (Beijing: Law Press, 2000). 沈涓. 合同准据法理论的解释[M]. 北京: 法律出版社, 2000.

(ed), *Private International Law* (Beijing: Social Sciences Academic Press, 2006). 沈涓. 国际私法[M]. 北京: 社会科学文献出版社, 2006.

Shen, Yiming, *Resolution of Disputes between Foreign Banks and Chinese Sovereign Borrowers: Public and Private International Law Aspects* (London: Kluwer Law International, 2000).

Shen Yong, 'The Application of Foreign Law in Foreign-Related Commercial Trial', in Zheng E (ed), *Research on Foreign-Related Commercial Trial (Volume 2)* (Beijing: Law Press, 2011) pp. 150–158. 沈湧. 找法的困惑——涉外商事审判中外国法适用的现状与思考[M]// 郑鄂. 中国涉外商事审判研究（第二辑）. 北京: 法律出版社, 2011: 150–158.

Shen Zongling, 'Legal Interpretation' (1993) 6 *China Legal Science* 57. 沈宗灵. 论法律解释[J]. 中国法学, 1993 (6): 57.

Shenzhen Intermediate People's Court of Guangdong Province, 'Summarising the Judicial Experience and Searching for Innovative Approaches to Further Develop Hong Kong- and Macao-related Commercial Trial', in The Fourth Division of Civil Case Trial of the SPC (ed), (2007) 2 *Guide on Foreign-related Commercial and Maritime Trial* (Beijing: People's Court Press, 2008) pp. 190–197. 广东省深圳市中级人民法. 总结审判经验 勇于探索创新 努力开创涉港澳商事审判新局面[M]// 最高人民法院民事审判第四庭. (2007) 2 涉外商事海事审判指导. 北京: 人民法院出版社, 2008: 190–197.

Si Yuzhuo (ed), *A Study on International Maritime Legislation Trends and China Countermeasures* (Beijing: Law Press, 2002). 司玉琢. 国际海事立法趋势及对策研究[M]. 北京: 法律出版社, 2002.

Si Yuzhuo and Li Zhiwen (eds), *Study on the Theories of Chinese Maritime Law* (Beijing: Peking University Press, 2009). 司玉琢, 李志文. 中国海商法基本理论专题研究[M]. 北京: 北京大学出版社, 2009.

Song Xiao, 'On the Ex Officio Application of Conflict of Laws Rules', in Huang Jin, Xiao Yongping and Liu Renshan (eds), *Chinese Yearbook of Private International Law and Comparative Law (10th Volume)* (Beijing: Peking University Press, 2007) pp. 141–158. 宋晓. 论冲突规范的依职权适用性质[M]// 黄进, 肖永平, 刘仁山. 中国国际私法与比较法年刊（第十卷）. 北京: 北京大学出版社, 2007: 141–158.

Story, Joseph, *Commentaries on the Conflict of Laws, Foreign and Domestic, in regard to Contracts, Rights, and Remedies, and especially in regard to*

Marriages, Divorces, Wills, Successions, and Judgments (Boston: Hilliard, Gray, and Co., 1834).

Sturley, Michael F., 'The Fair Opportunity Requirement under COGSA Section 4 (5): A Case Study in the Misinterpretation of the Carriage of Goods by Sea Act' (1988) 19 *Journal of Maritime Law and Commerce* 1.

Su Haopeng, *A Study on Standard Contract Clauses* (Beijing: China Renmin University Press, 2004). 苏号朋. 格式合同条款研究[M]. 北京: 中国人民大学出版社, 2004.

Sun Nanshen, 'Ordre Public in Inter-regional Conflict of Laws under the "One Country, Two Systems" Principle' (2005) 4 *ECUPL Journal* 73. 孙南申. 论一国两制下区际私法中的公共秩序保留[J]. 华东政法学院学报, 2005(4): 73.

Sun Yingzheng (ed), *Principles and Positive Analysis of Foreign-Related Civil and Commercial Law* (Beijing: People's Court Press, 2004). 孙应征. 涉外民商事法律原理与实证解析[M]. 北京: 人民法院出版社, 2004.

Symeonides, Symeon C., *The American Choice-of-Law Revolution: Past, Present and Future* (Leiden: Martinus Nijhoff Publishers, 2006a).

'Contracts Subject to Non-State Norms' (2006b) 54 *The American Journal of Comparative Law* 209.

Symeonides, Symeon C., Perdue, Wendy Collins and von Mehren, Arthur Taylor, *Conflict of Laws: American, Comparative, International: Cases and Materials* (Thomson West, 2nd edn, 2003).

Tai, Benny, 'The Chief Executive', in Chan and Lim (2015) Chapter 7.

Tang, Zheng Sophia, 'International Treaties in Chinese Private International Law' (2012a) 42 *Hong Kong Law Journal* 597.

'Effectiveness of Exclusive Jurisdiction Clauses in the Chinese Courts – A Pragmatic Study' (2012b) 61 *International and Comparative Law Quarterly* 459.

'Cross-border Enforcement of Gambling Contracts: A Comparative Study' (2014) 7(1) *International Journal of Private Law* 1.

Tang, Zheng Sophia, Xiao, Yongping and Huo, Zhengxin, *Conflict of Laws in the People's Republic of China* (Cheltenham: Edward Elgar Publishing, 2016).

Takeshita, Keisuke, 'Critical Analysis of Party Autonomy: From a Theoretical Perspective' (2015) 58 *Japanese Yearbook of International Law* 196.

Tay, Alice Erh-Soon, 'Law in Communist China (Part 3)' (1976) 7 (3) *Sydney Law Review* 400.

Tetley, William, 'Seven Rules of Interpretation (Construction) of Bills of Lading', in Serck, Marie-Paule (ed), *Liber Amicorum Robert Wijffels* (Antwerp: ETL, 2001) pp. 359–379.

Teubner, Gunther (ed), *Global Law without a State* (Aldershot: Dartmouth, 1997).

Tilbury, Michael, Davis, Gary and Opeskin, Brian, *Conflict of Laws in Australia* (South Melbourne: Oxford University Press, 2002).

Tsai, Wen-hui, 'Convergence and the Future of Reunification between Mainland China and Taiwan: A Developmental View' (1998) 4 *Occasional Papers/ Reprints Series in Contemporary Asian Studies* 1.

Tu, Guangjian, 'Arrangement on Mutual Recognition and Enforcement of Judgments in Civil and Commercial Matters between China and Macau: Inherent Problems, Six Years' Experience and the Way Forward' (2013) 43 *Hong Kong Law Journal* 349.

Private International Law in China (Singapore: Springer, 2016).

Tu Hong, *Foreign Exchange Control in China* (Hong Kong: CCH Hong Kong, 2nd edn, 2009).

Turner, Karen G., Feinerman, James V., and Guy, R. Kent (eds), *The Limits of the Rule of Law in China* (Seattle: University of Washington Press, 2000).

Vischer, F., 'The Antagonism between Legal Security and the Search for Justice in the Field of Contracts' (1974) 142 *Recueil des Cours* 1.

Vischer, Frank, 'General Course on Private International Law' (1992) 232 *Recueil des Cours* 9.

Vogenauer, Stefan and Kleinheisterkamp, Jan (eds), *Commentary on the Unidroit Principles of International Commercial Contracts (PICC)* (New York: Oxford University Press, 2009).

Wan E'xiang (ed), *Interpretation and Application of 'Law on the Application of Laws to Foreign-Related Civil Relationships of the People's Republic of China'* (Beijing: China Legal Publishing House, 2011a). 万鄂湘.《中华人民共和国涉外民事关系法律适用法》条文理解与适用[M]. 北京: 中国法制出版社, 2011.

(ed), *Interpretation and Application of 'Provisions of the SPC on Several Issues concerning the Trial of Disputes Involving Foreign-invested Enterprises (1)'* (Beijing: China Legal Publishing House, 2011b). 万鄂湘. 《最高人民法院关于审理外商投资企业纠纷案件若干问题的规定（一）》条文理解与适用[M]. 北京: 中国法制出版社, 2011.

'Speech at the National Conference on the Trial of Foreign-Related Commercial and Maritime Cases', in The Fourth Division of Civil Case Trial of the SPC (ed), (2002) 1 *Guide and Study on Foreign-Related Commercial and Maritime Trial* (Beijing: People's Court Press, 2002) pp. 40–59. 万鄂湘. 迎接入世 乘势而上 努力开创我国涉外商事海事审判工作的新局面——在全国涉外商事海事审判工作会议上的讲话[M]// 最高人民法院民事审判第四庭. (2002) 1 涉外商事海事审判指导与研究. 北京：人民法院出版社, 2002: 40–59.

'Speech at the Second National Conference on the Trial of Foreign-Related Commercial and Maritime Cases', in The Fourth Division of Civil Trial of the SPC (ed), (2005) 2 *Guide on Foreign-Related Commercial and Maritime Trial* (Beijing: People's Court Press, 2006) pp. 5–22. 万鄂湘. 在第二次全国涉外商事海事审判工作会议上的讲话[M]// 最高人民法院民事审判第四庭. (2005) 2 涉外商事海事审判指导. 北京: 人民法院出版社, 2006: 5–22.

'Strengthen the Work on Foreign-Related Trial, and Face up to the Challenges after China becomes a Member of the WTO', in The Fourth Division of Civil Trial of the SPC (ed), (2001) 1 *Guide and Research on Foreign-Related Commercial and Maritime Trial in China* (Beijing: People's Court Press, 2001) pp. 5–13. 万鄂湘. 加强涉外审判工作,全面迎接入世挑战[M]// 最高人民法院民事审判第四庭. (2001) 1中国涉外商事海事审判指导与研究. 北京: 人民法院出版社, 2001: 5–13.

Wang Changbin, 'Collection in the Greater China Area of Gambling Debts Generated in Macao' (2011) 3 *Macau Law Review* 43. 王长斌. 澳门赌债在大中华地区的追偿[J]. 澳门法学, 2011(3): 43.

Wang Changying (ed), *Theory and Practice of Chinese Private International Law* (Beijing: People's Court Press, 1993). 王常营. 中国国际私法理论与实践[M]. 北京: 人民法院出版社, 1993.

Wang, Guiguo and Leung, Priscilla M. F., 'One Country, Two Systems: Theory into Practice' (1998) 7 *Pacific Rim Law & Policy Journal* 279.

Wang Guohua, *Private International Law Issues in Maritime Law* (Beijing: Peking University Press, 2007). 王国华. 海事国际私法原论[M]. 北京: 北京大学出版社, 2007.

Wang Liming, *Studies on Contract Law* (Beijing: People's University Press, 2002), Volume 1. 王利明. 合同法研究[M]. 北京: 人民大学出版社, 2002.

New Issues of Contract Law (Beijing: China Social Science Press, 2003). 王利明. 合同法新问题研究[M]. 北京: 中国社会科学出版社, 2003.

Wang, Tay-sheng, *Legal Reform in Taiwan under Japanese Colonial Rule (1895–1945): The Reception of Western Law* (PhD Thesis submitted to the University of Washington in 1992).

Wang Jun and Chen Hongwu, *Contract Conflict of Laws* (Beijing: University of International Business and Economics Press, 2003). 王军, 陈洪武. 合同冲突法[M]. 北京: 对外经济贸易大学出版社, 2003.

Wang, Wei, *Law and Practice for the Delivery of Goods without Presentation of Original Bills of Lading – A Comparative Study on Relevant Legal Issues of International Carriage of Goods by Sea* (Beijing: Law Press, 2010). 王伟. 无正本提单交付货物的法律与实践——国际海上货物运输法若干问题的比较研究[M]. 北京: 法律出版社, 2010.

Wei Li, 'Judicial Interpretation in China' (1997) 5 *Willamette Journal of International Law & Dispute Resolution* 87.

Westlake, John, *A Treatise on Private International Law: with Principal Reference to its Practice in England* (London: Sweet & Maxwell, 7th edn/by Norman Bentwich, 1925).

Westlake, John and Bentwich, Norman, *A Treatise on Private International Law: With Principal Reference to Its Practice in England* (London: Sweet & Maxwell, 6th edn, 1922).

Wesley-Smith, Peter, *An Introduction to the Hong Kong Legal System* (New York: Oxford University Press, 3rd edn, 1998).

Williams, Professor Richard, 'The Rotterdam Rules: Winners and Losers' (2010) 16 (3) *The Journal of International Maritime Law* 191.

Wilson, John Furness, *Carriage of Goods by Sea* (New York: Pearson Longman, 7th edn, 2010).

Winship, Peter, 'Private International Law and the U.N. Sales Convention' (1988) 21 *Cornell International Law Journal* 487.

Wolff, Martin, *Private International Law* (Oxford: Clarendon Press, 2nd edn, 1950).

Wolff, Lutz-Christian, 'China's Private International Investment Law: One-Way Street into PRC Law?' (2008) 56 *The American Journal of Comparative Law* 1039.

Woo, Margaret Y. K., 'Law and Discretion in Contemporary Chinese Courts', in Turner, Feinerman and Guy (2000) pp. 163–195.

Working Group for the Preparation of Principles for International Commercial Contracts, *Summary Records of the Meeting Held in Miami from 6 to 10 January 1992 (P.C. - Misc. 18).*

Wu, Zhaoxiang, 'The Application of Comparative Law in Judicial Interpretations' (paper presented at the Conference on the Chinese Judge and International and Comparative Law at the University of Hong Kong on 2 November 2007), cited in Ip (2011) p. 401.

Xiao Fang, *Proof of Foreign Law: A Comparative Study from the Chinese Law Perspective* (Beijing: Peking University Press, 2010). 肖芳. 论外国法的查明——中国法视角下的比较法研究[M]. 北京: 北京大学出版社, 2010.

Xiao Weiyun, 'The Hong Kong Basic Law: A Masterpiece of Creative Legislation' (1995) 3 *China Law* 87.

Xiao, Yongping and Huo, Zhengxin, 'Ordre Public in China's Private International Law' (2005) 53 *American Journal of Comparative Law* 653.

Xiao Yongping and Long Weidi, 'Contractual Party Autonomy in Chinese Private International Law' (2009) 11 *Yearbook of Private International Law* 193.

Xie Hui, 'On Normative Analysis' (2009) 2 *Chinese Jurisprudence* 36. 谢晖. 论规范分析方法[J]. 中国法学, 2009(2): 36.

Xing Gang, 'The Design Ideas and Comment of Chinese Private International Law Legislation' (2009) 2 *Legal Forum* 75. 刑钢. 中国国际私法立法的设计思路及其评析[J]. 法学论坛, 2009(2): 75.

Xu Chongde, *Introduction to the Theory of 'One Country, Two Systems'* (Beijing: China Democracy and Legal System Publishing House, 2010). 许崇德. "一国两制"理论助读[M]. 北京: 中国民主法制出版社, 2010.

Xu Guojian, 'Contract in Chinese Private International Law' (1989) 38 *International and Comparative Law Quarterly* 648.

Xu Hong, *International Judicial Assistance in Civil Matters* (Wuchang: Wuhan University Press, 1996). 徐宏. 国际民事司法协助[M]. 武昌: 武汉大学出版社, 1996.

Xu Jintang, *Empirical Research on Parties' Choice of Law by Agreement – From the Perspective of the Foreign-Related Judicial Practice in China* (Beijing: People's Press, 2010). 徐锦堂. 当事人合意选法实证研究——以我国涉外审判实践为中心[M]. 北京: 人民出版社, 2010.

Xuan Zengyi and Wang Yanyan, 'Application of UN Convention of International Sale of Goods (CISG) in China Courts' (2012) 5 *Law Science Magazine* 125. 宣增益, 王延妍. 我国法院对《联合国国际货物销售合同公约》的适用[J]. 法学杂志, 2012(5): 125.

Xue Hanqin and Jin Qian, 'International Treaties in the Chinese Domestic Legal System' (2009) 8 (2) *Chinese Journal of International Law* 299.

Yan Jianguo and Liang Yuxia, *Foreign-Related and Taiwan-, Hong Kong- and Macao-related Legal Issues* (Beijing: Beijing Broadcasting College Press, 1992). 阎建国, 梁玉霞. 最新涉外涉台港澳法律顾问大全[M]. 北京:北京广播学院出版社, 1992.

Yan Yingfeng, 'Ordre Public in Inter-regional Conflict of Laws relating to Hong Kong and Macao', in Lv Botao (ed), *Study on Questions of Commercial Trials Involving Hong Kong and Macao's Affairs* (Beijing: Law Press, 2006) pp. 156–161. 颜映丰. 涉港澳区际冲突法中的公共秩序保留[M]// 吕伯涛. 涉港澳商事审判热点问题探析. 北京: 法律出版社, 2006: 156–161.

Yang, Fan, 'The Application of the CISG in the Current PRC Law and CIETAC Arbitration Practice' (2006) 2 *Nordic Journal of Commercial Law* 1.

Contracts for the International Sale of Goods in China (Hong Kong: CCH Hong Kong, 2012).

Yang·Hongkui, *Selected Cases of Private International Law* (Beijing: Law Press, 1996). 杨洪逵. 国际私法案例选编[M]. 北京: 法律出版社, 1996.

Yang Lixin and Zhang Zebing (eds), *Judicial Policies on Taiwan- and Hong Kong-related Civil Disputes* (Changchun: Jilin People's Press, 1993). 杨立新, 张泽兵. 涉台、港民事纠纷司法对策[M]. 长春: 吉林人民出版社, 1993.

Ye Dan, *On the Public Policy in Chinese Foreign Judicial Practice Relating to Civil and Commercial Matters* (Beijing: Law Press, 2012). 叶丹. 公共秩序保留在我国涉外民商事司法实务中之适用[M].北京: 法律出版社, 2012.

Yeo, TM, 'Breach of Agreements on Choice of Law' (2010) *Lloyd's Maritime and Commercial Law Quarterly* 194.

Yiannopoulos, Athanassios N., *Negligence Clauses in Ocean Bills of Lading: Conflict of Laws and the Brussels Convention of 1924 – A Comparative Study* (New Orleans: Louisiana State University Press, 1962).

Yntema, Hessel E., '"Autonomy" in Choice of Law' (1952) 1 *American Journal of Comparative Law* 341.

Yuan, Arthur Anyuan, 'Enforcing and Collecting Money Judgments in China from a US Judgment Creditor's Perspective' (2004) 35 *George Washington International Law Review* 757.

Zhang Lei, 'Analysis of the Problems in Legislation and Judicial Practice concerning Ascertainment of Foreign Law' (2003) 1 – 2 *Journal of Law Application* 96. 张磊. 外国法的查明之立法及司法问题探析[J]. 法律适用, 2003(1–2): 96.

Study on Guarantee Involving Foreign Elements in Private International Law: From Perspective of PRC Judicial Practice (Beijing: Law Press, 2012). 张磊. 涉外保证的国际私法问题研究: 以中国司法实践为视角[M]. 北京: 法律出版社, 2012.

Zhang, Mo, 'International Civil Litigation in China: A Practical Analysis of the Chinese Judicial System' (2002) 25 *Boston College International and Comparative Law Review* 59.

Chinese Contract Law: Theory and Practice (Leiden: Martinus Nijhoff Publishers, 2006a).

'Choice of Law in Contracts: A Chinese Approach' (2006b) 26 *Northwestern Journal of International Law & Business* 289.

'Codified Choice of Law in China: Rules, Processes and Theoretic Understandings' (2011) 37 *North Carolina Journal of International Law and Commercial Regulation* 83.

Zhang, Qianfan, *The Constitution of China: A Contextual Analysis* (Oxford: Hart Publishing, 2012).

Zhang Shangjin (ed), *Private International Law* (Beijing: China Renmin University Press, 2000). 章尚锦. 国际私法[M]. 北京: 中国人民大学出版社, 2000.

Zhang Yongjian, 'Speech at the National Conference of Chief Judges of People's Courts' Divisions Responsible for Foreign-Related Commercial and Maritime Trial', in The Fourth Division of Civil Trial of the SPC (ed), (2016) 1 *Guide on Foreign-Related Commercial and Maritime Trial* (Beijing: People's Court Press, 2017) pp. 15–25. 张勇健. 在全国涉外商事海事审判庭长座谈会上的讲话[M]// 最高人民法院民事审判第四庭. (2016) 1 涉外商事海事审判指导. 北京: 人民法院出版社, 2017: 15–25.

Zhang Wanming, *An Overview of Taiwan-related Issues* (Beijing: Law Press, 2nd edn, 2009). 张万明. 涉台法律问题总论[M]. 北京: 法律出版社, 2009.

Zhou Daoluan, 'Reflections on the History of Judicial Interpretation in China since 1949 and Its Improvement (Preface)', in Research Institute of the SPC (ed), *Collection of the Judicial Interpretations of the People's Republic of China Volume 2 (1993.7–1996.6)* (Beijing: People's Court Press, 1997) pp. 1–27. 周道鸾. 新中国司法解释工作的回顾与完善司法解释工作的思考（代序）[M]// 最高人民法院研究室. 中华人民共和国最高人民法院司法解释全集第二卷(1993.7–1996.6). 北京: 人民法院出版社, 1997: 1–27.

Zhao Hong, *Selection of Cases Adjudicated by the Shanghai Maritime Court in Thirty Years (1984 – 2014)* (Beijing: Law Press, 2015). 赵红. 上海海事法院三十年案例精选(1984 – 2014)[M]. 北京:法律出版社, 2015.

Zhao Jianwen, 'The Status of International Treaties in Chinese Legal System' (2010) 6 *Chinese Journal of Law* 190. 赵建文. 国际条约在中国法律体系中的地位[J]. 法学研究, 2010(6): 190.

Zhao, Liang and Chan, Felix W. H., 'Incorporating the Charterparty's Applicable Law Clause into Bills of Lading: The Dolphina' (2012) 4 *Lloyd's Maritime and Commercial Law Quarterly* 481.

Zheng Xinjian and Zhang Lei, 'On the Ascertainment of Foreign Law in Mainland China', available at www.ccmt.org.cn/showexplore.php?id=811 accessed on 26 March 2013. 郑新俭, 张磊. 中国内地域外法查明制度之研究[EB/OL]. (2005–05–25) [2013–03–26] www.ccmt.org.cn/showexplore.php?id=811.

Zhong Jianhua & Yu Guanghua, 'Establishing the Truth on Facts: Has the Chinese Civil Process Achieved this Goal?' (2004) 13 (2) *Journal of Transnational Law & Policy* 393.

Zhou Qiang, 'To Plan Carefully for the Improvement of Foreign-Related Commercial and Maritime Trial in the Context of the Advance of the Rule of Law in China', *People's Court Daily*, 19 November 2014. 周强. 在全面推进依法治国大局中科学谋划和推进涉外商事海事审判工作[N]. 人民法院报, 2014–11–19 (1).

Zhu, Guobin, 'Inter-regional Conflict of Laws under "One Country, Two Systems": Revisiting Chinese Legal Theories and Chinese and Hong Kong Law, with Special Reference to Judicial Assistance' (2002) 32 *Hong Kong Law Journal* 615.

Zhu Jie, 'The Legal Obstacles in Regional Cooperation between Mainland China and Macao SAR and the Solution' (2013) 66 *Wuhan University Journal (Philosophy and Social Sciences)* 60. 祝捷. 论内地与澳门区域合作法律障碍及其解决机制[J]. 武汉大学学报(哲学社会科学版), 2013(66): 60.

Zweigert, Konrad, 'Some Reflections on the Sociological Dimensions of Private International Law or What Is Justice in Conflict of Laws?' (1973) *University of Colorado Law Review* 283.

Zweigert, Konrad and Kötz, Hein, *Introduction to Comparative Law* (Oxford: Clarendon Press, 3rd edn, 1998).

Statutes and Administrative Rules

Announcement No. 13 [2014] of the People's Bank of China—Announcement on Repealing Relevant Rules and Regulatory Documents (issued by the Bank of China on 8 June 2014).

中国人民银行公告[2014]第13号——关于废止有关规章和规范性文件的公告.

Anti-Monopoly Law of the People's Republic of China (adopted at the 29th meeting of the Standing Committee of the 10th NPC on 30 August 2007, effective on 1 August 2008).

中华人民共和国反垄断法.

The Basic Law of the Hong Kong Special Administrative Region of the People's Republic of China (adopted at the 3rd Session of the 7th National People's Congress on 4 April 1990, effective on 1 July 1997).
中华人民共和国香港特别行政区基本法.

The Basic Law of the Macao Special Administrative Region of the People's Republic of China (adopted at the 1st Session of the 8th NPC on 31 March 1993, effective on 20 December 1999).
中华人民共和国澳门特别行政区基本法.

Catalogue of Industries for Guiding Foreign Investment (2017 Revision) (issued by the National Development and Reform Commission and Ministry of Commerce on 28 June 2017, effective on 28 July 2017).
外商投资产业指导目录 (2017年修订).

Civil Aviation Law of the People's Republic of China (adopted at the 6th Meeting of the Standing Committee of the 8th NPC on 30 October 1995; amended for the first time at the 10th meeting of the Standing Committee of the 11th NPC on 27 August 2009, amended for the second time at the 14th Meeting of the Standing Committee of the 12th NPC on 24 April 2015 and amended for the third time at the 30th Meeting of the Standing Committee of the 12th NPC on 4 November 2017.)
中华人民共和国民用航空法

Civil Procedure Law of the People's Republic of China (adopted at the 4th Session of the 7th NPC on 9 April 1991, amended for the first time at the 30th Meeting of the Standing Committee of the 10th NPC on 28 October 2007, amended for the second time at the 28th Meeting of the Standing Committee of the 11th NPC on 31 August 2012 and amended for the third time at the 28th Meeting of the Standing Committee of the 12th NPC on 27 June 2017).
中华人民共和国民事诉讼法.

Contract Law of the People's Republic of China (adopted by the 2nd Session of the 9th NPC on 15 March 1999, effective on 1 October 1999).
中华人民共和国合同法.

Constitution of the People's Republic of China (adopted at the 5th Session of the 5th NPC and promulgated for implementation by the Announcement of the NPC on 4 December 1982, amended in accordance with the Amendments to the Constitution of the People's Republic of China adopted respectively at the 1st Session of the 7th NPC on 12 April 1988, the 1st Session of the 8th NPC on 29 March 1993, the 2nd Session of the 9th NPC on 15 March 1999 and the 2nd Session of the 10th NPC on 14 March 2004).
中华人民共和国宪法.

Criminal Law of the People's Republic of China (adopted at the 2nd Session of the 5th NPC on 1 July 1979, revised at the 5th Session of the 8th NPC on 14 March 1997, amended for the first time at the 13rd Meeting of the Standing Committee of the 9th NPC on 25 December 1999, for the second time at the 23rd Meeting of the Standing Committee of the 9th NPC on 31 August 2001, for the third time at the 25th Meeting of the Standing Committee of the 9th NPC on 29 December 2001, for the fourth time at the 31st Meeting of the Standing Committee of the 9th NPC on 28 December 2002, for the fifth time at the 14th Meeting of the Standing Committee of the 10th NPC on 28 February 2005, for the sixth time at the 22nd Meeting of the Standing Committee of the 10th NPC on 29 June 2006, for the seventh time at the 7th Meeting of the Standing Committee of the 11th NPC on 28 February 2009, for the eighth time at the 19th Meeting of the Standing Committee of the 11th NPC on 25 February 2011, for the ninth time at the 16th Meeting of the Standing Committee of the 12th NPC on 29 August 2015 and for the tenth time at the 30th Meeting of the Standing Committee of the 12th NPC on 4 November 2017).

中华人民共和国刑法.

Customs Law of the People's Republic of China (adopted at the 19th Meeting of the Standing Committee of the 6th NPC on 22 January 1987, amended for the first time on 8 July 2000, amended for the second time 29 June 2013, amended for the third time on 28 December 2013, amended for the fourth time on 7 November 2016 and amended for the fifth time on 4 November 2017).

中华人民共和国海关法.

Decision of the National People's Congress on Authorizing the State Council to Formulate Interim Provisions or Regulations Concerning the Reform of the Economic Structure and the Open Policy (adopted at the 3rd Session of the 6th NPC on 10 April 1985).

全国人民代表大会关于授权国务院在经济体制改革和对外开放方面可以制定暂行的规定或者条例的决定.

Decision of the Standing Committee of the National People's Congress on the Methods for Selecting the Chief Executive and Forming the Legislative Council of the Hong Kong Special Administrative Region in 2012 and Issues on Universal Suffrage (adopted at the 31st Conference of the Standing Committee of the 10th NPC on 29 December 2007).

全国人民代表大会常务委员会关于香港特别行政区2012年行政长官和立法会产生办法及有关普选问题的决定.

Decision of the Standing Committee of the National People's Congress on Issues concerning the Selection of the Chief Executive of the Hong Kong Special Administrative Region by Universal Suffrage and on the Method for the Formation of the Legislative Council of the Hong Kong Special Administrative Region in 2016 (adopted at the 10th Session of the Standing Committee of the 12th NPC on 31 August 2014).

全国人大常委会关于香港特别行政区行政长官普选问题和 2016 年立法会产生办法的决定.

Detailed Rules for the Implementation of the Administrative Measures for the Provision of Foreign Guarantees by Domestic Institutions (issued by State Administration of Foreign Exchange on 11 December 1997, repealed by the State Administration of Foreign Exchange on 12 May 2014 through Annex 3 of

Notice of the State Administration of Foreign Exchange on Issuing the Provisions on the Foreign Exchange Administration of Cross-border Guarantees. The provisions therein supersede the previous rules issued by the same Administration which contradicted this Notice).
境内机构对外担保管理办法实施细则.

Environmental Protection Law of the People's Republic of China (adopted at the 11th Meeting of the Standing Committee of the 7th NPC on 26 December 1989 and revised at the 8th Meeting of the Standing Committee of the 12th NPC on 24 April 2014).
中华人民共和国环境保护法.

Food Safety Law of the People's Republic of China (adopted at the 7th Meeting of the Standing Committee of the 11th NPC on 28 February 2009 and revised at the 14th Meeting of the Standing Committee of the 12th NPC on 24 April 2015).
中华人民共和国食品安全法.

Foreign-Related Economic Contract Law of the People's Republic of China (adopted at the 10th Meeting of the Standing Committee of the 6th National People's Congress on 21 March 1985, effective on 1 July 1985, superseded by the Contract Law on 1 October 1999).
中华人民共和国涉外经济合同法.

The General Principles of Civil Law of the People's Republic of China (adopted at the 4th Session of the 6th NPC on 12 April 1986, effective on 1 January 1987, amended at the 10th Meeting of the Standing Committee of the 11th NPC on 27 August 2009).
中华人民共和国民法通则.

The General Provisions of Civil Law of the People's Republic of China (adopted at the 5th Session of the 12th NPC on 15 March 2017, effective on 1 October 2017).
中华人民共和国民法总则.

Insurance Law of the People's Republic of China (adopted at the 14th Meeting of the Standing Committee of the 8th NPC on 30 June 1995, amended for the first time on 28 October 2002, revised on 28 February 2009, amended for the second time on 31 August 2014 and amended for the third time on 24 April 2015).
中华人民共和国保险法.

Interim Measures for Record-filing Administration of the Establishment and Change of Foreign-invested Enterprises (2017 Revision, issued by the Ministry of Commerce on 30 July 2017).
外商投资企业设立及变更备案管理暂行办法 (2017 修订).

The Interpretation of Articles 22(4) and 24(2)(3) of the Basic Law of the Hong Kong Special Administrative Region of the People's Republic of China by the

Standing Committee of the National People's Congress (adopted by at the 10th Meeting of the Standing Committee of the 9th NPC on 26 June 1999).
全国人民代表大会常务委员会关于《中华人民共和国香港特别行政区基本法》第二十二条第四款和第二十四条第二款第(三)项的解释.

The Interpretation of Article 104 of the Basic Law of the Hong Kong Special Administrative Region of the People's Republic of China by the Standing Committee of the National People's Congress (adopted at the 24th Meeting of the Standing Committee of the 12th NPC on 7 November 2016).
全国人大常委会关于《中华人民共和国香港特别行政区基本法》第一百零四条的解释.

Law of the People's Republic of China on Chinese-Foreign Equity Joint Ventures (adopted at the 2nd Session of the 5th NPC on 1 July 1979 and revised for the first time at the 3rd Session of the 7th NPC on 4 April 1990, revised for the second time at the 4th Session of the 9th NPC on 15 March 2001, revised for the third time at the 22nd Meeting of the Standing Committee of the 12th NPC on 3 September 2016).
中华人民共和国中外合资经营企业法.

Law of the People's Republic of China on the Procedure of Conclusion of Treaties (adopted at the 17th Meeting of the Standing Committee of the 7th NPC on 28 December 1990, effective on 28 December 1990).
中华人民共和国缔结条约程序法.

Law on the Application of Laws to Foreign-Related Civil Relationships of the People's Republic of China (adopted at the 17th Meeting of the Standing Committee of the 11th NPC on 28 October 2010, effective on 1 April 2011).
中华人民共和国涉外民事关系法律适用法.

Law on Judges of the People's Republic of China (adopted at the 12th Meeting of the Standing Committee of the 8th NPC on 28 February 1995, amended for the first time at the 22nd Meeting of the Standing Committee of the 9th NPC on 30 June 2001 and amended for the second time at the 29th Meeting of the Standing Committee of the 12th NPC on 1 September 2017).
中华人民共和国法官法.

Law on Legislation of the People's Republic of China (adopted at the 3rd Session of the 9th NPC on 15 March 2000, and amended at the 3rd Session of the 12th NPC 15 March 2015).
中华人民共和国立法法.

Lottery Regulations (issued by the State Council on 4 May 2009, effective on 1 July 2009).
彩票管理条例.

Mainland and Hong Kong Closer Economic Partnership Arrangement (signed in Hong Kong on 29 June 2003, effective on the same date).
内地与香港关于建立更紧密经贸关系的安排.

Mainland and Macao Closer Economic Partnership Arrangement (signed in Macao on 17 October 2003, effective on the same date).
内地与澳门关于建立更紧密经贸关系的安排.

Maritime Code of the People's Republic of China (adopted at the 28th Meeting of the Standing Committee of the 7th NPC on 7 November 1992, effective on 1 July 1993).
中华人民共和国海商法.

Negotiable Instruments Law of the People's Republic of China (adopted at the 13th Meeting of the Standing Committee of the 8th NPC on 10 May 1995, amended at the 11th Meeting of the Standing Committee of the 10th NPC on 28 August 2004).
中华人民共和国票据法.

Notice of the General Office of the State Council on the Establishment of the Security Review System for Mergers and Acquisitions of Domestic Enterprises by Foreign Investors (issued by the General Office of the State Council on 2 March 2011, effective on 3 March 2011).
国务院办公厅关于建立外国投资者并购境内企业安全审查制度的通知.

Notice of the State Administration of Foreign Exchange on Issuing the Provisions on the Foreign Exchange Administration of Cross-border Guarantees (issued by the State Administration of Foreign Exchange on 12 May 2014, effective on 1 June 2014).
国家外汇管理局关于发布《跨境担保外汇管理规定》的通知.

Notice of the State Council on the Further Regulation of the Futures Market (issued by the State Council on 1 August 1998).
国务院关于进一步整顿和规范期货市场的通知.

The One-China Principle and the Taiwan Issue (White Paper on the Taiwan Issue issued by the Taiwan Affairs Office of the State Council of the PRC on 21 February 2000).
一个中国的原则与台湾问题（台湾问题白皮书）.

Opinions of the State Council on Further Utilising Foreign Investment (issued by the State Council on 6 April 2010).
国务院关于进一步做好利用外资工作的若干意见.

Organic Law of the People's Courts of the People's Republic of China (adopted at the 2nd Session of the 5th NPC on 1 July 1979, amended for the first time at the 2nd Session of the 6th NPC on 2 September 1983, amended for the second time at the 18th Session of the 6th NPC on 2 December 1986, and amended for the third time at the 24th Meeting of the Standing Committee of the 10th NPC on 31 October 2006).
中华人民共和国人民法院组织法.

Procedures for the Administration of Guarantees Overseas by Institutions within the Chinese Territory (issued by the People's Bank of China on 25 September 1996,

effective on 1 October 1996, repealed by the People's Bank of China on 8 June 2014 through Announcement No. 13 [2014] of the People's Bank of China—Announcement on Repealing Relevant Rules and Regulatory Documents).
境内机构对外担保管理办法.

Provisions of the State Council of the People's Republic of China for Encouraging Taiwan Compatriots to Invest in the Mainland (issued by the State Council on 3 July 1988).
国务院关于鼓励台湾同胞投资的规定.

Provisions on Guiding the Orientation of Foreign Investment (issued by the State Council on 11 February 2002, effective on 1 April 2002.).
指导外商投资方向规定.

Public Security Administration Punishments Law of the People's Republic of China (adopted at the 17th Meeting of the Standing Committee of the 10th NPC on 28 August 2005, effective on 1 March 2006, amended at the 29th Meeting of the Standing Committee of the 11th NPC on 26 October 2012).
中华人民共和国治安管理处罚法.

Regulations for the Implementation of the Law of the PRC on Chinese-Foreign Equity Joint Ventures (issued by the State Council on 20 September 1983, revised on 15 January 1986, 21 December 1987, 22 July 2001, 8 January 2011 and 19 February 2014 by the State Council).
中华人民共和国中外合资经营企业法实施条例.

Regulation of the People's Republic of China on Foreign Exchange Administration (2008 Revision) (issued by the State Council on 5 August 2008, effective on the same date).
中华人民共和国外汇管理条例.

Regulation of the People's Republic of China on International Maritime Transportation (issued by the State Council on 11 December 2001, effective on 1 January 2002, revised for the first time on 18 July 2013, revised for the second time on 6 February 2016).
中华人民共和国国际海运条例.

Resolution of the Standing Committee of the National People's Congress Regarding the Improvement of Interpretation of Law (adopted at the 19th Meeting of the Standing Committee of the 5th NPC on 10 June 1981).
全国人民代表大会常务委员会关于加强法律解释工作的决议.

Regulations on Encouragement of Investments from Overseas Chinese and Hong Kong and Macao Compatriots (issued by the State Council on 19 August 1990).
国务院关于鼓励华侨和香港澳门同胞投资的规定.

Report of the Financial Ministry concerning the Distribution and Use of the Lottery Public Welfare Fund in 2014 (issued by the Ministry of Finance on 26 August 2015).
财政部公告2015年第59号——关于2014年彩票公益金筹集分配情况和中央集中彩票公益金安排使用情况的公告.

Several Opinions of the State Council on Promoting the Construction and Development of the Hainan International Tourism Island (issued by the State Council on 31 December 2009).

国务院关于推进海南国际旅游岛建设发展的若干意见.

The Taiwan Issue and Reunification of China (White Paper on Taiwan Issue issued by the Taiwan Affairs Office of the State Council of the PRC on 1 September 1993).

台湾问题与中国统一（台湾问题白皮书）.

Judicial Interpretations and Other Documents Issued by the Supreme People's Court

Arrangement between the Mainland and the Macao Special Administrative Region on the Mutual Recognition and Enforcement of Civil and Commercial Judgments (issued by the SPC on 21 March 2006, effective on 1 April 2006).

最高人民法院关于内地与澳门特别行政区相互认可和执行民商事判决的安排.

Arrangement between the Mainland and the Macao SAR on Reciprocal Recognition and Enforcement of Arbitration Awards (issued by the SPC on 12 December 2007, effective on 1 January 2008).

最高人民法院关于内地与澳门特别行政区相互认可和执行仲裁裁决的安排.

Arrangement of the Supreme People's Court between the Mainland and the HKSAR on Reciprocal Recognition and Enforcement of the Decisions of Civil and Commercial Cases under Consensual Jurisdiction (issued by the SPC on 3 July 2008, effective on 1 August 2008).

最高人民法院关于内地与香港特别行政区法院相互认可和执行当事人协议管辖的民商事案件判决的安排.

Arrangement of the Supreme People's Court for Mutual Authorisation between Courts in Mainland and Macao SAR for Service of Judicial Documents and Obtainment of Evidence in Civil And Commercial Cases (issued by the SPC on 27 August 2001, effective on 25 September 2001).

最高人民法院关于内地与澳门特别行政区法院就民商事案件相互委托送达司法文书和调取证据的安排.

Arrangement of the Supreme People's Court on the Mutual Enforcement of Arbitral Awards between the Mainland and the Hong Kong Special Administrative Region (issued by the SPC on 24 January 2000, effective on 1 February 2000).

最高人民法院关于内地与香港特别行政区相互执行仲裁裁决的安排.

Arrangement on Mutual Taking of Evidence in Civil and Commercial Matters between the Courts of the Mainland and the Hong Kong Special Administrative Region (issued by the SPC on 27 February 2017, effective on 1 March 2017).
关于内地与香港特别行政区法院就民商事案件相互委托提取证据的安排.

Arrangement on Reciprocal Recognition and Enforcement of Civil Judgments in Matrimonial and Family Cases by the Courts of the Mainland and of the Hong Kong Special Administrative Region (issued by the SPC on 20 June 2017, to be effective after both sides have completed their respective internal procedures).
最高人民法院、香港特别行政区政府关于内地与香港特别行政区法院相互认可和执行婚姻家庭民事案件判决的安排.

Agreement on Joint Cross-Strait Crime-Fighting and Mutual Judicial Assistance (signed on 26 April 2009, effective on 25 June 2009).
海峡两岸共同打击犯罪及司法互助协议.

The Catalogue of the Relevant Judicial Interpretations Issued before the End of 1999 Which Would Be Invalidated by the Supreme People's Court (the Third Batch) (issued by the SPC on 13 July 2000 and effective on 25 July 2000).
最高人民法院予以废止的1999年底以前发布的有关司法解释目录（第三批）.

The Catalogue of the Relevant Judicial Interpretations Issued between 1 July 1997 and 31 December 2011 That Would Be Invalidated by the Supreme People's Court (the Tenth Batch) (issued by the SPC on 26 February 2013 and effective on 8 April 2013).
最高人民法院关于废止1997年7月1日至2011年12月31日期间发布的部分司法解释和司法解释性质文件（第十批）的决定.

Circular of the Supreme People's Court on Transmitting Certain Issues of the Ministry of Foreign Trade and Economic Cooperation in Connection with the Implementation of United Nations Convention on Contracts for the International Sale of Goods (Circular of the SPC Concerning the Implementation of the CISG) (issued by the SPC on 10 December 1987).
最高人民法院转发对外经济贸易部《关于执行联合国国际货物销售合同公约应注意的几个问题》的通知.

Decision of the Supreme People's Court on Invalidating the Relevant Judicial Interpretations (the Seventh Batch) Promulgated before the End of 2007.
最高人民法院关于废止2007年底以前发布的有关司法解释(第七批)的决定.

Detailed Rules for the Implementation of the Provisions of the Supreme People's Court on Case Guidance (issued by the SPC on 13 May 2015, effective on the same date).
《最高人民法院关于案例指导工作的规定》实施细则.

Guiding Opinions of the Supreme People's Court on Carrying out the Case Quality Evaluation Work (for Trial Implementation) (issued by the SPC on 11 January 2008).

最高人民法院关于开展案件质量评估工作的指导意见(试行).

Guiding Opinions on Several Issues Concerning the Trial of Civil and Commercial Contract Disputes under Current Circumstances (issued by the SPC on 7 July 2009).

关于当前形势下审理民商事合同纠纷案件若干问题的指导意见.

Interpretation of the Supreme People's Court and Supreme People's Procuratorate about Some Issues Concerning the Application of Law in Gambling Criminal Cases (issued by the SPC and the Supreme People's Procuratorate on 11 May 2005, effective on 13 May 2005).

最高人民法院、最高人民检察院关于办理赌博刑事案件具体应用法律若干问题的解释.

Interpretation of the Supreme People's Court on Certain Issues Concerning the Application of the 'Law of the People's Republic of China on the Application of Laws to Foreign-Related Civil Relations' (1) (issued by the SPC on 28 December 2012, effective on 7 January 2013).

最高人民法院关于适用《中华人民共和国涉外民事关系法律适用法》若干问题的解释（一）.

Interpretation of the Supreme People's Court on the Application of Civil Procedure Law of the People's Republic of China (issued by the SPC on 30 January 2015, effective on 4 February 2015).

最高人民法院关于适用《中华人民共和国民事诉讼法》的解释.

Interpretation of the Supreme People's Court on Some Issues Regarding the Application of Security Law (issued by the SPC on 8 December 2000, effective on 13 December 2000).

最高人民法院关于适用《中华人民共和国担保法》若干问题的解释.

Interpretation of Supreme People's Court Regarding Law Application Matters of the Contract Law of the People's Republic of China (1) (issued on 19 December 1999, effective on 29 December 1999).

最高人民法院关于适用《中华人民共和国合同法》若干问题的解释（一）.

Interpretation of the Supreme People's Court Regarding Law Application Matters of the Contract Law of the PRC (2) (Interpretation of Contract Law (2) (issued by the Supreme People's Court on 24 April 2009, effective on 13 May 2009).

最高人民法院关于适用《中华人民共和国合同法》若干问题的解释（二）.

Measures for the People's Courts' Implementation of the Provisions on the Recording and Accountability of Staff Members of Judicial Organs for Their

Intervention in Case Handling (issued by the SPC on 19 August 2015, effective on 20 August 2015).
人民法院落实《司法机关内部人员过问案件的记录和责任追究规定》的实施办法.
Minutes of the National Conference on Foreign-, Hong Kong- and Macao-Related Economic Trials in Coastal Areas (issued by the SPC on 12 June 1989).
全国沿海地区涉外、涉港澳经济审判工作座谈会纪要.
Minutes of the Second National Conference on Foreign-Related Commercial and Maritime Trial (issued by the SPC on 26 December 2005).
第二次全国涉外商事海事审判工作会议纪要.
Notice Concerning Several Issues in the Adjudication and Enforcement of Foreign-related Civil and Commercial Cases (issued by the SPC on 17 April 2000).
最高人民法院关于审理和执行涉外民商事案件应当注意的几个问题的通知.
Notice on Several Issues Concerning People's Courts' Handling of Foreign-Related and Foreign Arbitration (issued by the SPC on 28 August 1995, the sequential number of the relevant article of the Civil Procedure Law cited in it was revised by the SPC on 16 December 2008 after the NPCSC's Amendment of the Civil Procedure Law on 28 October 2007).
最高人民法院关于人民法院处理与涉外仲裁及外国仲裁事项有关问题的通知.
Notice on Strengthening the Work of Jurisdiction over Foreign-Related Commercial Cases (issued by the SPC on 29 December 2004).
最高人民法院关于加强涉外商事案件诉讼管辖工作的通知.
Notice of Issuance of the Guiding Opinions on Several Issues in Foreign-Related Commercial Trials (issued by the Guangdong Higher People's Court on 17 December 2004, effective on the same date).
广东省高级人民法院关于印发《关于涉外商事审判若干问题的指导意见》的通知.
Notice of the Supreme People's Court on Earnestly Studying and Implementing 'Provisions of the Supreme People's Court on Certain Issues Concerning Jurisdiction over Civil and Commercial Cases Involving Foreign Elements' (issued by the SPC on 1 March 2002).
最高人民法院关于认真学习贯彻《关于涉外民商事案件诉讼管辖若干问题的规定》的通知.
Notice of the Supreme People's Court on the Implementation of the Convention on the Recognition and Enforcement of Foreign Arbitral Awards (issued on 10 April 1987).
最高人民法院关于执行我国加入的《承认及执行外国仲裁裁决公约》的通知.
Opinions of the Supreme People's Court on Comprehensively Carrying Forward the Strategy of Producing Fine Works on the Trial of Foreign-Related

Commercial and Maritime Cases to Provide Effective Judicial Safeguard for Establishing an Open Economic System and Building up a Maritime Power (issued by the SPC on 14 July 2015).
最高人民法院关于全面推进涉外商事海事审判精品战略为构建开放型经济体制和建设海洋强国提供有力司法保障的意见.

Opinion of the Supreme People's Court on Deepening Reform of the People's Courts Comprehensively: Outline of the Fourth Five-Year Reform of the People's Courts (2014–2018) (issued by the SPC on 26 February 2015).
最高人民法院关于全面深化人民法院改革的意见——人民法院第四个五年改革纲要（2014–2018）.

Opinions of the Supreme People's Court on Enforcing the Judicial Accountability System and Improving the Adjudication Supervision and Administration Mechanism (for Trial Implementation) (issued by the SPC on 12 April 2017, effective on 1 May 2017).
最高人民法院关于落实司法责任制完善审判监督管理机制的意见（试行）.

Opinions of the Supreme People's Court on Improving the Judicial Accountability System of People's Courts (issued by the SPC on 21 September 2015, effective on the same date).
最高人民法院关于完善人民法院司法责任制的若干意见.

Opinions on Several Issues Concerning the Implementation of the General Principles of Civil Law of the People's Republic of China (Provisional) (issued by the SPC on 2 April 1988; Articles 88, 94, 115, 117, 118 and 177 therein were invalidated by the SPC on 18 December 2008 in 'Decision of the Supreme People's Court on Invalidating the Relevant Judicial Interpretations (the Seventh Batch) Promulgated before the End of 2007' (issued on 18 December 2008, effective on 24 December 2009)).
最高人民法院关于贯彻执行《中华人民共和国民法通则》若干问题的意见（试行）(第88条、第94条、第115条、第117条、第118条、第177条已被《最高人民法院关于废止2007年底以前发布的有关司法解释(第七批)的决定》所废止).

Provisions of the Supreme People's Court on the Application of Law in the Trial of Taiwan-Related Civil and Commercial Cases (issued by the SPC on 27 December 2010, effective on 1 January 2011).
最高人民法院关于审理涉台民商事案件法律适用问题的规定.

Provisions of the Supreme People's Court on Certain Issues Concerning Jurisdiction over Foreign-Related Civil and Commercial Cases (issued by the SPC on 25 February 2002, effective on 1 March 2002).
最高人民法院关于涉外民商事案件诉讼管辖若干问题的规定.

Provisions of the Supreme People's Court on Citation of Such Normative Legal Documents as Laws and Regulations in the Judgments (issued on 26 October 2009, effective on 4 November 2009).

最高人民法院关于裁判文书引用法律、法规等规范性法律文件的规定.

Notice of the Supreme People's Court on Legally and Properly Hearing Cases on Disputes over Private Lending to Promote Economic Development and Maintain Social Stability (issued by the SPC on 2 December 2011, effective on the same date).

最高人民法院关于依法妥善审理民间借贷纠纷案件促进经济发展维护社会稳定的通知.

Provisions of the Supreme People's Court on the Judicial Interpretation Work (issued on 23 March 2007).

最高人民法院关于司法解释工作的规定.

Provisions of the Supreme People's Court on People's Courts' Handling of Cases of Mutual Judicial Assistance in Terms of Serving Legal Documents, Investigation and Evidence Collection between Both Sides of the Taiwan Strait (issued by the SPC on 14 June 2011, effective on 25 June 2011).

最高人民法院关于人民法院办理海峡两岸送达文书和调查取证司法互助案件的规定.

Provisions of the Supreme People's Court on the People's Courts' Recognition of the Civil Judgments Made by Courts of the Taiwan Region (issued by the SPC on 22 May 1998, effective on 26 May 1998, repealed by Provisions of the Supreme People's Court on Recognition and Enforcement of the Civil Judgments of Courts of the Taiwan Region (issued by the SPC on 29 June 2015, effective on 1 July 2015)).

最高人民法院关于人民法院认可台湾地区有关法院民事判决的规定（已被《最高人民法院关于认可和执行台湾地区法院民事判决的规定》所废止).

Provisions of the Supreme People's Court on Recognition and Enforcement of the Civil Judgments of Courts of the Taiwan Region (issued by the SPC on 29 June 2015, effective on 1 July 2015).

最高人民法院关于认可和执行台湾地区法院民事判决的规定.

Provisions of the Supreme People's Court on Several Issues Concerning the Trial of Disputes Involving Foreign-Invested Enterprises (1) (issued by the SPC on 5 August 2010, effective on 16 August 2010).

最高人民法院关于审理外商投资企业纠纷案件若干问题的规定(一).

Provisions of the Supreme People's Court on Several Issues Concerning the Application of Law in the Trial of Private Lending Cases (issued by the SPC on 6 August 2015, effective on 1 September 2015).

最高人民法院关于审理民间借贷案件适用法律若干问题的规定.

Provisions of the Supreme People's Court on Some Issues Concerning the Trial of Cases of Disputes over Letter of Credit (issued by the SPC on 14 November 2005, effective on 1 January 2006).

最高人民法院关于审理信用证纠纷案件若干问题的规定.

Provisions on Case Guidance (issued by the SPC on 26 November 2010, effective on the same date).

关于案例指导工作的规定.

Provisions on the Procedural Issues Concerning the Application of Chinese Citizens for the Recognition and Enforcement of Foreign Divorce Judgments (issued by the SPC on 13 August 1991).

关于中国公民申请承认外国法院离婚判决程序问题的规定.

Provisions on Several Issues Concerning the Application of the Law in Trials of Foreign-Related Civil and Commercial Contract Disputes (issued on 23 July 2007 and effective on 8 August 2007, invalidated by The Catalogue of the Relevant Judicial Interpretations issued between 1 July 1997 and 31 December 2011 that would be Invalidated by the Supreme People's Court (the Tenth Batch) (issued by the SPC on 26 February 2013 and effective on 8 April 2013)).

关于审理涉外民事或商事合同纠纷案件法律适用若干问题的规定（已被《最高人民法院关于废止1997年7月1日至2011年12月31日期间发布的部分司法解释和司法解释性质文件（第十批）的决定》所废止).

The Reply of the Supreme People's Court Regarding Whether to Protect the Obligation Created in Hong Kong between Xia Qinrui and Wu Zhixiang, in Research Office of the SPC (1997) pp. 574–575.

最高人民法院关于夏勤锐与吴志翔在香港发生的债务应否保护问题的批复.

Response of the Supreme People's Court to Certain Questions Concerning the Adjudication of Cases involving Hong Kong- and Macao-related Economic Disputes (issued by the SPC on 19 October 1987, invalidated by Decision of the Supreme People's Court on Invalidating the Judicial Interpretations issued between 1 January 1980 and 30 June 1997 (the Ninth Batch) (promulgated on 13 July 2000 and effective on 25 July 2000)).

最高人民法院关于审理涉港澳经济纠纷案件若干问题的解答(已被《最高人民法院关于废止1980年1月1日至1997年6月30日期间发布的部分司法解释和司法解释性质文件(第九批)的决定》所废止).

Response of the Supreme People's Court to Certain Questions Concerning the Application of the Foreign Economic Contract Law (issued on 19 October 1987 by the SPC; invalidated by the SPC in 'The Catalogue of the Relevant Judicial Interpretations issued before the End of 1999 which would be Invalidated by the Supreme People's Court (the Third Batch)' (adopted at the 1119th meeting of the Judicial Committee of the SPC on 16 June 2000, promulgated on 13 July 2000 and effective on 25 July 2000)).

最高人民法院关于适用《涉外经济合同法》若干问题的解答(已被《最高人民法院予以废止的1999年底以前发布的有关司法解释目录（第三批）》所废止).

Responses to Questions in Foreign-Related Commercial and Maritime Trial (1), in The Fourth Division of Civil Case Trial of the SPC (ed), (2004) 1 *Study on Foreign-Related Commercial and Maritime Trial* (Beijing: People's Court Press, 2004), pp. 45–83.

涉外商事海事审判实务问题解答（一）. 最高人民法院民事审判第四庭. 涉外商事海事审判指导. 北京: 人民法院出版社, 2004: 45–83.

Several Opinions Regulating the Relationship between Higher and Lower Courts in Adjudicative Work (issued by the SPC on 28 December 2010, effective on the same day).

关于规范上下级人民法院审判业务关系的若干意见.

Some Provisions of the Supreme People's Court on Evidence in Civil Procedure (issued by the SPC on 21 December 2001, effective on 1 April 2002; revised on 16 December 2008).

最高人民法院关于民事诉讼证据的若干规定.

Supplementary Provisions of the Supreme People's Court on the People's Courts' Recognition of Civil Judgments Made by the Courts of the Taiwan Region (issued on 24 April 2009 by the SPC, effective on 14 May 2009, repealed by Provisions of the Supreme People's Court on Recognition and Enforcement of the Civil Judgments of Courts of the Taiwan Region (issued by the SPC on 29 June 2015, effective on 1 July 2015)).

最高人民法院关于人民法院认可台湾地区有关法院民事判决的补充规定 (已被《最高人民法院关于认可和执行台湾地区法院民事判决的规定》所废止).

Whitepaper on Judicial Reform in China (issued by the SPC on 29 February 2016).

中国法院的司法改革白皮书.

International Conventions and Foreign Law

International Conventions and Instruments

Convention on the Recognition and Enforcement of Foreign Arbitral Awards (New York, 1958).

International Convention for the Unification of Certain Rules of Law Relating to Bills of Lading (Brussels, 25 August 1924).

Protocol to Amend the International Convention for the Unification of Certain Rules of Law Relating to Bills of Lading (Brussels, 23 February 1968).

United Nations Convention on Contracts for the International Sale of Goods (prepared by the United Nations Commission on International Trade Law (UNCITRAL) and adopted by a diplomatic conference on 11 April 1980).

United Nations Convention on Contracts for the International Carriage of Goods Wholly or Partly by Sea (adopted by the United Nations General Assembly on 11 December 2008).

United Nations Convention on the Carriage of Goods by Sea (Hamburg, 31 March 1978).

Vienna Convention on the Law of Treaties (concluded at Vienna on 23 May 1969, opened for signature on the same date and entered into force on 27 January 1980).

EU Legislation

1968 Brussels Convention on Jurisdiction and Enforcement of Judgments in Civil and Commercial Matters.

1980 Rome Convention on the Law Applicable to Contractual Obligations (Rome Convention).

Council Regulation (EC) No 44/2001 of 22 December 2000 on Jurisdiction and the Recognition and Enforcement of Judgments in Civil and Commercial Matters (Brussels I Regulation).

Regulation of the European Parliament and of the Council on the Law Applicable to Contractual Obligations (Rome I Regulation).

Regulation (EU) No 1215/2012 of the European Parliament and of the Council of 12 December 2012 on Jurisdiction and the Recognition and Enforcement of Judgments in Civil and Commercial Matters (Recast) (Brussels I Regulation Recast).

Hong Kong SAR

Cap. 148 Gambling Ordinance

Macao SAR

Regulation on Gambling or Betting Credit in Casinos, Law No.5/2004.
娱乐场所博彩或投注信贷法律制度，第5/2004 号法律.

Macao Civil Code, Law No.33/99/M.
澳门《民法典》，第39/99/M 号法令.

Cases

Australia

Ace Insurance Ltd. *v.* Moose Enterprise Ltd. [2009] NSWSC 724

Allstate Life Insurance Co. *v.* Australia & New Zealand Banking Group Ltd. [No 6] (1996) 64 FCR 79

Oceanic Sun Line Special Shipping Company Inc. *v.* Fay (1988) 165 CLR 197

European Court of Justice

Coreck Maritime GmbH *v.* Handelsveem BV and Others, Case C-387/98, [2000] ECR I-9337

Mainschiffahrts-Genossenschaft e.G. (MSG) *v.* Les Gravières Rhénanes S.a.r.l., Case C-106/95, [1997] Q.B. 731

Partenreederei ms. Tilly Russ and Another *v.* Haven & Vervoebedrijf Nova N.V. and Another, Case 71/83, [1984] ECR 2417

Trasporti Castelletti Spedizioni Internazionali SpA *v.* Hugo Trumpy SpA, Case C-159/97, [1999] ECR I-1636

Hong Kong SAR

Chen Li Hung and Another *v.* Ting Lei Miao and Others [2000] 1 HKC 461

Democratic Republic of the Congo *v.* FG Hemisphere Associates LLC (No. 1) (2011) 14 HKCFAR 95

Las Vegas Hilton Corporation *v.* Lo Yuk Leung [1998] HKCU 33 (1997, No. A8739, 19 January 1998)

Lau Kong Yung *v.* Director of Immigration [1999] 4 HKC 731

Ng Ka Ling *v.* Director of Immigration [1999] 1 HKC 291

Ng Ka Ling *v.* Director of Immigration (No. 2) [1999] 1 HKC 425

Vallejos *v.* Commissioner of Registration (2013) 16 HKCFAR 45

Mainland China

A Case Concerning the Transfer of Shares between Zhang and a Company (17 July 2013, Hubei Higher People's Court, the names of the parties not revealed in the judgment).
张某与某甲公司等股权转让纠纷上诉案

American President Lines Ltd. *v.* Feida Appliance Company, Feili Industry Co. Ltd. & Changcheng Industry Company (25 June 2002, Supreme People's Court) (This judgment is published in (2005) 7 *Gazette of the Supreme People's Court of the People's Republic of China* at pp. 175–178, and also in The Fourth Division of Civil Case Trial of the SPC (ed), (2002) 2 *Guide and Study on Foreign-Related Commercial and Maritime Trial* (Beijing: People's Court Press, 2002) pp. 186–193. The published versions of the SPC's judgment are slightly different in the above two sources. The discussion of the case in this book is based on the version published in the Gazette of the SPC.)
美国总统轮船公司与万宝集团广州菲达电器厂、菲利（广州）工业有限公司、中国长城工业广州公司无单放货纠纷再审案

Awell Logistics Group, Inc. *v.* Baron Motorcycles, Inc. (20 September 2010, Shanghai Higher People's Court)
美顺国际货运有限公司与巴润摩托车有限公司海上货物运输合同纠纷上诉案
The Application of B&T Ceramic Group s.r.1. Co. Ltd. for the Recognition and Enforcement of an Italian Bankruptcy Judgment (application made on 18 December 2000 to Foshan Intermediate People's Court, the date of the judgment not clear)
B&T Ceramic Group s. r. 1. 有限公司申请承认和执行意大利法院破产判决案
Baining Group *v.* Yangzhou Yongfengli Fashion Co. Ltd. (17 June 2014, Yangzhou Intermediate People's Court)
百宁集团有限公司诉扬州永丰利时装有限公司企业借贷纠纷案
Bank of China (Hong Kong) Co. Ltd. *v.* Fujian Longhai Power Co. and Fujian Longhai Government (28 July 2005, Fujian Higher People's Court)
中国银行（香港）有限公司诉福建省龙海市电力公司、福建省龙海市人民政府担保合同纠纷案
Bank of China (Hong Kong) Co. Ltd. *v.* Guangzhou Southern Steelworks (Guangdong Higher People's Court, the date of the judgment not clear), in Guangdong Higher People's Court (2006) pp. 117–127
中国银行(香港)有限公司与广州南方钢厂借款担保合同纠纷上诉案
Bank of China (Hong Kong) Co. Ltd. *v.* Shantou Hongye Co. Ltd. and Shantou Xinye Co. Ltd. (9 July 2004, Supreme People's Court)
中银香港公司诉宏业公司等担保合同纠纷案
Bank of China (Hong Kong) Co. Ltd. *v.* Sonic Printing and Carton Co. Ltd. et al (15 December 2008, Shenzhen Bao'an District People's Court)
中国银行(香港)有限公司诉三某印刷瓦通制品有限公司等借款担保合同纠纷案
Case on the Application of Gomi Akira (a Japanese Citizen) to Chinese Court for Recognition and Enforcement of Japanese Judicial Decision (5 November 1994, Dalian Intermediate People's Court)
日本公民五味晃申请中国法院承认和执行日本法院判决案
China Ocean Shipping (Group) Company *v.* Ryoshin Lease International (Panama) S.A., Beijing Lucky Tower Co. Ltd. and Kingsun Holding Pte. Ltd. (18 December 2001, Beijing Higher People's Court)
中国远洋运输总公司与菱信租赁国际（巴拿马）有限公司借款合同纠纷案
Chongqing Lifan Industry Group and Chongqing Zhonglv Carriage and Trade Co. Ltd. *v.* Guangdong Yongbang Jingmao International Forwarding Co. Ltd., Maolin Express (Hong Kong) Co. Ltd. and Guangdong Zhongwaiyun

Huangpu Storage and Forwarding Co. Ltd. (20 May 2004, Guangzhou Maritime Court)

重庆力帆实业（集团）进出口有限公司等诉广东永邦经贸国际货运代理有限公司等海上货物运输合同货物交付纠纷案

DBS Bank (Hong Kong) Ltd. *v.* Shengwang Clothes-Making Co. Ltd. and Shenzhen Tongyihe Shengwang Clothes Processing Factory (15 September 2006, Yantian District People's Court of Shenzhen), in Deng (2008) pp. 156–160.

星展银行（香港）有限公司与盛旺制衣有限公司及深圳市同益和盛旺制衣来料加工厂融资租赁合同纠纷案

Delixy Energy Pte. Ltd. *v.* Dongming Zhongyou Petrochemical Co. Ltd. (28 December 2016, Shandong Higher People's Court)

德力西能源私人有限公司与东明中油燃料石化有限公司国际货物运输合同纠纷上诉案

Fugong Tenghong Foreign Trade Co. Ltd. *v.* Li Changkui (22 December 2015, Yunnan Higher People's Court)

福贡腾鸿外贸有限责任公司与李昌奎建设工程合同纠纷上诉案

Hong Kong Jingchuan International Shipping Group *v.* Huawei Offshore Shipping Ltd. and Rescue and Salvage Bureau of Ministry of Transport of PRC (Shanghai) (Guangzhou Maritime Court). See also Jin (1998) pp. 466–472. From the available reports about this case on the Internet and in the book, no information is provided as to when the judgment was made. It was only mentioned in the reports that the plaintiff sued the defendants on 20 July 1997.

"昌鑫" 轮拖航合同纠纷案

Foshan Chancheng District Government *v.* Bank of Communications (Hong Kong) Co. Ltd. (22 January 2003, Guangdong Higher People's Court)

佛山市禅城区人民政府与交通银行香港分行借款担保合同纠纷上诉案

Fujian Provincial Arts & Crafts Xiamen Import and Export Corp. *v.* Greating Marine Ltd. and Xiamen Yuli Container Services Ltd. (20 December 2004, Xiamen Maritime Court; 20 March 2005, Fujian Higher People's Court)

福建省工艺品厦门进出口公司因其记名提单项下货物被无单放给记名收货人诉裕利航运有限公司等海上货物运输合同无单放货纠纷案

German Reconstruction Bank *v.* Abu Dhabi Container Lines P.J.S.C. (21 June 2002, Shanghai Maritime Court)

德国再建设银行诉阿布达比集装箱航运公司船舶抵押贷款合同欠款案

Guangzhou Zhaoying Metals Co. Ltd. *v.* Beijing Expeditors Transport Agency Guangzhou Branch, Beijing Expeditors Transport Agency and Jinda Transport Agency Co. Ltd. (7 April 2005, Guangzhou Maritime Court, 9 October 2005, Guangdong Higher People's Court)

广州市兆鹰五金有限公司诉北京康捷空货运代理有限公司广州分公司等海上货物运输无提单交付货物案

Hangzhou Shengke Electrics Co. Ltd. *v.* Westconsolidators Inc. and Shenzhen Hualian International Transportation Agency Co. Ltd. (20 April 2010, Shanghai Maritime Court)

杭州声科电器有限公司诉美国华志货运有限公司等海上货物运输合同纠纷案

Hemofarm D.D., MAG International Trade Ltd. and Sulame Media Ltd. *v.* Jinan Yongning Pharmaceutical Co. Ltd. (Reply of the Supreme People's Court to a Request for Instructions on the Non-recognition and Non-enforcement of an Arbitration Award of the ICC International Court of Arbitration [2 June 2008, Supreme People's Court])

最高人民法院关于不予承认和执行国际商会仲裁院仲裁裁决的请示的复函

Industrial and Commercial Bank of China (Shenzhen Branch) *v.* Karsing (Holding) Ltd., Karsing Investment Co. Ltd. and Guangzhou Dongyi Real Estate Co. Ltd. (26 March 2002, Guangdong Higher People's Court)

中国工商银行深圳市分行与嘉星(集团)有限公司等被告借款纠纷案

ING Bank (Shanghai Branch) *v.* SIP Shell Gas Holland (6 September 2000, Jiangsu Higher People's Court)

荷兰商业银行上海分行诉苏州工业园区壳牌燃气有限公司担保合同偿付纠纷案

Japanese Pipe Centre Co. Ltd. *v.* Beijing Zhuangsheng Real Estate Development Co. Ltd. (6 July 2009, Beijing Higher People's Court)

日本管材中心株式会社与北京庄胜房地产开发有限公司买卖合同纠纷案

Jiangsu Hongye Co. Ltd. *v.* CTS International Logistics Co. Ltd. (29 March 2011, Shanghai Maritime Court)

江苏弘业股份有限公司与港中旅华贸国际物流股份有限公司海上货物运输合同纠纷案

Jiangsu Light Industrial Products Import & Export Group Co. Ltd. *v.* Jiangsu Brilliant Globe Logistics & United States Brilliant Globe Logistics Inc. (25 December 2001, Wuhan Maritime Court)

江苏省轻工业品进出口集团股份有限公司与江苏环球国际货运有限公司、美国博联国际有限公司海上货物运输合同纠纷案

Jiangsu Textile Import & Export Group Co. Ltd. *v.* Beijing Farenco Freight Services Co. Ltd. Shanghai Branch & Farenco Freight Services Ltd. (20 May 2004, Shanghai Maritime Court, 11 November 2004, Shanghai Higher People's Court)

江苏省纺织品进出口集团股份有限公司诉北京华夏企业货运有限公司上海分公司等海上货物运输合同无单放货赔偿案

JP Morgan Chase Bank *v.* Seastream Shipping Inc. (25 July 2002, Guangzhou Maritime Court)

美国JP摩根大通银行与利比里亚海流航运公司船舶抵押权纠纷案

Kincheng-Tokyo Finance Company Ltd. *v.* Fullrate Enterprises Ltd. (19 September 1991, Shenzhen Intermediate People's Court)

香港金东财务有限公司诉香港富雷企业有限公司贷款合同纠纷案

Kogee International Group and Kogee Co. Ltd. *v.* DSL Star Express Inc., Maersk Logistics (China) Co. Ltd., Panama Greencompass Marine S.A., Copenhagen A.P. Moller-Maersk and CMA CGM S.A. (18 December 2007, Guangzhou Maritime Court)

台山市志高休闲用品制造有限公司等诉DSL 星运公司等海上货物运输合同货物交付纠纷案

Kreditanstalt für Wiederaufbau *v.* Abu Dhabi Container Lines P.J.S.C. (21 June 2002, Shanghai Maritime Court)

德国再建设银行与阿布达比集装箱航运公司船舶抵押贷款合同欠款纠纷案

Kwak Yong Pil *v.* KMC Co. Ltd. (23 November 2005, Shanghai Maritime Court)

郭龙必与KMC株式会社船员劳务合同欠款纠纷案

Lai *v.* Li (Nanwan Circuit Tribunal of Xiangzhou People's Court in Zhuhai, reported in *People's Court Daily*, 13 May 2012)

韩芳，任慧娟，苏倩文. 涉澳审判三难题 南湾法庭"对对碰"[N]. 人民法院报, 2012-05-13(3)

Lianyungang Koufu Food Co. Ltd. *v.* Industrial Bank of Korea Seoul (Head Office Seoul) and Bank of China (Lianyungang Nuclear Power Station Branch) (30 December 2002, Nanjing Intermediate People's Court, 23 December 2003, Jiangsu Higher People's Court)

韩国中小企业银行（汉城总行）与连云港口福食品有限公司信用证纠纷上诉案

Mediterranean Shipping Company S.A. *v.* Qingdao Jieyunda International Logistics Co. Ltd. (11 June 2010, Tianjin Higher People's Court)

上诉人地中海航运公司因与被上诉人青岛捷运达国际物流有限公司海上货物运输合同纠纷案

Nanjing Jindao Clothing Co. Ltd. *v.* The Ultimate Freight Management Corporation (9 April 2010, Shanghai Higher People's Court)

南京金岛服装有限公司与雅得美运通有限公司海上货物运输合同纠纷上诉案

Ningbo Congzhongxiao Gifts Co. Ltd. *v.* Banca Nazionale Del Lavoro S.P.A. (11 January 2007, Zhejiang Higher People's Court)

宁波市江北丛中笑礼品有限公司诉意大利国民劳动银行股份有限公司信用证付款纠纷案

Ningbo Market Union International Trade Company *v.* Tianjin Huafeng Transport Agency Shanghai Branch (2009, Shanghai Maritime Court, the specific date of the judgment not indicated), in Zhao (2015) pp. 391–396
宁波凯越国际贸易有限公司诉天津华丰货运代理有限责任公司上海分公司等海上货物运输合同纠纷案

OCBC Wing Hang Bank Limited *v.* Diyuan Trading Ltd. (6 November 2015, Foshan Shunde People's Court)
华侨永亨银行有限公司诉迪源贸易有限公司等融资租赁合同纠纷案

ORIX Ship Resources Pte. Ltd. *v.* Shenzhen Huaxin Co. Ltd. and Shenzhen Xingpeng Shipping Industrial Company Ltd. (2 July 2002, Guangzhou Maritime Court, 2 June 2003, Guangdong Higher People's Court)
新加坡欧力士船务有限公司诉深圳市华新股份有限公司等应依光船租赁权益转让合同给付欠付租金案

PICC Property Insurance Company Zhanjiang Economic and Technological Development Zone Branch *v.* Cross Seas Shipping Corporation, Croatia Line and Lucky Seaway Service SPTE Ltd. (29 December 2000, Guangzhou Maritime Court, 9 July 2002, Guangdong Higher People's Court)
中保财产保险有限公司湛江经济技术开发区支公司与越海航运公司、克罗地亚航运公司、幸运海路服务有限公司海上货物运输货损、货差纠纷案

Ping An Insurance (Group) Company of China Ltd. (Beijing Branch) *v.* Dongnama Shipping Co. Ltd. (24 March 2003, Tianjin Maritime Court)
中国平安保险股份有限公司诉东南亚船务有限公司海上货物运输合同代位求偿纠纷案

SEoIL Shipping Co. Ltd. *v.* Tangshan Ganglu Iron & Steel Co. Ltd. (12 December 2012, Tianjin Higher People's Court)
赛奥尔航运有限公司与唐山港陆钢铁有限公司错误申请海事强制令损害赔偿纠纷案

Shanghai Dongshen Import & Export Corporation *v.* The Shanghai Branch of the Jiangsu Unite Transport Co. and Oceanic Bridge International Inc. (24 October 2005, Shanghai Maritime Court)
上海东申进出口公司与江苏省联运有限公司上海分公司、海桥运通国际有限公司海上货物运输合同无单放货损害赔偿纠纷案

Shanghai Gramter Shipping Co. Ltd. *v.* China Oriental Local Products and Livestock Import and Export Co. Ltd. and Others (27 May 2009, Shandong Higher People's Court)
上海进航船务有限公司与中土畜东方进出口有限责任公司海上货物运输合同无单放货纠纷

Shanghai Lansheng Co. Ltd. *v.* Citibank N.A. and OCBC Bank Shanghai Branch (25 April 2000, Shanghai Second Intermediate People's Court, 2 August 2001, Shanghai Higher People's Court)
花旗银行与上海兰生股份有限公司等国际托收纠纷上诉案

Shantou Ocean Enterprise Group Co. *v.* Bank of China (Hong Kong) Co. Ltd. (17 January 2012, Supreme People's Court)
汕头海洋（集团）公司等与中国银行（香港）有限公司担保合同纠纷上诉案

Shen Hua's Application for Recognition of Foreign Judgment (27 July 2009, Chengdu Intermediate People's Court)
沈华申请承认外国判决纠纷案

Shengli Shipping Co. (Germany) *v.* Junye International Trade Co. Ltd. (Tianjin) (30 January 2002, Tianjin Higher People's Court)
德国胜利航运公司诉俊业（天津）国际贸易有限公司无正本提单放货损失赔偿纠纷案

Shenglun Import and Export Co. Ltd. *v.* Tianjin-Inchon International Passenger & Cargo Co. Ltd. and Tianjin-Inchon International Passenger & Cargo Co. Ltd. (Tianjin) (30 July 2002, Tianjin Maritime Court)
河北圣仑进出口股份有限公司诉津川国际客货航运有限公司、津川国际客货航运（天津）有限公司无单放货纠纷案

Shenzhen Cereals Group Co. Ltd. *v.* Future E.N.E (20 November 2004, Qingdao Maritime Court)
深圳市粮食集团有限公司诉美景伊恩伊公司提单运输货物损害纠纷案

Shenzhen Yihe Import & Export Co. Ltd. *v.* MSC Mediterranean Shipping Company S.A., Go-Trans (Hong Kong) Co. Ltd. and Go-Trans Express Co. Ltd. (25 December 2003, Guangzhou Maritime Court)
深圳市怡禾进出口股份有限公司诉MSC地中海航运有限公司等海上货物运输合同货物交付纠纷案

Sinochem International (Overseas) Pte. Ltd. *v.* ThyssenKrupp Metallurgical Products Gmbh (30 June 2014, Supreme People's Court)
中化国际（新加坡）有限公司与蒂森克虏伯冶金产品有限责任公司国际货物买卖合同纠纷案

Sitic America Inc. *v.* Kunlun Properties Inc. (16 May 2003, Shandong Higher People's Court, 20 October 2005, Supreme People's Court)
鲁信有限公司与凯伦实业有限公司股权转让协议纠纷案

Societe Air France *v.* Geo Logistics Limited (12 March 2010, Shanghai First Intermediate People's Court)
法国航空公司与智傲物流有限公司货物运输合同违约赔偿纠纷上诉案

Song Kai *v.* Li Shilong (1 November 2015, Shanxi Higher People's Court, 28 March 2016, Supreme People's Court)
宋恺与李世隆股权转让纠纷案

Standard Chartered (Asia) Ltd. *v.* Guangxi Zhuang Autonomous Region Huajian Company (18 November 1992, Nanning Intermediate People's Court, 20 September 1993, Guangxi Zhuang Autonomous Region Higher People's Court)
渣打（亚洲）有限公司诉广西壮族自治区华建公司借款合同担保案

Standard Chartered China (Beijing Branch) *v.* Tian Qixin (19 August 2011, The Second Intermediate People's Court of Beijing)
渣打银行（中国）有限公司北京分行诉田启新借款合同纠纷案

Starflower Investment Services Co. Ltd. *v.* Hangzhou Jinma Real Estate Co. Ltd. and Hangzhou Weilai Shijie Recreation Co. Ltd. (21 February 2006, Supreme People's Court)
星花投资服务有限公司诉杭州金马房地产有限公司，杭州未来世界游乐有限公司债务及担保合同纠纷案

The Oriental Scientific Instrument Zhejiang Import and Export Corporation *v.* Zim Israel Navigation Co. Ltd. (16 July 2001, Ningbo Maritime Court)
浙江东方科学仪器进出口公司诉以星轮船有限公司海上货物运输合同货损赔偿纠纷案

The SPC's Reply concerning the Refusal to Enforce the Arbitral Award Made by the ICC International Court of Arbitration (No. 18295/CYK) (22 March 2016, Supreme People's Court)
最高人民法院关于不予执行国际商会仲裁院第18295/CYK号仲裁裁决一案请示的复函

The SPC's Reply to Haikou Intermediate People's Court Concerning the Non-Recognition and Non-Enforcement of the Award Made by the Arbitration Institute of the Stockholm Chamber of Commerce in Sweden (13 July 2005, Supreme People's Court)
最高人民法院关于对海口中院不予承认和执行瑞典斯德哥尔摩商会仲裁院仲裁裁决请示的复函

The SPC's Reply to the Request on the Application by ED&F (Hong Kong) Co. Ltd. for the Recognition and Enforcement of the Arbitral Award Made by London Sugar Association (1 July 2003, Supreme People's Court)
最高人民法院关于ED&F 曼氏（香港）有限公司申请承认和执行伦敦糖业协会仲裁裁决案的复函

Tongchuan Xinguang Aluminum Ltd. *v.* Bank of China (Hong Kong) Ltd. (8 May 2004, Guangdong Higher People's Court)
铜川鑫光铝业有限公司与中国银行(香港)有限公司担保合同纠纷上诉案

United Overseas Bank (China) Shanghai Branch and The Hong Kong and Shanghai Banking Corporation Limited (Shanghai Branch) *v.* Shanghai Golden Real Estate Co. Ltd. (7 June 2010, Shanghai Higher People's Court)
大华银行(中国)有限公司上海分行等诉上海黄金置地有限公司金融借款合同纠纷案

The United States Joint Enterprises Ltd. *v.* Shandong Foreign Trade Corporation Yantai Branch (8 August 2000, Supreme People's Court)
美国联合企业有限公司与中国山东省对外贸易总公司烟台公司购销合同纠纷案

USA Productions and Tom Hulett & Associates *v.* China Women Travel Agency (Reply of the Supreme People's Court to a Request for Instructions on the Non-Recognition and Non-Enforcement of an Arbitration Award Concerning USA Productions and Tom Hulett & Associates *v.* China Women Travel Agency (26 December 1997, Supreme People's Court))
最高人民法院关于北京市第一中级人民法院不予执行美国制作公司和汤姆·胡莱特公司诉中国妇女旅行社演出合同纠纷仲裁裁决请示的批复

Wing Hang Bank *v.* Hong Kong Yuan Feng Color Printing Limited (18 December 2014, Fuzhou Intermediate People's Court)
永亨银行有限公司诉香港源峰彩印有限公司等融资租赁合同纠纷案

Xiamen Branch of Industry and Commercial Bank of China *v.* Liao Jinghui, Zeng Baiqi and Zeng Baixiong (12 March 2013, Haicang District People's Court of the Xiamen City, Fujian Province)
中国工商银行股份有限公司厦门市分行诉廖静惠等信用卡纠纷案

Xingchen Bank (Hong Kong) Co. Ltd. *v.* Shengwang Clothes-Making Co. Ltd. and Shenzhen Tongyihe Shengwang Clothes Processing Factory (15 September 2006, Yantian District People's Court of Shenzhen)
星辰银行 (香港) 有限公司与盛旺制衣有限公司及深圳市同益和盛旺制衣来料加工厂融资租赁合同纠纷案

Xu Wen *v.* Hu Guisheng (15 December 2014, Guiyang Intermediate People's Court, 15 June 2016, Guizhou Higher People's Court)
徐文与胡贵生确认合同效力纠纷案

Xue Yong's Application for Recognition of Foreign Judgment (30 November 2009, Chengdu Intermediate People's Court)
薛勇申请承认外国判决纠纷案

Yu Jinhong *v.* Liang Yangjiao (13 November 2013, Foshan Intermediate People's Court, the judgment is on file with the author)
佛山市中级人民法院民事判决书 (2013) 佛中法民二终字第820号

Zhoushan Shichuang Seafood Co. Ltd. *v.* Kyungnam Bank (2009, Zhoushan Intermediate People's Court, 17 June 2010, Zhejiang Higher People's Court)
舟山市世创水产有限公司与株式会社庆南银行信用证纠纷上诉案

Zhu Guiqing *v.* Fan Huiqiang (23 July 2013, Nanning Intermediate People's Court of Guangxi Zhuang Autonomous Region)
上诉人朱桂青与被上诉人范惠强民间借贷纠纷案

Zhu Niankuan *v.* Dongguan Steel Structure Engineering Co. Ltd. (19 September 2014, Dongguan Intermediate People's Court)
祝年宽与东莞美源钢结构工程有限公司劳动合同纠纷上诉案

Permanent Court of International Justice

Dissenting Opinion by Judge De Bustamante in the Serbian and Brazilian Loans cases, (1929) PCIJ Serious A, Nos. 20 – 21, Judgment No. 14

United Kingdom

Adamastos Shipping Co. Ltd. *v.* Anglo-Saxon Petroleum Co. Ltd. [1959] A.C. 133 (H.L.)

AIG Europe S.A. *v.* QBE International Insurance Ltd. [2001] 2 Lloyd's Rep. 268

AIG Europe (UK) Ltd. and Others *v.* The Ethniki [2000] 2 All ER 566 (C.A.)

Akai Pty Ltd. *v.* People's Insurance Co. Ltd. [1999] I.L.Pr. 24

Ascherberg, Hopwood & Crew Ltd. *v.* Casa Musicale Sonzogno [1971] 1 All ER 577 (C.A.)

A/S Tallinna Laevauhisus and Others *v.* Estonian State Steamship Line and Another (1947) 80 Ll. L. R. 99 (C.A.)

Compagnie Tunisienne de Navigation S.A. *v.* Compagine d'Armement Maritime SA [1971] A.C. 572

Earl Nelson *v.* Lord Bridport (1845) 8 Beavan 527

The Freights Queen [1977] 2 Lloyd's Rep. 140

G.E. Dobell & Co. *v.* S.S. Rossmore Co. Ltd. [1895] 2 Q.B. 408

Golodetz *v.* Kersten, Hunik & Co. (1926) 24 Ll. L. Rep. 374

Habas Sinai ve Tibbi Gazlar Isthisal Endustri A.S. *v.* Sometal SAL [2010] EWHC 29 (Comm); [2010] 1 Lloyd's Rep. 661

Halpern *v.* Halpern (Nos. 1 and 2) [2008] Q.B. 195.

Joseph Constantine Steamship Line Ltd. *v.* Imperial Smelting Corp. Ltd. [1942] A.C. 154 (H.L.)

King of Spain *v.* Machado (1827) 4 Russ. 225

Mackender and Others *v.* Feldia A.G. and Others [1967] 2 Q.B. 590

Marifortuna Naviera S.A. *v.* Government of Ceylon [1970] 1 Lloyd's Rep. 247

MCC Proceeds *v.* Bishopsgate [1999] C.L.C. 417 (C.A.)

Morgan Grenfell Ltd. *v.* SACE [2001] EWCA Civ 1932 (C.A.)
Mostyn *v.* Fabrigas (1774) 1 Cowp. 161
O.T. Africa Line Ltd. *v.* Hijazy and Others [2001] 1 Lloyd's Rep. 76
Ocean Steamship Co. Ltd. *v.* Queensland State Wheat Board [1941] 1 K.B. 402 (C.A.)
Parkasho *v.* Singh [1968] P. 233
Robinson *v.* Bland (1760) 2 Burr. 1077
Sabah Flour and Feedmills Sdn Bhd *v.* Comfez Ltd. [1988] 2 Lloyd's Rep. 18 (C.A.)
Shamil Bank of Bahrain E.C. *v.* Beximco Pharmaceuticals Ltd. [2004] 1 W.L.R. 1784
Siboti K/S *v.* BP France S.A. [2003] EWHC 1278 (Comm); [2003] 2 Lloyd's Rep. 364
The Stolt Sydness [1997] 1 Lloyd's Rep. 273
Trasporti Castelletti Spedizioni Internazionali SpA *v.* Hugo Trumpy SpA [1999] I.L.Pr. 492
Vita Food Products Inc. *v.* Unus Shipping Co. Ltd. [1939] A.C. 277 (P.C.)
W.R. Varnish & Co. Ltd. *v.* Kheti (Owners) (1949) 82 Ll. L. Rep. 525

United States

Associated Metals & Minerals Corp *v.* M/V Vishva Shobha 530 F.2d 714 (6th Cir. 1976)
Continental Coal Co. *v.* Birdsall, 108 F. 882 (C.C.A. 4th Cir. 1901)
Eames *v.* H.B. Claflin Co., 239 F. 631 (C.C.A. 2nd Cir. 1917)
Elijah Goodenow *v.* John E. Tyler 7 Mass. 36 (1810)
Federal Reserve Bank of Richmond *v.* Malloy, 264 U.S. 160 (US Supreme Court, 1924)
Frigaliment Importing Co. *v.* B.N.S. International Sales Corp. 190 F. Supp. 116 (S.D. N.Y. 1960)
Gamma-10 Plastics, Inc. *v.* American President Lines, Ltd., 32 F.3d 1244 (8th Cir. 1994)
Joseph N. Ermolieff *v.* R.K.O. Radio Pictures, Inc. 19 Cal. 2d 543 (1942)
Mori Seiki USA, Inc. *v.* M.V. Alligator Triumph 990 F.2d 444 (9th Cir. 1993)
Mullins Lumber Co. *v.* Williamson & Brown Land & Lumber Co., 246 F. 232 (C.C.A. 4th Cir. 1917)
Nanakuli Paving and Rock Co. *v.* Shell Oil Co., Inc., 664 F.2d 772, 32 U.C.C. Rep. Serv. 1025 (9th Cir. 1981)
Navieros Oceanikos, S.A. *v.* S.T. Mobil Trader 554 F.2d 43 (2nd Cir. 1977)
Pacific Grape Products Co. *v.* C.I.R., 219 F.2d 862 (9th Cir. 1955)
US Naval Institute *v.* Charter Communications, Inc. 687 F. Supp. 115 (S.D. N.Y. 1988), judgment reversed, 875 F.2d 1044 (2nd Cir. 1989)
US Shipping Board Emergency Fleet Corp. *v.* Levensaler 290 F. 297 (App. D.C. 1923), affirmed, 1 F.2d 1021 (App. D.C. 1924)

INDEX